THE AMERICAN SISTERHOOD

WENDY MARTIN
Queens College of the City University of New York

THE AMERICAN SISTERHOOD

Writings of the Feminist Movement from Colonial Times to the Present

Harper & Row, Publishers
New York, Evanston, San Francisco, London

Photograph credits are as follows: title spread, left, *Michael Hardy*, right, *"The Revolt of American Women" by Oliver Jensen (Harcourt Brace Jovanovich); p. 1*, bottom left and far right, *Michel Cosson; p. 8*, left, *Brown Brothers; p. 8*, top right, *Photoworld-FPG; p. 8* bottom right, *Photoworld-FPG; p. 9*, top, *New York Times; p. 9*, bottom, *United Press International; p. 10*, middle left, *Brown Brothers; p. 10*, middle right, *Wide World; p. 10*, bottom, *The Byron Collection, Museum of the City of New York; p. 11*, *Werner Wolff from Black Star; p. 12*, top left, *Barnard College; p. 12*, top right, *Esther Bubley from Children's Bureau, Department of Health, Education, and Welfare; p. 12*, bottom, *Wide World; p. 13*, top, *S. F. Press Club/United Press International; p. 13*, bottom, *Wide World; p. 190*, top, *Culver Pictures; p. 190*, bottom, *Culver Pictures; p. 191*, top left, *Sybil Shelton from Monkmeyer; p. 191*, top right, *Wide World, p. 191*, bottom, *Mimi Forsyth from Monkmeyer; p. 192*, top, *New York Times; p. 192*, middle, *United Press International; p. 192*, bottom, *Photoworld-FPG; p. 193*, © *Dennis Stock from Magnum; p. 194*, top left, *United Press International; p. 194*, bottom left, *United Press International; p. 194*, right, *United Press International; p. 195*, top, *Caraballo from Monkmeyer p. 195*, bottom, *Bettman Archive.*

Contents

Preface

Much of the material in this volume has not been available to the general public since its initial printing and is now quite difficult to obtain. Many of these essays can only be found in special collections or in rare book rooms and have generally been overlooked by most historians and literary scholars. By making this material available, I wish to encourage scholars and students to begin the long overdue study of these women who have had a major impact on the intellectual, political, and social life of the United States from the colonial times to the present. Also, I hope that political activists will read these selections with care because in addition to clarifying revolutionary values and goals, an historical perspective is the best defense against the ignorant and egoistic whether they be in the camps of the conservative, liberal, or radical.

I wish to thank my many colleagues and students as well as my family and friends particularly Elaine Showalter of Douglass College and Cecelia Tichi of Boston University for encouraging me to undertake this project. I also thank the students of "The Feminine Mystique in American Fiction" and "The Feminist Movement"—two of the courses I taught at Queens College in the spring of 1971—many of whom have contributed significantly to my knowledge of feminism. In fact, several of the women represented in this volume such as Crystal Eastman and Emma Goldman were brought to my attention by students in these courses. Finally, my special gratitude goes to Janet Baine and Harriet Friendlich for their editorial assistance and to Peter Merner for his help in the preparation of the manuscript.

This anthology provides an historical and intellectual framework for American feminism, the conviction that women should have political, economic, and social rights equal to those of men, which has its roots in colonial America. More than three centuries have passed since the first American feminists, Anne Hutchinson, Sarah Kemble Knight, Mary Rowlandson, and Anne Bradstreet raised their voices. These voices were heard once again in the nineteenth century, in the lectures, speeches, and tracts of Elizabeth Cady Stanton, Susan B. Anthony, Lucy Stone, and Margaret Fuller and are still heard today in the critical writings of Kate Millett, Sally Kempton, Shulamith Firestone, and Robin Morgan.

From the time that a court of church elders expelled Anne Hutchinson from the ranks of the saved and exiled her from the Massachusetts Bay Colony for insisting on the efficacy of her conscience—her inner light—in interpreting the Bible, men have severely criticized and even chastized those women who have insisted on the right to think for themselves. John Winthrop, governor of the Massachusetts Bay Colony, condemned Anne Hutchinson as "a haughty and fierce carriage, of a nimble wit and active spirit, and a very voluble tongue, more bold than a man, though in understanding and judgment, inferior to many women."[1] Echoing Winthrop, Norman Mailer, novelist and self-proclaimed guru of good sex, recently said of Kate Millett, author of Sexual Politics, *"Well, it could be said for Kate that she was nothing if not a pug-nosed wit" and, designating her the prophetess of technological sex, dismisses her analysis of sexual relationships in fiction as "pure left totalitarian."[2]*

Orestes A. Brownson in his article entitled "The Women Question," written in 1873, elaborates the male supremacist point of view:

We do not believe women, unless we acknowledge individual exceptions, are fit to have their own head. The most degraded of the savage tribes are those in which women rule, and descent is reckoned from a mother instead of a father. Revelation asserts, and universal experience proves that man is the head of women, and that the woman is for the man, not the man for the woman; and his greatest error, as well as the primal curse of society is that he abdicates his headship, and allows himself to be governed, we might say, deprived of his reason, by

[1] *Antinomianism in the Colony of Massachusetts Bay, 1636–1638*, Vol. 21, Prince Society Publications, 1894, p. 158.
[2] Norman Mailer, "The Prisoner of Sex," *Harper's Magazine*, March 1971, 60.

woman, herself seduced by the serpent, that man fell, and brought sin and all our woe into the world.[3]

Brownson's diatribe reveals the rationale behind the bitter invective of Winthrop and Mailer: woman is responsible for the original sin that resulted in man's exile from the garden of Eden and loss of eternal bliss and cannot be trusted; to prevent her from deceiving man again, she must be denied her independence and remain subservient to him. Brownson elaborates further:

She has all the qualities that fit her to be a help-meet of man, to be the mother of his children, to be their nurse, their early instructress, their guardian, their life-long friend; to be his companion, his comforter, his consoler in sorrow, his friend in trouble, his ministering angel in sickness; but as an independent existence, free to follow her own fancies and vague longings, her own ambition and natural love of power, without masculine direction or control, she is out of her element, and a social anomaly, sometimes a hideous monster, which men seldom are, excepting through a woman's influence. This is no excuse for men, but it proves that women need a head, and the restraint of father, husband, or the priest of God."[4]

Brownson insists that as long as woman remains in her proper sphere as a dedicated helpmeet and mother, she approaches the angelic; once she strays from the home, her designated arena, she unleashes demonic forces on man. This insistence on woman's role as nurturing angel is the basis for the cult of true womanhood that reigned in the middle of the nineteenth century and also for the feminine mystique, which Betty Friedan has analyzed, of the mid-twentieth century.

Just as Winthrop and Mailer imply that Anne Hutchinson and Kate Millett are sexual anomalies rather than true women, Brownson states that a woman (in this case a probable reference to Margaret Fuller), is a "hideous monster," an unnatural woman, if she disobeys man's dictates. This undercutting of the independent woman's sexuality, a relatively subtle form of psychological warfare, has been the time-honored method of engendering anxiety and self-doubt in a woman who challenges man's authority and mastery: The charge of "hideous monster" is intended to keep her in her place.

The mixture of fear and hatred directed toward women is inherent in our Judeo-Christian world-view, and our paternalistic legal, social, and political systems are all too often an expression of the need to punish women for committing original sin that resulted in the loss of primal gratification. However, throughout American history there have always been women who have demanded full equality as human beings in a world ruled not by the angry God of the Old Testament but, in reality, by men

[3] Orestes A. Brownson, "The Woman Question," *Brownson's Quarterly Review*, October 1873, in Henry F. Brownson, ed., *The Works of Orestes Brownson*, XVIII, Detroit, 1885, p. 403.
[4] Ibid.

*who frequently use the argument of feminine frailty in order
to help secure their social prerogatives and economic advantages.
In spite of the doctrines that insist on women's physical and
spiritual inferiority or the efforts to enmesh them in obfuscatory
mystiques, however lyrical, about the powers of the womb,
women such as those represented in this volume have refused
to be defined solely by their reproductive organs. Chafing under
the edicts of political and/or psychological subservience, which
has an economic rather than divine origin, and believing in their
ability to think for themselves, these women have demanded
equality for all their sisters.*

*It is important to realize that American women have not
always been confined to a circumscribed domestic setting and
that women have participated equally with men in society*
whenever her labor was economically necessary. *The shortage
of labor in colonial America required that women do the same
work as men: Not only did women supervise the production,
processing, and preparation of food; they butchered animals,
made textiles, and acted as physicians, midwives, and nurses.
Women operated printing presses, were owners of general stores
and bookstores, were proprietresses of taverns; women were
accomplished in the glass, metal, wood, and leather crafts.
Women were shippers as well as bakers, and there were even
a few women blacksmiths. Women were also lawyers, morticians,
owners of saw mills, flour mills, and cider mills. In fact, one
woman is recorded as owning and operating a whaling business.*[5]

*The fact that women and men often functioned alike did not
impair women's femininity. William Byrd, while surveying the
Virginia–North Carolina boundary line, encountered a "very
civil woman" who reflected:*

"nothing of ruggedness or immodesty in her carriage, yet she
will carry a gun in the woods and kill deer, turkeys, etc. and
shoot down wild cattle, catch and tye hogs, knock down
beeves [bee hives] with an axe and perform most exercises
as well as most men in these parts."[6]

*In most settlements single women and widows had head-of-
household status and were given land grants equal to those
of men. In Maryland, married women were given land grants as
well. Because the right to vote was based on property ownership,
women voted, held power of attorney, and had rights to their
earnings as "Feme Sole" under the law of Couvert de Baron of*

---

[5] For extensive background on colonial women see Eugenie Andruss
Leonard, Sophie Hutchinson Drinker, and Miriam Young Holden, *The
American Women in Colonial and Revolutionary Times*, Philadelphia,
University of Pennsylvania Press, 1962.

[6] "Boundary Line Proceedings," *Virginia Magazine*, n.d., p. 236.

1419, which was extended to German, French, Dutch as well as British women. Only after the need for labor was reduced because of the industrial revolution were women confined to the home. Thus, the nineteenth-century myth of the frail woman provided an ideology that prevented women from competing with men on the labor force, or, worse, that provided a rationale for the inhuman exploitation of women in industrial sweatshops.

The competence and ability of women to perform the most arduous task is demonstrated whenever her labor is necessary: Consider the women riveters, welders, streetcar operators, truck drivers, and ice vendors of World War II—ironically, in mobilizing this country for war, there was no job that was not performed by women. With the return of the troops, women retreated to their homes under the aegis of the feminine mystique. But the accomplishments of women during periods of relative labor scarcity proved that they do not have to be the frail sisters prescribed by the nineteenth-century cult of true womanhood, nor do they have to be the decorative toys defined by the feminine mystique.

In the nineteenth century, women rebelling against restrictions of "true womanhood" demanded the vote and the right to an education, as well as property rights; in the twentieth century, they are demanding equal pay for equal work (not yet a reality despite the Equal Pay for Women Act passed in 1963 and Title VII of the Equal Rights Act of 1964), revision of marriage and divorce laws, free abortion, and community controlled child-care centers. Like Anne Hutchinson, many women today listen to their inner voices and reject the ideal of passive femininity: Their anger against sexist society is articulated in such underground journals as Up from Under, Off Our Backs, It Ain't Me, Babe, Ain't I a Woman?, *and* No More Fun and Games, *just as the grievances of their nineteenth-century sisters were spelled out in* The Revolution *(a feminist newspaper with the motto "Men Their Rights and Nothing More; Women Their Rights and Nothing Less," edited by Susan B. Anthony),* The Lily *(edited by Amelia Bloomer),* The Una, *and* The Woman's Advocate.

Anne Hutchinson's discussion groups have spawned a host of women's rights groups ranging from the National Woman's Suffrage Association in 1869, to the National Organization of Women founded in 1966 to "bring women into full participation with the mainstream of society ... exercising all the privileges and responsibilities thereof in truly equal participation with men," to New York Radical Feminists, W.I.T.C.H., B.I.T.C.H., Radical Lesbians, and Older Women's Liberation, as well as the thousands of consciousness-raising groups, women's communes, and collectives throughout the country today. From the Seneca Falls Convention in 1848 to the First and Second Congress to Unite Women held in New York City in 1969 and 1970, women have been resisting the infantilization of their personalities and the fragmentation of their lives.

In the nineteenth century,
suffragettes marched down New
York City's Fifth Avenue and held
vigils for the vote in Washington,
D.C. Frequenly, these feminists were
heckled and jeered, their banners
and posters torn, and the entrances
to their stores and meeting places
such as the International Suffrage
Shop were blocked.

Women have been traditionally used as a source of cheap labor, and have been encouraged to work at "feminine" tasks or those low in status. Clerical work, once preferred by men in the late nineteenth and early twentieth centuries, has been redefined as subservient, and is now performed mainly by women. Often, only in periods of labor shortage are women able to demonstrate their wide range of skills, as the "farmerettes" of World War I showed. Today, women are protesting male chauvinism in the labor market and are demanding equal pay for equal work, as well as equal opportunities.

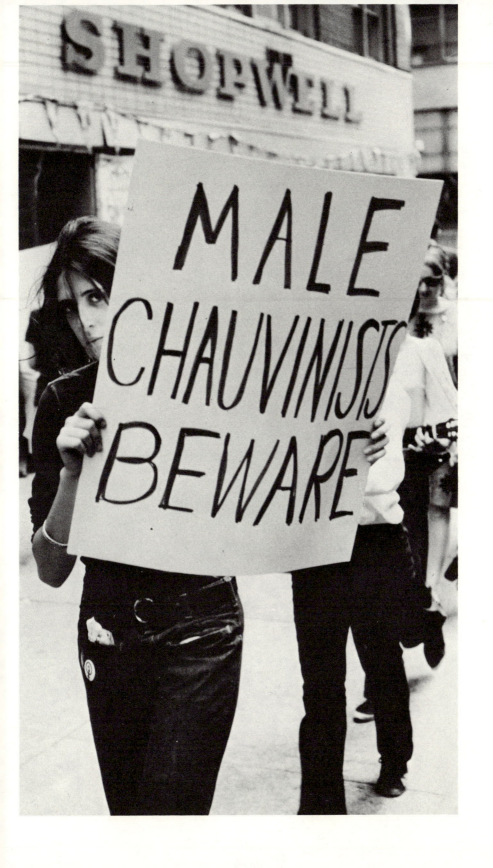

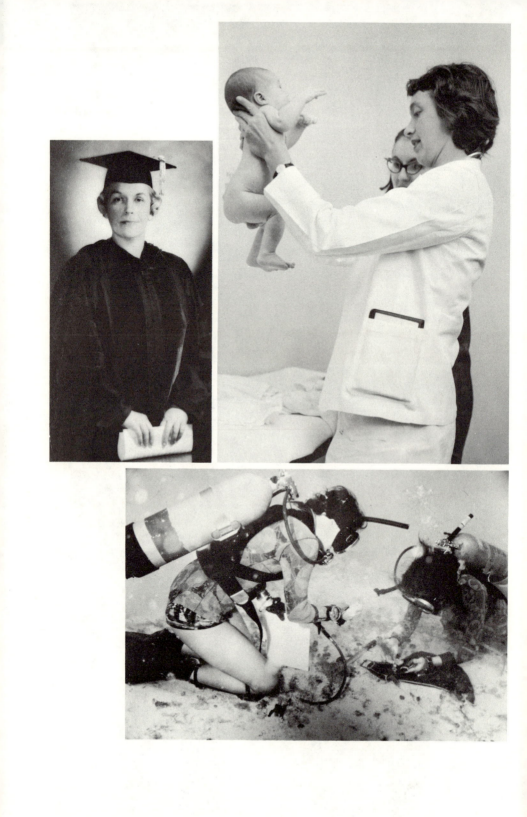

For the most part, women have been barred from the professions that are essentially "boys' clubs." However, the fact that a few women have succeeded in breaking the barriers of discrimination to become doctors, lawyers, professors, business executives, and even aquanauts and pilots, proves that women are capable of succeeding in a "man's world." One of the major platforms of the feminist movement in the twentieth century is that women should have equal professional opportunities and equal responsibility for national and international political, social, and economic decisions.

Anne Hutchinson

EXCERPTS FROM THE FIRST TRIAL OF ANNE HUTCHINSON, 1636

The struggle for equality of women with men in early colonial America was an integral part of the struggle for greater religious freedom. Anne Hutchinson, a woman of unique ability, combined the moral and physical courage of a religious martyr with the intellectual and charismatic faculties of a gifted leader.

Born in Lincolnshire, England, in 1591, she was the daughter of an orthodox Anglican Minister with "dangerous" Puritan leanings; her father suffered censure and loss of a ministry for fifteen years as punishment for his nonconformity. It was therefore ironic that Anne's persecutors in the New World were the Puritan elders who had founded a theocracy that she found particularly intolerable to women.

After her marriage to William Hutchinson, she bore fourteen children in twenty-two years, eleven of whom were alive when the family emigrated to the colony of Massachusetts in 1634. The uprooting of her family was reputed to be because of her decision to follow her minister, Reverend Joseph Cotton, an earnest Puritan who could no longer bear the persecution and restriction of his religious convictions in England.

Anne was herself suspected of unorthodoxy and not immediately admitted to membership in the Puritan congregation despite her kindliness, capable ministering to the sick, and thorough knowledge of the Bible.

SOURCE
David D. Hall, The Antinomian Controversy, 1636–1638, *The Wesleyan University Press, 1968. This essay first appeared in Charles Francis Adams*, Antinomianism in the Massachusetts Bay Colony, 1636–1638, *Boston, Prince Society, 1894.*
Portrait: Culver Pictures.

In the first year of their Boston residency, Anne organized weekly meetings in her home for women to discuss the sermon of the preceding Sabbath. Women were segregated at church and expected to remain silent while the men participated in prayers and testimonials and discussed matters that concerned the community. Church attendance was the colonists' most important social activity and took place three times weekly.

In a theocracy, church and state are one, and great intolerance exists for the slightest nonconformity. Only members of the church voted or held office, and they obviously had to be male. Women at church meetings were not permitted to ask a question or express an opinion.

The weekly meetings in Anne's home were so eagerly attended that they increased to three a week and attendance grew to eighty women; eventually men also attended. Anne Hutchinson taught the Bible and argued that nowhere in the scriptures was there a law restricting the freedom to worship as one wished. She argued against the Puritanical thesis called the "covenant of works," which viewed man as fallen and God as judge, with the minister as arbiter of justice. Her "covenant of grace" was opposed to the authority of man over man and substituted conscience and brotherly love as intermediaries between God and man. Anne's meetings served as a forum for discussion and criticism and provided the necessary social intercourses that were otherwise denied to women.

Under heartless circumstances her trial soon followed and resulted in the banishment of the family from Massachusetts colony by the Puritan Governor Winthrop. A difficult journey brought them to Rhode Island, where they lived for five years until her husband's death. Moving then to southern New York State, they were barely settled before the entire family was massacred by Indians. Only one child survived—an eight-year-old daughter who was later ransomed by the Dutch.

Long before legal or civil rights for women were ever considered, Anne Hutchinson initiated a struggle for human rights that would have liberated women from their oppressed condition even as it broke the bonds of religious intolerance.

Mrs. H. No, Sir, that was no rule to me but if you look upon the rule in Titus it is a rule to me. If you convince me that it is no rule I shall yield.

Gov. You know that there is no rule that crosses another, but this rule crosses that in the Corinthians.[1] But you must take it in this sense that elder women must instruct the younger about their business, and to love their husbands and not to make them to clash.

Mrs. H. I do not conceive but that it is meant for some publick times.

Gov. Well, have you no more to say but this?

Mrs. H. I have said sufficient for my practice.

Gov. Your course is not to be suffered for, besides that we find such a course as this to be greatly prejudicial to the state, besides the occasion that it is to seduce many honest persons that are called to those meetings and your opinions being known to be different from the word of God may seduce many simple souls that resort unto you, besides that the occasion which hath come of late hath come from none but such as have frequented your meetings, so that now they are flown off from magistrates and ministers and this since they have come to you, and besides that it will not well stand with the commonwealth that families should be neglected for so many neighbours and dames and so much time spent, we see no rule of God for this, we see not that any should have authority to set up any other exercises besides what authority hath already set up and so what hurt comes of this you will be guilty of and we for suffering you.

Mrs. H. Sir, I do not believe that to be so.

Gov. Well, we see how it is we must therefore put it away from you, or restrain you from maintaining this course.

Mrs. H. If you have a rule for it from God's word you may.

Gov. We are your judges, and not you ours and we must compel you to it.

Mrs. H. If it please you by authority to put it down I will freely let you for I am subject to your authority.

Mr. Bradstreet.[2] I would ask this question of Mrs. Hutchinson, whether you do think this is lawful? for then this will follow that all other women that do not are in a sin.

Mrs. H. I conceive this is a free will offering.

[1] 1 Corinthians 14.34, 35.
[2] Simon Bradstreet, an assistant in the General Court.

Bradst. If it be a free will offering you ought to forbear it because it gives offence.

Mrs. H. Sir, in regard of myself I could, but for others I do not yet see light but shall further consider of it.

Bradst. I am not against all women's meetings but do think them to be lawful.

Mr. Dudley, dep. gov.[3] Here hath been much spoken concerning Mrs. Hutchinson's meetings and among other answers she saith that men come not there, I would ask you this one question then, whether never any man was at your meeting?

Gov. There are two meetings kept at their house.

Dep. Gov. How; is there two meetings?

Mrs. H. Ey Sir, I shall not equivocate, there is a meeting of men and women and there is a meeting only for women.

Dep. Gov. Are they both constant?

Mrs. H. No, but upon occasions they are deferred.

Mr. Endicot.[4] Who teaches in the men's meetings none but men, do not women sometimes?

Mrs. H. Never as I heard, not one.

Dep. Gov. I would go a little higher with Mrs. Hutchinson. About three years ago we were all in peace. Mrs. Hutchinson from that time she came hath made a disturbance, and some that came over with her in the ship did inform me what she was as soon as she was landed. I being then in place dealt with the pastor and teacher of Boston and desired them to enquire of her, and then I was satisfied that she held nothing different from us, but within half a year after, she had vented divers of her strange opinions and had made parties in the country, and at length it comes that Mr. Cotton and Mr. Vane were of her judgment, but Mr. Cotton hath cleared himself that he was not of that mind, but now it appears by this woman's meeting that Mrs. Hutchinson hath so forestalled the minds of many by their resort to her meeting that now she hath a potent party in the country. Now if all these things have endangered us as from that foundation and if she in particular hath disparaged all our ministers in the land that they have preached a covenant of works, and only Mr. Cotton a covenant of grace, why this is not to be suffered, and therefore being driven to the foundation and it being found that Mrs. Hutchinson is she that hath depraved all the ministers and hath been the cause of what is fallen out, why we must take away the foundation and the building will fall.

Mrs. H. I pray, Sir, prove it that I said they preached nothing but a covenant of works.

Dep. Gov. Nothing but a covenant of works, why a Jesuit may preach truth sometimes.

Mrs. H. Did I ever say they preached a covenant of works then?

Dep. Gov. If they do not preach a covenant of grace clearly, then they preach a covenant of works.

[3] Thomas Dudley, then deputy governor of the colony.
[4] John Endicot, an assistant in the General Court.

Mrs. H. No, Sir, one may preach a covenant of grace more clearly than another, so I said.

D. Gov. We are not upon that now but upon position.

Mrs. H. Prove this then, Sir, that you say I said.

D. Gov. When they do preach a covenant of works do they preach truth?

Mrs. H. Yes, Sir, but when they preach a covenant of works for salvation, that is not truth.

D. Gov. I do but ask you this, when the ministers do preach a covenant of works do they preach a way of salvation?

Mrs. H. I did not come hither to answer to questions of that sort.

D. Gov. Because you will deny the thing.

Mrs. H. Ey, but that is to be proved first.

D. Gov. I will make it plain that you did say that the ministers did preach a covenant of works.

Mrs. H. I deny that.

D. Gov. And that you said they were not able ministers of the new testament, but Mr. Cotton only.

Mrs. H. If ever I spake that I proved it by God's word.

Court. Very well, very well.

Mrs. H. If one shall come unto me in private, and desire me seriously to tell them what I thought of such an one, I must either speak false or true in my answer.

D. Gov. Likewise I will prove this that you said the gospel in the letter and words holds forth nothing but a covenant of works and that all that do not hold as you do are in a covenant of works.

Mrs. H. I deny this for if I should so say I should speak against my own judgment.

Mr. Endicot. I desire to speak seeing Mrs. Hutchinson seems to lay something against them that are to witness against her.

Gover. Only I would add this. It is well discerned to the court that Mrs. Hutchinson can tell when to speak and when to hold her tongue. Upon the answering of a question which we desire her to tell her thoughts of she desires to be pardoned.

Mrs. H. It is one thing for me to come before a public magistracy and there to speak what they would have me to speak and another when a man comes to me in a way of friendship privately there is difference in that.

Gov. What if the matter be all one.

Mr. Hugh Peters.[5] That which concerns us to speak unto as yet we are sparing in unless the court command us to speak, then we shall answer to Mrs. Hutchinson notwithstanding our brethren are very unwilling to answer.

---

[5] Hugh Peter (1599–1660), minister at Salem, 1636–1641. His role in the Antinomian Controversy is described by Raymond Stearns in *The Strenuous Puritan, Hugh Peter*, Urbana, Ill., 1954, pp. 112–124.

Govern. This speech was not spoken in a corner but in a public assembly, and though things were spoken in private yet now coming to us, we are to deal with them as public.

Mr. Peters. We shall give you a fair account of what was said and desire that we may not be thought to come as informers against the gentlewoman, but as it may be serviceable for the country and our posterity to give you a brief account. This gentlewoman went under suspicion not only from her landing, that she was a woman not only difficult in her opinions, but also of an intemperate spirit. What was done at her landing I do not well remember, but as soon as Mr. Vane and ourselves came[6] this controversy began yet it did reflect upon Mrs. Hutchinson and some of our brethren had dealt with her, and it so fell out that some of our ministry doth suffer as if it were not according to the gospel and as if we taught a covenant of works instead of a covenant of grace. Upon these and the like we did address ourselves to the teacher of that church, and the court then assembled being sensible of these things, and this gentlewoman being as we understood a chief agent, our desire to the teacher was to tell us wherein the difference lay between him and us, for the spring did then arise as we did conceive from this gentlewoman, and so we told him. He said that he thought it not according to God to commend this to the magistrates but to take some other course, and so going on in the discourse we thought it good to send for this gentlewoman, and she willingly came, and at the very first we gave her notice that such reports there were that she did conceive our ministry to be different from the ministry of the gospel, and that we taught a covenant of works, &c. and this was her table talk and therefore we desired her to clear herself and deal plainly. She was very tender at the first. Some of our brethren did desire to put this upon proof, and then her words upon that were The fear of man is a snare why should I be afraid.[7] These were her words. I did then take upon me to ask her this question. What difference do you conceive to be between your teacher and us? She did not request us that we should preserve her from danger or that we should be silent. Briefly, she told me there was a wide and broad difference between our brother Mr. Cotton and our selves. I desired to know the difference. She answered that he preaches the covenant of grace and you the covenant of works, and that you are not able ministers of the New Testament and know no more than the apostles did before the resurrection of Christ. I did then put it to her, What do you conceive of such a brother? She answered he had not the seal of the spirit. And other things we asked her but generally the frame of her course was this, that she did conceive that we were not able ministers of the gospel. And that day being past our brother Cotton was sorry that she

[6] Hugh Peter and Sir Henry Vane both arrived in Massachusetts in early October 1635, Winthrop, *History, 1*, pp. 202–203.
[7] Proverbs 29.25.

should lay us under a covenant of works, and could have wished she had not done so. The elders being there present we did charge them with her, and the teacher of the place said they would speak further with her, and after some time she answered that we were gone as far as the apostles were before Christ's ascension. And since that we have gone with tears some of us to her.

Mrs. H. If our pastor would shew his writings you should see what I said, and that many things are not so as is reported.

Mr. Wilson. Sister Hutchinson, for the writings you speak of I have them not, and this I must say I did not write down all that was said and did pass betwixt one and another, yet I say what is written I will avouch.

Dep. Gov. I desire that the other elders will say what Mr. Peters hath said.

Mr. Weld. Being desired by the honoured court, that which our brother Peters had spoken was the truth and things were spoken as he hath related and the occasion of calling this sister and the passages that were there among us. And myself asking why she did cast such aspersions upon the ministers of the country though we were poor sinful men and for ourselves we cared not but for the precious doctrine we held forth we could not but grieve to hear that so blasphemed. She at that time was sparing in her speech. I need not repeat the things they have been truly related. She said the fear of man is a snare and there-fore I will speak freely and she spake her judgment and mind freely as was before related, that Mr. Cotton did preach a cove-nant of grace and we a covenant of works. And this I remember she said we could not preach a covenant of grace because we were not sealed, and we were not able ministers of the New Testament no more than were the disciples before the resurrec-tion of Christ.

Mr. Phillips.[8] For my own part I have had little to do in these things only at that time I was there and yet not being privy to the ground of that which our brother Peters hath men-tioned but they procuring me to go along with them telling me that they were to deal with her; at first she was unwilling to answer but at length she said there was a great deal of difference between Mr. Cotton and we. Upon this Mr. Cotton did say that he could have wished that she had not put that in. Being asked of particulars she did instance in Mr. Shephard that he did not preach a covenant of grace clearly, and she instanced our brother Weld. Then I asked her of myself (being she spake rashly of them all) because she never heard me at all. She like-wise said that we were not able ministers of the New Testament and her reason was because we were not sealed.

[8] George Phillips (1593–1644), minister of Watertown, 1630–1644.

Mr. Simmes.[9] For my own part being called to speak in this case to discharge the relation wherein I stand to the commonwealth and that which I stand in unto God, I shall speak briefly. For my acquaintance with this person I had none in our native country, only I had occasion to be in her company once or twice before I came, where I did perceive that she did slight the ministers of the word of God. But I came along with her in the ship, and it so fell out that we were in the great cabin together and therein did agree with the labours of Mr. Lothrop[10] and myself, only there was a secret opposition to things delivered. The main thing that was then in hand was about the evidencing of a good estate, and among the rest about that place in John concerning the love of the brethren.[11] That which I took notice of was the corruptness and narrowness of her opinions, which I doubt not but I may call them so, but she said, when she came to Boston there would be something more seen than I said, for such speeches were cast about and abused as that of our saviour, I have many things to say but you cannot bear them now. And being come and she desiring to be admitted as a member, I was desired to be there, and then Mr. Cotton did give me full satisfaction in the things then in question. And for things which have been here spoken, as far as I can remember they are the truth, and when I asked her what she thought of me, she said alas you know my mind long ago, yet I do not think myself disparaged by her testimony and I would not trouble the court, only this one thing I shall put in, that Mr. Dudley and Mr. Haines[12] were not wanting in the cause after I had given notice of her.

Mr. Wilson. I desire you would give me leave to speak this word because of what has been said concerning her entrance into the church. There was some difficulty made, but in her answers she gave full satisfaction to our teacher and myself, and for point of evidencing justification by sanctification she did not deny, but only justification must be first. Our teacher told her then that if she was of that mind she would take away the scruple: for we thought that matter, for point of order we did not greatly stand upon, because we hoped she would hold with us in that truth as well as the other.

Mr. Shephard. I am loth to speak in this assembly concerning this gentlewoman in question, but I can do no less than speak what my conscience speaks unto me. For personal reproaches I take it a man's wisdom to conceal. Concerning the reproaches of the ministry of our's there hath been many in the country, and this hath been my thoughts of that. Let men speak what they will not only against persons but against ministry, let

[9] Zechariah Symmes (1599–1671), minister of Charlestown, 1634–1671.
[10] John Lothrop (1584–1653), who emigrated to New England in 1634 on the same ship as Symmes, was minister in Scituate and Barnstable.
[11] 1 John 3.14, a text invoked frequently in the Controversy.
[12] John Haynes, governor of Massachusetts 1635–1636, emigrated to Connecticut in May 1637.

that pass, but let us strive to speak to the consciences of men, knowing that if we had the truth with us we shall not need to approve our words by our practice and our ministry to the hearts of the people, and they should speak for us and therefore I have satisfied myself and the brethren with that. Now for that which concerns this gentlewoman at this time I do not well remember every particular, only this I do remember that the end of our meeting was to satisfy ourselves in some points. Among the rest Mrs. Hutchinson was desired to speak her thoughts concerning the ministers of the Bay. Now I remember that she said that we were not able ministers of the New Testament. I followed her with particulars, she instanced myself as being at the lecture and hearing me preach when as I gave some means whereby a Christian might come to the assurance of God's love.[13] She instanced that I was not sealed. I said why did she say so. She said because you put love for an evidence. Now I am sure she was in an error in this speech for if assurance be an holy estate then I am sure there are not graces wanting to evidence it.

Mr. Eliot.[14] I am loth to spend time therefore I shall consent to what hath been said. Our brethren did intreat us to write and a few things I did write the substance of which hath been here spoken and I have it in writing therefore I do avouch it.

Mr. Shephard. I desire to speak this word, it may be but a slip of her tongue, and I hope she will be sorry for it, and then we shall be glad of it.

Dep. Gov. I called these witnesses and you deny them. You see they have proved this and you deny this, but it is clear. You said they preached a covenant of works and that they were not able ministers of the New Testament; now there are two other things that you did affirm which were that the scriptures in the letter of them held forth nothing but a covenant of works and likewise that those that were under a covenant of works cannot be saved.

Mrs. H. Prove that I said so. (*Gov.*) Did you say so?

Mrs. H. No, Sir, it is your conclusion.

D. Gov. What do I do charging of you if you deny what is so fully proved?

Gov. Here are six undeniable ministers who say it is true and yet you deny that you did say that they did preach a covenant of works and that they were not able ministers of the gospel, and it appears plainly that you have spoken it, and whereas you say that it was drawn from you in a way of friendship, you did pro-

---

[13] The sermons Shepard was preaching during these years were later published as *The Parable of the Ten Virgins Opened & Applied*, London, 1660. For Shepard's doctrine of assurance, see p. 19.

[14] John Eliot (1604–1690), minister of Roxbury, 1632–1690.

fess then that it was out of conscience that you spake and said The fear of man is a snare wherefore should I be afraid, I will speak plainly and freely.

Mrs. H. That I absolutely deny, for the first question was thus answered by me to them. They thought that I did conceive there was a difference between them and Mr. Cotton. At the first I was somewhat reserved, then, said Mr. Peters, I pray answer the question directly as fully and as plainly as you desire we should tell you our minds. Mrs. Hutchinson, we come for plain dealing and telling you our hearts. Then I said I would deal as plainly as I could, and whereas they say I said they were under a covenant of works and in the state of the apostles why these two speeches cross one another. I might say they might preach a covenant of works as did the apostles, but to preach a covenant of works and to be under a covenant of works is another business.

Dep. Gov. There have been six witnesses to prove this and yet you deny it.

Mrs. H. I deny that these were the first words that were spoken.

Gov. You make the case worse, for you clearly shew that the ground of your opening your mind was not to satisfy them but to satisfy your own conscience.

Mr. Peters. We do not desire to be so narrow to the court and the gentlewoman about times and seasons, whether first or after, but said it was.

Dep. Gov. For that other thing I mentioned for the letter of the scripture that it held forth nothing but a covenant of works, and for the latter that we are in a state of damnation, being under a covenant of works, or to that effect, these two things you also deny. Now the case stands thus. About three quarters of a year ago I heard of it, and speaking of it there came one to me who is not here, but will affirm it if need be, as he did to me that he did hear you say in so many words. He set it down under his hand and I can bring it forth when the court pleases. His name is subscribed to both these things, and upon my peril be it if I bring you not in the paper and bring the minister (meaning Mr. Ward[15]) to be deposed.

Gov. What say you to this, though nothing be directly proved, yet you hear it may be.

Mrs. H. I acknowledge using the words of the apostle to the Corinthians unto him, that they that were ministers of the letter and not the spirit did preach a covenant of works. Upon his saying there was no such scripture, then I fetched the Bible and shewed him this place 2 Cor. iii. 6. He said that was the letter of the law. No said I it is the letter of the gospel.[16]

---

[15] Nathaniel Ward, in Massachusetts from 1634–1646, part of the time as minister of Ipswich.

[16] 2 Corinthians 3.6: Who also hath made us able ministers of the new testament: not of the letter, but of the spirit: for the letter killeth, but the spirit giveth life.

Gov. You have spoken this more than once then.

Mrs. H. Then upon further discourse about proving a good estate and holding it out by the manifestation of the spirit he did acknowledge that to be the nearest way, but yet said he, will you not acknowledge that which we hold forth to be a way too wherein we may have hope; no truly if that be a way it is a way to hell.

Gov. Mrs. Hutchinson, the court you see hath laboured to bring you to acknowledge the error of your way that so you might be reduced, the time now grows late, we shall therefore give you a little more time to consider of it and therefore desire that you attend the court again in the morning.

The next morning.

Gov. We proceeded the last night as far as we could in hearing of this cause of Mrs. Hutchinson. There were divers things laid to her charge, her ordinary meetings about religious exercises, her speeches in derogation of the ministers among us, and the weakening of the hands and hearts of the people towards them. Here was sufficient proof made of that which she was accused of in that point concerning the ministers and their ministry, as that they did preach a covenant of works when others did preach a covenant of grace, and that they were not able ministers of the New Testament, and that they had not the seal of the spirit, and this was spoken not as was pretended out of private conference, but out of conscience and warrant from scripture alledged the fear of man is a snare and seeing God had given her a calling to it she would freely speak. Some other speeches she used, as that the letter of the scripture held forth a covenant of works, and this is offered to be proved by probable grounds. If there be anything else that the court hath to say they may speak.

Mrs. H. The ministers come in their own cause. Now the Lord hath said that an oath is the end of all controversy; though there be a sufficient number of witnesses yet they are not according to the word, therefore I desire they may speak upon oath.

Gov. Well, it is in the liberty of the court whether they will have an oath or no and it is not in this case as in case of a jury. If they be satisfied they have sufficient matter to proceed.

Mrs. H. I have since I went home perused some notes out of what Mr. Wilson did then write and I find things not to be as hath been alledged.

Gov. Where are the writings?

Mrs. H. I have them not; it may be Mr. Wilson hath.

Gov. What are the instructions that you can give, Mr. Wilson?

Mr. Wilson. I do say that Mr. Vane desired me to write the discourse out and whether it be in his own hands or in some body's else I know not. For my own copy it is somewhat imperfect, but I could make it perfect with a little pains.

Gov. For that which you alledge as an exception against the elders it is vain and untrue, for they are no prosecutors in this cause but are called to witness in the cause.

Mrs. H. But they are witnesses of their own cause.

Gov. It is not their cause but the cause of the whole country and they were unwilling that it should come forth, but that it was the glory and honour of God.

Mrs. H. But it being the Lord's ordinance that an oath should be the end of all strife, therefore they are to deliver what they do upon oath.

Mr. Bradstreet. Mrs. Hutchinson, these are but circumstances and adjuncts to the cause, admit they should mistake you in your speeches you would make them to sin if you urge them to swear.

Mrs. H. That is not the thing. If they accuse me I desire it may be upon oath.

Gov. If the court be not satisfied they may have an oath.

Mr. Nowel.[17] I should think it convenient that the country also should be satisfied because that I do hear it affirmed, that things which were spoken in private are carried abroad to the publick and thereupon they do undervalue the ministers of congregations.

Mr. Brown.[18] I desire to speak. If I mistake not an oath is of a high nature, and it is not to be taken but in a controversy, and for my part I am afraide of an oath and fear that we shall take God's name in vain, for we may take the witness of these men without an oath.

Mr. Endicot. I think the ministers are so well known unto us, that we need not take an oath of them, but indeed an oath is the end of all strife.

Mrs. H. There are some that will take their oaths to the contrary.

Mr. Endicot. Then it shall go under the name of a controversy; therefore we desire to see the notes and those also that will swear.

Gov. Let those that are not satisfied in the court speak.

Many say.—We are not satisfied.

Gov. I would speak this to Mrs. Hutchinson. If the ministers shall take an oath will you sit down satisfied?

Mrs. H. I can't be notwithstanding oaths satisfied against my own conscience.

Mr. Stoughton. I am fully satisfied with this that the ministers do speak the truth but now in regard of censure I dare not hold up my hand to that, because it is a course of justice, and I cannot satisfy myself to proceed so far in a way of justice, and therefore I should desire an oath in this as in all other things.

[17] Increase Nowell of Charlestown, an official of the colony.
[18] Richard Brown, a deputy from Watertown to the General Court.

I do but speak to prevent offence if I should not hold up my hand at the censure unless there be an oath given.

Mr. Peters. We are ready to swear if we see a way of God in it.[19]

Here was a parley between the deputy governor and Mr. Stoughton about the oath.

Mr. Endicot. If they will not be satisfied with a testimony an oath will be in vain.

Mr. Stoughton. I am persuaded that Mrs. Hutchinson and many other godly minded people will be satisfied without an oath.

Mrs. H. An oath, Sir, is an end of all strife and it is God's ordinance.

Mr. Endicot. A sign it is what respect she hath to their words, and further, pray see your argument, you will have the words that were written and yet Mr. Wilson saith he writ not all, and now you will not believe all these godly ministers without an oath.

Mrs. H. Mr. Wilson did affirm that which he gave in to the governor that then was to be true. (*Some reply.*) But not all the truth.

Mr. Wilson. I did say so far as I did take them they were true.

Mr. Harlakenden.[20] I would have the spectators take notice that the court doth not suspect the evidence that is given in, though we see that whatever evidence is brought in will not satisfy, for they are resolved upon the thing and therefore I think you will not be unwilling to give your oaths.

Gov. I see no necessity of an oath in this thing seeing it is true and the substance of the matter confirmed by divers, yet that all may be satisfied, if the elders will take an oath they shall have it given them.

Dep. Gov. Let us join the things together that Mrs. Hutchinson may see what they have their oaths for.

Mrs. H. I will prove by what Mr. Wilson hath written that they never heard me say such a thing.

Mr. Sims. We desire to have the paper and have it read.

Mr. Harlakenden. I am persuaded that is the truth that the elders do say and therefore I do not see it necessary now to call them to oath.

---

[19] Puritans took the third commandment seriously. "Whosoever taketh an Oath," declared the Westminster Confession, "ought duly to consider the weightiness of so solemn an act, and therein to avouch nothing but what he is fully perswaded is the truth." The ministers were simply not *that* sure of what had been said eleven months ago, hence their reluctance to take the oath.

[20] Roger Harlakenden of Cambridge, an assistant in the General Court.

Gov. We cannot charge any thing of untruth upon them.

Mr. Harlakenden. Besides, Mrs. Hutchinson doth say that they are not able ministers of the New Testament.

Mrs. H. They need not swear to that.

Dep. Gov. Will you confess it then?

Mrs. H. I will not deny it nor say it.

Dep. Gov. You must do one.

Mrs. H. After that they have taken an oath, I will make good what I say.

Gov. Let us state the case and then we may know what to do. That which is laid to Mrs. Hutchinson's charge is that, that she hath traduced the magistrates and ministers of this jurisdiction, that she hath said the ministers preached a covenant of works and Mr. Cotton a covenant of grace, and that they were not able ministers of the gospel, and she excuses it that she made it a private conference and with a promise of secrecy, &c. now this is charged upon her, and they therefore sent for her seeing she made it her table talk, and then she said the fear of man was a snare and therefore she would not be affeared of them.

Mrs. H. This that yourself hath spoken, I desire that they may take their oaths upon.

Gov. That that we should put the reverend elders unto is this that they would deliver upon oath that which they can remember themselves.

Mr. Shephard. I know no reason of the oath but the importunity of this gentlewoman.

Mr. Endicot. You lifted up your eyes as if you took God to witness that you came to entrap none and yet you will have them swear.

Mr. Harlakenden. Put any passage unto them and see what they say.

Mrs. H. They say I said the fear of man is a snare, why should I be afraid. When I came unto them, they urging many things unto me and I being backward to answer at first, at length this scripture came into my mind 29th Prov. 15. The fear of man bringeth a snare, but whoso putteth his trust in the Lord shall be safe.

Mr. Harlakenden. This is not an essential thing.

Gov. I remember his testimony was this.

Mrs. H. Ey, that was the thing that I do deny for they were my words and they were not spoken at the first as they do alledge.

Mr. Peters. We cannot tell what was first or last, we suppose that an oath is an end of all strife and we are tender of it, yet this is the main thing against her that she charged us to be unable ministers of the gospel and to preach a covenant of works.

Gover. You do understand the thing, that the court is clear for we are all satisfied that it is truth but because we would take away all scruples, we desire that you would satisfy the spectators by your oath.

Mr. Bishop.[21] I desire to know before they be put to oath whether their testimony be of validity.

Dep. Gov. What do you mean to trouble the court with such questions. Mark what a flourish Mrs. Hutchinson puts upon the business that she had witnesses to disprove what was said and here is no man to bear witness.

Mrs. H. If you will not call them in that is nothing to me.

Mr. Eliot. We desire to know her and her witnesses what they deny and then we shall speak upon oath. I know nothing we have spoken of but we may swear to.

Mr. Sims. Ey, and more than we have spoken to.

Mr. Stoughton. I would gladly that an oath should be given that so the person to be condemned should be satisfied in her conscience, and I would say the same for my own conscience if I should join in the censure . . . [*two or three lines in the manuscript are defaced and not legible*].

Mr. Coggeshall.[22] I desire to speak a word—It is desired that the elders would confer with Mr. Cotton before they swear.

Govern. Shall we not believe so many godly elders in a cause wherein we know the mind of the party without their testimony?

Mr. Endicot to Mr. Coggeshall. I will tell you what I say. I think that this carriage of yours tends to further casting dirt upon the face of the judges.

Mr. Harlakenden. Her carriage doth the same for she doth not object any essential thing, but she goes upon circumstances and yet would have them sworn.

Mrs. H. This I would say unto them. Forasmuch as it was affirmed by the deputy that he would bring proof of these things, and the elders they bring proof in their own cause, therefore I desire that particular witnesses be for these things that they do speak.

Gov. The elders do know what an oath is and as it is an ordinance of God it should be used.

Mrs. H. That is the thing I desire and because the deputy spake of witnesses I have them here present.

Mr. Colborn.[23] We desire that our teacher may be called to hear what is said.—Upon this Mr. Cotton came and sat down by Mrs. Hutchinson.

Mr. Endicot. This would cast some blame upon the ministers.—Well, but whatsoever he will or can say we will believe the ministers.

Mr. Eliot and Mr. Shephard. We desire to see light why we should take an oath.

---

[21] Townsend Bishop, a deputy from Salem to the General Court.
[22] John Cogshall, a deputy from Boston who had previously signed the remonstrance protesting the Court's action against Wheelwright.
[23] William Coluburn, a deputy from Boston to the General Court. He had also signed the remonstrance.

Mr. Stoughton. Why it is an end of all strife and I think you ought to swear and put an end to the matter.

Mr. Peters. Our oath is not to satisfy Mrs. Hutchinson but the court.

Mr. Endicot. The assembly will be satisfied by it.

Dep. Gov. If the country will not be satisfied you must swear.

Mr. Shephard. I conceive the country doth not require it.

Dep. Gov. Let her witness be called.

Gov. Who be they?

Mrs. H. Mr. Leveret and our teacher and Mr. Coggeshall.

Gov. Mr. Coggeshall was not present.

Mr. Coggeshall. Yes but I was, only I desired to be silent till I should be called.

Gov. Will you, Mr. Coggeshall, say that she did not say so?

Mr. Coggeshall. Yes, I dare say that she did not say all that which they lay against her.

Mr. Peters. How dare you look into the court to say such a word?

Mr. Coggeshall. Mr. Peters takes upon him to forbid me. I shall be silent.

Mr. Stoughton. Ey, but she intended this that they say.

Gov. Well, Mr. Leveret, what were the words? I pray speak.

Mr. Leveret.[24] To my best remembrance when the elders did send for her, Mr. Peters did with much vehemency and intreaty urge her to tell what difference there was between Mr. Cotton and them, and upon his urging of her she said. The fear of man is a snare, but they that trust upon the Lord shall be safe. And being asked wherein the difference was, she answered that they did not preach a covenant of grace so clearly as Mr. Cotton did, and she gave this reason of it because that as the apostles were for a time without the spirit so until they had received the witness of the spirit they could not preach a covenant of grace so clearly.

Gov. Don't you remember that she said they were not able ministers of the New Testament?

Mrs. H. Mr. Weld and I had an hour's discourse at the window and then I spake that, if I spake it.

Mr. Weld. Will you affirm that in the court? Did not I say unto you, Mrs. Hutchinson, before the elders? When I produced the thing, you then called for proof. Was not my answer to you, leave it there, and if I cannot prove it you shall be blameless?

Mrs. H. This I remember I spake, but do not you remember that I came afterwards to the window when you was writing and there spake unto you?

Mr. Weld. No truly.

Mrs. H. But I do very well.

Gov. Mr. Cotton, the court desires that you declare what you do remember of the conference which was at that time and is now in question.

---

[24] Thomas Leverett, ruling elder of the Boston Church.

Mr. Cotton. I did not think I should be called to bear witness in this cause and therefore did not labour to call to remembrance what was done; but the greatest passage that took impression upon me was to this purpose. The elders spake that they had heard that she had spoken some condemning words of their ministry, and among other things they did first pray her to answer wherein she thought their ministry did differ from mine, how the comparison sprang I am ignorant, but sorry I was that any comparison should be between me and my brethren and uncomfortable it was, she told them to this purpose that they did not hold forth a covenant of grace as I did, but wherein did we differ? why she said that they did not hold forth the seal of the spirit as he doth. Where is the difference there? say they, why saith she speaking to one or other of them, I know not to whom. You preach of the seal of the spirit upon a work and he upon free grace without a work or without respect to a work, he preaches the seal of the spirit upon free grace and you upon a work. I told her I was very sorry that she put comparisons between my ministry and theirs, for she had said more than I could myself, and rather I had that she had put us in fellowship with them and not have made that discrepancy. She said, she found the difference. Upon that there grew some speeches upon the thing and I do remember I instanced to them the story of Thomas Bilney in the book of martyrs[25] how freely the spirit witnessed unto him without any respect unto a work as himself professes. Now upon this other speeches did grow. If you put me in mind of any thing I shall speak it, but this was the sum of the difference, nor did it seem to be so ill taken as it is and our brethren did say also that they would not so easily believe reports as they had done and withal mentioned that they would speak no more of it, some of them did; and afterwards some of them did say they were less satisfied than before. And I must say that I did not find her saying they were under a covenant of works, nor that she said they did preach a covenant of works.

Gov. You say you do not remember, but can you say she did not speak so . . . [*Here two lines again defaced*].

Mr. Cotton. I do remember that she looked at them as the apostles before the ascension.

Mr. Peters. I humbly desire to remember our reverend teacher. May it please you to remember how this came in. Whether do you not remember that she said we were not sealed with the spirit of grace, therefore could not preach a covenant of grace, and she said further you may do it in your judgment but not in experience, but she spake plump that we were not sealed.

Mr. Cotton. You do put me in remembrance that it was asked her why cannot we preach a covenant of grace? Why, saith

[25] See above.

she, because you can preach no more than you know, or to that purpose, she spake. Now that she said you could not preach a covenant of grace I do not remember such a thing. I remember well that she said you were not sealed with the seal of the spirit.

Mr. Peters. There was a double seal found out that day which never was.

Mr. Cotton. I know very well that she took the seal of the spirit in that sense for the full assurance of God's favour by the holy ghost, and now that place in the Ephesians[26] doth hold out that seal.

Mr. Peters. So that was the ground of our discourse concerning the great seal and the little seal.

Mr. Cotton. To that purpose I remember somebody speaking of the difference of the witness of the spirit and the seal of the spirit, some to put a distinction called it the broad seal and the little seal. Our brother Wheelright answered if you will have it so be it so.

Mrs. H. Mr. Ward said that.

Some three or four of the ministers. Mr. Wheelwright said it.

Mr. Cotton. No, it was not brother Wheelwright's speech but one of your own expressions, and as I remember it was Mr. Ward.

Mr. Peters. . . .

Mr. Cotton. Under favour I do not remember that.

Mr. Peters. Therefore her answer clears it in your judgment but not in your experience.

Mrs. H. My name is precious and you do affirm a thing which I utterly deny.

D. Gov. You should have brought the book with you.

Mr. Nowell. The witnesses do not answer that which you require.

Gov. I do not see that we need their testimony any further.

Books about Anne Hutchinson

BATTIS, EMERY. *Saints and Sectaries.* Chapel Hill: The University of North Carolina Press, 1962.

HALL, DAVID D. *The Antinomian Controversy, 1636–1638.* Middletown, Conn.: Wesleyan University Press, 1968.

RUGG, WINNIFRED KING. *Unafraid: A Life of Anne Hutchinson.* Freeport, N.Y.: Books for Libraries Press, 1970.

WINTHROP, JOHN. *History of New England.* James Savage, ed. Boston: 1853.

[26] Ephesians 1.13, 14.

Sarah Grimké

LEGAL DISABILITIES OF WOMEN, 1837

2

Sarah Moore Grimké was born November 26, 1792, in Charleston, South Carolina, to Judge John Faucheraud Grimké and Mary Smith Grimké, wealthy, conservative slaveholders. On a trip to Philadelphia at the age of twenty-seven, Sarah came into contact with the Quakers. She and her younger sister Angelina (1805–1879) moved from their birthplace to Philadelphia and became members of the Society of Friends, but they later left because of the church's inactivity in dealing with the abolition of slavery.

To further the cause of abolition, Sarah joined the American Anti-Slavery Society, and she and Angelina, under the society's sponsorship, made public speeches, creating such excitement that their lectures, along with other women reformers and preachers, were denounced by the Pastoral Letter *of the General Association of Congregational Ministers of Massachusetts. The dismissal that met their efforts stimulated Sarah and Angelina to advocate women's rights: Sarah wrote the* Letters on the Equality of the Sexes and the Condition of Women *(1838), and Angelina, the* Appeal to the Women of the Nominally Free States *(1837).*

Sarah's Letters *began to appear in July 1837 in the New England* Spectator; *fifteen in all, they provided some of the first*

SOURCE
Sarah Grimké, "Legal Disabilities of Women," June 9, 1837, Letters on the Equality of the Sexes and the Condition of Women, *Boston, Isaac Knapp, 1838.*
Portrait: Brown Brothers.

reasoned arguments in America for women's rights. In them Sarah surveyed the condition of women throughout history and throughout the world, and concluded that "the page of history teems with women's wrongs." She carefully demolished the prevalent notion that the words of the Bible sanctioned women's inferior position in society; she inveighed against the inferior education women received and the wage inequalities between men and women.

In 1838 Sarah and Angelina, after having been awarded slaves as their shares of the family estate, freed them immediately; the same year saw the marriage of Angelina to abolitionist Theodore Dwight Weld. By now both women were beginning to moderate their concern for women's rights in order to further the abolitionist cause. Angelina helped her husband to prepare American Slavery As It Is *(1839), and both women aided him in conducting an integrated school in Belleville, New Jersey. Sarah and Angelina continued to work for the abolition of slavery until their deaths.*

Sarah Grimké wrote An Epistle to the Clergy of the Southern States, *an antislavery statement, in 1836, and finished a translation of Lamartine's* Joan of Arc *in 1838.*

My Dear Sister, There are few things which present greater obstacles to the improvement and elevation of woman to her appropriate sphere of usefulness and duty, than the laws which have been enacted to destroy her independence, and crush her individuality; laws which, although they are framed for her government, she has had no voice in establishing, and which rob her of some of her *essential rights*. Woman has no political existence. With the single exception of presenting a petition to the legislative body, she is a cipher in the nation; or, if not actually so in representative governments, she is only counted, like the slaves of the South, to swell the number of law-makers who form decrees for her government, with little reference to her benefit, except so far as her good may promote their own. I am not sufficiently acquainted with the laws respecting women on the continent of Europe, to say anything about them. But Prof. Follen, in his essay on "The Cause of Freedom in our Country," says, "Woman, though fully possessed of that rational and moral nature which is the foundation of all rights, enjoys amongst us fewer legal rights than under the civil law of continental Europe." I shall confine myself to the laws of our country. These laws bear with peculiar rigor on married women. Blackstone, in the chapter entitled "Of husband and wife," says:—

By marriage, the husband and wife are one person in law;
that is, *the very being, or legal existence of the woman*
is suspended during the marriage, or at least is incorporated
and consolidated into that of the husband under whose wing,
protection and cover she performs everything. For this reason,
a man cannot grant anything to his wife, or enter into
covenant with her; for the grant would be to suppose her
separate existence, and to covenant with her would be to
covenant with himself; and therefore it is also generally true,
that all compacts made between husband and wife when
single, are voided by the intermarriage. A woman indeed may
be attorney for her husband, but that implies no separation
from, but is rather a representation of, her love.

Here now, the very being of a woman, like that of a slave, is absorbed in her master. All contracts made with her, like those made with slaves by their owners, are a mere nullity. Our kind defenders have legislated away almost all our legal rights, and in the true spirit of such injustice and oppression, have kept us in ignorance of those very laws by which we are governed.

They have persuaded us, that we have no right to investigate the laws, and that, if we did, we could not comprehend them; they alone are capable of understanding the mysteries of Blackstone, &c. But they are not backward to make us feel the practical operation of their power over our actions.

The husband is bound to provide his wife with necessaries by law, as much as himself; and if she contracts debts for them, he is obliged to pay for them; but for anything besides necessaries, he is not chargeable.

Yet a man may spend the property he has acquired by marriage at the ale-house, the gambling table, or in any other way that he pleases. Many instances of this kind have come to my knowledge; and women, who have brought their husbands handsome fortunes, have been left, in consequence of the wasteful and dissolute habits of their husbands, in straitened circumstances, and compelled to toil for the support of their families.

If the wife be indebted before marriage, the husband is bound afterwards to pay the debt; for he has adopted her and her circumstances together.

The wife's property is, I believe, equally liable for her husband's debts contracted before marriage.

If the wife be injured in her person or property, she can bring no action for redress without her husband's concurrence, and his name as well as her own: neither can she be sued, without making her husband a defendant.

This law that "a wife can bring no action," &c., is similar to the law respecting slaves. "A slave cannot bring a suit against his master, or any other person, for an injury—his master, must bring it." So if any damages are recovered for an injury committed on a wife, the husband pockets it; in the case of the slave, the master does the same.

In criminal prosecutions, the wife may be indicted and punished separately, unless there be evidence of coercion from the fact that the offence was committed in the presence, or by the command of her husband. A wife is excused from punishment for theft committed in the presence, or by the command of her husband.

It would be difficult to frame a law better calculated to destroy the responsibility of woman as a moral being, or a free agent. Her husband is supposed to possess unlimited control over her; and if she can offer the flimsy excuse that he bade her steal, she may break the eighth commandment with impunity, as far as human laws are concerned.

Our law, in general, considers man and wife as one person; yet there are some instances in which she is separately considered, as inferior to him and acting by his compulsion. Therefore, all deeds executed, and acts done by her during her coverture (i.e., marriage) are void, except it be a fine,

or like matter of record, in which case she must be solely
and secretly examined, to learn if her act be voluntary.

Such a law speaks volumes of the abuse of that power which
men have vested in their own hands. Still the private examination of a wife, to know whether she accedes to the disposition of
property made by her husband is, in most cases, a mere form;
a wife dares not do what will be disagreeable to one who is, in
his own estimation, her superior, and who makes her feel, in
the privacy of domestic life, that she has thwarted him. With
respect to the nullity of deeds or acts done by a wife, I will
mention one circumstance. A respectable woman borrowed of a
female friend a sum of money to relieve her son from some dis-
tressing pecuniary embarrassment. Her husband was from home,
and she assured the lender, that as soon as he returned, he
would gratefully discharge the debt. She gave her note, and the
lender, entirely ignorant of the law that a man is not obliged to
discharge such a debt, actually borrowed the money, and lent it
to the distressed and weeping mother. The father returned home,
refused to pay the debt, and the person who had loaned the money
was obliged to pay both principal and interest to the friend
who lent it to her. Women should certainly know the laws by
which they are governed, and from which they frequently suffer;
yet they are kept in ignorance, nearly as profound, of their legal
rights, and of the legislative enactments which are to regulate
their actions, as slaves.

The husband, by the old law, might give his wife moderate
correction, as he is to answer for her misbehavior. The law
thought it reasonable to entrust him with this power of
restraining her by domestic chastisement. The courts of law
will still permit a husband to restrain a wife of her liberty,
in case of any gross misbehavior.

What a mortifying proof this law affords, of the estimation
in which woman is held! She is placed completely in the hands
of a being subject like herself to the outbursts of passion, and
therefore unworthy to be trusted with power. Perhaps I may be
told respecting this law, that it is a dead letter, as I am sometimes told about the slave laws; but this is not true in either
case. The slaveholder does kill his slave by moderate correction,
as the law allows; and many a husband, among the poor, exercises the right given him by the law, of degrading woman by
personal chastisement. And among the higher ranks, if actual
imprisonment is not resorted to, women are not unfrequently
restrained of the liberty of going to places of worship by irre-
ligious husbands, and of doing many other things about which,
as moral and responsible beings, *they* should be the *sole* judges.
Such laws remind me of the reply of some little girls at a
children's meeting held recently at Ipswich. The lecturer told

them that God had created four orders of beings with which he had made us acquainted through the Bible. The first was angels, the second was man, the third beasts; and now, children, what is the fourth? After a pause, several girls replied "Women."

A woman's personal property by marriage becomes absolutely her husband's, which, at his death, he may leave entirely away from her.

And farther, all the avails of her labor are absolutely in the power of her husband. All that she acquires by her industry is his; so that she cannot, with her own honest earnings, become the legal purchaser of any property. If she expends her money for articles of furniture, to contribute to the comfort of her family, they are liable to be seized for her husband's debts: and I know an instance of a woman, who by labor and economy had scraped together a little maintenance for herself and a do-little husband, who was left, at his death, by virtue of his last will and testament, to be supported by charity. I knew another woman, who by great industry had acquired a little money which she deposited in a bank for safe keeping. She had saved this pittance whilst able to work, in hopes that when age or sickness disqualified her for exertion, she might have something to render life comfortable, without being a burden to her friends. Her husband, a worthless, idle man, discovered this hid treasure, drew her little stock from the bank, and expended it all in extravagance and vicious indulgence. I know of another woman, who married without the least idea that she was surrendering her rights to all her personal property. Accordingly, she went to the bank as usual to draw her dividends, and the person who paid her the money, and to whom she was personally known as an owner of shares in that bank, remarking the change in her signature, withdrew the money, informing her that if she were married, she had no longer a right to draw her dividends without an order from her husband. It appeared that she intended having a little fund for private use, and had not even told her husband that she owned this stock, and she was not a little chagrined, when she found that it was not at her disposal. I think she was wrong to conceal the circumstance. The relation of husband and wife is too near and sacred to admit of secrecy about money matters, unless positive necessity demands it; and I can see no excuse for any woman entering into a marriage engagement with a design to keep her husband ignorant that she was possessed of property. If she was unwilling to give up her property to his disposal, she had infinitely better have remained single.

The laws above cited are not very unlike the slave laws of Louisiana.

All that a slave possesses belongs to his master; he possesses nothing of his own, except what his master chooses he should possess.

By the marriage, the husband is absolutely master of the profits of the wife's lands during the coverture, and if he has had a living child, and survives the wife, he retains the whole of those lands, if they are estates of inheritance, during his life; but the wife is entitled only to one third if she survives, out of the husband's estates of inheritance. But this she has, whether she has had a child or not. With regard to the property of women, there is taxation without representation; for they pay taxes without having the liberty of voting for representatives.

And this taxation, without representation, be it remembered, was the cause of our Revolutionary war, a grievance so heavy, that it was thought necessary to purchase exemption from it at an immense expense of blood and treasure, yet the daughters of New England, as well as of all the other States of this free Republic, are suffering a similar injustice—but for one, I had rather we should suffer any injustice or oppression, than that my sex should have any voice in the political affairs of the nation. The laws I have quoted, are, I believe, the laws of Massachusetts, and, with few exceptions, of all the States in this Union. "In Louisiana and Missouri, and possibly, in some other southern States, a woman not only has half her husband's property by right at his death, but may always be considered as possessed of half his gains during his life; having at all times power to bequeath that amount." That the laws which have generally been adopted in the United States, for the government of women, have been framed almost entirely for the exclusive benefit of men, and with a design to oppress women, by depriving them of all control over their property, is too manifest to be denied. Some liberal and enlightened men, I know, regret the existence of these laws; and I quote with pleasure an extract from Harriet Martineau's *Society in America*, as a proof of the assertion. "A liberal minded lawyer of Boston, told me that his advice to testators always is to leave the largest possible amount to the widow, subject to the condition of her leaving it to the children; but that it is with shame that he reflects that any woman should owe that to his professional advice, which the law should have secured to her as a right." I have known a few instances where men have left their whole property to their wives, when they have died, leaving only minor children; but I have heard more instances of the friend and helper of many years, being portioned off like a salaried domestic, instead of having a comfortable independence secured to her, while the children were amply provided for.

As these abuses do exist, and women suffer intensely from them, our brethren are called upon in this enlightened age, by every sentiment of honor, religion and justice, to repeal these unjust and unequal laws, and restore to woman those rights which they have wrested from her. Such laws approximate too nearly to the laws enacted by slaveholders for the government of their slaves, and must tend to debase and depress the mind of that being, whom God created as a help meet for man, or "helper like unto himself," and designed to be his equal and his companion. Until such laws are annulled, woman never can occupy that exalted station for which she was intended by her Maker. And just in proportion as they are practically disregarded, which is the case to some extent, just so far is woman assuming that independence and nobility of character which she ought to exhibit.

The various laws which I have transcribed, leave women very little more liberty, or power, in some respects, than the slave. "A slave," says the civil code of Louisiana, "is one who is in the power of a master, to whom he belongs. He can possess nothing, nor acquire anything, but what must belong to his master." I do not wish by any means to intimate that the condition of free women can be compared to that of slaves in suffering, or in degradation; still, I believe the laws which deprive married women of their rights and privileges, have a tendency to lessen them in their own estimation as moral and responsible beings, and that their being made by civil law inferior to their husbands, has a debasing and mischievous effect upon them, teaching them practically the fatal lesson to look unto man for protection and indulgence.

Ecclesiastical bodies, I believe, without exception, follow the example of legislative assemblies, in excluding woman from any participation in forming the discipline by which she is governed. The men frame the laws, and, with few exceptions, claim to execute them on both sexes. In ecclesiastical, as well as civil courts, woman is tried and condemned, not by a jury of her peers, but by beings, who regard themselves as her superiors in the scale of creation. Although looked upon as an inferior, when considered as an intellectual being, woman is punished with the same severity as man, when she is guilty of moral offences. Her condition resembles, in some measure, that of the slave, who, while he is denied the advantages of his more enlightened master, is treated with even greater rigor of the law. Hoping that in the various reformations of the day, women may be relieved from some of their legal disabilities, I remain,

Thine in the bonds of womanhood,
Sarah M. Grimké

Books by Sarah Grimké

An Epistle to the Clergy of the Southern States. New York: n.n., 1836.
Letters on the Equality of the Sexes and the Condition of Women. Boston: Isaac Knapp, 1838.

Books about Sarah Grimké

AUSTIN, GEORGE LOWELL. "The Grimké Sisters." *The Bay State Monthly* III, no. 3 (August 1885).

BARNES, G. H., AND DUMOND, D. W., eds. *Letters of Theodore Dwight Weld, Angelina Grimké Weld and Sarah Grimké: 1822–1844.* 2 vols. New York: Appleton-Century-Crofts, 1934.

BIRNEY, CATHERINE. *The Grimké Sisters: Sarah and Angelina Grimké, the First Women Advocates of Abolition and Woman's Rights.* Boston: Lee & Sheppard, 1885.

JONES, DUDLEY F. "The Grimké Sisters." *The Proceedings of the South Carolina Historical Association* (1933), 12–21.

LERNER, GERDA. *The Grimké Sisters from South Carolina.* Boston: Houghton Mifflin, 1967.

WILLARD, FRANCES, AND LIVERMORE, MARY. "Grimké, Sarah." *A Woman of the Century.* Buffalo, Chicago, and New York: Charles Wells Moulton, 1893. Republished Detroit, 1967.

Seneca Falls Convention

DECLARATION OF SENTIMENTS AND RESOLUTIONS, 1848

Outraged by the refusal to seat American women delegates at the World Anti-Slavery Convention held in 1840 in London, women began to demand the vote. Led by Elizabeth Cady Stanton and Lucretia Mott, the Seneca Falls Convention in 1848—described by Stanton as "the first organized protest against the injustice which had brooded for ages over the character and destiny of half the race"—has been called the first woman suffrage convention in the United States. The Declaration of Sentiments, one of the most important documents in American feminism, was passed at this convention. Modeled after the Declaration of Independence, it demanded the same basic and inalienable rights, asserting that the democratic freedoms won by the French and American Revolutions should also be applied to women. In the following ten years, Susan B. Anthony and Elizabeth Cady Stanton formed the Radical National Woman Suffrage Association, opposing the Fifteenth Amendment, which extended the vote to Negro men but not to women—black or white.

Although woman suffrage was finally won in 1920 with the passing of the Nineteenth Amendment, economic, political, and social discrimination has persisted, and once again women are protesting the denial of their rights. The First and Second Congress to Unite Women, held in New York City in November 1969 and May 1970, are the twentieth-century counterparts of the Seneca Falls Convention.

SOURCE
"Declaration of Sentiments and Resolutions," Seneca Falls Convention, July 1848, in History of Woman Suffrage, I, pp. 70–73.

Declaration of Sentiments

When, in the course of human events, it becomes necessary for one portion of the family of man to assume among the people of the earth a position different from that which they have hitherto occupied, but one to which the laws of nature and of nature's God entitle them, a decent respect to the opinions of mankind requires that they should declare the causes that impel them to such a course.

We hold these truths to be self-evident: that all men and women are created equal; that they are endowed by their Creator with certain inalienable rights; that among these are life, liberty, and the pursuit of happiness; that to secure these rights governments are instituted, deriving their just powers from the consent of the governed. Whenever any form of government becomes destructive of these ends, it is the right of those who suffer from it to refuse allegiance to it, and to insist upon the institution of a new government, laying its foundation on such principles, and organizing its powers in such form, as to them shall seem most likely to effect their safety and happiness. Prudence, indeed, will dictate that governments long established should not be changed for light and transient causes; and accordingly all experience hath shown that mankind are more disposed to suffer, while evils are sufferable, than to right themselves by abolishing the forms to which they are accustomed. But when a long train of abuses and usurpations, pursuing invariably the same object, evinces a design to reduce them under absolute despotism, it is their duty to throw off such government, and to provide new guards for their future security. Such has been the patient sufferance of the women under this government, and such is now the necessity which constrains them to demand the equal station to which they are entitled.

The history of mankind is a history of repeated injuries and usurpations on the part of man toward woman, having in direct object the establishment of an absolute tyranny over her. To prove this, let facts be submitted to a candid world.

He has never permitted her to exercise her inalienable right to the elective franchise.

He has compelled her to submit to laws, in the formation of which she had no voice.

He has withheld from her rights which are given to the most ignorant and degraded men—both natives and foreigners.

Having deprived her of this first right of a citizen, the elective franchise, thereby leaving her without representation in the halls of legislation, he has oppressed her on all sides.

He has made her, if married, in the eye of the law, civilly dead.

He has taken from her all right in property, even to the wages she earns.

He has made her, morally, an irresponsible being, as she can commit many crimes with impunity, provided they be done in the presence of her husband. In the covenant of marriage, she is compelled to promise obedience to her husband, he becoming, to all intents and purposes, her master—the law giving him power to deprive her of her liberty, and to administer chastisement.

He has so framed the laws of divorce, as to what shall be the proper causes, and in case of separation, to whom the guardianship of the children shall be given, as to be wholly regardless of the happiness of women—the law, in all cases, going upon the false supposition of the supremacy of man, and giving all power into his hands.

After depriving her of all rights as a married woman, if single, and the owner of property, he has taxed her to support a government which recognizes her only when her property can be made profitable to it.

He has monopolized nearly all the profitable employments, and from those she is permitted to follow, she receives but a scanty remuneration. He closes against her all the avenues to wealth and distinction which he considers most honorable to himself. As a teacher of theology, medicine, or law, she is not known.

He has denied her the facilities for obtaining a thorough education, all colleges being closed against her.

He allows her in Church, as well as State, but a subordinate position, claiming Apostolic authority for her exclusion from the ministry, and, with some exceptions, from any public participation in the affairs of the Church.

He has created a false public sentiment by giving to the world a different code of morals for men and women, by which moral delinquencies which exclude women from society, are not only tolerated, but deemed of little account in man.

He has usurped the prerogative of Jehovah himself, claiming it as his right to assign for her a sphere of action, when that belongs to her conscience and to her God.

He has endeavored, in every way that he could, to destroy her confidence in her own powers, to lessen her self-respect, and to make her willing to lead a dependent and abject life.

Now, in view of this entire disenfranchisement of one-half the people of this country, their social and religious degradation —in view of the unjust laws above mentioned, and because women do feel themselves aggrieved, oppressed, and fraudulently deprived of their most sacred rights, we insist that they have immediate admission to all the rights and privileges which belong to them as citizens of the United States.

In entering upon the great work before us, we anticipate no small amount of misconception, misrepresentation, and ridicule; but we shall use every instrumentality within our power to effect our object. We shall employ agents, circulate tracts, petition the State and National legislatures, and endeavor to enlist the pulpit and the press in our behalf. We hope this Convention will be followed by a series of Conventions embracing every part of the country.

Resolutions

WHEREAS, The great precept of nature is conceded to be, that "man shall pursue his own true and substantial happiness." Blackstone in his Commentaries remarks, that this law of Nature being coeval with mankind, and dictated by God himself, is of course superior in obligation to any other. It is binding over all the globe, in all countries and at all times; no human laws are of any validity if contrary to this, and such of them as are valid, derive all their force, and all their validity, and all their authority, mediately and immediately, from this original; therefore,

Resolved, That such laws as conflict, in any way, with the true and substantial happiness of woman, are contrary to the great precept of nature and of no validity, for this is "superior in obligation to any other."

Resolved, That all laws which prevent woman from occupying such a station in society as her conscience shall dictate, or which place her in a position inferior to that of man, are contrary to the great precept of nature, and therefore of no force or authority.

Resolved, That woman is man's equal—was intended to be so by the Creator, and the highest good of the race demands that she should be recognized as such.

Resolved, That the women of this country ought to be enlightened in regard to the laws under which they live, that they may no longer publish their degradation by declaring themselves satisfied with their present position, nor their ignorance, by asserting that they have all the rights they want.

Resolved, That inasmuch as man, while claiming for himself intellectual superiority, does accord to woman moral superiority, it is pre-eminently his duty to encourage her to speak and teach, as she has an opportunity, in all religious assemblies.

Resolved, That the same amount of virtue, delicacy, and refinement of behavior that is required of woman in the social state, should also be required of man, and the same transgressions should be visited with equal severity on both man and woman.

Resolved, That the objection of indelicacy and impropriety, which is so often brought against woman when she addresses a public audience, comes with a very ill-grace from those who encourage, by their attendance, her appearance on the stage, in the concert, or in feats of the circus.

Resolved, That woman has too long rested satisfied in the circumscribed limits which corrupt customs and a perverted application of the Scriptures have marked out for her, and that it is time she should move in the enlarged sphere which her great Creator has assigned her.

Resolved, That it is the duty of the women of this country to secure to themselves their sacred right to the elective franchise.

Resolved, That the equality of human rights results necessarily from the fact of the identity of the race in capabilities and responsibilities.

Resolved, therefore, That, being invested by the Creator with the same capabilities, and the same consciousness of responsibility for their exercise, it is demonstrably the right and duty of woman, equally with man, to promote every righteous cause by every righteous means; and especially in regard to the great subjects of morals and religion, it is self-evidently her right to participate with her brother in teaching them, both in private and in public, by writing and by speaking, by any instrumentalities proper to be used, and in any assemblies proper to be held; and this being a self-evident truth growing out of the divinely implanted principles of human nature, any custom or authority adverse to it, whether modern or wearing the hoary sanction of antiquity, is to be regarded as a self-evident falsehood, and at war with mankind.

[All the above resolutions had been drafted by Elizabeth Cady Stanton. At the last session of the convention Lucretia Mott offered the following, which, along with all the other resolutions except the ninth, was adopted unanimously.—*Ed.*]

Resolved, That the speedy success of our cause depends upon the zealous and untiring efforts of both men and women, for the overthrow of the monopoly of the pulpit, and for the securing to woman an equal participation with men in the various trades, professions, and commerce.

Lucy Stone

SPEECH BEFORE THE NATIONAL WOMEN'S RIGHTS CONVENTION OF 1855

Lucy Stone was born August 13, 1818, into a male-dominated farming family; her father ruled the household, her mother devoting herself to a quiet, feminine domesticity. Lucy, however, was independent in thought and challenged her mother's docile submission, working hard enough to prove herself equal, and often superior, to her brother scholastically. But, because she was a female, she did not share the right to the recognition and opportunities that she deserved; Lucy realized that, in addition to this curtailment, a woman's rights were further denied in the eyes of God and the civil law.

Lucy's father, firmly believing that intellectual growth was unnecessary to a woman, refused to finance his daughter's higher education. Thus Lucy was forced to work, for negligible wages, as a teacher. From an early age she recognized the inequalities in the prevailing laws of education, occupational opportunity, and suffrage, when applied to women. Entering Oberlin College in 1843, Lucy used her earlier church experience to shape her course of study; she selected Hebrew and Greek to enable her to examine the Bible for laws that supported women's rights. In 1847, she was graduated from Oberlin and was the first Massachusetts woman to earn a college degree.

SOURCE
Lucy Stone, speech before the National Woman's Rights Convention in Cincinnati in October 1855, History of Woman Suffrage, I, *pp. 165–166.*

Lucy began to lecture for the Anti-Slavery Society, and, although an ardent abolitionist, she could not help mentioning women's rights issues in her speeches. The Anti-Slavery Society, unfortunately, was not willing to share its cause with another, so Lucy presented free-lance feminist speeches during the week, devoting her lecture time to the Anti-Slavery Society on weekends. In her own words: "I was a woman before I was an abolitionist . . . I must speak for the women."

During the 1850s Lucy Stone devoted great effort to the feminist movement, dealing with the problems of wages, education, suffrage, job oportunities, and property rights among others. At this time, she began to speak extensively on the status of married and widowed women, and was especially concerned with the legal and financial independence of women; always, of course, she urged suffrage as a means of eliminating unfair and biased legislation. While working for change, she believed in marriage, and married Henry Browne Blackwell in 1855.

In 1858 Lucy staged a tax protest at her New Jersey home; she refused, as a woman, to allow further "taxation without representation." Throughout the next ten years, she campaigned, recruited, and organized all over the United States: A fight was waged over the elimination of the term "male" from the Fourteenth Amendment. Lucy organized and was appointed to the American Equal Rights Association in 1866; in 1867 and 1868 she organized the New Jersey and the New England Woman's Suffrage Association. Another battle over the Fifteenth Amendment caused a split in the AERA. Lucy organized the American Woman Suffrage Association, which operated in opposition to the National Woman's Suffrage Association until 1890, when the two factions united to form the National American Woman Suffrage Association.

In 1870 Lucy Stone founded and edited The Woman's Journal, the principal reform newspaper for women's suffrage in the United States for fifty years. The Woman's Journal was "devoted to [women's] educational, industrial, legal and political Equality, and especially to the right of suffrage." Most of Lucy's editorials dealt with the legal status of women in marriage and business, and although she continued to give speeches, this newspaper was Lucy Stone's major concern until her death.

The last speaker alluded to this movement as being that of a few disappointed women. From the first years to which my memory stretches, I have been a disappointed woman. When, with my brothers, I reached forth after the sources of knowledge, I was reproved with "It isn't fit for you; it doesn't belong to women." Then there was but one college in the world where women were admitted, and that was in Brazil. I would have found my way there, but by the time I was prepared to go, one was opened in the young State of Ohio—the first in the United States where women and Negroes could enjoy opportunities with white men. I was disappointed when I came to seek a profession worthy an immortal being—every employment was closed to me, except those of the teacher, the seamstress, and the housekeeper. In education, in marriage, in religion, in everything, disappointment is the lot of woman. It shall be the business of my life to deepen this disappointment in every woman's heart until she bows down to it no longer. I wish that women, instead of being walking show-cases, instead of begging of their fathers and brothers the latest and gayest new bonnet, would ask of them their rights.

The question of Woman's Rights is a practical one. The notion has prevailed that it was only an ephemeral idea; that it was but women claiming the right to smoke cigars in the streets, and to frequent bar-rooms. Others have supposed it a question of comparative intellect; others still, of sphere. Too much has already been said and written about woman's sphere. Trace all the doctrines to their source and they will be found to have no basis except in the usages and prejudices of the age. This is seen in the fact that what is tolerated in woman in one country is not tolerated in another. In this country women may hold prayer-meetings, etc., but in Mohammedan countries it is written upon their mosques, "Women and dogs, and other impure animals, are not permitted to enter." Wendell Phillips says, "The best and greatest thing one is capable of doing, that is his sphere." I have confidence in the Father to believe that when He gives us the capacity to do anything He does not make a blunder. Leave women, then, to find their sphere. And do not tell us before we are born even, that our province is to cook dinners, darn stockings, and sew on buttons. We are told woman has all the rights she wants; and even women, I am ashamed to say, tell us so. They mistake the politeness of men for rights—seats while men stand in this hall to-night, and their adulations;

49

but these are mere courtesies. We want rights. The flour-merchant, the house-builder, and the postman charge us no less on account of our sex; but when we endeavor to earn money to pay all these, then, indeed, we find the difference. Man, if he have energy, may hew out for himself a path where no mortal has ever trod, held back by nothing but what is in himself; the world is all before him, where to choose; and we are glad for you, brothers, men that it is so. But the same society that drives forth the young man, keeps woman at home—a dependent—working little cats on worsted, and little dogs on punctured paper; but if she goes heartily and bravely to give herself to some worthy purpose, she is out of her sphere and she loses caste. Women working in tailor-shops are paid one-third as much as men. Some one in Philadephia has stated that women make fine shirts for twelve and a half cents apiece; that no woman can make more than nine a week, and the sum thus earned, after deducting rent, fuel, etc., leaves her just three and a half cents a day for bread. Is it a wonder that women are driven to prostitution? Female teachers in New York are paid fifty dollars a year, and for every such situation there are five hundred applicants. I know not what you believe of God, but I believe He gave yearnings and longings to be filled, and that He did not mean all our time should be devoted to feeding and clothing the body. The present condition of woman causes a horrible perversion of the marriage relation. It is asked of a lady, "Has she married well?" "Oh, yes, her husband is rich." Woman must marry for a home, and you men are the sufferers by this; for a woman who loathes you may marry you because you have the means to get money which she cannot have. But when woman can enter the lists with you and make money for herself, she will marry you only for deep and earnest affection. . . .

Books about Lucy Stone

BLACKWELL, ALICE STONE. *Lucy Stone: Pioneer Woman Suffragist*. Boston, 1930.

CATT AND SHULER. *Woman Suffrage and Politics*. New York: 1926.

HAYS, ELINOR. *Morning Star: A Biography of Lucy Stone*.

RIEGEL, ROBERT. *American Feminists*.

Lucy Stone and Henry B. Blackwell

MARRIAGE CONTRACT, 1855

Even though Lucy Stone strongly opposed the status
conferred on married women, characterized by no property or
contract rights, and the acceptance of wife beating, she married
Henry Browne Blackwell in 1855. In defiance of the debilitating,
degrading, and inhuman condition of the married woman, Henry
Blackwell and Lucy Stone issued a joint statement denouncing
her limited, slavish existence. In fact, Lucy became the first
woman to retain her maiden name in marriage, refusing to
substitute her husband's surname for her own.

SOURCE
Lucy Stone and Henry B. Blackwell, "1855 Marriage Contract," in
History of Woman Suffrage, I, pp. 260–261.

While acknowledging our mutual affection by publicly assuming the relationship of husband and wife, yet in justice to ourselves and a great principle, we deem it a duty to declare that this act on our part implies no sanction of, nor promise of voluntary obedience to such of the present laws of marriage, as refuse to recognize the wife as an independent, rational being, while they confer upon the husband an injurious and unnatural superiority, investing him with legal powers which no honorable man would exercise, and which no man should possess. We protest especially against the laws which give to the husband:

1. The custody of the wife's person.

2. The exclusive control and guardianship of their children.

3. The sole ownership of her personal, and use of her real estate, unless previously settled upon her, or placed in the hands of trustees, as in the case of minors, lunatics, and idiots.

4. The absolute right to the product of her industry.

5. Also against laws which give to the widower so much larger and more permanent an interest in the property of his deceased wife, than they give to the widow in that of the deceased husband.

6. Finally, against the whole system by which "the legal existence of the wife is suspended during marriage," so that in most States, she neither has a legal part in the choice of her residence, nor can she make a will, nor sue or be sued in her own name, nor inherit property.

We believe that personal independence and equal human rights can never be forfeited, except for crime; that marriage should be an equal and permanent partnership, and so recognized by law; that until it is so recognized, married partners should provide against the radical injustice of present laws, by every means in their power.

We believe that where domestic difficulties arise, no appeal should be made to legal tribunals under existing laws, but that all difficulties should be submitted to the equitable adjustment of arbitrators mutually chosen.

Thus reverencing law, we enter our protest against rules and customs which are unworthy of the name, since they violate justice, the essence of law.

(Signed), *Henry B. Blackwell,*
Lucy Stone

Lucretia Mott

DISCOURSE ON WOMEN, 1849

6

Lucretia Mott, one of the first advocates of equality for women, was born January 3, 1793, in Massachusetts into a family of seagoing Nantucket Quakers; Nantucket women were expected to manage all domestic and business affairs while their husbands were on long voyages. Lucretia, the most responsible and clever of the Coffin children, was mistress of the house when her father was away, and her mother visiting far from home.

When Lucretia was fifteen, her father ended his seafaring to begin a new career in the business world and sent his children to a public school in Boston. There he hoped they would benefit; but he discovered the educational attitudes of the school unjust and prejudiced, as compared with the Quakers. He then sent Lucretia to the Quaker Seminary in Nine Partners, New York, a coeducational school where boys and girls lived in separate houses and were taught and kept strictly apart. Lucretia soon qualified as a teacher, but she met with sexual discrimination: Her stipend would be half of that accorded to young men assistant teachers similarly trained. At the Seminary Lucretia met her future husband, James Mott; they were married in 1811, Lucretia then eighteen, and James, twenty-three.

By the middle 1820s, Lucretia, in her position as the Nine Partners congregational minister and the founder and teacher

SOURCE
Lucretia Mott, Discourse on Women, *December 1849, pp. 12–20.*

53

of her own community school, had become a respected, prominent woman. Slavery was a predominating problem in many states; the more conservative members of the congregation were opposed to giving equal rights to Negro slaves. More liberal members, such as Elias Hicks, supported the abolitionists. In 1827, the Motts decided to separate from the main branch of Quakers to join the new Quaker branch, the Hicksites. Within three years, an antislavery convention was created in Philadelphia, and both James and Lucretia were invited, Lucretia becoming the first woman to speak before a delegation of men. This meeting, with its principal issue of slavery, served as the springboard for Lucretia's later work to free women from their slavery to men.

In 1833 Lucretia helped found the first female American Anti-Slavery Society in Philadelphia, following several years of preaching throughout the United States on reform subjects, especially slavery and women's rights. In 1840, she and her husband were asked to represent the United States at the world Anti-Slavery Convention in London, but she was barred from entrance because of her sex. Elizabeth Cady Stanton, receiving the same discriminatory treatment, became Lucretia's friend, and they aligned to crusade for women's freedom. Eight years after their fateful rebuff in London, they called the women's convention at Seneca Falls, New York, that initiated the formal feminist movement in the United States.

Always active in the antislavery movement, Lucretia Mott made her home, from 1850 until her death, a refuge for runaway slaves and continued to aid the reform causes. During her lifetime she was known as the "Great Woman" by members of the Quaker sect and the "Lioness" by representatives who were impressed by her dedicated work at conventions.

The question is often asked, "What does woman want, more than she enjoys? What is she seeking to obtain? Of what rights is she deprived? What privileges are withheld from her? I answer, she asks nothing as favor, but as right, she wants to be acknowledged a moral, responsible being. She is seeking not to be governed by laws, in the making of which she has no voice. She is deprived of almost every right in civil society, and is a cypher in the nation, except in the right of presenting a petition. In religious society her disabilities, as already pointed out, have greatly retarded her progress. Her exclusion from the pulpit or ministry—her duties marked out for her by her equal brother man, subject to creeds, rules, and disciplines made for her by him—this is unworthy her true dignity. In marriage, there is assumed superiority, on the part of the husband, and admitted inferiority, with a promise of obedience, on the part of the wife. This subject calls loudly for examination, in order that the wrong may be redressed. Customs suited to darker ages in Eastern countries, are not binding upon enlightened society. The solemn covenant of marriage may be entered into without these lordly assumptions, and humiliating concessions and promises.

There are large Christian denominations who do not recognise such degrading relations of husband and wife. They ask no magisterial or ministerial aid to legalize or to sanctify this union. But acknowledging themselves in the presence of the Highest, and invoking his assistance, they come under reciprocal obligations of fidelity and affection, before suitable witnesses. Experience and observation go to prove, that there may be as much harmony, to say the least, in such a union, and as great purity and permanency of affection, as can exist where the more common custom of form is observed. The distinctive relations of husband and wife, of father and mother of a family are sacredly preserved, without the assumption of authority on the one part, or the promise of obedience on the other. There is nothing in such a marriage degrading to woman. She does not compromise her dignity or self-respect; but enters married life upon equal ground, by the side of her husband. By proper education, she understands her duties, physical, intellectual and moral; and fulfilling these, she is a help meet, in the true sense of the word.

I tread upon delicate ground in alluding to the institutions of religious associations; but the subject is of so much importance, that all which relates to the position of woman, should be examined, apart from the undue veneration which ancient usage receives.

> Such dupes are men to custom, and so prone
> To reverence what is ancient, and can plead
> A course of long observance for its use,
> That even servitude, the worst of ills,
> Because delivered down from sire to son,
> Is kept and guarded as a sacred thing.

So with woman. She has so long been subject to the disabilities and restrictions, with which her progress has been embarrassed, that she has become enervated, her mind to some extent paralysed; and, like those still more degraded by personal bondage, she hugs her chains. Liberty is often presented in its true light, but it is liberty for man.

> Whose freedom is by suffrance, and at will
> Of a superior—he is never free.
> Who lives, and is not weary of a life
> Exposed to manacles, deserves them well.

I would not, however, go so far, either as regards the abject slave or woman; for in both cases they may be so degraded by the crushing influences around them, that they may not be sensible of the blessing of Freedom. Liberty is not less a blessing, because oppression has so long darkened the mind that it cannot appreciate it. I would therefore urge, that woman be placed in such a situation in society, by the yielding of her rights, and have such opportunities for growth and development, as shall raise her from this low, enervated and paralysed condition, to a full appreciation of the blessing of entire freedom of mind.

It is with reluctance that I make the demand for the political rights of woman, because this claim is so distasteful to the age. Woman shrinks, in the present state of society, from taking any interest in politics. The events of the French Revolution, and the claim for woman's rights are held up to her as a warning. But let us not look at the excesses of women alone, at that period; but remember that the age was marked with extravagances and wickedness in men as well as women. Indeed, political life abounds with these excesses, and with shameful outrage. Who knows, but that if woman acted her part in governmental affairs, there might be an entire change in the turmoil of political life. It becomes man to speak modestly of his ability to act without her. If woman's judgment were exercised, why might she not aid in making the laws by which she is governed? Lord Brougham remarked that the works of Harriet Martineau upon Political Economy were not excelled by those of any political writer of the present time. The first few chapters of her "Society in America," her views of a Republic, and of Government generally, furnish evidence of woman's capacity to embrace subjects of universal interest.

Far be it from me to encourage woman to vote, or to take an active part in politics, in the present state of our government. Her right to the elective franchise however, is the same, and should be yielded to her, whether she exercise that right or not. Would that man too, would have no participation in a government based upon the life-taking principle—upon retaliation and the sword. It is unworthy a Christian nation. But when, in the diffusion of light and intelligence, a convention shall be called to make regulations for self-government on Christian, non-resistant principles, I can see no good reason, why woman should not participate in such an assemblage, taking part equally with man.

Walker, of Cincinnati, in his Introduction to American Law, says: "With regard to political rights, females form a positive exception to the general doctrine of equality. They have no part or lot in the formation or administration of government. They cannot vote or hold office. We require them to contribute their share in the way of taxes, to the support of government, but allow them no voice in its direction. We hold them amenable to the laws when made, but allow them no share in making them. This language, applied to males, would be the exact definition of political slavery; applied to females, custom does not teach us so to regard it." Woman, however, is beginning so to regard it.

"The law of husband and wife, as you gather it from the books, is a disgrace to any civilized nation. The theory of the law degrades the wife almost to the level of slaves. When a woman marries, we call her condition coverture, and speak of her as a *femme convert*. The old writers call the husband baron, and sometimes, in plain English, lord. . . . The merging of her name in that of her husband is emblematic of the fate of all her legal rights. The torch of Hymen serves but to light the pile, on which these rights are offered up. The legal theory is, that marriage makes the husband and wife one person, and that person is the *husband*. On this subject, reform is loudly called for. There is no foundation in reason or expediency, for the absolute and slavish subjection of the wife to the husband, which forms the foundation of the present legal relations. Were woman, in point of fact, the abject thing which the law, in theory, considers her to be when married, she would not be worthy the companionship of man."

I would ask if such a code of laws does not require change? If such a condition of the wife in society does not claim redress? On no good ground can reform be delayed. Blackstone says, "The very being and legal existence of woman is suspended during marriage,—incorporated or consolidated into that of her husband, under whose protection and cover she performs every thing." Hurlbut, in his Essays upon Human Rights, says: "The laws touching the rights of woman are at variance with the laws of the Creator. Rights are human rights, and pertain to human beings, without distinction of sex. Laws should not be made for man or for woman, but for mankind. Man was not born to command, nor woman to obey. . . . The law of France, Spain, and Holland, and one of our own States, Louisiana, recognizes the wife's right to property, more than the common law of England. . . . The law depriving woman of the right of property is handed down to us from dark and feudal times, and not consistent with the wiser, better, purer spirit of the age. The wife is a mere pensioner on the bounty of her husband. Her lost rights are appropriated to himself. But justice and benevolence are abroad in our land, awakening the spirit of inquiry and innovation; and the Gothic fabric of the British law will fall before it, save where it is based upon the foundation of truth and justice."

May these statements lead you to reflect upon this subject, that you may know what woman's condition is in society—what her restrictions are, and seek to remove them. In how many cases in our country, the husband and wife begin life together, and by equal industry and united effort accumulate to themselves a comfortable home. In the event of the death of the wife, the household remains undisturbed, his farm or his workshop is not broken up, or in any way molested. But when the husband dies, he either gives his wife a *portion* of their joint accumulation, or the law apportions to her a *share*; the homestead is broken up, and she is dispossessed of that which she earned equally with him; for what she lacked in physical strength, she made up in constancy of labor and toil, day and evening. The sons then coming into possession of the property, as has been the custom until of latter time, speak of having to *keep* their mother, when she in reality is aiding to keep them. Where is the justice of this state of things? The change in the law of this State and of New York, in relation to the property of the wife, go to a limited extent, toward the redress of these wrongs; but they are far more extensive, and involve much more, than I have time this evening to point out.

On no good ground can the legal existence of the wife be suspended during marriage, and her property surrendered to her husband. In the intelligent ranks of society, the wife may not in point of fact, be so degraded as the law would degrade her; because public sentiment is above the law. Still, while the law stands, she is liable to the disabilities which it imposes. Among the ignorant classes of society, woman is made to bear heavy burdens, and is degraded almost to the level of the slave.

There are many instances now in our city, where the wife suffers much from the power of the husband to claim all that she can earn with her own hands. In my intercourse with the poorer class of people, I have known cases of extreme cruelty, from the hard earnings of the wife being thus robbed by the husband, and no redress at law.

. . .

In visiting the public school in London, a few years since, I noticed that the boys were employed in linear drawing, and instructed upon the black board, in the higher branches of arithmetic and mathematics; while the girls, after a short exercise in the mere elements of arithmetic, were seated, during the bright hours of the morning, *stitching wristbands*. I asked, Why there should be this difference made; why they too should not have the black board? The answer was, that they would not probably fill any station in society requiring such knowledge.

But the demand for a more extended education will not cease, until girls and boys have equal instruction, in all the departments of useful knowledge. We have as yet no high school for girls in this state. The normal school may be a preparation for such an establishment. In the late convention for general education, it was cheering to hear the testimony borne to woman's capabilities for head teachers of the public schools. A resolution there offered for equal salaries to male and female teachers, when equally qualified, as practised in Louisiana, I regret to say was checked in its passage, by Bishop Potter; by him who has done so much for the encouragement of education, and who gave his countenance and influence to that convention. Still the fact of such a resolution being offered, augurs a time coming for woman, which she may well hail. At the late examination of the public schools in this city, one of the alumni delivered an address on Woman, not as is too common, in eulogistic strains, but directing the attention to the injustice done to woman in her position in society, in a variety of ways. The unequal wages she receives for her constant toil, &c., presenting facts calculated to arouse attention to the subject.

Women's property has been taxed, equally with that of men's, to sustain colleges endowed by the states; but they have not been permitted to enter those high seminaries of learning. Within a few years, however, some colleges have been instituted, where young women are admitted, nearly upon equal terms with young men; and numbers are availing themselves of their long denied rights. This is among the signs of the times, indicative of an advance for women. The book of knowledge is not opened to her in vain. Already is she aiming to occupy important posts of honor and profit in our country. We have three female editors in our state—some in other states of the Union. Numbers are entering the medical profession—one received a diploma last year; others are preparing for a like result.

Let woman then go on—not asking as favor, but claiming as right, the removal of all the hindrances to her elevation in the scale of being—let her receive encouragement for the proper cultivation of all her powers, so that she may enter profitably into the active business of life; employing her own hands, in ministering to her necessities, strengthening her physical being by proper exercise, and observance of the laws of health. Let her not be ambitious to display a fair hand, and to promenade the fashionable streets of our city, but rather, coveting earnestly the best gifts, let her strive to occupy such walks in society, as will befit her true dignity in all the relations of life. No fear that she will then transcend the proper limits of female delicacy. True modesty will be as fully preserved, in acting out those important vocations to which she may be called, as in the nursery or at the fireside, ministering to man's self-indulgence.

Then in the marriage union, the independence of the husband and wife will be equal, their dependence mutual, and their obligations reciprocal.

In conclusion, let me say, "Credit not the old fashioned absurdity, that woman's is a secondary lot, ministering to the necessities of her lord and master! It is a higher destiny I would award you. If your immortality is as complete, and your gift of mind as capable as ours, of increase and elevation, I would put no wisdom of mine against God's evident allotment. I would charge you to water the undying bud, and give it healthy culture, and open its beauty to the sun—and then you may hope, that when your life is bound up with another, you will go on equally, and in a fellowship that shall pervade every earthly interest."

Books about Lucretia Mott

BURNETT, CONSTANCE BUEL. *Five for Freedom*. New York: 1953.

HALLOWELL, ANNA DAVIS, ed. *James and Lucretia Mott: Life and Letters*. Cambridge: 1884.

TOLLES, FREDERICK B., ed. *Slavery and "The Woman Question."* Haverford, Pa.: 1952.

WHITTON, MARY ORMSBEE, *These Were the Women, U.S.A., 1776–1860*. New York: 1954.

Amelia Bloomer

LETTER TO WOMAN'S CONVENTION, 1851

7

Amelia Jenks Bloomer, editor of what was probably the first journal published by a woman, was born in Homer, Cortland County, New York, May 27, 1818.

She married Dexter C. Bloomer in 1840, and together they joined the Independent Temperance Total-Abstinence Society. For several years the Bloomers published a semimonthly periodical in Seneca Falls, New York, and Bloomer urged his wife to send her articles on temperance, anonymously, to newspapers.

Women were now permitted to attend temperance meetings and contribute to the cause, but they were given almost no opportunity to voice their opinions. So Amelia and a number of women, in 1849, established their own newspaper, The Lily, *in the interests of temperance reform and women's rights. Lasting from 1849 to 1854, the paper eventually became the sole responsibility of Mrs. Bloomer.*

Early articles in The Lily *were concerned with temperance literary events, and the raising of children, but Amelia's outrage at the 1850 Tennessee Legislature decision, stating that women*

SOURCE
Dexter Bloomer, The Life and Writings of Amelia Bloomer, *Boston, 1895. Letter published in* The Lily, *August 1851, from Amelia Bloomer, editor, to the Woman's Convention held at Akron, Ohio, May 28, 1851.*

lacked a soul and had no right to property, prompted her to write her first editorial on the subject of women's rights. The Mott–Stanton convention of 1848 also impressed her with the great injustices suffered by women, in the hands of the shapers of society, men. Elizabeth Cady Stanton contributed many articles to The Lily, whose publication was resumed in Mount Vernon, Ohio, where Amelia moved in 1853; Mrs. Bloomer also became associate editor of The Western Home Journal.

The Bloomers moved two years later to Council Bluffs, Iowa, where Bloomer helped to organize the state's Republican Party and became a federal official and a judge. Mrs. Bloomer continued her reformatory work for many years, but much of her publicity resulted from her radical style of dress, donned in an attempt to reform women's apparel. Because of the discomfort caused by current styles, Mrs. Bloomer wore instead a costume devised by Mrs. Elizabeth Smith Miller; it consisted of a short dress and trousers gathered at the ankle. Although she had not invented it, the style was given Amelia's name, and "Bloomer" became a symbol of the cause of woman suffrage, "Bloomer girls" being synonymous with feminists.

Amelia Bloomer's adoption of a "sensible" dress for women was only an episode in her life; the primary causes to which she devoted herself were women's right to equal education, employment, and legal privileges; temperance; and the abolition of slavery. The inscription on her gravestone reads:

IN MEMORIAM
AMELIA JENKS, WIFE OF D.C. BLOOMER
DIED DECEMBER 30th 1894
AGED 76 YEARS, 7 MONTHS & 3 DAYS
A PIONEER IN WOMAN'S ENFRANCHISEMENT

Ladies:—

I am deeply impressed with a sense of the great wrong done to woman in every branch of her education, and I hail with pleasurable feelings every movement, which has for its object her emancipation from ignorance and bondage.

It was from contemplating the condition of the oppressed and downtrodden of my own sex who are victims to the cruelties of the liquor traffic, that I was first led to see upon how wrong a basis society at present rests. We see many a woman who has been cradled in luxury, and reared with tenderness, now spurned from the society of the good and respectable, as a thing too low to receive even respectful kindness. Her feelings are as tender now as ever—her heart as pure, but alas, she has been unfortunate in wedding one whom the laws of this enlightened land have made a drunkard. No matter how highly educated— no matter how wealthy—no matter in how high a circle she moved previous to the time when her identity was merged in him, she is now a drunkard's wife; and no words can express more of sorrows, degradation, and wretchedness than is implied in those two words—a drunkard's wife. We see her now poor, dejected, and forlorn, toiling early and late to earn a subsistence, and then often compelled by fear and brutal force to yield up the pittance she has earned to an idle and dissolute being whom the law calls her husband, that he may with it imbrute his soul still deeper in infamy. She is outraged in her every feeling, her affections trampled upon, her person subjected to the most violent abuse, her children corrupted and destroyed, or left to starve before her eyes. She has been deprived of every right, stripped of every comfort, compelled to toil like a very slave to earn the necessaries of life, and at last driven forth, to beg or starve, or what is equally degrading, end her days in a poor house, or a brothel. All this, and more, has woman suffered from the legalized traffic in strong drinks; while they who have caused it all, have been respected of men, and shielded by law from the punishment and scorn they so richly deserve.

It is surprising that women have so long submitted to these indignities instead of rising en masse and demanding relief and protection. And yet what could they do? They have ever been taught that they are weak and powerless, and that the will of their masters must be their law: hence we see them silently submitting to man's dictates, and bending their backs to the burthen he has heaped upon them. They have been taught that

God created them inferior, and designed them to occupy an inferior and subordinate position; and that to rebel against man's rule, was to rebel against God. Many minds are so impressed with this belief, that notwithstanding the hardness of their fate, they feel that they must meekly bow their necks to the yoke which their Great Master has laid upon them. They never stop to ask if, or why this is so, or to endure whether a just and holy God can with justice require so much at their hands.

Those who dare speak out against this injustice, and come in earnest before the people claiming that the rights which have been wrested from them shall be restored, are met with ridicule, scoffs, and abuse. They may beg, they may plead, they may pray—it avails them not!—Their law makers turn a deaf ear, and the rumseller spurns from his presence. They may endure every hardship, labor in the most menial employment, expose themselves to the gaze of licentious men upon the theatrical stage, become paupers or public prostitutes, and nobody cares; they are within their "sphere." But let them come forth like true women, pleading in the name of God and humanity that their wrongs may be redressed, and their rights restored, and they are at once condemned. They have outstepped their sphere and become "manish."

Men claim the right to represent us, and to legislate for us, but alas! we have had too much of their legislation. We have never been faithfully represented—we have never even been consulted as to our opinions and wishes. They have made laws to suit their own views and interests, and then exacted obedience from us.—Methinks if woman had a voice in making the laws she would guard her own interests better than they have ever yet been guarded. She knows better than man can know, what her interests are, and he has no right to exclude her from a participation in framing the laws by which she is to be governed.

Another instance of the great wrong done to woman is seen in her circumscribed sphere of industry, and the meagre wages she receives for her labor. Men call us angels, and boast of the deference they pay to our weakness! They give us their seats in church, in cars and omnibusses, at lectures and concerts, and in many other ways show us great respect where nothing but form is concerned. This is all mere complimentary politeness, and is well enough so far as it goes; but at the same time they are defrauding us of our just rights by crowding us out of every lucrative employment, and subjecting us to virtual slavery. Menial occupations, and menial compensation is thought well enough for woman. She can earn only as much, and sometimes only half as much, in a week, by the closest application, as a man can earn in one day. And yet with a family of little ones to support, she must pay as much for rent, fire wood, and other necessaries out of these meagre earnings, as he pays with his six or ten fold wages. Not a cent can be laid by for sickness, or a "rainy day"; when these come she must suffer from abject poverty, and to prevent starvation seek a home for herself and little ones in the poor house. Young girls, of whom there are thousands in our free country who are compelled to support themselves—instead of being suffered to share with their brothers in the various opportunities for gain—instead of having opened to them the professions, the arts and sciences, and many other kinds of business to which their capacities are so well suited, are crowded out of them all and driven either to the drudgery of the kitchen, to die by consumption over their needles, to drag out weary lives amid the din and stench of a factory, or submit to the loathesome life of prostitution. Men monopolize every lucrative branch of business and unfeelingly deny woman's equal right to share their employment and their wages. She has the same right to accumulate, and the same necessity for doing so, that he has; and the same opportunities, and the same encouragement, should be given her to participate in the active business of life.

Again, the great wrong done the married woman in depriving her of a right to property, is a just cause of complaint. True, recent legislation has done something for her, by suffering her to retain what she owned before marriage; yet this is going but little way. The great majority of girls have nothing at marriage, but by economy and industry may assist their husbands to accumulate a sum sufficient to make them comfortable for life, if not independent.

Yet by existing laws, at the husband's death the wife must be deprived of all but a life interest in one-third of this property, while the remaining two thirds, in case there are no children, goes to some distant relation of her husband, who can have no shadow of right to it, and who may be better able to give her thousands, than she is to part with hundreds. It frequently happens that the "widow's third" is not enough for her supoprt; and then she must still toil for it, or become a town charge; while the money honestly hers, and which should have kept her from dependence and want, is wrested from her and given to another. If there are children, the two-thirds goes to them, and if the mother's third is not sufficient for her maintenance, she becomes a charge to them, and is often treated with unfilial regard, and even her death longed for, that they may be rid of the burthen, and possess themselves of the little she has.

But I need not dwell upon particular cases where woman has been treated as an inferior and subordinate being. They are so many, and so various, that much time would be required to depict them all. I consider the great wrongs she has endured as but legitimate fruits of the false education she has received. By education I mean not mere book learning, but the whole moral, intellectual, physical, domestic, and civil education: these have been almost entirely neglected, and only the ornamental cultivated. She has never been taught to think or act for herself, or to have any higher purpose than to display her accomplishments, and catch a husband. Her education, from childhood up, has been entirely superficial, and not commensurate with the wants and capacities of her mind. Our colleges have been closed against her, as if her presence would profane their sacred halls. The state has largely endowed these institutions, and women have been taxed for their support, that men may be fitted to perform their part in life's great drama; but women must be content with the senseless balderdash taught in our female seminaries, and fashionable boarding schools. A little music, a little French, a great deal of self-conceit and vanity and the young lady is considered educated, and is sent forth, to take her part, also, in the drama of life! How far she is fitted by these accomplishments to cope with the world and perform her part of life's duties, every day's history will tell us! How far she is fitted to be the helpmate and bosom companion of man, his treatment of her too truly tells us! There is nothing useful— nothing practical in her education: and can it be wondered at that she is considered inferior in intellect, or that looking to man's superior wisdom she should learn to think him superior? Can it be wondered at that she falls a victim to his seducive wiles, or that she bears his indignities in silence? Is it not strange, that men are so loath to improve and cultivate the powers of her mind, and to teach her to rely more upon herself, since they know that in whatever sphere she is destined to move, she will need through life "all the energy, strength, and endurance, of which her system shall be capable"? Is it not strange that they are so unwilling to admit our equality, so long as we are so nearly associated with them in this life, and must share with them joys of immortality?

But woman is herself aroused to a sense of her wrongs, and sees the necessity of action on her part if she would have justice done her! A brighter day has dawned for her! a spirit of enquiry has awakened in her bosom, which neither ridicule or taunts can quench! Henceforth her course is upward and onward! Her mind is capable of grasping things hitherto thought beyond her reach, and she will not weary of the chase till she has reached the topmost round in the ladder of science! She will yet prove conclusively that she possesses the same God-given faculties which belong to man, and that she is endowed with powers of mind and body suitable for any emergency in which she may be placed!

But I will conclude with the prayer, that the blessing of God may rest upon, and guide you in your deliberation.

Yours in every good cause,
Amelia Bloomer

To C. D. Smalley,
M. L. Gilbert,
E. Robinson,
Committee

Amelia Bloomer

LETTER TO MRS. JANNEY, 1872

Feb. 9, 1872

Dear Mrs. Janney,

Noticing your call for the annual gathering of the friends of woman's suffrage in Ohio, on the 15 & 16th inst., I cannot forbear sending you a few words of greeting and encouragement. It does one good to see the names of old and tried workers in woman's cause connected with such meetings, and to know that the pioneers in the movement have never wearied or faltered in their purpose to emancipate woman from the thralldom of ignorance and civil inferiority in which all past ages have held her. Weak and timid ones may falter by the way and drop out of the ranks; but you and I, and others who entered this work with us a score of years ago from a full conviction of the right and justice of the cause we espoused, enlisted for the war and must die with harness on, unless those who have the rule over us soon grant our demands and release us from our work. Little we thought years ago when pleading the cause of the slave as well as our own, that he would be given the boon of freedom and the rights of citizenship before us. Yet such has been the justice of our rulers. The sons of Africa, just freed from bondage, and steeped in ignorance, are elevated above us, with power to make laws for our governance without our consent. And

SOURCE
New York Historical Society.

these rights were given them unasked, while all our pleading and demands have been in vain.

No, not all in vain—for though our cause makes very slow progress, as it seems to us, yet much has been gained in the way of more liberal law codes, greater educational advantages, and wider fields of employment. We have gained too, in an increased public sentiment in our favor, and the addition to our ranks of some of the ablest minds of the country. The days of ridicule are past, and the subject can no longer be set aside with a sneer. Clouds have settled over us of late, and have obscured in part the brightness of our prospects, but as "it is always darkest just before day," so let us believe that these clouds will soon be lifted, and show us their "silver linings," and that men will see more clearly than ever before what is due to woman from their hands.

I wish I could report to your convention just what we expect to do in this State, but it is a little too early for me to give definite information. Two years ago the Legislature passed a resolution giving suffrage to woman. By the law of this state that resolution must be ratified by the present Legislature before it can go to the people. The question has not yet been taken up, but will probably be brought forward at an early day. Should it pass, it will be voted on by the people at the next general election; but should it fail, nothing more can be done for ten years to come.

At the time of the passage of the Resolution two years ago, and even up to six months ago, the friends of the cause were very sanguine of success both in the Legislature and at the polls. We have believed that Iowa would be the first state to do justice to its women. But I am sorry to say that the cloud now rests upon us here, as elsewhere. The unwise and foolish "social theories" of one who has but recently allied herself to the movement have caused a scare in the minds of many; and strange as it may seem to all intelligent and true woman suffragists, this attempt to saddle obnoxious doctrines upon our cause has had the effect to drive some away, and to make others doubt and hesitate as to the expediency of placing in woman's hand the power to protect and represent herself.

A few days more and the fate of the Resolution in the Legislature will be decided. Should it pass there and go to the people, then we shall need all the aid in the months to come that the friends of the cause can bestow. Should it fail there, we must bide our time and try again.

Though somewhat disheartened by the adverse influences which have been at work, we yet have full faith in the justice and righteousness of our cause, and of its final triumph over the obstacles which ignorance, cowardice, and prejudice now throw in our way

Wishing you success in your convention, and in all your undertakings.

I am Most Truly Yours,
Amelia Bloomer

Elizabeth Cady Stanton

SPEECH BEFORE THE LEGISLATURE, 1860

Elizabeth Cady Stanton was born November 12, 1815, in
Johnstown, New York, to a stern Presbyterian family and was
raised in an atmosphere of religious severity. She was, by
special permission, the first girl to be admitted to Boys Academy
of Johnstown, where she received second prize in Greek. Unable
to continue her schooling at Union College because of the
restriction on women's higher education, she went to the Emma
Willard Seminary in Troy and was graduated in 1832.

    Elizabeth studied law briefly with her father, Judge Daniel
Cady, but was prevented from admission to the bar and from
practice because of her sex; during this time she realized the
inequity of a legal system that was male-oriented and
discriminatory to females. An entry in her diary, "The tears and
complaints of the women who came to my father for legal
advice touched my heart and early drew my attention to the
injustice and cruelty of the laws," marked a beginning of her
advocacy of women's rights. Greatly influenced by her cousin,
Gerrit Smith, Elizabeth also became interested in temperance
activities and in the antislavery movement.

    Upon marriage to well-known abolitionist Henry Brewster
Stanton, on May 10, 1840, Elizabeth insisted that the word
"obey" be omitted from the ceremony. "I obstinately refused

SOURCE
Elizabeth Cady Stanton, "Speech Before the Legislature, February,
1860," in History of Woman Suffrage, I, pp. 679–685.

to obey one with whom I supposed I was entering into an equal relationship," she wrote. She would later champion the rights of women to property and to easy divorce, but her major concern was always women's suffrage.

At the first world Anti-Slavery Convention in London, in the summer of 1840, Elizabeth met Lucretia Mott, and both discovered that women delegates were denied participation at the conference. They vowed to hold a women's rights convention denouncing such bias upon their return to the United States. Although delayed, the convention was held eight years later on July 13, 1848, at Seneca Falls, New York, and the "Declaration of Sentiments and Resolutions," containing the grievances of women against existing discriminatory laws and customs, was read by Elizabeth Stanton. The demand for women's suffrage, however, proved most controversial and was finally resolved, after much effort, with the help of black leader Frederick Douglass.

In 1851 Elizabeth's acquaintance with Susan B. Anthony broadened into a mutual crusade for temperance reform, and in 1868 they, with the help of Parker Pillsbury, founded The Revolution, a radical weekly newspaper. Elizabeth was chosen the first president of the newly formed National Woman's Suffrage Association and held the post for twenty-one years. The NWSA had emerged from splits between radicals and others but realigned itself in 1890 as the National American Woman Suffrage Association. Mrs. Stanton was again elected president.

During her presidency, Elizabeth gained a reputation as an eloquent speaker, writer, and contributor to feminist thought. She co-authored The Woman's Bible, published in two parts in 1895 and 1898; with Susan B. Anthony and Matilda Joslyn Gage, she compiled the momentous six-volume History of Woman Suffrage between 1881 to 1886. Eighty Years and More, her reminiscences, was published in 1898.

Elizabeth Cady Stanton, the mother of seven and a pioneer for women's rights, died on October 26, 1906. The first volume of the History of Woman Suffrage contains a moving speech delivered to the New York Legislature on February 18, 1860, in which the undaunted Mrs. Stanton appealed for woman's equality in the courts: "Leave us alone," she said, "strike out the words 'white male' from your constitution." She demanded a new image of womanhood, one of courage and independence, to replace the age-old conception of a beautiful being "without rights, or hopes, or fears."

On the 18th of February 1860 Mrs. Stanton addressed the Legislature on woman's right of suffrage and the bill then pending in the Senate. A magnificent audience greeted her in the Capitol. She occupied the Speaker's desk, and was introduced by Senator Hammond, and spoke as follows:

Gentlemen of the Judiciary:—There are certain natural rights as inalienable to civilization as are the rights of air and motion to the savage in the wilderness. The natural rights of the civilized man and woman are government, property, the harmonious development of all their powers, and the gratification of their desires. There are a few people we now and then meet who, like Jeremy Bentham, scout the idea of natural rights in civilization, and pronounce them mere metaphors, declaring that there are no rights aside from those the law confers. If the law made man too, that might do, for then he could be made to order to fit the particular niche he was designed to fill. But inasmuch as God made man in His own image, with capacities and powers as boundless as the universe, whose exigencies no mere human law can meet, it is evident that the man must ever stand first; the law but the creature of his wants; the law giver but the mouthpiece of humanity. If, then, the nature of a being decides its rights, every individual comes into this world with rights that are not transferable. He does not bring them like a pack on his back, that may be stolen from him, but they are a component part of himself, the laws which insure his growth and development. The individual may be put in the stocks, body and soul, he may be dwarfed, crippled, killed, but his rights no man can get; they live and die with him.

Though the atmosphere is forty miles deep all round the globe, no man can do more than fill his own lungs. No man can see, hear, or smell but just so far; and though hundreds are deprived of these senses, his are not the more acute. Though rights have been abundantly supplied by the good Father, no man can appropriate to himself those that belong to another. A citizen can have but one vote, fill but one office, though thousands are not permitted to do either. These axioms prove that woman's poverty does not add to man's wealth, and if, in the plenitude of his power, he should secure to her the exercise of all her God-given rights, her wealth could not bring poverty to him. There is a kind of nervous unrest always manifested by those in power, whenever new claims are started by those out of their own immediate class. The philosophy of this is very plain. They imagine that if the rights of this new class be granted, they must, of necessity, sacrifice something of what they already possess. They can not divest themselves of the idea that rights are very much like lands, stocks, bonds, and mortgages, and that if every new claimant be satisfied, the supply of human rights must in time run low. You might as well carp at the birth of every child, lest there should not be enough air left to inflate your lungs; at the success of every scholar, for fear that your draughts at the fountain of knowledge could not be so long and deep; at the glory of every hero, lest there be no glory left for you. . . .

If the object of government is to protect the weak against the strong how unwise to place the power wholly in the hands of the strong. Yet that is the history of all governments, even the model republic of these United States. You who have read the history of nations, from Moses down to our last election, where have you ever seen one class looking after the interests of another? Any of you can readily see the defects in other governments, and pronounce sentence against those who have sacrificed the masses to themselves; but when we come to our own case, we are blinded by custom and self-interest. Some of you who have no capital can see the injustice which the laborer suffers; some of you who have no slaves, can see the cruelty of his oppression; but who of you appreciate the galling humiliation, the refinements of degradation, to which women (the mothers, wives, sisters, and daughters of freemen), are subject, in this the last half of the nineteenth century? How many of you have ever read even the laws concerning them that now disgrace your statute-books? In cruelty and tyranny, they are not surpassed by any slaveholding code in the Southern States; in fact they are worse, by just so far as woman, from her social position, refinement, and education, is on a more equal ground with the oppressor.

Allow me just here to call the attention of that party now so much interested in the slave of the Carolinas, to the similarity in his condition and that of the mothers, wives, and daughters of the Empire State. The negro has no name. He is Cuffy Douglas or Cuffy Brooks, just whose Cuffy he may chance to be. The woman has no name. She is Mrs. Richard Roe or Mrs. John Doe, just whose Mrs. she may chance to be. Cuffy has no right to his earnings; he can not buy or sell, or lay up any thing that he can call his own. Mrs. Roe has no rights to her earnings; she can neither buy nor sell, make contracts, nor lay up anything that she can call her own. Cuffy has no right to his children; they can be sold from him at any time. Mrs. Roe has no right to her children; they may be bound out to cancel a father's debts of honor. The unborn child, even by the last will of the father, may be placed under the guardianship of a stranger and a foreigner. Cuffy has no legal existence; he is subject to restraint and moderate chastisement. Mrs. Roe has no legal existence; she has not the best right to her own person. The husband has the power to restrain, and administer moderate chastisement.

Blackstone declares that the husband and wife are one, and learned commentators have decided that that one is the husband. In all civil codes you will find them classified as one. Certain rights and immunities, such and such privileges are to be secured to white male citizens. What have women and negroes to do with rights? What know they of government, war, or glory?

The prejudice against color, of which we hear so much, is no stronger than that against sex. It is produced by the same cause, and manifested very much in the same way. The negro's skin and the woman's sex are both *prima facie* evidence that they were intended to be in subjection to the white Saxon man. The few social privileges which the man gives the woman, he makes up to the negro in civil rights. The woman may sit at the same table and eat with the white man; the free negro may hold property and vote. The woman may sit in the same pew with the white man in church; the free negro may enter the pulpit and preach. Now, with the black man's right to suffrage, the right unquestioned, even by Paul, to minister at the altar, it is evident that the prejudice against sex is more deeply rooted and more unreasonably maintained than that against color. As citizens of a republic, which should we most highly prize, social privileges or civil rights? The latter, most certainly.

To those who do not feel the injustice and degradation of the condition, there is something inexpressibly comical in man's "citizen woman." It reminds me of those monsters I used to see in the old world, head and shoulders woman, and the rest of the body sometimes fish and sometimes beast. I used to think, What a strange conceit! but now I see how perfectly it represents man's idea! Look over all his laws concerning us, and you will see just enough of woman to tell of her existence; all the rest is submerged, or made to crawl upon the earth. Just imagine an inhabitant of another planet entertaining himself some pleasant evening in searching over our great national compact, our Declaration of Independence, our Constitutions, or some of our statute books; what would he think of those "women and negroes" that must be so fenced in, so guarded against? Why, he would certainly suppose we were monsters, like those fabulous giants or Brobdignagians of olden times, so dangerous to civilized man, from our size, ferocity, and power. Then let him take up our poets, from Pope down to Dana; let him listen to our Fourth of July toasts, and some of the sentimental adulations of social life, and no logic could convince him that this creature of the law, and his angel of the family altar, could be one and the same being. Man is in such a labyrinth of contradictions with his marital and property rights; he is so befogged on the whole question of maidens, wives, and mothers, that from pure benevolence we should relieve him from this troublesome branch of legislation. We should vote, and make laws for ourselves. Do not be alarmed, dear ladies! You need spend no time reading Grotius, Coke, Puffendorf, Blackstone, Bentham, Kent, and Story to find out what you need. We may safely trust the shrewd selfishness of the white man, and consent to live under the same broad code where he has so comfortably ensconced himself. Any legislation that will do for man, we may abide by most cheerfully. . . .

But, say you, we would not have woman exposed to the grossness and vulgarity of public life, or encounter what she must at the polls. When you talk, gentlemen, of sheltering woman from the rough winds and revolting scenes of real life, you must be either talking for effect, or wholly ignorant of what the facts of life are. The man, whatever he is, is known to the woman. She is the companion, not only of the accomplished statesman, the orator, and the scholar; but the vile, vulgar, brutal man has his mother, his wife, his sister, his daughter. Yes, delicate, refined, educated women are in daily life with the drunkard, the gambler, the licentious man, the rogue, and the villain; and if man shows out what he is anywhere, it is at his own hearthstone. There are over forty thousand drunkards in this State. All these are bound by the ties of family to some woman. Allow but a mother and a wife to each, and you have over eighty thousand women. All these have seen their fathers, brothers, husbands, sons, in the lowest and most debased stages of obscenity and degradation. In your own circle of friends, do you not know refined women, whose whole lives are darkened and saddened by gross and brutal associations? Now, gentlemen, do you talk to woman of a rude jest or jostle at the polls, where noble, virtuous men stand ready to protect her person and her rights, when, alone in the darkness and solitude and gloom of night, she has trembled on her own threshold, awaiting the return of a husband from his midnight revels?—when, stepping from her chamber, she has beheld her royal monarch, her lord and master—her legal representative—the protector of her property, her home, her children, and her person, down on his hands and knees slowly crawling up the stairs? Behold him in her chamber—in her bed! The fairy tale of "Beauty and the Beast" is far too often realized in life. Gentlemen, such scenes as woman has witnessed at her own fireside, where no eye save Omnipotence could pity, no strong arm could help, can never be realized at the polls, never equaled elsewhere, this side the bottomless pit. No, woman has not hitherto lived in the clouds, surrounded by an atmosphere of purity and peace—but she has been the companion of man in health, in sickness, and in death, in his highest and in his lowest moments. She has worshiped him as a saint and an orator, and pitied him as a madman or a fool. In Paradise, man and woman were placed together, and so they must ever be. They must sink or rise together. If man is low and wretched and vile, woman can not escape the contagion, and any atmosphere that is unfit for woman to breathe is not fit for man. Verily, the sins of the fathers shall be visited upon the children to the third and fourth generation. You, by your unwise legislation, have crippled and dwarfed womanhood, by closing to her all honorable and lucrative means of employment, have driven her into the garrets and dens of our cities, where she now revenges herself on your innocent sons, sapping the very foundations of national virtue and strength. Alas! for the young men just coming on the stage of action, who soon shall fill your vacant places—our future Senators, our Presidents, the expounders of our constitutional law! Terrible are the penalties we are now suffering for the ages of injustice done to woman.

Again, it is said that the majority of women do not ask for any change in the laws; that it is time enough to give them the elective franchise when they, as a class, demand it.

Wise statesmen legislate for the best interests of the nation; the State, for the highest good of its citizens; the Christian, for the conversion of the world. Where would have been our railroads, our telegraphs, our ocean steamers, our canals and harbors, our arts and sciences, if government had withheld the means from the far-seeing minority? This State established our present system of common schools, fully believing that educated men and women would make better citizens than ignorant ones. In making this provision for the education of its children, had they waited for a majority of the urchins of this State to petition for schools, how many, think you, would have asked to be transplanted from the street to the school-house? Does the State wait for the criminal to ask for his prison-house? the insane, the idiot, the deaf and dumb for his asylum? Does the Christian, in his love to all mankind, wait for the majority of the benighted heathen to ask him for the gospel? No; unasked and unwelcomed, he crosses the trackless ocean, rolls off the mountain of superstition that oppresses the human mind, proclaims the immortality of the soul, the dignity of manhood, the right of all to be free and happy.

No, gentlemen, if there is but one woman in this State who feels the injustice of her position, she should not be denied her inalienable rights, because the common household drudge and the silly butterfly of fashion are ignorant of all laws, both human and Divine. Because they know nothing of governments, or rights, and therefore ask nothing, shall my petitions be unheard? I stand before you the rightful representative of woman, claiming a share in the halo of glory that has gathered round her in the ages, and by the wisdom of her past words and works, her peerless heroism and self-sacrifice, I challenge your admiration; and, moreover, claiming, as I do, a share in all her outrages and sufferings, in the cruel injustice, contempt, and ridicule now heaped upon her, in her deep degradation, hopeless wretchedness, by all that is helpless in her present condition, that is false in law and public sentiment, I urge your generous consideration; for as my heart swells with pride to behold woman in the highest walks of literature and art, grows big enough to take in those who are bleeding in the dust.

Now do not think, gentlemen, we wish you to do a great many troublesome things for us. We do not ask our legislators to spend a whole session in fixing up a code of laws to satisfy a class of most unreasonable women. We ask no more than the poor devils in the Scripture asked, "Let us alone." In mercy, let us take care of ourselves, our property, our children, and our homes. True, we are not so strong, so wise, so crafty as you are, but if any kind friend leaves us a little money, or we can by great industry earn fifty cents a day, we would rather buy bread and clothes for our children than cigars and champagne for our legal protectors. There has been a great deal written and said about protection. We, as a class, are tired of one kind of protection, that which leaves us everything to do, to dare, and to suffer, and strips us of all means for its accomplishment. We would not tax man to take care of us. No, the Great Father has endowed all his creatures with the necessary powers for self-support, self-defense, and protection. We do not ask man to represent us; it is hard enough in times like these for many to carry backbone enough to represent himself. So long as the mass of men spend most of their time on the fence, not knowing which way to jump, they are surely in no condition to tell us where we had better stand. In pity for man, we would no longer hang like a millstone round his neck. Undo what man did for us in the dark ages, and strike out all special legislation for us; strike the words "white male" from all your constitutions, and then, with fair sailing, let us sink or swim, live or die, survive or perish together.

At Athens, an ancient apologue tells us, on the completion of the temple of Minerva, a statue of the goddess was wanted to occupy the crowning point of the edifice. Two of the greatest artists produced what each deemed his masterpiece. One of these figures was the size of life, admirably designed, exquisitely finished, softly rounded, and beautifully refined. The other was of Amazonian stature, and so boldly chiselled that it looked more like masonry than sculpture. The eyes of all were attracted by the first, and turned away in contempt from the second. That, therefore, was adopted, and the other rejected, almost with resentment, as though an insult had been offered to a discerning public. The favored statue was accordingly borne in triumph to the place for which it was designed, in the presence of applauding thousands, but as it receded from their upturned eyes, all, all at once agaze upon it, the thunders of applause unaccountably died away—a general misgiving ran through every bosom—the mob themselves stood like statues, as silent and as petrified, for as it slowly went up, and up the soft expression of those chiselled features, the delicate curves and outlines of the limbs and figure, became gradually fainter and fainter, and when at last it reached the place for which it was intended, it was a shapeless ball, enveloped in mist. Of course, the idol of the hour was now clamored down as rationally as it had been cried up, and its dishonored rival, with no good will and no good looks on the part of the chagrined populace, was reared in its stead. As it ascended, the sharp angles faded away, the rough points became smooth, the features full of expression, the whole figure radiant with majesty and beauty. The rude hewn mass, that before had scarcely appeared to bear even the human form, assumed at once the divinity which it represented, being so perfectly proportioned to the dimensions of the building, and to the elevation on which it stood, that it seemed as though Pallas herself had alighted upon the pinnacle of the temple in person, to receive the homage of her worshippers.

The woman of the nineteenth century is the shapeless ball in the lofty position which she was designed fully and nobly to fill. The place is not too high, too large, too sacred for woman, but the type that you have chosen is far too small for it. The woman we declare unto you is the rude, misshapen, unpolished object of the successful artist. From your stand-point, you are absorbed with the defects alone. The true artist sees the harmony between the object and its destination. Man, the sculptor, has carved out his ideal, and applauding thousands welcome his success. He has made a woman that from his low stand-point looks fair and beautiful, a being without rights, or hopes, or fears but in him—neither noble, virtuous, nor independent. Where do we see, in Church or State, in school-house or at the fireside, the much talked-of moral power of woman? Like those Athenians, we have bowed down and worshiped in woman, beauty, grace, the exquisite proportions, the soft and beautifully rounded outline, her delicacy, refinement, and silent helplessness—all well when she is viewed simply as an object of sight, never to rise one foot above the dust from which she sprung. But if she is to be raised up to adorn a temple, or represent a divinity—if she is to fill the niche of wife and counsellor to true and noble men, if she is to be the mother, the educator of a race of heroes or martyrs, of a Napoleon, or a Jesus—then must the type of womanhood be on a larger scale than that yet carved by man.

In vain would the rejected artist have reasoned with the Athenians as to the superiority of his production; nothing short of the experiment they made could have satisfied them. And what of your experiment, what of your wives, your homes? Alas! for the folly and vacancy that meet you there! But for your club-houses and newspapers, what would social life be to you? Where are your beautiful women? your frail ones, taught to lean lovingly and confidingly on man? Where are the crowds of educated dependents—where the long line of pensioners on man's bounty? Where all the young girls, taught to believe that marriage is the only legitimate object of a woman's pursuit—

they who stand listlessly on life's shores, waiting, year after year, like the sick man at the pool of Bethesda, for some one to come and put them in? These are they who by their ignorance and folly curse almost every fireside with some human specimen of deformity or imbecility. These are they who fill the gloomy abodes of poverty and vice in our vast metropolis. These are they who patrol the streets of our cities, to give our sons their first lessons in infamy. These are they who fill our asylums, and make night hideous with their cries and groans.

The women who are called masculine, who are brave, courageous, self-reliant and independent, are they who in the face of adverse winds have kept one steady course upward and onward in the paths of virtue and peace—they who have taken their gauge of womanhood from their own native strength and dignity—they who have learned for themselves the will of God concerning them. This is our type of womanhood. Will you help us raise it up, that you too may see its beautiful proportions— that you may behold the outline of the goddess who is yet to adorn your temple of Freedom? We are building a model republic; our edifice will one day need a crowning glory. Let the artists be wisely chosen. Let them begin their work. Here is a temple to Liberty, to human rights, on whose portals behold the glorious declaration, "All men are created equal." The sun has never yet shone upon any of man's creations that can compare with this. The artist who can mold a statue worthy to crown magnificence like this, must be godlike in his conceptions, grand in his comprehensions, sublimely beautiful in his power of execution. The woman—the crowning glory of the model republic among the nations of the earth—what must she not be? (Loud applause.)

Books about Elizabeth Cady Stanton

SINCLAIR, ANDREW. *The Emancipation of the American Woman.* New York: Harper & Row, 1965.

STANTON, THEODORE, AND BLATH, HARRIET, eds. *Elizabeth Cady Stanton,* New York: Arno, 1969.

LUTZ, ALMA. *Created Equal.* New York: John Day, 1940.

Elizabeth Cady Stanton

LETTER ON MARRIAGE AND DIVORCE, 1855

To the Editor of The New York Tribune:

Sir: At our recent National Woman's Rights Convention many were suprised to hear Wendell Phillips object to the question of Marriage and Divorce, as irrelevant to our platform. He said: "We had no right to discuss there any laws or customs but those where inequality existed in the sexes; that the laws on Marriage and Divorce rested equally on man and woman; that he suffered, as much as she possibly could, the wrongs and abuses of an ill-assorted marriage."

Now, it must strike every careful thinker, that an immense difference rests in the fact, that man has made the laws, cunningly and selfishly, for his own purpose. From Coke down to Kent, who can cite one clause of the marriage contract where woman has the advantage? When man suffers from false legislation, he has his remedy in his own hands. Shall woman be denied the right of protest against laws in which she has had no voice—laws which outrage the holiest affections of her nature—laws which transcend the limits of human legislation—in a Convention called for the express purpose of considering her wrongs? He might as well object to a protest against the injustice of hanging a woman, because capital punishment bears equally on man and woman.

The contract of marriage is by no means equal. The law permits the girl to marry at twelve years of age, while it requires several years more of experience on the part of the boy. In

SOURCE
Elizabeth Cady Stanton, Letter, May 30, 1855, History of Woman Suffrage, I, *pp. 738–740.*
Portrait: Brown Brothers.

entering this compact, the man gives up nothing that he before possessed—he is a man still; while the legal existence of the woman is suspended during marriage, and henceforth she is known but in and through the husband. She is nameless, purseless, childless—though a woman, an heiress, and a mother.

Blackstone says: "The husband and wife are one, and that one is the husband." Kent says: "The legal effects of marriage are generally deducible from the principle of common law, by which the husband and wife are regarded as one person, and her legal existence and authority lost or suspended during the continuance of the matrimonial union."—Vol. 2, p. 109. Kent refers to Coke on Littleton, 112, a. 187, B. Litt. sec. 168, 291.

The wife is regarded by all legal authorities as a *"feme-covert,"* placed wholly *sub potestate viri.* Her moral responsibility, even, is merged in the husband. The law takes it for granted that the wife lives in fear of her husband; that his command is her highest law: hence a wife is not punishable for theft committed in presence of her husband.—Kent, vol. 2, p. 127. An unmarried woman can make contracts, sue and be sued, enjoy the rights of property, to her inheritance—to her wages—to her person—to her children; but, in marriage, she is robbed by law of all and every natural and civil right. "The disability of the wife to contract, so as to bind herself, arises not from want of discretion, but because she has entered into an indissoluble connection, by which she is placed under the power and protection of her husband."—Kent, vol. 2, p. 127. She is possessed of certain rights until she is married; then all are suspended, to revive again the moment the breath goes out of the husband's body.—See "Cowen's Treatise," vol. 2, p. 709.

If the contract be equal, whence come the terms "marital power"—"marital rights"—"obedience and restraint"—"dominion and control"—"power and protection," etc., etc.? Many cases are stated, showing the exercise of a most questionable power over the wife, sustained by the courts.—See Bishop on Divorce, p. 489.

The laws on Divorce are quite as unequal as those of Marriage; yes, far more so. The advantages seem to be all on one side, and the penalties on the other. In case of divorce, if the husband be the guilty party, he still retains the greater part of the property. If the wife be the guilty party, she goes out of the partnership penniless.—Kent, vol. 2, p. 33; Bishop on Divorce, p. 492.

In New York and some other States, the wife of the guilty husband can now sue for a divorce in her own name, and the costs come out of the husband's estate; but, in the majority of the States, she is still compelled to sue in the name of another, as she has no means of paying costs, even though she may have brought her thousands into the partnership. "The allowance to the innocent wife of *ad interim* alimony and money to sustain the suit, is not regarded as strict right in her, but of sound discretion in the court."—Bishop on Divorce, p. 581.

"Many jurists," says Kent, vol. 2, p. 88, "are of opinion

that the adultery of the husband ought not to be noticed or made subject to the same animadversions as that of the wife, because it is not evidence of such entire depravity, nor equally injurious in its effects upon the morals, good order, and happiness of domestic life. Montesquieu, Pothier, and Dr. Taylor all insist that the cases of husband and wife ought to be distinguished, and that the violation of the marriage vow, on the part of the wife, is the most mischievous, and the prosecution ought to be confined to the offense on her part.—"Esprit des Loix," tom. 3, 186; "Traité du Contrat de Marriage," No. 516; "Elements of Civil Law," p. 254.

Say you, "These are but the opinions of men"? On what else, I ask, are the hundreds of women depending, who this hour demand in our courts a release from burdensome contracts? Are not these delicate matters left wholly to the discretion of courts? Are not young women from the first families dragged into the public courts—into assemblies of men exclusively—the judges all men, the jurors all men?—no true woman there to shield them by her presence from gross and impertinent questionings, to pity their misfortunes, or to protest against their wrongs?

The administration of justice depends far more on the opinions of eminent jurists, than on law alone, for law is powerless when at variance with public sentiment.

Do not the above citations clearly prove inequality? Are not the very letter and spirit of the marriage contract based on the idea of the supremacy of man as keeper of woman's virtue—her sole protector and support? Out of marriage, woman asks nothing at this hour but the elective franchise. It is only in marriage that she must demand her rights to person, children, property, wages, life, liberty, and the pursuit of happiness. How can we discuss all the laws and conditions of marriage, without perceiving its essential essence, end, and aim? Now, whether the institution of marriage be human or divine, whether regarded as indissoluble by ecclesiastical courts, or dissoluble by civil courts, woman, finding herself equally degraded in each and every phase of it, always the victim of the institution, it is her right and her duty to sift the relation and the compact through and through, until she finds out the true cause of her false position. How can we go before the Legislatures of our respective States, and demand new laws, or no laws, on divorce, until we have some idea of what the true relation is?

We decide the whole question of slavery by settling the sacred rights of the individual. We assert that man can not hold property in man, and reject the whole code of laws that conflicts with the self-evident truth of that assertion.

Again I ask, is it possible to discuss all the laws of a relation, and not touch the relation itself?

Yours respectfully,
Elizabeth Cady Stanton

Matilda Joslyn Gage

ARGUMENT FOR WOMAN'S SUFFRAGE, 1886

Matilda Joslyn Gage was born March 24, 1826, and spent her childhood in an intellectual atmosphere because of her father's interest in the reform movements of the time, such as temperance and the abolition of slavery. Following a liberal education, eighteen-year-old Matilda married Henry Gage and settled in Fayettesville. At a convention in Syracuse in 1852, Matilda Gage made her first public appearance as an advocate of women's rights, especially the right to vote.

Mrs. Gage became one of the most effective and forceful women's rights lecturers because of her research of the historical status of woman through the ages; Elizabeth Cady Stanton wrote that Matilda Gage "always had the knack of rummaging through old libraries, bringing more startling facts to light than any woman I ever knew." As president of several suffrage associations, Mrs. Gage's aim was to see "a nation in which the caste of sex shall fall down by the caste of color, and humanity alone be the criterion of all human rights." Speaking publicly, Matilda Gage urged women to protest injustices such as limited property rights, imposed by a male-dominated legal system, and to campaign for the recognition as man's political equal; on several occasions, she addressed congressional committees on the suffrage issue.

SOURCE
Matilda Joslyn Gage, "Argument for Woman's Suffrage," History of Woman Suffrage, *III, 1886, pp. 167–169.*

*Matilda Gage formed a triumvirate with the outstanding
leaders of the feminist movement, Elizabeth Cady Stanton
and Susan B. Anthony: Mrs. Gage served as the researcher of
woman's history, while Mrs. Stanton distinguished herself as a
writer and public speaker and Miss Anthony devoted her time
to organization. Besides publishing her own works pertaining
to the feminist cause, Mrs. Gage joined with Mrs. Stanton and
Miss Anthony in authoring and editing the* Woman's Declaration
of Rights *(1876) and the* History of Woman Suffrage *(vols. I–VI,
1881–1886). Mrs. Gage also wrote* Woman, Church and State,
*published in 1893, in which she points out the gradual
discrimination in favor of men, which crept in with the growth
of the church. Matilda Joslyn Gage ended her career as a
dedicated leader of the woman's rights movement, and the cause
of suffrage; she said, in a letter to Susan B. Anthony, "Into that
future I look with a prophetic eye to see woman no longer
enslaved."*

Mr. WILLITS of Michigan: *Mr. Chairman:* I would like to make a suggestion here. The regulation amendment, as it has heretofore been submitted, provided that the right of citizens of the United States to vote should not be abridged on account of sex. I notice that the amendment which the ladies here now propose has prefixed to it this phrase: "The right of suffrage in the United States shall be based on citizenship." I call attention to this because I would like to have them explain as fully as they may why they incorporate the phrase, "shall be based on citizenship." Is the meaning this, that all citizens shall have the right to vote, or simply that citizenship shall be the basis of suffrage? The words, "or for any reason not applicable to all citizens of the United States," also seem to require explanation. The proposition in the form in which it is now submitted, I understand, covers a little more than has been covered by the amendment submitted in previous years.

SARA A. SPENCER of Washington, D.C.: If the committee will permit me, I will say that the amendment in its present form is the concentrated wish of the women of the United States. The women of the country sent to congress petitions asking for three different forms of constitutional amendment, and when preparing the one now before the committee these three were concentrated in the one now before you (identical with that of the resolution offered in the House by Hon. George B. Loring and by Hon. T. W. Ferry in the Senate), omitting, at the request of each of the three classes of petitioners, all phrases which were regarded by any of them as objectionable. The amendment as now presented is therefore the combined wish of the women of the country, viz., that citizenship in the United States shall mean suffrage, and that no one shall be deprived of the right to vote for reasons not equally applicable to all citizens.

MATILDA JOSLYN GAGE said: It is necessary to refer to a remarkable decision of the Supreme Court. The case of Virginia L. Minor, claiming the right to vote under the fourteenth amendment, was argued before the Supreme Court of the United States, October term, 1874; decision rendered adversely by Chief-Justice Waite, March, 1875, upon the ground that "the United States had no voters in the States of its own creation." This was a most amazing decision to emanate from the highest judicial authority of the nation, and is but another proof how fully that body is under the influence of the dominant political party.

Contrary to this decision, I unhesitatingly affirm that the United States has possessed voters in States of its own creation from the very date of the constitution. In Article I, Sec. 2, the constitution provides that

The House of Representatives shall be composed of members chosen every second year by the people of the several States, and the electors in each State shall have the qualifications requisite for electors of the most numerous branch of the State legislature.

The persons so designated are voters under State laws; but by this section of the national constitution they are made United States voters. It is directed under what conditions of State qualification they may cast votes in their respective States for members of the lower house of Congress. The constitution here created a class of United States voters by adoption of an already voting class. Did but this single instance exist, it would be sufficient to nullify Chief-Justice Waite's decision, as Article VI, Sec. 2, declares

The constitution and the laws of the United States which shall be made in pursuance thereof . . . shall be the supreme law of the land.

This supreme law at its very inception created a class of United States voters. If in the Minor case alone, the premises of the Supreme Court and Chief-Justice Waite were wrong, the decision possesses no legal value; but in addition to this class, the United States, by special laws and amendments has from time to time created other classes of United States voters.

Under the naturalization laws citizenship is recognized as the basis of suffrage. No State can admit a foreigner to the right of the ballot, even under United States laws, unless he is already a citizen, or has formally declared his intention of becoming a citizen of the United States. The creation of the right here is national; its regulation, local.

Men who commit crimes against the civil laws of the United States forfeit their rights of citizenship. State law cannot rehabilitate them, but within the last five years 2,500 such men have been pardoned by congressional enactment, and thus again been made voters in States by United States law. Is it not strange that with a knowledge of these facts before him Chief-Justice Waite could base his decision against the right of a woman to the ballot, on the ground that the United States had no voters in the States of its own creation?

Criminals against the military law of the United States, who receive pardon, are still another class of voters thus created. A very large body of men, several hundred thousand, forfeited their rights of citizenship, their ballot, by participation in the rebellion; they were political criminals. When general amnesty was proclaimed they again secured the ballot. They had been deprived of the suffrage by United States law and it was restored to them by the same law.

It may be replied that the rebellious States had been reduced to the condition of territories, over whose suffrage the general government had control. But let me ask why, then, a large class of men remained disfranchised after these States again took up local government? A large class of men were especially exempted from general amnesty and for the restoration of their political rights were obliged to individually petition congress for the removal of their political disabilities, and these men then became "voters in States," by action of the United States. Here, again, the United States recognized citizenship and suffrage as synonymous. If the United States has no voters of its own creation in the States, what are these men? A few, the leaders in the rebellion, are yet disfranchised, and no State has power to change this condition. Only the United States can again make them voters in States.

Under the fourteenth and fifteenth amendments the colored men of the South, who never had possessed the ballot, and those colored men of the North over whom some special disqualification hung, were alike made voters by United States law. It required no action of Delaware, Indiana, New York, or any of those States in which the colored man was not upon voting equality with the white men, to change their constitutions or statutes in order to do away with such disqualifications. The fourteenth amendment created another class of United States voters in States, to the number of a million or more. The fourteenth amendment, and the act of Congress to enforce it, were at once recognized to be superior to State law—abrogating and repealing State constitutions and State laws contradictory to its provisions.

By an act of Congress March 3, and a presidential proclamation of March 11, 1865, all deserters who failed to report themselves to a provost marshall within sixty days, forfeited their rights of citizenship as an additional penalty for the crime of desertion, thus losing their ballot without possibility of its restoration except by an act of Congress. Whenever this may be done collectively or individually, these men will become State voters by and through the United States law.

As proving the sophistry used by legal minds in order to hide from themselves and the world the fact that the United States has power over the ballot in States, mention may be made of a case which, in 1866, came before Justice Strong, then a member of the Supreme Court of Pennsylvania, but since a justice of the Supreme Court of the United States. For sophistical reasoning it is a curiosity in legal decisions. One point made by Judge Strong was, that Congress may deprive a citizen of the opportunity to enjoy a right belonging to him as a citizen of a State even the right of voting, but cannot deprive him of the right itself. This is on a par with saying that congress may deprive a citizen of the opportunity to enjoy a right belonging to him as an individual, even the right of life, but cannot deprive him of life itself.

A still more remarkable class of United States voters than any yet mentioned, exists. Soon after the close of the war congress enacted a law that foreigners having served in the civil war and been honorably discharged from the army, should be allowed to vote. And this, too, without the announcement of their intention of becoming citizens of the republic. A class of United States voters were thus created out of a class of non-citizens.

I have mentioned eight classes of United States voters, and yet not one of the States has been deprived of the powers necessary to local self-government. To States belong all matters of strictly local interest, such as the incorporation of towns and cities, the settlement of county and other boundaries; laws of marriage, divorce, protection of life and property, etc. It has been said, the ordaining and establishment of a constitution for the government of a State is always the act of a State in its highest sovereign capacity, but if any question as to nationality ever existed, it was settled by the war. Even State constitutions were found unable to stand when in conflict with a law of the United States or an amendment to its constitution. All are bound by the authority of the nation.

This theory of State sovereignty must have a word. When the Union was formed several of the States did not even frame a constitution. Rhode Island had no constitution until 1842. Prior to these years the government of these States was administered under the authority of royal charters brought out from England.

Where was their State sovereignty? The rights even of suffrage enjoyed by citizens of these States during these respective periods of forty-two and sixty-six years, were either secured them by monarchial England or republican United States. If by the latter all voters in these two States during these years were United States voters. It is a historical fact that no State save Texas was ever for an hour sovereign or independent. The experience of the country proves there is but one real sovereignty. It has been said, with truth,

There is but one sovereign State on the American continent known to international or constitutional law, and that is the republic itself. This forms the United States and should be so called.

I ask for a sixteenth amendment because this republic is a nation and not a confederacy of States. I ask it because the United States not only possesses inherent power to protect its citizens but also because of its national duty to secure to all its citizens the exercise of their rights of self-government. I ask it because having created classes of voters in numberless instances, it is most flagrant injustice to deny this protection to woman. I ask it because the Nation and not the State is supreme.

Susan B. Anthony

SOCIAL PURITY, 1875

12

Susan Brownell Anthony, the daughter of Quakers, was born
in February 1820 in Adams, Massachusetts. Rebelling at the
rigid conventions for girls while at boarding school, she refused
to fit into a mold of demure, repressed femininity. The rational
ethics of her early environment, and her parents' advanced
views favoring economic independence for women through good
education, gave Susan the courage to violate the rules that
offended her dignity.

As a young teacher in her first position, she proved to be
"too liberal" and found her contract terminated after her first
term. Her courage and intelligence were recognized by others
and she was appointed principal, or dean of girls, at the
Canajoharie Academy (1846–1849). This was the highest position
in education that a woman could attain. Not content, she rose
from her seat in the audience at a teachers' convention and
demanded for women all the privileges that male teachers
enjoyed.

Although she was admired by many at the academy, the
proposals of marriage she received were not accepted. She never
felt it her destiny to be a wife or homemaker, preferring her
independence. Yet she was quick to say that women should
have the opportunity "to bake biscuits and learn algebra at the
same time."

SOURCE
Susan B. Anthony, "Social Purity," Chicago, 1875, in The Life and Work
of Susan B. Anthony, II, ed. Ida Harper, 1893, pp. 1006–1008.

Susan Anthony was a radical abolitionist and a militant agitator for women's rights who lectured and wrote with her friends, Elizabeth Cady Stanton and fiery Ernestine Rose. Distinctly individual in personality, they became prominent travelling throughout the country, opposing politicians and journalists as well as other backward, chauvinist males among their audience.

With her enormous store of energy, she helped to organize the Woman's Temperance Society of New York in 1852, the American Anti-Slavery Society in 1856, established a periodical on women's suffrage with her friend Elizabeth called The Revolution, *and served as president of the American Woman Suffrage Association (originally a rival group of her own National Woman's Suffrage Association, led by Lucy Blackwell) from 1892 until 1900, when she was 80 years old.*

Arrested with twelve other women in 1872 for attempting to vote in the presidential elections, Susan Anthony utilized the months before the trial to educate the voters, who would fill the jury box, about the issues involved. The judge dismissed the jurors before a decision was reached and fined her $100, which she refused to pay. She said, "I would ignore all law to help the slave and ignore it all to protect an enslaved woman."

Despite her somewhat puritan standards of behavior and her personal preference for celibacy, she fought for the right of mothers to remain the guardians of their children in case of divorce. She believed that only through equal rights with men could women work for the improvement of society. She knew this struggle would be unpopular at best, illegal, and hazardous to reputation, position, and health. Yet she was committed to it to the end of her life: "Cautious, careful people always casting about to preserve their reputation or social standards never can bring about a reform. Those who are really in earnest must be willing to be anything or nothing in the world's estimation and publicly and privately, in season and out, avow their sympathies with despised ideas and their advocates and bear the consequences."

In the olden times, when the daughters of the family, as well as the wife, were occupied with useful and profitable work in the household, getting the meals and washing the dishes three times in every day of every year, doing the baking, the brewing, the washing and the ironing, the whitewashing, the butter and cheese and soap making, the mending and the making of clothes for the entire family, the carding, spinning and weaving of the cloth—when everything to eat, to drink and to wear was manufactured in the home, almost no young women "went out to work." But now, when nearly all these handicrafts are turned over to men and to machinery, tens of thousands, nay, millions, of the women of both hemispheres are thrust into the world's outer market to earn their own subsistence. Society, ever slow to change its conditions, presents to these millions but few and meager chances. Only the barest necessaries, and oftentimes not even those, can be purchased with the proceeds of the most excessive and exhausting labor.

Hence, the reward of virtue for the homeless, friendless, penniless woman is ever a scanty larder, a pinched, patched, faded wardrobe, a dank basement or rickety garret, with the colder, shabbier scorn and neglect of the more fortunate of her sex. Nightly, as weary and worn from her day's toil she wends her way through the dark alleys toward her still darker abode, where only cold and hunger await her, she sees on every side and at every turn the gilded hand of vice and crime outstretched, beckoning her to food and clothes and shelter; hears the whisper in softest accents, "Come with me and I will give you all the comforts, pleasures and luxuries that love and wealth can bestow." Since the vast multitudes of human beings, women like men, are not born to the courage or conscience of the martyr, can we wonder that so many poor girls fall, that so many accept material ease and comfort at the expense of spiritual purity and peace? Should we not wonder, rather, that so many escape the sad fate?

Clearly, then, the first step toward solving this problem is to lift this vast army of poverty-stricken women who now crowd our cities, above the temptation, the necessity, to sell themselves, in marriage or out, for bread and shelter. To do that, girls, like boys, must be educated to some lucrative employment; women, like men, must have equal chances to earn a living. If the plea that poverty is the cause of woman's prostitution be not true, perfect equality of chances to earn honest bread will demonstrate the falsehood by removing that pretext and placing her on the same plane with man. Then, if she is found in the ranks

of vice and crime, she will be there for the same reason that
man is and, from an object of pity, she, like him, will become
a fit subject of contempt. From being the party sinned against,
she will become an equal sinner, if not the greater of the two.
Women, like men, must not only have "fair play" in the world
of work and self-support, but, like men, must be eligible to all
the honors and emoluments of society and government. Marriage, to women as to men, must be a luxury, not a necessity;
an incident of life, not all of it. And the only possible way to
accomplish this great change is to accord to women equal power
in the making, shaping and controlling of the circumstances of
life. That equality of rights and privileges is vested in the ballot,
the symbol of power in a republic. Hence, our first and most
urgent demand—that women shall be protected in the exercise
of their inherent, personal, citizen's right to a voice in the government, municipal, state, national.

Alexander Hamilton said one hundred years ago, "Give to a
man the right over my subsistence, and he has power over my
whole moral being." No one doubts the truth of this assertion
as between man and man; while, as between man and woman,
not only does almost no one believe it, but the masses of people
deny it. And yet it is the fact of man's possession of this right
over woman's subsistence which gives to him the power to dictate to her a moral code vastly higher and purer than the one
he chooses for himself. Not less true is it, that the fact of
woman's dependence on man for her subsistence renders her
utterly powerless to exact from him the same high moral code
she chooses for herself.

Of the 8,000,000 women over twenty-one years of age in the
United States, 800,000, one out of every ten, are unmarried, and
fully one-half of the entire number, or 4,000,000, support themselves wholly or in part by the industry of their own hands
and brains. All of these, married or single, have to ask man, as
an individual, a corporation, or a government, to grant to them
even the privilege of hard work and small pay. The tens of
thousands of poor but respectable young girls soliciting copying,
clerkships, shop work, teaching, must ask of men, and not seldom receive in response, "Why work for a living? There are
other ways!"

Whoever controls work and wages, controls morals. Therefore, we must have women employers, superintendents, committees, legislators; wherever girls go to seek the means of subsistence, there must be some woman. Nay, more; we must have
women preachers, lawyers, doctors—that wherever women go to
seek counsel—spiritual, legal, physical—there, too, they will be
sure to find the best and noblest of their own sex to minister
to them.

Independence is happiness. "No man should depend upon

another; not even upon his own father. By depend I mean, obey without examination—yield to the will of any one whomsoever." This is the conclusion to which Pierre, the hero of Madame Sand's "Monsieur Sylvestre," arrives, after running away from the uncle who had determined to marry him to a woman he did not choose to wed. In freedom he discovers that, though deprived of all the luxuries to which he had been accustomed, he is happy, and writes his friend that "without having realized it, he had been unhappy all his life; had suffered from his dependent condition; that nothing in his life, his pleasures, his occupations, had been of his own choice." And is not this the precise condition of what men call the "better half" of the human family?

Books about Susan B. Anthony

ANTHONY, SUSAN B. *History of Woman's Suffrage*. Elizabeth Cady Stanton, Susan B. Anthony, and Matilda J. Gage, eds. New York: Fowler and Wills, 1881–1922.

FLEXNER, E. *Century of Struggle*. New York: Atheneum, 1970.

HARPER, IDA. *The Life and Work of Susan B. Anthony*, II. Kansas City: Bowen and Merrill, 1898.

Susan B. Anthony

DEMAND FOR PARTY RECOGNITION, 1894

13

I come to you tonight not as a stranger, not as an outsider but, in spirit and in every sense, as one of you. I have been connected with you by the ties of relationship for nearly forty years. Twenty-seven years ago I canvassed this entire State of Kansas in your first woman suffrage campaign. During the last decade I have made a speaking tour of your congressional districts over and over again. Now I come once more to appeal to you for justice to the women of your State.

To preface, I want to say that when the rebellion broke out in this country, we of the woman suffrage movement postponed our meetings, and organized ourselves into a great National Women's Loyal League with headquarters in the city of New York. We sent out thousands of petitions praying Congress to abolish slavery, as a war measure, and to these petitions we obtained 365,000 signatures. They were presented by Charles Sumner, that noblest Republican of them all, and it took two stalwart negroes to carry them into the Senate chamber. We did our work faithfully all those years. Other women scraped lint, made jellies, ministered to sick and suffering soldiers and in every way worked for the help of the government in putting

SOURCE

Susan B. Anthony, "Demand for Party Recognition," May 4, 1894, in The Life and Work of Susan B. Anthony, II, *pp. 1015–1021. Delivered in Kansas City, Kansas at the opening of the campaign.*

down that rebellion. No man, no Republican leader, worked more faithfully or loyally than did the women of this nation in every city and county of the North to aid the government.

In 1865 I made my first visit to Kansas and, on the 2d of July, went by stage from Leavenworth to Topeka. O, how I remember those first acres and miles of cornfields I ever had seen; how I remember that ride to Topeka and from there in an open mail wagon to Ottumwa, where I was one of the speakers at the Fourth of July celebration. Those were the days, as you recollect, just after the murder of Lincoln and the accession to the presidential chair of Andrew Johnson, who had issued his proclamation for the reconstruction of Mississippi. So the question of the negro's enfranchisement was uppermost in the minds of leading Republicans, though no one save Charles Sumner had dared to speak it aloud. In that speech, I clearly stated that the government never would be reconstructed, that peace never would reign and justice never be uppermost until not only the black men were enfranchised but also the women of the entire nation. The men congratulated me upon my speech, the first part of it, every word I said about negro suffrage, but declared that I should not have mentioned woman suffrage at so critical an hour.

A little later the Associated Press dispatch came that motions had been made on the floor of the House of Representatives at Washington to insert the word "male" in the second clause of the Fourteenth Amendment. You remember the first clause, "All persons born or naturalized in the United States, and subject to the jurisdiction thereof, are citizens of the United States and of the State wherein they reside. No State shall make or enforce any law which shall abridge the privileges and immunities of citizens." That was magnificent. Every woman of us saw that it included the women of the nation as well as black men. The second section, as Thaddeus Stevens drew it, said, "If any State shall disfranchise any of its citizens on account of color, all that class shall be counted out of the basis of representation;" but at once the enemy asked, "Do you mean that if any State shall disfranchise its negro women, you are going to count all the black race out of the basis of representation?" And weak-kneed Republicans, after having fought such a glorious battle, surrendered; they could not stand the taunt. Charles Sumner said he wrote over nineteen pages of foolscap in order to keep the word "male" out of the Constitution; but he could not do it so he with the rest subscribed to the amendment: "If any State shall disfranchise any of its male citizens all of that class shall be counted out of the basis of representation."

There was the first great surrender and, in all those years of reconstruction, Elizabeth Cady Stanton, the great leader of our woman suffrage movement, declared that because the Republicans were willing to sacrifice the enfranchisement of the women of the nation they would lose eventually the power to protect the black man in his right to vote. But the leaders of the Republican party shouted back to us, "Keep silence, this is the negro's hour." Even our glorious Wendell Phillips, who said, "To talk to a black man of freedom without the ballot is mockery," joined in the cry, "This is the negro's hour;" but we never yielded the point that, "To talk to women of freedom without the ballot is mockery also." But timidity, cowardice and want of principle carried forward the reconstruction of the government with the women left out.

Then came in 1867 the submission by your Kansas legislature of three amendments to your constitution: That all men who had served in the rebel army should be disfranchised; that all black men should be enfranchised; and that all women should be enfranchised. The Democrats held their State convention and resolved they would have nothing to do with that "modern fanaticism of woman's rights." The Germans held a meeting in Lawrence, and denounced this "new-fangled idea." The Republicans held their State convention and resolved to be "neutral." And they were neutral precisely as England was neutral in the rebellion. While England declared neutrality, she allowed the *Shenandoah*, the *Alabama* and other pirate ships to be fitted up in her ports to maraud the seas and capture American vessels. The fact was not a single stump speaker appointed by the Republican committee advocated the woman suffrage amendment and, more than this, all spoke against it.

Then, of course, we had to make a woman suffrage campaign through the months of September and October. We did our best. Everywhere we had splendid audiences and I think we had a larger ratio of men in those olden times than we have nowadays. Election day came, that 5th day of November, 1867, when 9,070 men voted yes, and over 18,000 voted no. On the negro suffrage amendment, 10,500 voted yes and the remainder voted no. Both amendments were lost. All the political power of the national and State Republican party was brought to bear to induce every man to vote for negro suffrage; on the other hand, all the enginery and power of the Republican, as well as of the Democratic party, were against us; and many were so ignorant they absolutely believed that to vote for woman suffrage was to vote against the negro. It was exactly like declaring here tonight that if every woman in this house should fill her lungs with oxygen, she would rob all you men of enough to fill yours. Nobody is robbed by letting everybody have equal rights.

Since 1867 seven other States have submitted the question. Let me run them over.

[Miss Anthony then gave a graphic description of the campaigns in Michigan, 1874; Colorado, 1877; Nebraska, 1882; Oregon, 1884; Rhode Island, 1886; Washington, 1889; South Dakota, 1890; all of which failed for lack of support from the political platforms, editors and speakers.]

But at last in Colorado, in the second campaign, we won by the popular vote, *gained through party endorsement*, the enfranchisement of women. During the summer of 1893 nearly every Republican and Populist and not a few Democratic county conventions put approving planks in their platforms. When the fall campaign opened every stump orator was authorized to speak favorably upon the subject; no man could oppose it unless he ran counter to the principles laid down in his party platform. That made it a truly educational campaign to all the voters of the State. A word to the wise is sufficient. Let every man who wants the suffrage amendment carried, demand a full and hearty endorsement of the measure by his political party, be it Democrat, Republican, Populist or Prohibition, so that Kansas shall win as did her neighbor State, Colorado.

The Republicans of Kansas made the Prohibition amendment a party measure in 1880. After they secured the law they had planks in their platform for its enforcement from year to year, until they were tired of fighting the liquor dealers, backed by the Democrats in the State and on the borders. They wearied of being taunted with the fact that they had not the power to enforce the law. Then in 1887 they gave municipal suffrage to women as a sheer party necessity. Just as much as it was a necessity of the Republicans in reconstruction days to enfranchise the negroes, so was it a political necessity in the State of Kansas to enfranchise the women, because they needed a new balance of power to help them elect and re-elect officers who would enforce the law. Where else could they go to get that balance? Every man in the State, native and foreign, drunk and sober, outside of the penitentiary, the idiot and lunatic asylums, already had the right to vote. They had nobody left but the women. As a last resort the Republicans, by a straight party vote, extended municipal suffrage to women.

This political power was put into the hands of the women of this State by the old Republican party with its magnificent majorities—82,000, you remember, the last time you bragged. It was before you had the quarrel and division in the family; it was by that grand old party, solid as it was in those bygone days!

Last year, and two years ago, after the Peoples' party was organized, when their State convention was held, and also when the Republican convention was held, each put a plank in its platform declaring that the time had come for the submission of a proposition for full suffrage to women. What then could the women infer but that such action meant political help in carrying this amendment? If I had not believed this I never would have come to the State and given my voice in twenty-five or thirty political meetings, reminding the Republicans what a grand and glorious record they had made, not only in the enfranchisement of the black men but in furnishing all the votes on the floor of Congress ever given for women's enfranchisement there, and in extending municipal suffrage to the women of Kansas. I have vowed, from the time I began to see that woman suffrage could be carried only through party help, that I never would lend my influence to either of the two dominant parties that did not have a woman suffrage plank in its platform.

I consider, by every pledge of the past, by the passage of the resolution through the legislature when the representatives of the two parties, the Peoples' and Republican, vied with each other to see who would give the largest majority, that both promised to make this a party measure and I speak tonight to the two parties as the old Republican party. You are not the same men altogether, but you are the descendants, the children, of that party; and I am here tonight, and have come all the way from my home, to beg you to stand by the principles which have made you great and strong, and to finish the work you have so nobly begun.

The Republicans are to have their State convention the 6th of June. I shall be ashamed if the telegraph wires flash the word over the country, "No pledge for the amendment," as was flashed from the Republican League the other day. Should this happen, as I have heard intimated, and there is a woman in the State of Kansas who has any affiliation with the Republican party, any sympathy with it, who will float its banner after it shall have thus failed to redeem its pledge, I will disown her; she is not one of my sort.

The Populist convention is to be held the 12th of June. If it should shirk its responsibility, and not put a strong suffrage plank in its platform, pledging itself to use all its educational powers and all its party machinery to carry the amendment, then I shall have no respect for any woman who will speak of work for its success.

The Democrats have declared their purpose. They are going to fight us. What does the good Book say? "He that is not for me is against me." We know where the Democratic party is, it is against us. If the Republican and Peoples' parties say nothing for us, they say and do everything against us. No plank will be equivalent to saying to every woman suffrage Republican and Populist speaker, "You must not advocate this amendment, for to do so will lose us the whisky vote, it will lose us the foreign vote." Hence, no plank means no word for us, and no word for us means no vote for us. But while no word can be spoken in favor, every campaign orator, as in 1867, is free to speak in opposition.

Men of the Republican party, it comes your time first to choose whom you will have for your future constituents, to make up the bone and sinew of your party; whether you will have the most ignorant foreigners, just landed on our shores, who have not learned a single principle of free government—or the women of your own households; whether you will lose to-day a few votes of the high license or the low license Republicans, foreign or native, black or white, as the case may be, and gain to yourselves hereafter the votes of the women of the State. These are the alternatives. It has been stated that you can not have a suffrage plank in the Republican platform in Saline county because it would lose the votes of the Scandinavians. Will those 1,000 Scandinavian men be of more value to the Republicans than will be the votes of their own wives, mothers, daughters and sisters in all the years to come?

The crucial moment is upon you now, and I say unto you, men of both parties, you will have driven the last nail in the coffin of this amendment and banished all hope of carrying it at the ballot-box if you do not incorporate woman suffrage in your platforms. I know what the party managers will say, I have talked with and heard from many of them. I read Mr. Morrill's statement that "this question should go to the ballot-box on its merits and should not be spoken of in the political meetings or made a party measure."

The masses are rooted and grounded in the old beliefs in the inferiority and subjection of women, and consider them born merely to help man carry out his plans and not to have any of their own. Now, friends, because this is true, because no man believes in political equality for woman, except he is educated out of every bigotry, every prejudice and every usage that he was born into, in the family, in the church and in the state, so there can be no hope of the rank and file of men voting for this amendment, until they are taught the principles of justice and right; and there is no possibility that these men can be reached, can be educated, through any other instrumentality than that of the campaign meetings and campaign papers of the political parties. Therefore, when you say this is not to be a political question, not to be in your platform, not to be discussed in your meetings, not to be advocated in your papers, you make it impossible for its merits to be brought before the voters.

Who are the men that come to our women's meetings? We have just finished the tour of the sixty counties in the State of New York. We had magnificent gatherings, composed of people from the farthest townships in the county, and in many of them from every township, with the largest opera houses packed, hundreds going away who could not get in. Our audiences have been five-sixths women, and the one man out of the six, who was he? A man who already believed there was but one means of salvation for the race or the country, and that was through the political equality of women, making them the peers of men in every department of life. How are we going to reach the other five-sixths of the men who never come to women's meetings? There is no way except through the political rallies which are attended by all men. Now if you shut out of these the discussion of this question, then I say the fate of this amendment is sealed.

Even if it were possible to reach the men through separate meetings, the women of Kansas can not carry on a fall campaign. They can not get the money to do it unless you men furnish it.

Our eastern friends have already contributed to the extent of their ability to hold these spring meetings, and you very well know that after the husbands shall have paid their party assessments there will be nothing left for them to "give to their wives" to defray the expenses of a woman suffrage campaign. Therefore, no discussion in the regular political meetings means no discussion anywhere. But suppose there were plenty of money, and there could be a most thorough fall campaign, what then? Why, the same old story of "women talking to women," not one of whom can vote on the question.

Again, with what decency can either of the parties ask women to come to their political meetings to expound Populist or Republican doctrines after they have set their heels on the amendment? Do you not see that if it will lose votes to the parties to have the plank, it will lose votes to allow women to advocate the amendment on their platforms? And what a spectacle it would be to see women pleading with men to vote for the one or the other party, while their tongues were tied on the question of their own right to vote! Heaven and the Republican and Populist State Conventions spare us such a dire humiliation!

But should the Republicans refuse to insert the plank on June 6 and the Populists put a good solid one in their platform on June 12, what then? Do you suppose all the women in the State would shout for the Republicans and against the Populists? Would they pack the Republican meetings, where no word could be spoken for their liberty, and leave the benches empty in the Populist meetings where at every one hearty appeals were made to vote for woman's enfranchisement? My dear friends, woman surely will be able to see that her highest interest, her liberty, her right to a voice in government, is the great issue of this campaign, and overtops, outweighs, all material questions which are now pending between the parties.

I know you think your Kansas men are going to vote on this amendment independently of party endorsement. You are no more sanguine today than were the men and women, myself included, in 1867, that those Free State men, who had given up every comfort which human beings prize for the sake of liberty, who had fought not only through the border ruffian warfare but through the four years of the rebellion, would vote freedom to the heroic women of Kansas. Where would you ever expect to find a majority more ready to grant to women equal rights than among those old Free State men? You have not as glorious a generation of men in Kansas today as you had in 1867. I do not wish to speak disparagingly, but in the nature of things there can not be another race of men as brave as those. If you had told me then that a majority of those men would have gone to the ballot-box and voted against equal rights for women, I should have defended them with all my power; but they did it, two to one.

Do you mean to repeat the experiment of 1867? If so, do not put a plank in your platform; just have a "still hunt." Think of a "still hunt" when it must be necessarily a work of education! My friends, I know enough of this State, to feel that it is worth saving. I have given more time and money and effort to Kansas than to any other State in the Union, because I wanted it to be the first to make its women free. Women of Kansas, all is lost if you sit down and supinely listen to politicians and candidates. Both reckon what they will lose or what they will gain. They study expediency rather than principle. I appeal to you, men and women, make the demand imperative: "The amendment must be endorsed by the parties and advocated on the platform and in the press." Let me propose a resolution:

WHEREAS, From the standpoint of justice, political expediency and grateful appreciation of their wise and practical use of school suffrage from the organization of the State, and of municipal suffrage for the past eight years, we, Republicans and Populists, descendants of that grand old party of splendid majorities which extended these rights to the women of Kansas, in mass meeting assembled do hereby

Resolve, That we urgently request our delegates in their approaching State conventions to endorse the woman suffrage amendment in their respective platforms.

[The resolution was adopted by a unanimous vote.]

That vote fills my soul with joy and hope. Now I want to say to you, my good friends, I never would have made a 1,500 mile journey hither to appeal to the thinking, justice-loving men of Kansas. They already are converted, but they are a minority. We have to consider those whose votes can be obtained only by that party influence and machinery which politicians alone know how to use. This hearty response is a pledge that you will demand of your State conventions that the full power of this political machinery shall be used to carry the woman suffrage amendment to victory.

Sojourner Truth

THE NARRATIVE OF SOJOURNER TRUTH, 1878

Born a slave in Ulster County, New York, Sojourner Truth, whose given name was Isabella Van Wagner (from her kindest master), was sold four times in her first thirty years of life. The Abolition Law of New York State in 1827 freed her but was violated by her master, who sold her fifth child illegally. Her relentless struggle to recover her son brought her before the Grand Jury of New York, where she won her case.

Her religious indoctrination as a child spurred her militant spirit as she used the public platform to preach and teach abolitionism, equality of the races and sexes, temperance, prison reform, and revolutionary optimism. When Frederick Douglass completed a rather pessimistic speech in Boston's Faneuil Hall, Sojourner Truth cried out "Frederick, is God dead?"

SOURCE
Sojourner Truth, The Narrative of Sojourner Truth, *with a History of Her Labors and Correspondence drawn from her* Book of Life *by Frances W. Titus, 1878, by Oliver Gilbert, Arno, 1968.*
Portrait: Chicago Historical Society.

Her forthright manner, sharp wit, and self-appointed missionary role won her white audiences' support despite her shabby appearance and black folk-dialect.

Wendell Philips said he had never known anyone who could electrify and move an audience with as few words as she could. Harriet Beecher Stowe commented, "I never knew a person who possessed so much of that subtle controlling power called presence as Sojourner."

During the Civil War she met President Lincoln and urged him to enlist northern free black men to fight in the union armies. She remained in Washington, D.C., nursing the wounded soldiers and finding shelter and food for newly emancipated slaves.

Her abolitionist work brought her to her first feminist meeting sponsored by Lucretia Mott. Just as she was later to advocate homesteading for the black people as a simple and direct solution to their poverty and exploitation, she told the feminists, "Sisters, I aren't clear what ye'd be after. If women want any rights more than they got, why don't they just take 'em and not be talking about it?"

At the Women's Convention in Akron, she attacked the arguments of the men present who attempted to undermine the feminists' struggle by their repeated contentions that women had inferior reasoning power, inferior strength, and naturally carnal natures from the time of Eve. Sojourner Truth arose and reminded them of the physical endurance of slave women, and, as for intellect, she retorted, "What's dat got to do with women's rights or niggers' rights? If my cup won't hold but a pint and yourn holds a quart, wouldn't ye be mean not to let me have my little half-measure full?"

To support herself as she preached, she sold inexpensive photographs of herself saying, "I sells the shadow to support the substance." Her speeches and the story of her life were published in 1850 as The Narrative of Sojourner Truth: A Northern Slave. Together with the autobiographies of Frederick Douglass and a number of fugitive slaves, her biography became a powerful weapon against slavery. Hers was the only one which gave the woman slave's experience and an account of slavery in the North.

At 70 she attended the Women's Rights Convention in New York in 1867 and warned the women to get going because she didn't intend to die until she voted.

"Well, chilern, whar dar is so much racket dar must be something out o' kilter. I tink dat 'twixt de niggers of de Souf and de women at de Norf all a talkin' 'bout rights, de white men will be in a fix pretty soon. But what's all dis here talkin' 'bout? Dat man ober dar say dat women needs to be helped into carriages, and lifted ober ditches, and to have de best place every whar. Nobody eber help me into carriages, of ober mud puddles, or gives me any best place and ar'n't I a woman? Look at me! Look at my arm! I have plowed, and planted, and gathered into barns, and no man could head me—and ar'n't I a woman? I could work as much and eat as much as a man (when I could get it), and bear de lash as well—and ar'n't I a woman? I have borne thirteen chilern and seen 'em mos' all sold off into slavery, and when I cried out with a mother's grief, none but Jesus heard—and ar'n't I a woman? Den dey talks 'bout dis ting in de head—what dis dey call it? ("Intellect," whispered some one near.) Dat's it, honey. What's dat got to do with women's rights or niggers' rights? If my cup won't hold but a pint and yourn holds a quart, wouldn't ye be mean not to let me have my little half-measure full?" And she pointed her significant finger and sent a keen glance at the minister who had made the argument. The cheering was long and loud.

"Den dat little man in black dar, he say women can't have much rights as man, cause Christ wa'nt a woman. Whar did your Christ come from?" Rolling thunder could not have stilled that crowd as did those deep, wonderful tones, as she stood there with outstretched arms and eye of fire. Raising her voice still louder, she repeated, "Whar did your Christ come from? From God and a woman. Man had nothing to do with him." O! what a rebuke she gave the little man.

Turning again to another objector, she took up the defense of mother Eve. I cannot follow her through it all. It was pointed, and witty, and solemn, eliciting at almost every sentence deafening applause; and she ended by asserting that "if de fust woman God ever made was strong enough to turn the world upside down, all 'lone, den togedder (and she glanced her eye over us), ought to be able to turn it back and get it right side up again, and now dey is asking to do it, de men better let em." Long-continued cheering. "Bleeged to ye for hearin' on me, and now ole Sojourner ha'n't got nothing more to say."

Amid roars of applause, she turned to her corner, leaving more than one of us with streaming eyes and hearts beating with gratitude. She had taken us up to her strong arms and carried us safely over the slough of difficulty, turning the whole tide in our favor. I have never in my life seen anything like the magical influence that subdued the mobbish spirit of the day and turned the jibes and sneers of an excited crowd into notes of respect and admiration. Hundreds rushed up to shake hands, and congratulate the glorious old mother and bid her God speed on her mission of "testifying again concerning the wickedness of this 'ere people."

"It was about 8 o'clock A.M., when I called on the president. Upon entering his reception room we found about a dozen persons in waiting, among them two colored women. I had quite a pleasant time waiting until he was disengaged, and enjoyed his conversation with others; he showed as much kindness and consideration to the colored persons as to the whites—if there was any difference, more. One case was that of a colored woman who was sick and likely to be turned out of her house on account of her inability to pay her rent. The president listened to her with much attention, and spoke to her with kindness and tenderness. He said he had given so much he could give no more, but told her where to go and get the money, and asked Mrs. C—n to assist her, which she did.

The president was seated at his desk. Mrs. C. said to him, "This is Sojourner Truth, who has come all the way from Michigan to see you." He then arose, gave me his hand, made a bow, and said, "I am pleased to see you."

I said to him, "Mr. President, when you first took your seat I feared you would be torn to pieces, for I likened you unto Daniel, who was thrown into the lion's den; and if the lions did not tear you into pieces, I knew that it would be God that had saved you; and I said if he spared me I would see you before the four years expired, and he has done so, and now I am here to see you for myself."

He then congratulated me on my having been spared. Then I said, "I appreciate you, for you are the best president who has ever taken the seat." He replied: "I expect you have reference to my having emancipated the slaves in my proclamation. But," said he, mentioning the names of several of his predecessors (and among them emphatically that of Washington), "they were all just as good, and would have done just as I have done if the time had come. If the people over the river (pointing across the Potomac) had behaved themselves, I could not have done what I have; but they did not, which gave me the opportunity to do these things." I then said, "I thank God that you are the instrument selected by him and the people to do it. I told him that I had never heard of him before he was talked of for president." He smilingly replied, "I had heard of you many times before that."

He then showed me the Bible presented to him by the colored people of Baltimore, of which you have no doubt seen a description. I have seen it for myself, and it is beautiful beyond description. After I had looked it over, I said to him, "This is beautiful indeed; the colored people have given this to the head of the government, and that government once sanctioned laws that would not permit its people to learn enough to enable them to read this book. And for what? Let them answer who can."

I must say, and I am proud to say, that I never was treated by any one with more kindness and cordiality than were shown to me by that great and good man, Abraham Lincoln, by the grace of God president of the United States for four years more. He took my little book, and with the same hand that signed the death-warrant of slavery, he wrote as follows: "For Aunty Sojourner Truth, Oct. 29, 1864. A. Lincoln."

As I was taking my leave, he arose and took my hand, and said he would be pleased to have me call again. I felt that I was in the presence of a friend, and I now thank God from the bottom of my heart that I always have advocated his cause, and have done it openly and boldly. I shall feel still more in duty bound to do so in time to come. May God assist me.

Books about Sojourner Truth

BERNARD, JACQUELINE. *Journey Toward Freedom, the Story of Sojourner Truth*. New York: Grosset and Dunlap, 1969.

FAUSET, ARTHUR H. *Sojourner Truth, God's Faithful Pilgrim*. Chapel Hill: The University of North Carolina Press, 1938.

GILBERT, OLIVE. "Narrative of Sojourner Truth." *The American Negro, His History and Literature*. New York: Arno, 1968.

PAULI, HERTHA E. *Her Name Was Sojourner Truth*. New York: Appleton-Century-Crofts, 1962.

Alice Stone Blackwell

MAKING WOMEN INTO MEN, 1893

The daughter of ardent supporters of the feminist movement,
Alice Stone Blackwell was blessed with an unusually nutritive
environment. She was born in September 1857, ten years after
her mother had blazed a trail as the first woman to be graduated
from Oberlin College. Her parents, Henry and Lucy Blackwell,
were the publishers and writers of The Women's Journal. Aunt
Antoinette Brown Blackwell was the first woman minister; her
aunts Elizabeth and Emily Blackwell were the first and second
women physicians in the United States.

In 1881 she was graduated Phi Beta Kappa from Boston
University and worked for unity in the feminist movement,
helping to bring together her mother's American Woman
Suffrage Association with the rival group led by Susan B.
Anthony in 1890. When women won the right to vote in 1920 her
brains and courage were used for other causes, the struggle for
racial justice and the building of trade union solidarity.

SOURCE
Alice Stone Blackwell, "Making Women into Men," in The Women's
Journal, Boston, January 14, 1893.

Alice Blackwell worked on The Women's Journal *for 34 years as an assistant and as editor-in-chief. Her active involvement in the League of Women Voters, Suffrage Association, ACLU, the Women's International League for Peace and Freedom, and the Women's Trade Union League continued along with her writing career. She wrote (in collaboration) a biography of her mother, called* The Yellow Ribbon Speaker *in 1890. She mastered many languages and enjoyed translating foreign poetry into English. Her creative and intellectual talents were expressed in her translations of Armenian, Russian, Hungarian, Yiddish, and the more familiar Spanish and French poetry.*

She expressed her opposition to war in her articles in The Women's Journal, *pointing out how "armies take the very flower of youth" for destruction. In her calls for a lasting peace. she urged women to learn to influence government. The economic evils of maintaining standing armies were powerfully condemned.*

In her article Making Women into Men *(1893) Alice Blackwell attracted Charles Warner, one of the editors of* Harper's *magazine, who voiced his fear that women would become men if the feminists continued to struggle for equality. Miss Blackwell called on "experience" to prove whether "men will be less manly, or women less womanly, when men and women have equal rights before the law." In her statement we hear the early formulations, now revived by the Women's Liberation Movement, that working equality of the sexes will not hinder either from expressing their biological differentiation: "Not mankind, not womankind, but humankind."*

Her productive life spanned almost a century, and when she died in 1950 at the age of 93 The New York Times *was not alone in mourning her passing.*

Charles Dudley Warner, in the "Editor's Study" of *Harper's* magazine, says:

Being in possession of so much, we now expect to travel in the air, to read news in the sending mind before it is sent, to create force without cost, to be transported without time, and to make everybody equal in fortune and happiness to everybody else by act of Congress. Such confidence have we in the power of a "resolution" of the people and by the people that it seems feasible to make women into men.

Since no resolution to make women into men has ever been offered, either in Congress or elsewhere, and since resolutions to give women equal rights with men in regard to suffrage are often thus described by the unthinking, it is fair to suppose that suffrage is what Mr. Warner had in mind; especially as he is rather given to casting little slurs upon the women's rights movement. It is perhaps worth while to examine what substance there may be in this bugbear that if women vote they will be turned into men.

One estimable gentleman illustrated the same objection by comparing men and women to trees. He said an elm might be just as tall as an oak, but it could never become an oak, and if it tried to turn itself into an oak, it would only spoil itself for an elm. It did not seem to occur to him that we do not find it necessary to hedge off an elm into a separate corner of the field, or to grow it under glass, in order to keep it from turning into an oak. The same free growth and fresh air and sunlight that tend to make the oak a noble oak, tend also to make the elm a noble elm, but have never shown the slightest tendency to turn an elm into an oak. The advocates of equal rights believe that freedom and education and responsibility, which tend to develop a man into a noble man, will also tend to develop a woman into a noble woman, but will never in the least tend to turn a woman into a man. Nature has a way of looking out for herself.

We believe that the differences between men and women are natural, not artificial. As Rev. Dr. Gregg says, "Sex is dyed in wool." It is not the result of women's disfranchisement. Moreover, we find that every man comes away from the polls just about the same sort of man that he was when he went there. The mysterious act of voting does not make a good man bad, or a refined man brutal, a sweet-tempered man bearish, a loud man quiet, or a timid man bold. The fact that all men have equal rights before the law does not wipe out natural differences of temperament and disposition between one man and another.

Why should a similar equality of legal status be expected to wipe out the natural differences of temperament and disposition between men and women? Of all the silly objections that have been urged against equal suffrage—and they are many—there is none sillier than this.

The same fearful prediction, that women would be turned into men, has been made before each successive step of the equal rights movement. It was made before in regard to higher education, in regard to the opening of colleges and of the professions; but hitherto it has proved groundless. In Wyoming and in England, when women have been voting since 1869, they are not perceptibly less womanly than before. Experience is the best of tests; and experience thus far has borne out Whittier's prediction, made years ago: "I have no fear that men will be less manly, or women less womanly, when men and women have equal rights before the law."

Books by Alice Stone Blackwell

The Yellow Ribbon Speaker in collaboration with Lucy E. Anthony and Anne Howard Show, 1890.

The Little Grandmother of the Russian Revolution—Life and Letters of Catherine Breshkovsky, 1917.

Songs of Russia, a collection of Russian poems, 1906.

Songs of Grief and Gladness, translated from the Yiddish, 1908.

Crystal Eastman

STATEMENT TO THE FIRST FEMINIST CONGRESS, 1919

Crystal Eastman Benedict, a brilliant pioneer in feminist education, was one of the few who made the connection between labor's struggle and the liberation of women. In her two books on labor conditions, Employers' Liability: A Criticism Based on Facts *(1909) and* Work–Accidents and the Law *(1910), she documented the need for safety standards, plant inspection, and workers' insurance.*

As campaign manager for the Political Equality League in 1911, she gained enough experience to lead a Washington demonstration of 5000 women (on the day before Wilson's inauguration) for passage of the Federal Suffrage Amendment. This "parade" helped to begin the work of Alice Paul's lobby for woman suffrage, the Congressional Union.

SOURCE
Crystal Eastman, in The Liberator, a Journal of Revolutionary Progress, *May 1919.*

In 1913 Crystal Eastman helped to organize the Woman's Peace Party of New York, which became a nationwide organization by 1915. Frequently overshadowed by Jane Addams, many tended to forget that Miss Eastman was the first to fight the prewar advocates of military preparations. With her New York group of women, she arranged public debates and wrote legislation opposing military involvement in the coming world war. This opposition was later used by Jane Addams.

Under the auspices of the American Union Against Militarism, she urged President Wilson to help organize a World Federation, where continuous mediation among nations would prevent an outbreak of war. After U.S. involvement in World War I, the New York Women's Peace Party agitated for an early peace by resisting conscription, conducting classes on world politics, and distributing an antiwar magazine soon impounded by the post office.

With her radical-socialist brother Max Eastman, she coedited The Liberator, *a Journal of Revolutionary Progress between 1918 and 1920, writing on labor struggles, Russian Bolshevism, and the continuing battle for women's liberation. Not satisfied with merely obtaining the vote, Crystal Eastman sought the more substantial "freedom of choice in occupation" and "individual economic independence" for all women.*

In her article "Now We Can Begin," published in The Liberator *(December 1920), she saw the fundamental lesson for women to be:*

how to arrange the world so that women can be human beings, with a chance to exercise their infinitely varied gifts in infinitely varied ways, instead of being destined by their sex to one field of activity—housework and child nursing. . . .

The proposals Crystal Eastman advanced were very radical and are now receiving the forum they deserve. She called for feminist education for husbands and children, voluntary motherhood, requiring free birth control education and "motherhood endowment," and wages for women who labor at housework. She believed the feminist movement should "create conditions of outward freedom in which a free woman's soul can be born and grow."

111

For two years the whole western world has been talking about freedom and democracy. Now that the war is over and it is possible to think calmly once more, we must examine these popular abstractions, and consider (especially here in America where boasting has been the loudest)—how much freedom and democracy we actually have. Above all it behooves women to determine frankly what their status is in this republic.—

Four-fifths of us are still denied the elementary political right of voting.

Only one woman has held a seat in the United States . Congress.

Only twenty-one women are sitting in our 48 state legislatures.

With rare exceptions all the higher executive offices in both state and federal governments are, by law or rigid precedent, open only to men.

In only six states do women sit on juries.

With half a dozen exceptions in the lower courts, there are no women judges.

In all government work, federal, state, county and city, —(notoriously in public school teaching),—women are paid much less than men for the same work.

In private industry, where it is estimated that twelve million women are now employed, the wages of women both skilled and unskilled (except in a few trades) are on a scale of their own, materially lower than the wages of men, even at work where their productive capacity is equal or greater.

Most of the strong labor unions, except in trades where women are in the majority, still close their doors to women workers.

Marriage laws in many states (including the guardianship of children) are designed to perpetuate the economic dependence of a wife on her husband. And nothing has been done in this country by way of maternity insurance or by giving to a wife legal right to a share of her husband's earnings in recognition of her services as houseworker and nurse, to modify that dependence. And the vital importance of potential economic independence has yet to become a recognized principle of modern education for girls.

Voluntary motherhood is an ideal unrealized in this country. Women are still denied by law the right to that scientific knowledge necessary to control the size of their families, which means that among the poor where the law is effective, marriage can become virtual slavery for women.

Laws, judges, courts, police, and social custom still disgrace, punish and "regulate" the woman prostitute and leave uncensured the man who trades with her,—though in case of all other forbidden vices the buyers as well as the seller suffer if caught.

From this brief statement of facts it is fairly clear that women in America today not only share the wholesale denial of civil liberty which came with the war and remains to bless our victory, but carry a special burden of restrictive legislation and repressive social customs,—(not in any way relieved by the war for freedom nor affected by the two years' crusade of democratic eloquence)—a burden which halts them in almost every field of endeavor, and effectually marks them as an inferior class. This is stated without any bitterness and with full recognition of the fact that women by their passivity have made these things possible. But it is stated for a purpose.

It is my hope that this first Women's Freedom Conference, held in New York City, will see the birth of a new spirit in American women—a spirit of humane and intelligent self-interest, a spirit of determined pride—which will lead them to declare:

"We will not wait for the Social Revolution to bring us the freedom we should have won in the 19th century."

Books by Crystal Eastman

The Woman's Peace Party Yearbook, 1916.

Marlene Dixon

WHY WOMEN'S LIBERATION? 1969

Marlene Dixon is a professor of sociology at McGill University and an activist in the Women's Liberation Movement.

SOURCE
Marlene Dixon, "Why Women's Liberation?" Ramparts, *December 1969, pp. 58–63.*
Portrait: United Press International.

The 1960's has been a decade of liberation; women have been swept up by that ferment along with blacks, Latins, American Indians and poor whites—the whole soft underbelly of this society. As each oppressed group in turn discovered the nature of its oppression in American society, so women have discovered that they too thirst for free and fully human lives. The result has been the growth of a new women's movement, whose base encompasses poor black and poor white women on relief, working women exploited in the labor force, middle class women incarcerated in the split level dream house, college girls awakening to the fact that sexiness is not the crowning achievement in life, and movement women who have discovered that in a freedom movement they themselves are not free. In less than four years women have created a variety of organizations, from the nationally based middle class National Organization of Women (NOW) to local radical feminist groups in every major city in North America. The new movement includes caucuses within nearly every New Left group and within most professional associations in the social sciences. Ranging in politics from reform to revolution, it has produced critiques of almost every segment of American society and constructed an ideology that rejects every hallowed cultural assumption about the nature and role of women.

As is typical of a young movement, much of its growth has been underground. The papers and manifestos written and circulated would surely comprise two very large volumes if published, but this literature is almost unknown outside of women's liberation. Nevertheless, where even a year ago organizing was slow and painful, with small cells of six or ten women, high turnover, and an uphill struggle against fear and resistance, in 1969 all that has changed. Groups are growing up everywhere with women eager to hear a hard line, to articulate and express their own rage and bitterness. Moving about the country, I have found an electric atmosphere of excitement and responsiveness. Everywhere there are doubts, stirrings, a desire to listen, to find out what it's all about. The extent to which groups have become politically radical is astounding. A year ago the movement stressed male chauvinism and psychological oppression; now the emphasis is on understanding the economic and social roots of women's oppression, and the analyses range from social democracy to Marxism. But the most striking change of all in the last year has been the loss of fear. Women are no longer afraid that their rebellion will threaten their very identity as women. They are not frightened by their own militancy, but liberated by it. Women's Liberation is an idea whose time has come.

The old women's movement burned itself out in the frantic decade of the 1920s. After a hundred years of struggle, women won a battle, only to lose the campaign: the vote was obtained, but the new millennium did not arrive. Women got the vote and achieved a measure of legal emancipation, but the real social and cultural barriers to full equality for women remained untouched.

For over 30 years the movement remained buried in its own ashes. Women were born and grew to maturity virtually ignorant of their own history of rebellion, aware only of a caricature of blue stockings and suffragettes. Even as increasing numbers of women were being driven into the labor force by the brutal conditions of the 1930's and by the massive drain of men into the military in the 1940's, the old ideal remained: a woman's place was in the home and behind her man. As the war ended and men returned to resume their jobs in factories and offices, women were forced back to the kitchen and nursery with a vengeance. This story has been repeated after each war and the reason is clear: women form a flexible, cheap labor pool which is essential to a capitalist system. When labor is scarce, they are forced onto the labor market. When labor is plentiful, they are forced out. Women and blacks have provided a reserve army of unemployed workers, benefiting capitalists and the stable male white working class alike. Yet the system imposes untold suffering on the victims, blacks and women, through low wages and chronic unemployment.

With the end of the war the average age at marriage declined, the average size of families went up, and the suburban migration began in earnest. The political conservatism of the '50s was echoed in a social conservatism which stressed a Victorian ideal of the woman's life: a full womb and selfless devotion to husband and children.

As the bleak decade played itself out, however, three important social developments emerged which were to make a rebirth of the women's struggle inevitable. First, women came to make up more than a third of the labor force, the number of working women being twice the prewar figure. Yet the marked increase in female employment did nothing to better the position of women, who were more occupationally disadvantaged in the 1960's than they had been 25 years earlier. Rather than moving equally into all sectors of the occupational structure, they were being forced into the low paying service, clerical and semi-skilled categories. In 1940, women had held 45 per cent of all professional and technical positions; in 1967, they held only 37 per cent. The proportion of women in service jobs meanwhile rose from 50 to 55 per cent.

Second, the intoxicating wine of marriage and suburban life was turning sour; a generation of women woke up to find their children grown and a life (roughly 30 more productive years) of housework and bridge parties stretching out before them like a wasteland. For many younger women, the empty drudgery they saw in the suburban life was a sobering contradiction to adolescent dreams of romantic love and the fulfilling role of woman as wife and mother.

Third, a growing civil rights movement was sweeping thousands of young men and women into a moral crusade—a crusade which harsh political experience was to transmute into the New Left. The American Dream was riven and tattered in Mississippi and finally napalmed in Viet-Nam. Young Americans were drawn not to Levittown, but to Berkeley, the Haight-Ashbury and the East Village. Traditional political ideologies and cultural myths, sexual mores and sex roles with them, began to disintegrate in an explosion of rebellion and protest.

The three major groups which make up the new women's movement—working women, middle class married women and students—bring very different kinds of interests and objectives to women's liberation. Working women are most concerned with the economic issues of guaranteed employment, fair wages, job discrimination and child care. Their most immediate oppression is rooted in industrial capitalism and felt directly through the vicissitudes of an exploitative labor market.

Middle class women, oppressed by the psychological mutilation and injustice of institutionalized segregation, discrimination and imposed inferiority, are most sensitive to the dehumanizing consequences of severely limited lives. Usually well educated and capable, these women are rebelling against being forced to trivialize their lives, to live vicariously through husbands and children.

Students, as unmarried middle class girls, have been most sensitized to the sexual exploitation of women. They have experienced the frustration of one-way relationships in which the girl is forced into a "wife" and companion role with none of the supposed benefits of marriage. Young women have increasingly rebelled not only against passivity and dependency in their relationships but also against the notion that they must function as sexual objects, being defined in purely sexual rather than human terms, and being forced to package and sell themselves as commodities on the sex market.

Each group represents an independent aspect of the total institutionalized oppression of women. Their differences are those of emphasis and immediate interest rather than of fundamental goals. All women suffer from economic exploitation, from exploitive sexuality. Within women's liberation there is a growing understanding that the common oppression of women provides the basis for uniting across class and race lines to form a powerful and radical movement.

Clearly, for the liberation of women to become a reality it is necessary to destroy the ideology of male supremacy which asserts the biological and social inferiority of women in order to justify massive institutionalized oppression. Yet we all know that many women are as loud in their disavowal of this oppression as are the men who chant the litany of "a woman's place is in the home and behind her man." In fact, women are as trapped in their false consciousness as were the mass of blacks 20 years ago, and for much the same reason.

As blacks were defined and limited socially by their color, so women are defined and limited by their sex. While blacks, it was argued, were preordained by God or nature, or both, to be hewers of wood and drawers of water, so women are destined to bear and rear children, and to sustain their husbands with obedience and compassion. The Sky-God tramples through the heavens and the Earth/Mother-Goddess is always flat on her back with her legs spread, putting out for one and all.

Indeed, the phenomenon of male chauvinism can only be understood when it is perceived as a form of racism, based on stereotypes drawn from a deep belief in the biological inferiority of women. The so-called "black analogy" is no analogy at all; it is the same social process that is at work, a process which both justifies and helps perpetuate the exploitation of one group of human beings by another.

The very stereotypes that express the society's belief in the biological inferiority of women recall the images used to justify the oppression of blacks. The nature of women, like that of slaves, is depicted as dependent, incapable of reasoned thought, childlike in its simplicity and warmth, martyred in the role of mother, and mystical in the role of sexual partner. In its benevolent form, the inferior position of women results in paternalism; in its malevolent form, a domestic tyranny which can be unbelievably brutal.

It has taken over 50 years to discredit the scientific and social "proof" which once gave legitimacy to the myths of black racial inferiority. Today most people can see that the theory of the genetic inferiority of blacks is absurd. Yet few are shocked by the fact that scientists are still busy "proving" the biological inferiority of women.

In recent years, in which blacks have led the struggle for liberation, the emphasis on racism has focused only upon racism against blacks. The fact that "racism" has been practiced against many groups other than blacks has been pushed into the background. Indeed, a less forceful but more accurate term for the phenomenon would be "social Darwinism." It was the opinion of the social Darwinists that in the natural course of things the "fit" succeed (i.e., oppress) and the "unfit" (i.e., the biologically inferior) sink to the bottom. According to this view, the very fact of a group's oppression proves its inferiority and the inevitable correctness of its low position. In this way each successive immigrant group coming to America was decked out in the garments of "racial" or biological inferiority until the group was sufficiently assimilated, whereupon Anglo-Saxon venom would turn on a new group filling up the space at the bottom. Now two groups remain, neither of which has been assimilated according to the classic American pattern: the "visibles"—blacks and women. It is equally true for both: "it won't wear off."

Yet the greatest obstacle facing those who would organize women remains women's belief in their own inferiority. Just as all subject populations are controlled by their acceptance of the rightness of their own status, so women remain subject because they believe in the rightness of their own oppression. This dilemma is not a fortuitous one, for the entire society is geared to socialize women to believe in and adopt as immutable necessity their traditional and inferior role. From earliest training to the grave, women are constrained and propagandized. Spend an evening at the movies or watching television, and you will see a grotesque figure called woman presented in a hundred variations upon the themes of "children, church, kitchen" or "the chick sex-pot."

For those who believe in the "rights of mankind," the "dignity of man," consider that to make a woman a person, a human being in her own right, you would have to change her sex: imagine Stokely Carmichael "prone and silent"; imagine Mark Rudd as a Laugh-In girl; picture Rennie Davis as Miss America. Such contradictions as these show how pervasive and deep-rooted is the cultural contempt for women, how difficult it is to imagine a woman as a serious human being, or conversely, how empty and degrading is the image of woman that floods the culture.

Countless studies have shown that black acceptance of white stereotypes leads to mutilated identity, to alienation, to rage and self-hatred. Human beings cannot bear in their own hearts the contradictions of those who hold them in contempt. The ideology of male supremacy and its effect upon women merits as serious study as has been given to the effects of prejudice upon Jews, blacks, and immigrant groups.

It is customary to shame those who would draw the parallel between women and blacks by a great show of concern and chest beating over the suffering of black people. Yet this response itself reveals a refined combination of white middle class guilt and male chauvinism, for it overlooks several essential facts. For example, the most oppressed group within the feminine population is made up of black women, many of whom take a dim view of the black male intellectuals' adoption of white male attitudes of sexual superiority (an irony too cruel to require comment). Neither are those who make this pious objection to the racial parallel addressing themselves very adequately to the millions of white working class women living at the poverty level, who are not likely to be moved by this middle class guilt-ridden one-upmanship while having to deal with the boss, the factory, or the welfare worker day after day. They are already dangerously resentful of the gains made by blacks, and much of their "racist backlash" stems from the fact that they have been forgotten in the push for social change. Emphasis on the real mechanisms of oppression—on the commonality of the process—is essential lest groups such as these, which should work in alliance, become divided against one another.

White middle class males already struggling with the acknowledgment of their own racism do not relish an added burden of recognition: that to white guilt must soon be added "male." It is therefore understandable that they should refuse to see the harshness of the lives of most women—to honestly face the facts of massive institutionalized discrimination against women. Witness the performance to date: "Take her down off the platform and give her a good fuck," "Petty Bourgeois Revisionist Running Dogs," or in the classic words of a Berkeley male "leader," "Let them eat cock."

Among whites, women remain the most oppressed—and the most unorganized—group. Although they constitute a potential mass base for the radical movement, in terms of movement priorities they are ignored; indeed they might as well be invisible. Far from being an accident, this omission is a direct outgrowth of the solid male supremacist beliefs of white radical and left-liberal men. Even now, faced with both fact and agitation, leftist men find the idea of placing any serious priority upon women so outrageous, such a degrading notion, that they respond with a virulence far out of proportion to the modest requests of movement women. This only shows that women must stop wasting their time worrying about the chauvinism of men in the movement and focus instead on their real priority: organizing women.

Marriage: Genesis of Women's Rebellion

The institution of marriage is the chief vehicle for the perpetuation of the oppression of women; it is through the role of wife that the subjugation of women is maintained. In a very real way the role of wife has been the genesis of women's rebellion throughout history.

Looking at marriage from a detached point of view one may well ask why anyone gets married, much less women. One answer lies in the economics of women's position, for women are so occupationally limited that drudgery in the home is considered to be infinitely superior to drudgery in the factory. Secondly, women themselves have no independent social status. Indeed, there is no clearer index of the social worth of a woman in this society than the fact that she has none in her own right. A woman is first defined by the man to whom she is attached, but more particularly by the man she marries, and secondly by the children she bears and rears—hence the anxiety over sexual attractiveness, the frantic scramble for boyfriends and husbands. Having obtained and married a man the race is then on to have children, in order that their attractiveness and accomplishments may add more social worth. In a woman, not having children is seen as an incapacity somewhat akin to impotence in a man.

Beneath all of the pressures of the sexual marketplace and the marital status game, however, there is a far more sinister organization of economic exploitation and psychological mutilation. The housewife role, usually defined in terms of the biological duty of a woman to reproduce and her "innate" suitability for a nurturant and companionship role, is actually crucial to industrial capitalism in an advanced state of technological development. In fact, the housewife (some 44 million women of all classes, ethnic groups and races) provides, unpaid, absolutely essential services and labor. In turn, her assumption of all household duties makes it possible for the man to spend the majority of his time at the workplace.

It is important to understand the social and economic exploitation of the married woman, since the real productivity of her labor is denied by the commonly held assumption that she is dependent on her husband, exchanging her keep for emotional and nurturant services. Margaret Benston, a radical women's liberation leader, points out: "In sheer quantity, household labor, including child care, constitutes a huge amount of socially necessary production. Nevertheless, in a society based on commodity production, it is not usually considered even as 'real work' since it is outside of trade and the marketplace. This assignment of household work as the function of a special category 'women' means that this group *does* stand in a different relationship to production. . . . The material basis for the inferior status of women is to be found in just this definition of women. In a society in which money determines value, women are a group who work outside the money economy. Their work is not worth money, is therefore valueless, is therefore not even real work. And women themselves, who do this valueless work, can hardly be expected to be worth as much as men, who work for money."

Women are essential to the economy not only as free labor, but also as consumers. The American system of capitalism depends for its survival on the consumption of vast amounts of socially wasteful goods, and a prime target for the unloading of this waste is the housewife. She is the purchasing agent for the family, but beyond that she is eager to buy because her own identity depends on her accomplishments as a consumer and her ability to satisfy the wants of her husband and children. This is not, of course, to say that she has any power in the economy.

Although she spends the wealth, she does not own or control it—it simply passes through her hands.

In addition to their role as housewives and consumers, increasing numbers of women are taking outside employment. These women leave the home to join an exploited labor force, only to return at night to assume the double burden of housework on top of wage work—that is, they are forced to work at two full-time jobs. No man is required or expected to take on such a burden. The result: two workers from one household in the labor force with no cutback in essential female functions—three for the price of two, quite a bargain.

Frederick Engels, now widely read in women's liberation, argues that, regardless of her status in the larger society, within the context of the family the woman's relationship to the man is one of proletariat to bourgeoisie. One consequence of this class division in the family is to weaken the capacity of men and women oppressed by the society to struggle together against it.

In all classes and groups, the institution of marriage functions to a greater or lesser degree to oppress women; the unity of women of different classes hinges upon our understanding of that common oppression. The 19th century women's movement refused to deal with marriage and sexuality, and chose instead to fight for the vote and elevate the feminine mystique to a political ideology. That decision retarded the movement for decades. But 1969 is not 1889. For one thing, there now exist alternatives to marriage. The most original and creative politics of the women's movement has come from a direct confrontation with the issue of marriage and sexuality. The cultural revolution —experimentation with life-styles, communal living, collective child-rearing—have all come from the rebellion against dehumanized sexual relationships, against the notion of women as sexual commodities, against the constriction and spiritual strangulation inherent in the role of wife.

Lessons have been learned from the failures of the earlier movement as well. The feminine mystique is no longer mistaken for politics, nor gaining the vote for winning human rights. Women are now all together at the bottom of the work world, and the basis exists for a common focus of struggle for all women in American society. It remains for the movement to understand this, to avoid the mistakes of the past, to respond creatively to the possibilities of the present.

Women's oppression, although rooted in the institution of marriage, does not stop at the kitchen or the bedroom door. Indeed, the economic exploitation of women in the workplace is the most commonly recognized aspect of the oppression of women.

Most women who enter the labor force do not work for "pin money" or "self-fulfillment." Sixty-two per cent of all women working in 1967 were doing so out of economic need (i.e., were either alone or with husbands earning less than $5000 a year). In 1963, 36 per cent of American families had an income of less than $5000 a year. Women from these families work because they must; they contribute 35 to 40 per cent of the family's total income when working full-time, and 15 to 20 per cent when working part-time.

Despite their need, however, women have always represented the most exploited sector of the industrial labor force. Child and female labor were introduced during the early stages of industrial capitalism, at a time when most men were gainfully employed in crafts. As industrialization developed and craft jobs were eliminated, men entered the industrial labor force, driving women and children into the lowest categories of work and pay. Indeed, the position of women and children industrial workers was so pitiful, and their wages so small, that the craft unions refused to organize them. Even when women organized themselves and engaged in militant strikes and labor agitation—from the shoemakers of Lynn, Massachusetts, to the International Ladies' Garment Workers and their great strike of 1909—male unionists continued to ignore their needs. As a result of this male supremacy in the unions, women remain essentially unorganized despite the fact that they are becoming an even larger part of the labor force.

The trend is clearly toward increasing numbers of women entering the work force: women represented 55 per cent of the growth of the total labor force in 1962, and the number of working women rose from 16.9 million in 1957 to 24 million in 1962. There is every indication that the number of women in the labor force will continue to grow as rapidly in the future.

Job discrimination against women exists in all sectors of work, even in occupations which are predominantly made up of women. This discrimination is reinforced in the field of education, where women are being short-changed at a time when the job market demands higher educational levels. In 1962, for example, while women constituted 53 per cent of the graduating high school class, only 42 per cent of the entering college class were women. Only one in three people who received a B.A. or M.A. in that year was a woman, and only one in ten who received a Ph.D. was a woman. These figures represent a decline in educational achievement for women since the 1930s, when women received two out of five of the B.A. and M.A. degrees given, and one out of seven of the Ph.Ds. While there has been a dramatic increase in the number of people, including women, who go to college, women have not kept pace with men in terms of educational achievement. Furthermore, women have lost ground in professional employment. In 1960 only 22 per cent of the faculty and other professional staff at colleges and universities were women—down from 28 per cent in 1949, 27 per cent in 1930, 26 per cent in 1920. 1960 does beat 1919 with only 20 per cent—"you've come a long way, baby"—right back to where you started! In other professional categories: 10 per cent of all scientists are women, 7 per cent of all physicians, 3 per cent of all lawyers, and 1 per cent of all engineers.

Even when women do obtain an education, in many cases it does them little good. Women, whatever their educational level, are concentrated in the lower paying occupations. The figures in Chart A tell a story that most women know and few men will admit: most women are forced to work at clerical jobs, for which they are paid, on the average, $1600 less per year than men doing the same work. Working class women in the service and operative (semi-skilled) categories, making up 30 per cent of working women, are paid $1900 less per year on the average than are men. Of all working women, only 13 per cent are professionals (including low-pay and low-status work such as teaching, nursing and social work), and they earn $2600 less per year than do professional men. Household workers, the lowest category of all, are predominantly women (over 2 million) and predominantly black and third world, earning for their labor barely over $1000 per year.

CHART A

Comparative Statistics For Men and Women in the Labor Force, 1960

Occupation	Percentage of working women in each occupational category	Income of year-round full-time workers		Numbers of workers (in millions)	
		Women	Men	Women	Men
Professional	13%	$4358	$7115	3	5
Managers, Officials and Proprietors	5	3514	7241	1	5
Clerical	31	3586	5247	7	3
Operatives	15	2970	4977	4	9
Sales	7	2389	5842	2	3
Service	15	2340	4089	3	3
Private Household	10	1156	—	2	—

Sources: U.S. Department of Commerce, Bureau of the Census, Current Population Reports, P-60, No. 37; U.S. Department of Labor, Bureau of Labor Statistics, and U.S. Department of Commerce, Bureau of the Census.

CHART B

Median Annual Wages For Men and Women by Race, 1960

Workers	Median Annual Wage
Males, White	$5137
Males, Non-White	$3075
Females, White	$2537
Females, Non-White	$1276

Source: U.S. Department of Commerce, Bureau of the Census. Also see: President's Commission on the Status of Women, 1963.

Not only are women forced onto the lowest rungs of the occupational ladder, they are in the lowest income levels as well. The most constant and bitter injustice experienced by all women is the income differential. While women might passively accept low status jobs, limited opportunities for advancement, and discrimination in the factory, office and university, they choke finally on the daily fact that the male worker next to them earns more, and usually does less. In 1965 the median wage or salary income of year-round full-time women workers was only 60 per cent that of men, a 4 per cent loss since 1955. Twenty-nine per cent of working women earned less than $3000 a year as compared with 11 per cent of the men; 43 per cent of the women earned from $3000 to $5000 a year as compared with 19 per cent of the men; and 19 per cent of the women earned $7000 or more as compared with 43 per cent of the men.

What most people do not know is that in certain respects, women suffer more than do non-white men, and that black and third world women suffer most of all.

Women, regardless of race, are more disadvantaged than are men, including non-white men. White women earn $2600 less than white men and $1500 less than non-white men. The brunt of the inequality is carried by 2.5 million non-white women, 94 per cent of whom are black. They earn $3800 less than white men, $1900 less than non-white men, and $1200 less than white women.

There is no more bitter paradox in the racism of this country than that the white man, articulating the male supremacy of the white male middle class, should provide the rationale for the oppression of black women by black men. Black women constitute the largest minority in the United States, and they are the most disadvantaged group in the labor force. The further oppression of black women will not liberate black men, for black women were never the oppressors of their men—that is a myth of the liberal white man. The oppression of black men comes from institutionalized racism and economic exploitation; from the world of the white man. Consider the following facts and figures.

The percentage of black working women has always been proportionately greater than that of white women. In 1900, 41 per cent of black women were employed, as compared to 17 per cent for white women. In 1963, the proportion of black women employed was still a fourth greater than that of whites. In 1960, 44 per cent of black married women with children under six years were in the labor force, in contrast to 29 per cent for white women. While job competition requires ever higher levels of education, the bulk of illiterate women are black. On the whole, black women—who often have the greatest need for employment —are the most discriminated against in terms of opportunity. Forced by an oppressive and racist society to carry unbelievably heavy economic and social burdens, black women stand at the bottom of that society, doubly marked by the caste signs of color and sex.

The rise of new agitation for the occupational equality of women also coincided with the re-entry of the "lost generation" —the housewives of the 1950's—into the job market. Women from middle class backgrounds, faced with an "empty nest" (children grown or in school) and a widowed or divorced rate of one-fourth to one-third of all marriages, returned to the workplace in large numbers. But once there they discovered that women, middle class or otherwise, are the last hired, the lowest paid, the least often promoted, and the first fired. Furthermore, women are more likely to suffer job discrimination on the basis of age, so the widowed and divorced suffer particularly, even though their economic need to work is often urgent. Age discrimination also means that the option of work after child-rearing is limited. Even highly qualified older women find themselves forced into low-paid, unskilled or semi-skilled work—if they are lucky enough to find a job in the first place.

The realities of the work world for most middle class women —that they become members of the working class, like it or not —are understandably distant to many young men and women in college who have never had to work, and who tend to think of the industrial "proletariat" as a revolutionary force, to the exclusion of "bourgeois" working women. Their image of the "pampered middle class woman" is factually incorrect and politically naive. It is middle class women forced into working class life who are often the first to become conscious of the contradiction between the "American Dream" and their daily experience.

Faced with discrimination on the job—after being forced into the lower levels of the occupational structure—millions of women are inescapably presented with the fundamental contradictions in their unequal treatment and their massive exploitation. The rapid growth of women's liberation as a movement is related in part to the exploitation of working women in all occupational categories.

Male supremacy, marriage, and the structure of wage labor —each of these aspects of women's oppression has been crucial to the resurgence of the women's struggle. It must be abundantly clear that radical social change must occur before there can be significant improvement in the social position of women. Some form of socialism is a minimum requirement, considering the changes that must come in the institutions of marriage and the family alone. The intrinsic radicalism of the struggle for women's liberation necessarily links women with all other oppressed groups.

The heart of the movement, as in all freedom movements, rests in women's knowledge, whether articulated or still only an illness without a name, that they are not inferior—not chicks, nor bunnies, nor quail, nor cows, nor bitches, nor ass, nor meat. Women hear the litany of their own dehumanization each day.

Yet all the same, women know that male supremacy is a lie. They know they are not animals or sexual objects or commodities. They know their lives are mutilated, because they see within themselves a promise of creativity and personal integration. Feeling the contradiction between the essentially creative and self-actualizing human being within her, and the cruel and degrading less-than-human role she is compelled to play, a woman begins to perceive the falseness of what her society has forced her to be. And once she perceives this, she knows that she must fight.

Women must learn the meaning of rage, the violence that liberates the human spirit. The rhetoric of invective is an equally essential stage, for in discovering and venting their rage against the enemy—and the enemy in everyday life is men—women also experience the justice of their own violence. They learn the first lessons in their own latent strength. Women must learn to know themselves as revolutionaries. They must become hard and strong in their determination, while retaining their humanity and tenderness.

There is a rage that impels women into a total commitment to women's liberation. That ferocity stems from a denial of mutilation; it is a cry for life, a cry for the liberation of the spirit. Roxanne Dunbar, surely one of the most impressive women in the movement, conveys the feelings of many: "We are damaged—we women, we oppressed, we disinherited. There are very few who are not damaged, and they rule. . . . The oppressed trust those who rule more than they trust themselves, because self-contempt emerges from powerlessness. Anyway, few oppressed people believe that life could be much different. . . . We are damaged and we have the right to hate and have contempt and to kill and to scream. But for what? . . . Do we want the oppressor to admit he is wrong, to withdraw his misuse of us? He is only too happy to admit guilt—then do nothing but try to absorb and exorcize the new thought. . . . That does not make up for what I have lost, what I never had, and what all those others who are worse off than I never had. . . . Nothing will compensate for the irreparable harm it has done to my sisters. . . . How could we possibly settle for anything remotely less, even take a crumb in the meantime less, than total annihilation of a system which systematically destroys half its people. . . ."

Alice Rossi

WOMEN—TERMS OF LIBERATION, 1970

Alice Rossi is a professor of sociology at Goucher College, Maryland.

SOURCE
Alice Rossi, "Women—Terms of Liberation," Dissent, November–
December 1970, pp. 531–541.
Portrait: Peter Eric Rossi.

At least for the moment, Women's Liberation is "in." Its advocates get wide publicity in the mass media, and there is talk, mostly not very serious, about what "those women" want. On campuses, as in professional organizations, there has been mounting pressure to hire and promote more women, to provide child-care facilities for married women students and employees, and to offer courses on the history and the status of women. The voicing of these demands will increase significantly at professional conventions. I predict comparable increases in the political and economic realms, as women organize and demonstrate to change laws and employer practices that discriminate on the grounds of sex. Among activist women there is clearly a new note of optimism.

This optimistic sense does not, however, seem to be shared by many men. The majority of American men appear to be convinced that if they wait out the storm, activism will die down and they can then continue to run government agencies, businesses, and universities. I do not share the view that the women's rights movement has not yet reached its crest, though I also believe it faces hard times. What follows is an attempt to sketch both the encouraging and discouraging developments that may mark the women's movement in the next decade.

At the outset I shall draw on my personal experiences in academic and private life, upon participation in several reform movements in recent years, and upon a commitment to fundamental change in America society.

Personal-Political Background

As an undergraduate and graduate student, I had no particular interest in the status of women, sex roles, or occupational choice. I entered college as an English major, pragmatism dictating an occupational choice of high school English teacher, but romanticism prompting a hope I might become a famous writer. I was one of those thousands of bright, eager New York students attending the city colleges, in my case, Brooklyn College. My first sociology instructor was Louis Schneider, and he began his course by reading a Whitman poem and raising the question: who was this man? what does the poem tell about his time, his place on this globe? I found the sociological dimension of literature so fascinating that I fell in love with the field, and began a life-long affair of the heart and mind that is second only to my own marriage and the three children of that marriage. As a graduate student at Columbia, I was interested in the macroscopic analysis of social institutions; in family and kinship systems rather than the roles of women within family systems; in reference groups, through work with Robert Merton, and in studies of the professions. The occupational role I chose to study in Kingsley Davis's seminar was that of the politician, though not once did I think to look into the sex-linked nature of occupational choice.

No woman in 1970, I hope, could be the total innocent I was in 1950 concerning sex discrimination. I dreamed of being one day the president of the American Sociological Society, and of writing a major opus that would be built on the strengths of my two mentors in theory and research. I discounted as peevish envy the claim of my male peers that I would not get a fellowship "because I was a woman," and then, when I was awarded one, the counterclaim that "someone on the faculty must be trying to make you."

It would have been congenial for me to move from graduate training to an academic position as a teacher and secondarily a researcher. But this is a path difficult for a married woman in academia, particularly if, like myself, she is married to a sociologist. So I spent ten years as a research associate, following not my own interests so much as the availability of funds and openings: intergroup relations at Cornell, generational differences in the Soviet Union at Harvard, kinship in the middle class at the University of Chicago.

Through these research undertakings, I developed a fascination with a problem seldom adequately stated within sociological theory itself: what are the connections, the strains and accommodations between involvement in the family on the one hand, and the occupational system on the other? I was taking a first step away from the predominant theory that the family and occupational systems require "mechanisms of segregation" with only one member of the family participating significantly in the occupational system—a theory I now view as an intellectual put-down providing a rationale for men as the prime movers in work and politics.

The source of this growing interest was not only research and scholarship; it was also my own personal experience as a faculty wife and mother of young children. As a faculty wife, I had ample opportunity to observe that some sociological theorists did a good job of preventing two members of a family from holding significant positions in the occupational system. At Harvard and again at Chicago, I saw numerous instances of women being kept off the academic turf their husbands claimed as their own. I had offended one such theorist by negotiating an appointment at Harvard without first clearing such a horrendous step with him, then my husband's department chairman. I watched women friends leave the university when they became pregnant and being kept out when they tried to return after their children entered school. And during the two years I had my first two children I learned from personal experience the truth of the existential thesis that "one becomes what one does," for I realized with horror that I was resenting my husband's freedom to continue his full-time academic work despite the addition of parental responsibilities, and even more that I was actually trying to prevent his playing an intimate role in the lives of the children, so that I might at least have ascendancy in parenthood to complement his ascendancy in our profession.

But it took a return to academia, involving a traumatic encounter with the discrimination academic women so often suffer, to jar me out of my innocence. I began a long process of reestablishing connections with my earlier life: intellectual exposure to the ideas of Robert Lynd and C. Wright Mills, personal experiences in a variety of working-class and white-collar clerical jobs, and involvement in radical politics (as an undergraduate in the 1930s and early 1940s). I began to draw together these older layers of the self and to focus the ideas, the personal experience, and the political commitment I now have.

My own trial by fire involved a not untypical story of a bright woman Ph.D. accepting a research associateship to do a study the male principal investigator was not competent to do on his own, and in which he had very little interest. At least initially his interest was low, until I had designed the study, fielded it, and partially analyzed the results. At that point he realized he had a good thing going, and simply announced, despite verbal agreements about co-authorship, that my services were no longer needed. I was a salaried research associate, he a full professor, and as the dean put it bluntly to me, "he is valuable university property; you, unfortunately, are expendable."

My own concern for the status of women, the analysis of sex roles, the study of and active participation in abortion law and divorce reform, I date to the "slow burn" that began in that first major encounter with sex discrimination in academia. It immediately precipitated the scholarship and writing that led me down the path of immodesty to my first essay on sex equality.

The varied response to that *Daedalus* essay was itself a revealing commentary on American academia. Several male colleagues accused me of troubling their marriages. Young women wrote to say they had decided to return to graduate school instead of having another baby. My husband received a sympathetic bereavement card from a West Coast sociologist for having such an upstart wife. A more recent example of this kind was the reaction of male sociologists to the roles my husband and I played at the sociology convention in the fall of 1969. As secretary of the association, my husband was on the platform while I delivered a speech and submitted resolutions for the women's caucus. In the months since then, I have had offers for academic appointments based on the premise that my husband and I are about to be divorced. My husband has been asked how he felt when I delivered that speech, with his male colleagues not knowing how to take his response that he felt pride! During earlier years, my university colleagues criticized me for "not sticking to my last" as research sociologist instead of writing analytic social criticism. Others said it was inappropriate and would "ruin your career" to get involved in the "woman thing," or to be publicly visible as an organizer for abortion law reform, or to write in a woman's magazine that "motherhood was not enough." Nowhere did one hear anything about responsibility for reaching the larger public, nor did one have any sense that there was an obligation for a family sociologist to "do something" about contraception, abortion, or women's rights.

As you may know from reading Eli Ginsberg on life styles of educated women, a supportive husband is an absolute requirement for professional women. Unfortunately, Ginsberg does not understand how a woman gets a supportive husband. It is not a "condition" she is fortunate to have as a base for being something more than homemaker, mother, and husband-relaxer. He is something she looks for, and when she finds him, she marries him. It didn't just happen that my husband is supportive: I chose him in part because he *was*.

From 1964 to the fall of 1969 I enjoyed an unusual status under a research award from the National Institute of Mental Health. This award gave me an academic umbrella to legitimize my status in the university and the independence to undertake my own research. The best education I ever had I acquired on my own during the first year or so of that award: the luxury of getting lost in libraries again, free to acquire that delicious "itch to know," to tackle new fields, turn down any lecture, paper, or course offering that did not interest me. Midway into that five-year award, I undertook a major research study of family and career roles of women college graduates. What time I had beyond this research and family responsibilities was invested in active attempts at social, legal, and political change to benefit women. By early 1969, however, I felt increasingly out of rapport with most of my colleagues in empirical sociology and restless for direct contact with the college-age generation. I had studied these young people; now I wanted to teach them. In the fall of 1969, I therefore shifted from research sociology at Johns Hopkins to undergraduate teaching at Goucher College.

Background of Current Women's Movement

It has become fashionable to link the emergence of the women's liberation movement to the participation of younger women in the civil rights movement. These young women, one reads, drew the conclusion their ancestors did from involvement in the abolitionist cause of the nineteenth century: that the arguments developed and the battles waged to free the black American could apply to American women, even though women in the abolitionist as in the civil rights movement all too often found themselves treated as second-class creatures good for cooking, typing, and comforting their male leaders. Without detracting from this point at all, I would only remark that the women's liberation movement is a bit more than two years old, and there were important, though less visible, changes among American women earlier in the 1960s.

In fact, I would argue that it was the changed composition of the female labor force during the period beginning with 1940 but rapidly peaking in the 1950s that provided the momentum leading to the establishment of the Kennedy Commission on the Status of Women and the formation of new women's rights organizations in the mid-1960s. So long as women worked mostly before marriage or after marriage only until a first pregnancy, or lived within city limits where there was a diversity of cultural activities to engage them, there were but feeble grounds for a significant movement among women, since their motivation for working was short-lived. Only among women who are relatively permanent members of the work force could daily experience force an awareness of economic inequities based on sex and a determination to do something about them. It was the women who served on the numerous committees of the Kennedy commission, followed by the thousands who worked with the state commissions established during the Kennedy and Johnson administrations, who experienced and then stimulated a mood of rising expectations among American women.

These were committed, knowledgeable, largely middle-aged women who had high hopes, as they filed their reports, that American society would finally do something to improve the status of women. Their hopes were dashed by the treatment they experienced at the spring 1966 conference of representatives from the state commissions brought together by the Department of Labor in Washington. From that frustrating experience, a number of women concluded that little significant change could be expected until a strong organization was built that would be completely independent of the political establishment. This was how the National Organization for Women was formed in the fall of 1966. The range of women's problems that NOW is concerned with has broadened greatly since 1966, but the core continues to be equal treatment in hiring and promotion.

NOW includes lively, dedicated women who are pressing hard against the barriers that restrict women in American society. Except for its action in behalf of airline stewardesses, however, it has had relatively little public or media attention outside of New York, at least if compared to the extraordinary press coverage given to the women's liberation groups this past year. Why so? The answer, I think, lies in differences of stress and outlook between these two tendencies within the women's movement.

A fundamental assumption of American society is that men's primary social roles are in work and women's primary social roles in the family. It is conventionally supposed that all men will want to work at a challenging job. Nothing is so threatening to conventional values as a man who does not want to work or does not want to work at a challenging job, and most people are disturbed if a man in a well-paying job indicates ambivalence or dislike toward it. The counterpart for women is any suggestion that they feel ambivalent toward maternity, marriage, or homemaking, probably in that order. In more sociological terms, we might put this as follows: social roles vary in the extent to which it is culturally permissible to express ambivalence or negative feelings toward them. Ambivalence can be admitted most readily toward those roles that are optional, least where they are considered primary. Thus men repress negative feelings toward work and feel freer to express negative feelings toward leisure, sex and marriage, while women are free to express negative feelings toward work but tend to repress them toward family roles.

Applying these hypotheses to the issues that triggered public attention to the women's movement helps explain why reactions are more intense to the women's liberation groups than to women's rights organizations like NOW. There was widespread concern in manpower, government, and university circles when many bright middle-class young men began to depart from an unthinking acceptance of occupational aspirations like those of their fathers, either shifting away from business, engineering, and science toward teaching, social science, and the humanities, or by indicating that their desire was for a life style with more time spent away from the job. The movie *The Graduate* symbolized this generational contrast in dramatic form. Universities were concerned when men students expressed resentment to advanced training as a preparation for the adult rat race. But I doubt that anyone would have worried if only women had expressed such resentment. They would simply have been told that if they could not take the academic pressure, they should go home.

Public airing of ambivalence or a shift of values toward the place of work in the lives of men touches a vital nerve in American society. For women, the counterpart is any airing of ambivalence toward what the culture has defined as *their* primary roles, in marriage and maternity. However, once even a minority of women begin to reject their role as sex object, postpone or reject marriage, stop smiling over a shiny waxed floor or, heaven forbid, question the desirability of having children or rearing them themselves as a full-time job, then they touch an equivalent nerve in American society.

Hence, it is when men question work and women question family commitment that we find public responses ranging from a shiver of distaste to a convulsion of hate. It has been the ques-

tioning of family roles among women's liberation groups that
has triggered the current widespread attention to the "woman
issue." NOW's focus on employment issues, dealing with an
"optional" role for women, cannot compete for media attention
with antimarriage and antisexism campaigns by the women's
lib spokesmen.

Employment

What, now, are the immediate problems and possibilities? Let
me start with the bread-and-butter issue of women's employment. We must first look at a critical determinant of the changed
profile of women's participation in the labor force. A lot of
nonsense has been written in the past decade to account for the
flow of older married women into the labor force. The emphasis
has been on the impact of homemaking simplification via frozen
foods and complex gadgetry on the one hand, and the search for
self-fulfillment and a solution to the "problem without a name"
on the other. This is to look for explanations on the supply side
of the economic equation. But in an economy as hard-nosed as
ours, such a stress is naive, for there must be powerful factors
on the demand side that prompted employers to open their
doors to older women.

A significant factor underlying this willingness lies in the
peculiarities of the demographic structure of the American population between 1940 and 1970. Young women were staying in
school longer and marrying at an earlier age, thus shrinking the
size of the traditional labor pool of young unmarried women.
Even more important, the young women of the 1950s were born
in the 1930s, when the birth rate was very low, while at the same
time there was a vast increase in the number of young children
born during the baby boom of those postwar years. As a result
of the rippling effect of this low-fertility cohort, employers *had*
to seek women workers from other sources than the young
unmarried. Consequently, the trigger was in the first place far
more a matter of employer demand than of assertive women
pressing to enter into the labor force.

These were also years of vast expansion in precisely those
segments of the occupational system in which women have traditionally been prominent. Because schools were flooded with the
baby-boom children, women college graduates were assured a
welcome as teachers despite age, marital and family status. Colleges and universities were expanding at a rapid rate, and married women were taken on as part-time instructors and full-time
researchers. Clerical, sales, and service occupations were expanding, and women with high school degrees were able to choose
among the available jobs.

This fortunate circumstance is now changing. In the 1970s there will be a reversal in the demographic pattern. The birth rate is now on the decline, the age at marriage creeping upward, and the time interval between marriage and childbearing widening. In the 1970s there will be more young unmarried and childless married women seeking jobs, for they will be the baby-boom females grown to maturity. At the same time, graduate schools will be producing large numbers of young people with advanced degrees, who will face a very different job market from the one that young Ph.D.'s faced during the past 20 years. Up to 1970 the supply of Ph.D.'s was far below the demand in institutions of higher education, but the reverse will hold from 1970 onward: the supply will exceed the demand in universities. This will be especially true for the natural sciences, less so for the social sciences until late in the 1970s. Which is not to say that the society cannot absorb or does not need highly trained people. From one point of view, the excess supply means an opportunity for reducing class size, providing students with better learning experiences, changing graduate curricula to prepare students for nonacademic jobs, etc. On the other hand, higher education is facing a financial crisis due to the cutbacks in government funding, corporations are pruning staffs of "frills," and government agencies are on an internal economy drive.

It is therefore of critical importance that women press hard during the next few years to secure equal protection of the law and to assure adequate representation in all segments of the economy. There is already a first sign that women are withdrawing from the labor force: in the last quarter of 1969 the Bureau of Labor Statistics showed a drop in the unemployment rate, though the drop occurred not because people found jobs, but because unemployed young people and women were ceasing to look for jobs.

What women must do in the next several years does not require new legislation, though passage of an equal rights amendment to the Constitution would cover a wide range of sex inequities in law and practice. Short of such passage, however, it is true that there has been a legal revolution during the 1960s in regard to protection of women's economic rights. Title VII of the Civil Rights Act of 1964 prohibits discrimination based on sex by all employers of 25 or more employees, employment agencies and unions with 25 or more members, with the exception of educational institutions. The Equal Pay Act of 1963 requires equal wages and salaries for men and women doing equal work. Amended Executive Order 11375 prohibits discrimination based on sex by federal government contractors and subcontractors. The Age Discrimination in Employment Act of 1967 prohibits discrimination based on age between 40 and 65. While this act does not prohibit sex discrimination, it could play a significant role in enlarging employment opportunities for women over 40 who wish to return to the labor market or change jobs. Municipal and state Fair Employment Practices commissions and agencies administering state equal pay legislation can also be used to protect employment rights. Women in colleges and universities are not covered by the Civil Rights Act, but women lawyers in activist groups are now working through the channels provided by Executive Order 11375 rather than pressing for congressional change in the educational institutions exemption in the 1964 act. WEAL, the Women's Equity Action League, has mounted an important campaign designed to apply pressure on colleges and universities to comply with this executive order or face cancellation and future loss of government contracts— something no institution of higher education would care to risk. Labor Department guidelines were announced in June 1970 to assure equal job opportunities for women on work paid for under federal contract.

The mere existence of such laws does not solve anything unless women press for their implementation, first by concerted efforts to educate their sex, and second by developing test cases that will bring real changes in women's employment status. Though unglamorous and hard work, and rarely making a flashy news story, this is of greater long-range significance than any amount of bra-burning or antimen speech-making.

Right now it is not clear how national policies in the coming decade will affect the lives of women. In the post-Sputnik decade, there was a widespread campaign to persuade women to enter the labor force, with the government serving as spokesman for short-handed employers trying to meet personnel needs. The laws serving to strengthen women's economic rights were passed during the '60s. It is only in the past few years that Woman Power has emerged, with younger women questioning conventional women's roles. Even while expectations are rising, a reversal of national policy may lie ahead, as a brake is put on military expenditure, and as conservative political elements come into ascendancy with the new-old cry that women belong in the home instead of taking jobs away from men or making "outrageous" demands for maternity benefits and child-care facilities.

At the same time there will be mounting pressure for a national population policy. We are witnessing the advance wave of this policy with the unprecedented shift in opinion regarding abortion in the United States. Those of us who worked on this issue early in the 1960s are now gratified and disturbed by the ease with which total repeal of abortion laws looms as a reality: gratified because this represents the fruition of long, hard effort, disturbed by the quite mixed motivations behind the passage of such legislation.

Public dialogue on population is increasing significantly, and we begin to hear large families discussed as undesirable for individual couples and for society at large. But the problem is that women are being told to hold back on their fertility in the same era in which there may be a shift away from encouraging them to seek significant work in the economy, and when much volunteer work is being transformed into paid employment for the poor. Two such conflicting policies—low fertility and minimal participation in the labor force—can have serious consequences in undercutting the confidence of young women. It would be like putting them in a revolving door and spinning it: not permitting them easy entry or significant work *outside* the home, yet not permitting them fulfillment in a bountiful maternity *inside* the home. The social price of such a conflict could well be a rise in alienation, escape into drugs, alcoholism, or joyless sex and an even greater tendency to live vicariously through the few children they have.

I would like to think that women would take the lead in calling atttention to the human dimensions of national policies that have particular impact on the lives of women. For the organizations directly involved in action concerning women's rights, such a thorough analysis is difficult. It takes time and some distancing from the heat of battle, and hence becomes a special responsibility of women in academia. But their voices will not be heard nor will their analyses be pertinent unless they keep in close contact with the women's rights movement and national policy formation. A good example can be seen in the congressional hearings on the birth control pill this past spring, at which women's liberation spokesmen engaged in widely publicized protest. Their clamor was, in my judgment, ill-advised. We do not halt small-pox vaccinations because a dozen children die from them each year, or stop using antibiotics because 500 users die a year; by the same token, an element of risk in contraceptive pills is, in and of itself, no basis for calling a halt to their use. In no way is this to say that women should not have completely safe contraceptives, or that more emphasis should not be put on male contraceptives, sterilization, and abortion as acceptable procedures to control unwanted births. What I am urging is that women be more thorough and thoughtful in their analysis of a problem before rushing to the streets and into print with arguments that may appear sound superficially but are actually political posturing.

Sexuality

Research and education in human sexuality, and the implications of such research for the social roles of the sexes is another matter that merits increased attention in the 1970s. Fifty years of accepting Freudian concepts of female sexuality will not be quickly undone by current research on the human sexual response. Psychoanalytic theories have penetrated deep into the modern consciousness, and are reinforced a dozen times a day through commercials that attempt to sell everything from an Ohrbach dress to detergents. What concerns me equally is to be spared another 50 years of anti-Freudian polemics from the women's movement.

Very often such anti-Freudian analyses are couched in Marxist terms. It may serve unstated political ends, but it is historically false and analytically simplistic to claim that women's sexual role reflects the bourgeois notion of man's desire to possess and amass private property, or to charge that the second-class citizenship of women merely reflects capitalist society's need to coerce them into domestic slavery and conspicuous consumption. Marxist analyses of women and capitalism have an element of truth only if you substitute industrialization for capitalism. As the Communist nations have industrialized, the same hard pinch of double jobs is detectable in the lives of their employed married women, and the same loss of humane values in the work place. Nor is there much evidence that the relations between the sexes are particularly different in Communist nations from those in Western Europe or the United States. The major difference is merely one of intensity: no country can match the United States for media saturated with exploitative and male-dominant sex, typified so well by the infantile or cruel acts of physical rape that fill so many pages of Norman Mailer's books.

A number of radical-feminist analyses begin with a good critique of the Freudian fallacies concerning female sexuality. Let us now assume it to be established that there is no differentiation between a clitoral and vaginal orgasm; that the myth of women's relative asexuality has been shown to be a biological absurdity; and that women's sexuality has been suppressed through a socialization of gender roles that urges passivity and submission to men. Liberation group discussions of these points can be enormously helpful for the psychological release of the submerged sexual selves of many women. But one must also reckon with the fact that the Masters-Johnson research only illuminates the *physiological* dimension of human sexuality. It tells us nothing about the nonsexual components of human sexual behavior. Critiques of Freud's notions of female sexuality are now commonplace, but I have seen little as yet that suggests an alternative developmental theory, with the exception of recent work by John Gagnon and William Simon. I would suggest that more critical attention should be paid to two factors bearing upon sexual behavior in American society. One is the view that sex is an intense high-pressure drive that constrains the individual to seek sexual gratification either directly or indirectly. This view is apparent not only in psychoanalytic but in sociological literature as well. Kingsley Davis, for example, considers sex a high-intensity, social constant that must be channeled lest it find expression in behavior that threatens the maintenance of collective life. Part of the Freudian legacy, however, is that we have become extremely adept at weeding out the sexual ingredient in many forms of nonsexual behavior and symbolism while rarely engaging in what may be an equally fruitful analysis: an examination of sexual behavior as an agency for expressing nonsexual motives.

For in truth, sexual behavior in American society serves not merely sexual needs, but also power and status needs compensating for a lack of gratification in other areas of life. A further complication is the pressure on American adults to remain pegged at an adolescent stage of development and behavior. A man or woman of 45 is not the same person as a 20-year-old, and to perform sexually as if they were is to require that the man overperform sexually and that the woman persist in a girlish style that is equally inappropriate to her stage of sexual and social maturity. In the case of men, overperformance can be stoked by extra-marital adventures or self-stimulation via pornographic literature or dramatic productions. Men are good at such detached self-stimulation since they learn sexuality in part through masturbation, which itself paves the way for a greater detachment in the sexual act than women tend to have. It may also be the case that marital satisfaction and happiness decline with duration of marriage in American society largely because adults are expected to perform at 40 or 50 as they did at 20 or 25. This is a reflection of what Henry Murray has described as the retarded adolescent stage of development of American society. If, as a culture, we could move in the direction of mature interdependence between individuals, across social classes, religious, racial, and sexual lines, to say nothing of national boundaries, we might come to develop what Kenneth Boulding has described as "reconciling styles" in which we take primary pleasure in life from identifying with the process of change itself: watching and taking pleasure from our own individual growth and change, and the growth and change of our friends, spouses, and children.

What has this to do with the women's movement in the 1970s? I think we should be prepared for intense masculine backlash to the demands women make that are rooted not merely in the specific area of work or home management or parental responsibility, but in displacements from a deeper level. Demands for equality for women are threats to men's self-esteem and sense of sexual turf. Some feminists will say, fine and good: men have been our oppressors long enough, now they must give ground. But most women do not wish to live embattled and manless lives, and my impression is there are far more men in the younger generation than there were in my own who are eager to acquire a new life style, a gentler and more meaningful relationship with women. There is much need for research and sober analysis on the social correlates of varying styles of sexual behavior; following that, a great need for a rather different conception of sex education than anything we have seen in school curricula or gymnastic sex manuals to date.

Some women who have recently been active in women's caucuses in professional associations have begun to compare notes on the responses their demands are eliciting from male colleagues. One of the more interesting hypotheses emerging from these comparisons is that the men most resistant to and in some cases almost hysterical about women's pressure for equal treatment are men known to be sexually exploitative in their relations to women students. One such professor whose feathers were decidedly ruffled when the sociology women's caucus displaced a luncheon meeting he was to speak at, complained prettily, with an expectation that it would flatter rather than anger me: "But Alice, what is all the fuss about? There is always room in graduate departments for an extraordinary woman!" It was beyond his ability or willingness to understand that sex equality in academia would not be achieved until there was room for as many "average" women as for "average" men. Some of my caucus colleagues believe that, beneath the surface, men such as this are not able to relate to a woman colleague at the same or higher status rank and feel comfortable only in superordinate positions from which they can dispense professorial and sexual favors.

The male backlash is bound to come, and there are signs of it already. A male friend of mine recently sent me a xeroxed copy of a letter of recommendation to the chairman of his department. The applicant is an unmarried woman who had taught in the writer's department and taken graduate courses with him. He wrote:

When Miss X arrived she was somewhat lacking in self-confidence, uncertain whether there was a place for her in sociology. Now she recognizes that she can, as a female, contribute to the field without becoming a spinster or a swinger. I say this to emphasize that she is a mature person not swayed by the superficial values so evident on campuses today. In short, she is not a participant in the women's liberation movement but a competent sociologist. . . . She is neither seductive nor emasculating and will be a useful colleague.

I cite such examples to point out that we must have thick skins —at least as thick as those of our grandmothers in the suffrage, union, and socialist movements of an earlier day. We shall need every bit of sex solidarity we can get.

Women's Rights Organizations

Everyone knows there has already been a good deal of factionalism within the larger women's movement. We have WITCH, WEAL, Radical Feminists, FEW, NOW, WRAP, and there are undoubtedly more to come. Listening to men, one senses a glee-ful pleasure at seeing such sectarianism; many wishfully view this as a dissipation of effort in a noisy fizzle. But this need not be true so long as those who form a new group do not concentrate on fruitless attacks upon the group they left or on styles of protest directed mainly at getting attention from the press. Diversity within a movement can be a strength, for there is no one problem or one solution. Certain women's liberation groups may be trying to recruit for a political revolutionary movement yet find some of their members graduating from consciousness-raising group sessions to affiliation with a NOW chapter. In turn, many NOW chapters have lost members to the liberation groups. Women lawyers have on occasion separated from the more diffuse organizations, the better to focus on campaigns making greater use of their skills. Other groups may concentrate on demonstrations protesting sex imagery in the media or beauty pageants. There is far more risk in frantically dissipating one's efforts by doing a great variety of things than in organizational splitting.

Let me end with a comment concerning the relationship between the women's rights movement and movements of black Americans. There is a serious danger that the essentially middle-class and white women's groups will be as guilty of misunderstanding the problems confronting black men and women today as an earlier counterpart in the middle-class suffrage movement of the 19th century misunderstood the political efforts of working-class people.

In recent years, many women in the women's rights movement have taken up with great moral righteousness the task of informing black women that they should avoid the trap of moving through the same series of mistakes that middle-class women were subjected to in the past. A conference on women last February at Cornell culminated in a dramatic session on the black woman in America, in which the largely middle-class white audience hissed black women and men on a panel who spoke of the need for black women to give attention to the black man and his position in the community, to be supportive of their men's struggle for greater self-esteem and dignity. Renee Neblett of the Boston Black Panthers defined the black woman as a strong person who can act independently and make decisions but, most important of all, a woman with an ability to relate to men, one who would do anything to help her man retain or regain his manhood and insure the survival of her people.

In reading the transcript of this session, I felt anger and shame that the middle-class women in the audience had not appreciated the difference in the positions of the sexes among whites and blacks. John Dollard's description of caste in a Southern town is as relevant today as three decades ago, when he pointed out that within the white caste the man is in the superior position, and within the black caste the woman is more often in the superior position. If black women, largely poor but

still more advantageously placed than black men, have the
humanity and dignity to help raise the self-esteem of their men—
to realize, as one of my black students put it, that the black
female is no better than her man despite a history of educational and economic superiority—then this is a great tribute to
black women in America that unfortunately is not matched by a
comparable dedication on the part of white men toward their
women.

Nor do we sufficiently realize the continuing relevance of
class differences in the ways a problem is perceived and experienced. Abraham Maslow's need hierarchy thesis is helpful, for it
suggests that middle-class women, whose physical needs for
food, clothing, shelter, and sheer security of person are relatively
assured, are free to concentrate on a higher level of need. A
working-class person or group cannot indulge in such luxury
until needs for survival and security are met. I think, therefore,
that right now the middle-class women's rights movement can
find a collaborative arrangement with black women only on
such bread-and-butter issues as protecting and expanding economic and political rights. Beyond this, the white women's movement should try to deepen its understanding of the differences
between their relations to men and those of black women. Before
giving advice, one must understand. Listen, for example, to a
black poet's phrasing of the issue:

> blackwoman
> is an
> in and out
> rightsideup
> action-image
> of her man . . .
> in other
> (blacker) words;
> She's together,
> if
> he
> is.
>   —Don Lee

What white poet has yet said of a man, "he's together if she is."

Despite the optimists in our midst, or the pessimists who
anticipate revolution in the streets—after which, of course, a
magical transformation would follow—I think we are in for a
long and hard battle—cultural, legal, and political—before we
reach any goal of sex equality for black or white in this nation.
It will be won not by quickie-action skirmishes but by the per-
sistent beat of the hearts and work of the minds of at least
another generation.

Shirley Chisholm

THE 51% MINORITY, 1970

*Shirley Chisholm, the first black Congresswoman in the United
States, campaigned under the slogan "Unbought and Unbossed,"
which is also the title of her recently published autobiography.
As a representative of the people rather than a pawn of party
politics, she is an articulate champion of the rights of blacks
and Puerto Ricans, who elected her to the 91st Congress.
Intensely interested in the needs and rights of women, she has
worked for child-care centers, equal pay, and equal opportunities.*

SOURCE
Shirley Chisholm, The 51% Minority, *The Conference on Women's
Employment, January 1970.*

My sisters all, I am very glad to be here this afternoon because I think that we are beginning to recognize that indeed, women have to become very active in the social struggle that is occurring in the United States of America today, and that we too no longer must indulge in jargon and lots of words. We must now begin to suit the action to the words in order to acquire *our* unequivocal place in the American society just as black people are acting for their unequivocal share in American society.

Do women dare to take an active part in society? And particularly, do they dare to take a part in the present social revolution? I find the questions as much of an insult as I would the question, "Are you, as a black person, willing to fight for your rights?" America has been sufficiently sensitized to the answer, whether or not black people are willing to both die and fight for their rights, to make the question asinine and superfluous. America is not yet sufficiently aware that such a question, applied to women, is equally asinine and superfluous.

I am, as it is obvious, both black and a woman. And that is a good vantage point from which to view at least two elements of what is becoming a social revolution: the American black revolution and the women's liberation movement. But it is also a horrible disadvantage. It is a disadvantage because America as a nation is both racist and anti-feminist. Racism and anti-feminism are two of the prime traditions of this country. For any individual, breaking with social tradition is a giant step—a giant step because there are no social traditions which do not have corresponding social sanctions—the sole purpose of which are to protect the sanctity of those traditions.

That's when we ask the question, "Do women dare?" We're not asking whether women are capable of a break with tradition so much as we're asking whether they are capable of bearing the sanctions that will be placed upon them. Coupled with the hypothesis presented by some social thinkers and philosophers that in any given society, the most active groups are those who are nearest to the particular freedom that they desire, it does not surprise me that those women both active and vocal on the issue of freedom for women are those who are white and middle class. Nor is it too surprising that there are not more from that group involved in the women's liberation movement. There certainly are reasons why more women are not involved.

This country, as I have said, is both racist and anti-feminist. Few, if any, Americans are free of the psychological wounds imposed by racism and anti-feminism. A few months ago, while testifying before the Office of Federal Contract Compliance, I noted that anti-feminism, like every form of discrimination, is destructive both to those who perpetrate it and to their victims—that males with their anti-feminism, hurt both themselves and their women.

In *Soul On Ice*, Eldridge Cleaver pointed out how America's racial and sexual stereotypes were supposed to work. Whether his insight is correct or not, it bears close examination. Cleaver, in the chapter, "The Primeval Mitosis," describes in detail the four major roles. There is the white female, who he considers to be ultra-feminine, because she is required to present and project an image that is in sharp contrast to the white male's image as omnipotent administrator—all brains and no body.

He goes on to identify the black female as subfeminine, or amazon, by virtue of her assignment to the lowly household chores and those corresponding jobs of a tedious nature. He sums up the role of the black male as a supermasculine menial—all body and no brains—because he was expected to supply society with its store of brute power. What the roles and the interplay between them have led to in America Cleaver goes on to point out quite well.

But what he does not say, and what I think must be said is that because of the bizarre aspect of the roles and the influence that non-habitual contact between them has on this general society, black and white, male and female, must operate almost independently of each other in order to escape from the quicksand of psychological slavery.

Each—black male and black female, white male and white female—must escape first from their own intolerable trap before they can be fully effective in helping others to free themselves. Therein lies one of the major reasons that there are not more involved in the women's liberation movement. Women cannot, for the most part, operate independently of men because they often do not have sufficient economic freedom.

In 1966, the median earnings of women who worked full time for the whole year were less than the median income for males who worked full time for the whole year. In fact, white women workers made less than black male workers, and of course, black women workers made the least of all. Whether it is intentional or not, women are paid less than men for the same work, no matter what their chosen field of work. Whether it is intentional or not, employment for women is regulated more in terms of the jobs that are available to them. This is almost as true for white women as it is for black women. Whether it is intentional or not, when it becomes time for a high school girl to think about preparing for her career, her counselors, whether they be male or female, will think first of her so-called natural career—housewife and mother—and begin to program her for a field with which children and marriage will not unduly interfere.

That's exactly the same as the situation of the young black students whom the racist counselor advises to prepare for service-oriented occupations, because he does not think of them entering the professions. And the response of the average young female is precisely the same as the response of the average young black or Puerto Rican—tacit agreement—because the odds seem to be stacked against them.

This is not happening as much as it once did to young minority group people. It is not happening because they have been radicalized, and the country is becoming sensitized to its racist attitudes. Women must learn a lesson from that experience. They must rebel.

They must react to the traditional stereotyped education mapped out for them by society. Their education and training is programmed and planned for them from the moment the doctor says, "Mrs. Jones, it's a beautiful baby girl." And Mrs. Jones begins deleting mentally the things that she might have been, and adds the things that society says that she must be. That young woman—for society begins to see her as a stereotype the moment that her sex is determined—will be wrapped in a pink blanket—pink, because that's the color of her caste—and the unequal segregation of the sexes will have begun. Small wonder, then, that the young girl sitting across the desk from her counselor will not be able to say "No!" to educational, economic and social slavery. Small wonder—because she has been a psychological slave and programmed as such from the moment of her birth.

On May 20th of last year, I introduced legislation concerning the equal employment opportunity for women. And at that time I pointed out that there were three-and-one-half million more women than men in America. But women held only two per cent of the managerial positions; no women sat on the AFL-CIO council of the Supreme Court; only two women had ever held cabinet rank; and there were at that time only two women of ambassadorial rank in the diplomatic corps. I stated then as I do now: this situation is outrageous. In my speech on the floor that day, I said, "It is true that part of the problem has been that women have not been aggressive in demanding their rights. This was also true of the black population for many years. They submitted to oppression, and they even cooperated with it. Women have done exactly the same thing. But now there is an awareness of this situation, particularly among the younger segment of the population. As in the field of equal rights for blacks, Spanish Americans, the Indians, and other groups, laws will not change such deep-seated problems overnight, but they can be used to provide protection for those who are most abused, and begin the process of evolutionary change by compelling the insensitive majority to reexamine its unconscious attitudes."

The law cannot do it for us. *We must do it for ourselves.* Women in this country must become revolutionaries. We must refuse to accept the old, the traditional roles and stereotypes. We must reject the Greek philosopher's thought, "It is thy place, woman, to hold thy peace, and keep within doors." We must reject the thought of St. Paul, who said, "Let the woman learn silence." And we must reject the great German philosopher, Nietzsche, who said, "When a woman inclines to learning, there must be something wrong with her sexual apparatus." We must replace those thoughts and the concept that they symbolize with *positive values* based upon female experience.

A few short years ago, if you called most Negroes "blacks," it was tantamount to calling us niggers. But now black is beautiful, and black is proud. There are relatively few people, white or black, who do not recognize what has happened. Black people have freed themselves from the dead weight of albatross blackness that once hung around their necks. They have done it by picking it up in their arms and holding it out with pride for all the world to see. They have done it by embracing it, not in the dark of the moon, but in the searing light of the white sun. They have said "Yes!" to it, and they have found that the skin that was once seen as symbolizing their chains is in reality their badge of honor.

Now women must come to realize that the superficial symbolism that surrounds us, too, is negative only when we ourselves perceive and accept it as negative. We must replace the old, negative thoughts about our femininity with positive thoughts and positive action affirming it, and more. But we must also remember that we will be breaking with tradition, and so we must prepare ourselves educationally, economically, and psychologically in order that we will be able to accept and bear with the sanctions that society will immediately impose upon us.

I'm a politician. I detest the word because of the connotations that cling like slime to it. But for want of a better term, I must use it. I have been in politics for 20 years, and in that time I have learned a few things about the role of women in power. And the major thing that I have learned is that women are the backbone of America's political organizations. They are the letter writers, the envelope stuffers, the telephone answerers; they're the campaign workers and the organizers. Perhaps it is in America, more than any other country, that the inherent proof of the old bromide, "The power behind the throne is a woman" is most readily apparent.

Let me remind you once again of the relatively few women standard bearers on the American political scene. There are only 10 United States Representatives; one Senator; no cabinet members who are women; no women on the Supreme Court and only a small percentage of lady judges at the federal court level who might be candidates.

It is true that at the state level the picture is somewhat brighter, just as it is true that the North presents a service that is somewhat more appealing to the black American when compared to the South. But even though in 1967 there were 318 women who were in the state legislatures, the percentage is not good when compared with the fact that in almost all 50 states, there are more women of voting age than there are men and that in each state, the number of women of voting age is increasing at a greater rate than the number of men. Nor is it an encouraging figure when compared with the fact that in 1966 there were not 318 women in the state legislatures, as now, but there were 328, which shows that there has been a decline.

Secondly, I have learned that the attitude held by the high school counselors that I mentioned earlier is a general attitude held by many people. A few years ago a politician remarked to me about a potential young female candidate: "Why invest all the time and effort to build up the gal into a household name when she's pretty sure to drop out of the game to have a couple of kids just about the time we're ready to run her for mayor?"

I have pointed out time and time again that the harshest discrimination that I have encountered in the political arena is anti-feminism, both from males and brain-washed, Uncle Tom females. When I first announced that I was running for the United States Congress, both males and females advised me, as they had when I ran for the New York State legislature, to go back to teaching—a woman's vocation—and leave the politics to the men.

And one of the major reasons that I will not leave the American scene—that is, voluntarily—is because the number of women in politics is declining. There are at least 2,000,000 more women than men of voting age, but the fact is that while we get out the vote, we also do not get out *to* vote. In 1964, for example, 72% of registered males voted, while only 67% of the registered females voted. We seem to want to become a political minority by choice. I believe that women have a special contribution to make to help bring order out of chaos in our nation today because they have special qualities of leadership which are greatly needed today. And these qualities are the patience, tolerance, and perseverance which have developed in many women because of suppression. And if we can add to these qualities a reservoir of information about the techniques of community action, we can indeed become effective harbingers for change.

Women must participate more in the legislative process, because even of the contributions that I have just mentioned, the single greatest contribution that women could bring to American politics would be a spirit of moral fervor, which is sorely needed in this nation today. But unfortunately, women's participation in politics is declining, as I have noted.

And politics is not the only place where we're losing past gains. Columnist Clayton Fritchey, in a column, "Women in Office," noted that although more women are working, their salaries keep falling behind men's. Some occupations are still closed by law to women. Property laws still favor men. In 1940, women held 45% of all professional and technical positions as against 37% today. The decline is a general one. But it is because it is a decline that I believe that the true question is not whether or not woman dares. Women have always dared. The question which now faces us is: Will women dare in numbers sufficient to have an effect on their own attitudes toward themselves, and thus change the basic attitudes of males and general society?

Women will have to brave the social sanctions in great numbers in order to free themselves from the sexual, psychological, and emotional stereotyping that plagues us. Like black people, women will have to raise their albatross with pride. It is not feminine egoism to say that the future of mankind may very well be ours to determine.

It is simply a plain fact that the softness, the warmth, and the gentleness that are often used to stereotype us are positive human values—values that are becoming more and more important—like the general values that the whole of mankind seem to shift more and more out of kilter. And the strength that marked Christ, Gandhi, and Martin Luther King was a strength born not of violence, but of gentleness, understanding, and genuine human compassion. We must move outside the walls of our stereotypes, but we must retain the values on which they were built.

No, I'm not saying that we are inherently those things that the stereotypes impute that we are, but I am saying that because of the long-enforced roles that we have had to play, we should know by now that the values are good ones to hold. I am saying that by now we should have developed the capacity to not only hold them, but also to dispense them to those around us. This is the reason that we must free ourselves. This is the reason that we must become revolutionaries in the fashion of Christ, Gandhi, King, and the hundreds of other men and women who held those as the highest of human values. There is another reason. In working toward our own freedom, we can only allow our men to work towards their freedom from the trap of their stereotypes.

Your time is now, my sisters, as we never were before. From the past 20 years, with its decline for women in employment and government, it is clear that evolution is not necessarily always the process of positive forward motion. Susan B. Anthony, Carrie Nation, and Sojourner Truth were not evolutionaries. They were revolutionaries—as many of the young people are today. More and more women must join their ranks.

New goals and new priorities, not only for this country, but for all of mankind must be set. Formal education will not help us do that. We must therefore depend upon informal learning. We can do that by confronting people with their own humanity and their own inhumanity—confronting them wherever we meet them: in the church, in the classroom, on the floor of the Congress and the state legislatures, in the bars, and on the streets. We must reject not only the stereotypes that others hold of us, but also the stereotypes that we hold of ourselves.

In a speech made a few weeks ago to an audience that was predominately white and all female, I suggested the following, if they wanted to create change. You must start in your own homes, your own schools, and your own churches. I don't want you to go home and talk about integrated schools, churches, or marriages if the kind of integration you're talking about is black and white. I want you to go home and work for, fight for, the integration of male and female—human and human.

Franz Fanon pointed out in *Black Skin, White Mask* that the anti-semitic is eventually the anti-Negro. I want to say that both are eventually the anti-feminist. And even further, I want to indicate that all discrimination is eventually the same thing— anti-humanism. That is my charge to those of you in the audience today whether you are male or female. Thank you.

Faith Seidenberg

THE SUBMISSIVE MAJORITY, 1970

Modern Trends in the Law Concerning Women's Rights

20

*Faith Seidenberg is the president of the Syracuse chapter of
the National Organization for Women and received her doctor
of law degree at Syracuse University in 1954.*

SOURCE
*Faith A. Seidenberg, "The Submissive Majority: Modern Trends in the
Law Concerning Women's Rights,"* Cornell Law Review, *Vol. LV,
January 1970, pp. 262–272.*

The popular assumption that the law is even-handed does not hold true in the area of women's rights. Under the guise of paternalism (and you notice the word refers to a father), women have systematically been denied the equal protection of laws. Recently, however, there has been an upsurge of the feminist movement, and men are being forced to take a second look at some of the paternalistic laws they have propounded. Although challenge to the laws adversely affecting women is presently at about the same stage that the civil rights movement occupied in the 1930's, in the last few years there has nevertheless been a small beginning towards equal rights.

I Criminal Law

The idea that a "bad" woman is much worse than a "bad" man probably can be traced to the witch hunts that took place in the early days of the American Colonies; however, it survives to the present day. For example, it is a crime for a woman to engage in prostitution[1] but not for her customer to use her services. She is breaking the law, it seems, while he is only doing what comes naturally. However, in *City of Portland v. Sherill*[2] a city ordinance that punished women but not men who offered themselves for immoral purposes was held unconstitutional.

In addition, in several states higher penalties are imposed on a woman who commits a crime than on a man who commits the same crime.[3] The constitutionality of greater penalties for women was recently challenged in two cases. In *Commonwealth v. Daniels*[4] a woman was first sentenced to a term of from one to four years for the crime of robbery; one month later the sentence was vacated and the defendant resentenced to up to ten years under Pennsylvania's Muncy Act.[5] The Muncy Act provided that a woman imprisoned for a crime "punishable by

[1] See *The Social Evil* (Seligman ed. 1902); George, *Legal, Medical and Psychiatric Considerations in the Control of Prostitution*, 60 *Mich. L. Rev.* 717 (1962).
[2] No. M-47623 (Circuit Ct., Multnomah County, Ore., Jan. 9, 1967).
[3] E.g., Pennsylvania, Connecticut. See statutes upheld in *Ex parte* Gosselin, 141 Me. 412, 44 A.2d 882 (1945); Platt v. Commonwealth, 256 Mass. 539, 152 N.E. 914 (1926).
[4] 210 Pa. Super. 156, 232 A.2d 247 (1967).
[5] *Pa. Stat.* tit. 61, § 566 (1964), *as amended* (Supp. 1969).

imprisonment for more than a year" should be sentenced to an indeterminate period of up to three years except when the crime for which she was sentenced had a maximum of more than three years, in which case she had to receive the maximum sentence. That is, for a crime carrying a sentence of one to ten years, a man might have been sentenced to one to four years, but a woman could only be sentenced to an indefinite term of up to ten years. The discretion of the trial judge to set a maximum term for a woman of less than the maximum for the crime involved was thereby eliminated. The Superior Court of Pennsylvania affirmed the trial court's action, holding that longer incarceration for women is justifiable because of the "the physiological and psychological make-up of women . . . their roles in society [and] their unique vocational skills and pursuits. . . ."[6] Whatever their significance, these characteristics did not convince the Pennsylvania Supreme Court that the Muncy Act's classification was reasonable. The court held that women are entitled to the protection afforded by the equal protection clause of the United States Constitution and, since the maximum sentence is the real sentence, that a sentence of ten years for women as opposed to four years for men is unconstitutional.[7] In *United States ex. rel. Robinson v. York*[8] a federal district court held a Connecticut statute[9] similar to the Muncy Act unconstitutional. The decision was appealed by the state's Attorney General, but he withdrew the appeal after the decision came down in the *Daniels* case. Sixteen women, who had already served more time than a man's maximum sentence, were released.[10]

Criminal abortion statutes[11] are another example of the law's discrimination against women. That a woman has a right to control her own body is perhaps an idea whose time has yet to come, but there is at least a glimmering in some legal minds.

---

[6] 210 Pa. Super. at 164, 232 A.2d at 252. The philosophy of the statute is more cogently, if not convincingly, explained as follows: "There is little doubt in the minds of those who have had much experience in dealing with women delinquents, that the fundamental fact is that they belong to a class of women who lead sexually immoral lives. . . .

"[Such a statute] would remove permanently from the community the feeble-minded delinquents who are now generally recognized as a social menace, and would relieve the state from the ever increasing burden of the support of their illegitimate children."

Commonwealth v. Daniels, 210 Pa. Super. 156, 171 n.2, 232 A.2d 247, 255 n.2 (1967) (dissenting opinion). Oddly enough, the material quoted from the *Daniels* case was supplied by Philadelphia District Attorney Arlen Specter in a brief urging the *un*constitutionality of the Muncy Act.

[7] 430 Pa. 642, 243 A.2d 400 (1968). Shortly thereafter the Pennsylvania legislature enacted a statute that required the court to set a maximum sentence, but prohibited it from setting a minimum term. *Pa. Stat.* tit. 61, § 566 (Supp. 1969).

[8] 281 F. Supp. 8 (D. Conn. 1968).

[9] *Conn. Gen. Stat. Ann.* § 17-360 (1958).

[10] Middletown Press, Aug. 12, 1968, at 1, col. 1 (Middletown, Connecticut).

[11] E.g., *Cal. Penal Code* § 274 (West 1955). Prior to its liberalization in 1967, it was similar to statutes in 41 other jurisdictions. Leavy and Kummer, *Criminal Abortion: A Failure of Law*, 50 A.B.A.J. 52 n.2 (1964).

Most lawyers and legislators, if they are talking about the subject at all, are still talking in terms of abortion reform instead of abortion repeal.[12] They discuss a need for change, but they sound a cautious note.[13] One case moving against the prevailing winds, however, is *People v. Belous*,[14] recently decided in the Supreme Court of California. The defendant was convicted for performing an abortion, and an amicus curiae counsel argued that

[t]he right of reproductive autonomy sought to be protected here is clearly more basic and essential to a woman's dignity, self-respect and personal freedom than those personal rights . . . for which Constitutional protection has already been afforded. Probably, nothing except death itself can affect a woman's life more seriously than enforced bearing of children and enforced responsibility for them for perhaps the remainder of her and their lives. The choice must be that of the woman unless some overwhelming state interest requires otherwise, and those state interests generally adverted to will be shown below to be significantly, for constitutional purposes, less important than the interest of the woman herself. That right should be protected to the fullest by a holding that no state interest can control this field.[15]

In New York two bills, one for reform of abortion[16] and one for repeal,[17] were before the state legislature in the spring of 1969. Only the former had any chance of passing. Had it not been for the National Organization for Women coming out strongly in 1968 for abortion repeal,[18] followed by agreement by the State Council of Churches[19] and the American Civil Liberties Union[20] on this position, the bills would probably not have been considered at all. However, as is beginning to be seen in California, where the abortion laws were just reformed,[21] abortion reform is worse from the standpoint of freedom of choice for the woman than no reform at all.[22]

[12] But see Brief for Appellant as Amicus Curiae at 37–38, People v. Belous, 71 Cal. 2d 996, 458 P.2d 194, 80 Cal. Rptr. 354 (1969), reporting that Father Robert Drinan, Dean of Boston College Law School, has come out for repeal on the grounds that it should be a matter of individual conscience, not law.

[13] See, e.g., L. Kanowitz, *Women and the Law: The Unfinished Revolution* 27 (1969): "Though very few people would urge the legalization of all abortions, the principle of legal equality of the sexes is an additional reason for extending the circumstances under which therapeutic abortions should be legally justified."

[14] 71 Cal. 2d 996, 458 P.2d 194, 80 Cal. Rptr. 354 (1969).

[15] *Belous* Brief, *supra* note 12, at 10-11 (footnotes omitted).

[16] (1969) Assy. Int. No. 3473-A (Mr. Blumenthal).

[17] (1969) Assy. Int. No. 1061 (Mrs. Cook).

[18] See *2 Now Acts 14* (Winter-Spring 1969).

[19] New York State Council of Churches Leg. Release No. 8 (Feb. 10, 1969).

[20] American Civil Liberties Union Release (March 25, 1968).

[21] *Cal. Penal Code* § 274 (West Supp. 1968).

[22] Two actions were just filed in New York to have that state's abortion statutes declared unconstitutional. *New York Times*, Oct. 8, 1969, at 53, col. 1; *id.*, Oct. 1, 1969, at 55, col. 3.

For untold years there have been so-called "protective" laws regulating the working conditions of women. Necessary changes are beginning to be made, but the progress is slow; even legal experts do not always recognize the full dimensions of the problem. One commentator, for example, has remarked of women's working laws:

With regard to social policy, the initial reaction is that the modern woman should not be subjected to state protective restrictions on her right to work should she choose to experience the conditions from which she is being protected. However, it is clear that the extent to which sex differences constitute "discrimination" is a question of degree, depending upon what social mores it seems desirable to perpetuate. . . . [Here], *considerations of preserving femininity and motherhood appear.*[23]

Unfortunately, this misses the point. The net effect of these laws is to limit the advancement of women in industry and, since women are everywhere the majority, to ensure that there is always a large supply of poorly-paid persons.

California has a particularly stringent system of governing women's employment. Section 1350 of the California Labor Code,[24] for example, prohibits an employer from employing women workers for more than eight hours a day or forty-eight hours a week. The effect of this restriction is to prevent women, solely because of their sex, from pursuing certain better-paid occupations, such as running test equipment, doing final assembly work, and working as supervisors, and from earning overtime pay in the positions they now hold. In addition, paragraph 17 of the California Industrial Welfare Commission's Order No. 9-68[25] not only regulates wages, hours, and working conditions

[23] Oldham "Sex Discrimination and State Protective Laws," 44 *Denver L. Rev.* 344, 375 (1967) (emphasis added). But see R. Seidenberg, "Our Outraged Remnant," 6 *Psychiatric Opinion*, Oct. 1969, at 18: "The exaggeration of the difference between the sexes has been used to justify misogyny. Our young people want to make it difficult to distinguish between the sexes to show that everything feminine is not contemptible. One can wear long hair proudly; to be taken for a woman is not something to despair. Make the sexes undifferentiated, and then, perhaps, the mythology of 'feminine' and 'masculine' will be revealed for what it really is—a ruse to keep women subjugated and to guarantee men an unearned superiority."
[24] *Cal. Labor Code* § 1350 (West Supp. 1968): "No female shall be employed in any manufacturing, mechanical, or mercantile establishment or industry, laundry, . . . cleaning and dyeing establishment, hotel, public lodging house . . . in this state, more than eight hours during any one day of 24 hours or more than 48 hours in one week . . . ."
Females covered by the Fair Labor Standards Act, however, are exempt from the prohibitions of § 1350. *Id.* § 1350.5.
[25] *Cal. Admin. Code* tit. 8, § 11460 (1968). The division of public welfare is given specific enforcement power of § 1350. *Cal. Labor Code* § 1356 (West Supp. 1968).

of women and minors in the transportation industry but also limits the number of pounds a woman may lift to twenty-five.

This regulatory system was recently challenged. In *Mengelkoch v. Industrial Welfare Commission*[26] plaintiffs asked that a three-judge court be convened because the constitutionality of section 1350 was an important constitutional issue to be resolved. The request was denied. However, in a similar case, *Rosenfeld v. Southern Pacific Co.*,[27] the judge ruled in favor of plaintiff. This case concerned both section 1350 and paragraph 17. In it, plaintiff, a woman, applied for a job that had just opened up at the defendant company's facilities at Thermal, California. Although she was the most senior employee bidding for the position and was fully qualified, the company assigned a male with less seniority than plaintiff. The company never tested or evaluated plaintiff's ability to perform the work required, but argued that the appointment was within its discretion as an employer and, since plaintiff was a woman, that her assignment to the position would violate the California Labor Code. The court, however, held both that the California hours and weights legislation discriminates against women and is therefore unconstitutional and that defendant's refusal to assign plaintiff to Thermal was not a lawful exercise of its discretion as an employer.

Restrictions on the amount of weight a woman can legally lift[28] are under attack in other states. An employer's thirty-five pound limitation[29] was tested in *Bowe v. Colgate-Palmolive Co.*,[30] where the court held it legal and proper for an employer to fix a thirty-five pound maximum weight for carrying or lifting by female employees. In another case, *Weeks v. Southern Bell Telephone & Telegraph Co.*,[31] defendant company took the position that because the job of switchman required lifting weight in

---

[26] 284 F. Supp. 950 (C.D. Cal.), *vacated*, 393 U.S. 993 (1968).

[27] 293 F. Supp. 1219 (C.D. Cal. 1968).

[28] The typical restriction to 30 or 35 pounds is ironic if the goal is to preserve the femininity of women laborers; mothers commonly lift their children until they are 6 or 7 years old, when they weight at least 70 pounds.

[29] Originally instituted because of substantial female employment during World War II, this practice continued even when the men returned to work. Bowe v. Colgate-Palmolive Co., 272 F. Supp. 332, 340 (S.D. Ind. 1967).

[30] 272 F. Supp. 332 (S.D. Ind. 1967). The provision was also challenged in Sellers v. Colgate-Palmolive Co.,—F.2d—(7th Cir. 1969), which held in favor of the plaintiffs.

The *Bowe* court did hold, however, that use of a seniority list segregated by sex, which resulted in certain female employees being laid off from employment while males with less plant seniority were retained, resulted in discrimination in violation of the 1964 Civil Rights Act. 272 F. Supp. at 359.

[31] 408 F.2d 228 (5th Cir. 1969).

excess of thirty pounds, the legal limit in Georgia,[32] a woman could not hold the job. The company conceded that plaintiff had seniority over the male awarded the position and that she was paid $78 per week as opposed to the $135 she would receive if she were a switchman. The sole issue in the case was whether or not sex is a bona fide occupational qualification, entitling defendant to bar a woman, as such, from consideration for the job of switchman, her capacities notwithstanding. The lower court held for defendant, but the Fifth Circuit reversed, finding illegal discrimination based on sex.

Segregated "help wanted" advertisements are another aspect of discrimination against women. Although the Civil Rights Act of 1964 forbids most such ads to be placed in newspapers[33] and forbids discrimination by sex in employment, the Equal Employment Opportunity Commission guidelines[34] nonetheless allowed two columns classified by sex to stand in the newspapers. In July 1968, therefore, the National Organization for Women brought a mandamus suit against the EEOC to compel it to enforce the law as written. The court summarily dismissed the complaint, saying that obviously some jobs were better suited to men and others to women,[35] but the suit did cause the EEOC to change its guidelines to conform with the law.[36] The American Newspaper Publishers Association brought an action to enjoin enforcement of the guidelines;[37] both the district court and the court of appeals found for the EEOC. However, although the *New York Times* and some other New York newspapers have now desegregated their want ads, most newspapers around the country still refuse to abide by the law.

The public accommodations section[38] of the Civil Rights Act of 1964, unlike the employment section, does not forbid discrimi-

---

[32] Rule 59, promulgated by Georgia Commissioner of Labor, pursuant to Ga. Code Ann. § 54-122(d) (1961): "[f]or women and minors, not over 30 pounds." A more flexible rule, setting no specific limitations, replaced Rule 59 in 1968. See 408 F.2d at 233.

[33] Civil Rights Act of 1964, § 704(b), 78 Stat. 257, 42 U.S.C. § 2000e-3(b) (1964):

It shall be an unlawful employment practice for an employer, labor organization, or employment agency to print or publish or cause to be printed or published any notice or advertisement relating to employment by such an employer or membership in or any classification or referral for employment by such a labor organization, or relating to any classification or referral for employment by such an employment agency, indicating any preference, limitation, specification, or discrimination, based on race, color, religion, sex or national origin, except that such a notice or advertisement may indicate a preference, limitation, specification, or discrimination based on religion, sex, or national origin when religion, sex, or national origin is a bona fide occupational qualification for employment.

[34] 31 Fed. Reg. 6414 (1966).

[35] The court pointed out that secretaries are obviously female, despite the presence in front of the bench of the male stenographer.

[36] 29 C.F.R. § 1604.4 (1969).

[37] American Newspaper Pub. Ass'n v. Alexander, 294 F. Supp. 1100 (D.D.C. 1968).

[38] 42 U.S.C. § 2000a (1964).

nation on account of sex. A test case[39] was recently brought in
New York against a Syracuse hotel that does not allow women
to sit at the bar unescorted, and the action was dismissed. The
court emphasized, first, that there was no state action, since the
women who sat in at the bar were not arrested; and second,
because the public accommodation law does not forbid discrimination on the basis of sex, that the hotel could discriminate if it
so wished.[40]

The case was not appealed because the author, whose case it
was, thought it would be relatively easy to obtain state action
in an arrest. Accordingly, she and another member of the National Organization for Women sat in at several bars, including
one in New York City that has not served women for the last
one hundred and fourteen years. Although they suffered many
indignities, they were not arrested. The author then decided to
bring an action in a New York state court under a new section
of the state civil rights law[41] that makes it illegal to refuse to
serve a customer "without just cause." Summary judgment was
granted to defendants and the case was dismissed. The author
filed a third case, however, that was heard on August 6, 1969,
and that was decided in favor of plaintiff.

III Private Law

Some colleges have strict rules covering the hours when
coeds must be in their dormitories and an inflexible system of

---

[39] DeCrow v. Hotel Syracuse Corp., 288 F. Supp. 530 (N.D.N.Y. 1968).
[40] *Id.* at 532. It is interesting to note that the court did not find the
hotel's admitted discrimination offensive; this is in accord with public
opinion. The *Syracuse Post-Standard* said in a lead editorial:

The campaign waged for several months by the National Organization
for Women (NOW) against Hotel Syracuse for its long-standing policy
of refusing to serve drinks to unescorted women at the bar in the
Rainbow Lounge has reached another absurd point.
    All sororities at Syracuse University have been asked to refuse to
patronize Hotel Syracuse "because they discriminate against women at
their bar," in a letter from Faith A. Seidenberg, one of three directors
of the Central New York Chapter of NOW.
    . . .
    Hotel Syracuse has had the no-unescorted-women-at-the-bar rule
ever since Prohibition was repealed in an effort "to maintain the
dignity of the room" and to discourage undesirables and wouldbe
pickups from frequenting the Rainbow Lounge, which is at street level,
just off the main entrance to the hotel.
    . . .
    Hotel Syracuse should be commended for running a decent place,
instead of being subjected to the repeated persecution of sit-ins and
boycott efforts. Surely any women's rights group could find a better
cause than this!
Syracuse Post-Standard, Nov. 8, 1968, at 12, col. 1.
[41] N.Y. Civ. Rights Law § 40-e (McKinney Supp. 1969).

signing in and out.[42] Regulation is the product of the idea that a university stands *in loco parentis* to its students, an idea that is hopefully changing. After all, a married women of eighteen is considered to be "emancipated" from her parents under the law.[43] Why then is a college student living away from home not equally adult? But in any case, the rationale is not consistently applied; male students are not subjected to the same restrictions as women in the use of the dormitories, or even to the requirement that they live on campus. The Oneonta College curfew was challenged, but the case was dismissed on technical grounds without examination of the merits. Possibly because of the suit, however, the college voluntarily rescinded its curfew regulations,[44] so the students were the ultimate winners.

A double standard is also apparent in the law governing married women. Under present law, a married woman loses her name and becomes lost in the anonymity of her husband's name. Her domicile is his no matter where she lives,[45] which means she cannot vote or run for office in her place of residence if her husband lives elsewhere. If she wants an annulment and is over eighteen, in certain cases she cannot get one,[46] but her husband can until he is twenty-one.[47] In practice, if not in theory, she cannot contract for any large amount, borrow money, or get a credit card in her own name. She is, in fact, a non-person with no name.

Women receive little in exchange for this loss of status. Although in theory the husband and wife are one person, the relationship "has worked out in reality to mean . . . the one is the husband."[48] For example, husband and wife do not have equal rights to consortium,[49] the exclusive right to the services of the spouse and to his or her society, companionship, and conjugal affection.[50] Until recently it was everywhere the law that only the husband could recover for loss of consortium, and this is still the law in about two-thirds of the states.[51] The major breakthrough came in 1950 in *Hitaffer v. Argonne Co.*,[52] which reversed the prevailing rule. In a more recent case, *Karczewski v. Baltimore & O.R.R.*,[53] the court concluded, "[m]arriage is no

[42] E.g., Syracuse University at Syracuse, N.Y. Letter sent to parents of freshmen, January 1969 (freshman curfew); State University of New York at Oneonta, Experimental Women's House Policy, spring semester 1968 (freshman curfew).
[43] E.g., N.Y. Dom. Rel. Law § 140(b) (McKinney 1964).
[44] State University of New York at Oneonta, Experimental Women's Hours Policy (Rev. Sept. 1968).
[45] New York Trust Co. v. Riley, 24 Del. Ch. 354, 16 A.2d 772 (1940). But see N.Y. Dom. Rel. Law § 61 (McKinney 1964).
[46] E.g., Cal. Civ. Code §§ 56, 82 (West Supp. 1968).
[47] E.g., *id.*
[48] United States v. Yazell, 382 U.S. 341, 361 (1966) (dissenting opinion).
[49] Burk v. Anderson, 232 Ind. 77, 81, 109 N.E.2d 407, 480 (1952) (dictum).
[50] Smith v. Nicholas Bldg. Co., 93 Ohio 101, 112 N.E. 204 (1915).
[51] See Moran v. Quality Alum. Casting Co., 34 Wis. 2d 542, 549-50 nn.15 & 16, 150 N.W.2d 137, 140 nn.15 & 16 (1968); Simeone, *The Wife's Action for Loss of Consortium—Progress or No?* 4 St. Louis U.L.J. 424 (1957).
[52] 183 F.2d 811 (D.C. Cir. 1950).
[53] 274 F. Supp. 169 (N.D. Ill. 1967).

longer viewed as a 'master-servant relationship,' "[54] and in *Owen v. Illinois Baking Corp.*[55] the court held that denying a wife the right to sue for loss of consortium while permitting such suit to a husband violates the equal protection clause.[56]

The unreasonableness of denying an action for loss of consortium to the wife is well expressed by Michigan Supreme Court Justice Smith:

The gist of the matter is that in today's society the wife's position is analogous to that of a partner, neither kitchen slattern nor upstairs maid. Her duties and responsibilities in respect of the family unit complement those of the husband, extending only to another sphere. In the good times she lights the hearth with her own inimitable glow. But when tragedy strikes it is a part of her unique glory that, forsaking the shelter, the comfort, and warmth of the home, she puts her arm and shoulder to the plow. We are now at the heart of the issue. In such circumstances, when her husband's love is denied her, his strength sapped, and his protection destroyed, in short, when she has been forced by the defendant to exchange a heart for a husk, we are urged to rule that she has suffered no loss compensable at the law. But let some scoundrel dent a dishpan in the family kitchen and the law, in all its majesty, will convene the court, will march with measured tread to the halls of justice, and will there suffer a jury of her peers to assess the damages. Why are we asked, then, in the case before us, to look the other way? Is this what is meant when it is said that justice is blind?[57]

Conclusion

In theory all persons should be equal, but in practice women are less "equal" than men. In all phases of life women are second-class citizens leading legally sanctioned second-rate lives. The law, it seems, has done little but perpetuate the myth of the helpless female best kept on her pedestal. In truth, however, that pedestal is a cage bound by a constricting social system and hemmed in by layers of archaic and anti-feminist laws.

---

[54] *Id.* at 175. The court summarized the rationale of the prevailing rule:
The early status of women during the sixteenth and seventeenth centuries vitally affected the common law attitude toward relational marital interests. The wife was viewed for many purposes as a chattel of her husband, and he was entitled to her services in the eyes of the law. . . . The wife, however, as a "servant" was not entitled to sue for the loss of services of her husband, since in theory he provided none. *Id.* at 171.

[55] 260 F. Supp. 820 (W.D. Mich. 1966).

[56] "To draw such a distinction between a husband and wife is a classification which is unreasonable and impermissible." *Id.* at 822.

[57] Montgomery v. Stephan, 359 Mich. 33, 48-49, 101 N.W.2d 227, 234 (1960), *quoted with approval*, Millington v. Southeastern Elev. Co., 22 N.Y.2d 498, 503-04, 239 N.E.2d 897, 900, 293 N.Y.S.2d 205, 309 (1968).

Natalie Shainess

ABORTION IS NO MAN'S BUSINESS, 1970

As a psychotherapist whose practice was largely devoted to women, Natalie Shainess became aware of the "emotional problems and psychosomatic disturbances of woman." This prompted her to join civil rights attorneys Nancy Sterns, Diane Schulder, Florence Kennedy, and Carol Lefcourt in challenging the New York State abortion law. She received her degree in 1939 at the Medical College of Virginia in Richmond. She was a resident at New York State Psychiatric Institute and Hospital and the William Alanson White Institute. She has a daughter and a son who are attending medical school.

SOURCE
Natalie Shainess, M.D., "Abortion Is No Man's Business," Psychology Today, *May 1970.*

We all have enough strength to bear the misfortunes of others.
                          —Duc de la Rochefoucauld

Men have borne up well while forcing women to bear down in unwelcome labor and to bow down in lifetime subservience to the unwanted fruits of sex. Woman's condition of servitude has been rationalized in all sorts of ways; it has influenced our social and religious attitudes and has colored the male-dominated thinking of psychiatrists and psychoanalysts.

In all the consideration of abortion there has been almost no consideration of woman. She is regarded as nothing more than an encapsulating amniotic sac, and it is only the population explosion that has renewed interest in legalizing abortion. Demographer Christopher Tietze has noted the relationship between tolerance of abortion and the political wish to manipulate population size.

There was a time when survival of the species required that woman accept unwanted pregnancy. It is a measure of human absurdity that today, although our crowded planet will soon compel us to enforce limited reproduction for all, many still refuse to accept the limited population control that abortion offers.

When legalized abortion is suggested the anti-abortionist immediately cries "infanticide!" Yet his shrill voice is silent in the face of war and capital punishment and the violence and cruelty of the Saturday-morning-TV children's hour and the possession of guns and hunting—an unconscionable atavistic pleasure in today's world. Our society accepts war—a ritualized, institutionalized form of murder—and yet protests the removal of an unsentient cluster of cells.

If we are going to legislate on issues of human reproduction —and of course we should not—then we ought to deal with the important issues for the individual and for society. We should not permit an unwanted child to be born. An unwanted child destroys a woman's mastery of her life and creates great stress and anxiety, damaging to her and to all around her. But the real victim is the child. For we hide from the unpleasant fact that an unwanted child is a hated child and will be treated cruelly—by overprotection, by inattention, by destructiveness or abandonment, by child-battering, by murder. And ultimately society suffers: hated children become hate-filled adults, even more destructive to their own children.

It is true that pregnant women sometimes give up their unwanted children for adoption. This often means an orphanage or foster homes for the child—a dismal start in life. Then there are others who keep their children but find that they cannot help expressing rejection and hatred through their maternal actions. Theodore Lidz, formerly of Yale University Medical School, and anthropologist Jules Henry have documented their experiences while living with the families of schizophrenic children—children distorted by cruel, unloving, rejecting care. (Not all schizophrenic children are rejected children.) Where abortion is denied, unwelcome pregnancy results in unfortunate and disturbed children. The result of seeding an already hostile, overcrowded society with these unfortunates is to increase inadequacy, hostility and destructiveness within the society while distorting feminine lives.

Some primitive cultures practice couvade, the custom of placing the baby with the father and claiming that he has given birth. It is a sign of masculine envy. In the interesting couvade fantasy in Genesis, woman is created a second-class citizen, born out of man's side, a weaker vessel expected to endure greater pain and hardship, and denied mastery over her own life and body. That woman has accepted her secondary position derives in good measure from her physical weakness in relation to the male, her vulnerability to rape and her more or less perpetual state of pregnancy in earlier times. With these she has served the species' survival, as she has with her greater durability.

Impregnation is an accident of nature that shapes the life of the mother and creates what Robert Briffault calls the dyadic family: mother and child. Yet human beings continually alter nature; every scientific attempt to improve human life changes the natural course of events. But with regard to abortion—and to a lesser extent contraception—the attempt to eliminate chance has been deemed impermissible and a series of rationalizations has been constructed to bolster prevailing attitudes.

The procreative act is very different for man and for woman. Man's life continues essentially unchanged after sexual intercourse. If the woman is impregnated, her life is completely altered. And the role of the father is largely neglected. He has been an equal partner in procreation, sometimes has had a major share of the pleasure, and need accept virtually none of the responsibility.

This is obvious in the case of rape, but what about the complex uses of sexual intercourse in married life? Preventive and educational efforts should apply as much to the man as to the woman, although she is the necessary focus of attention.

When an unwelcome and unwanted pregnancy occurs, we refuse to restore a woman to her former state. We even bolster our lack of concern for her by insisting that she will be physically or psychologically damaged if we grant her relief. We further insist that the potential child live, no matter how miserable or unpleasant the life may be.

An unwelcome pregnancy is *never* accepted. Often the obvious is least understood. One of Freud's greatest contributions was his recognition that a negative feeling cannot simply be stored in the unconscious. Like an unseen infection deep within the body, it insists on expression through one symptom or another (the return of the repressed). It may erupt with force. In unwelcome pregnancy the alien germ may be buried deep, but it is never accepted. It always creates some degree of disturbance and negative imprint upon the personality and it manifests itself in an array of symptoms, initially affecting the mother, then spreading to the infant, the husband and the entire family.

Psychiatrists—among them Robert Laidlaw, Arthur Peck and John M. Cotton—have suggested that the physical and mental dangers of therapeutic abortion have been highly exaggerated. There is an imbalance in the equation of traditional psychiatric thinking. Serious reactions to abortion are much fewer than serious reactions to unwanted pregnancy. This was confirmed when Richard Rappaport and Peter Barglow studied 35 women who had undergone therapeutic abortion. Seventy-five per cent of the women reported improved emotional status, which was confirmed by psychiatric evaluation; 23 per cent believed that the abortion led to their emotional growth; and only two women wished they had not chosen to abort. The real danger lies in the condition of the woman who is driven to self-induced or illegal abortion. These quests for abortion often take on the quality of hopeless struggles against unknown and unfathomable odds— the kind of struggles we associate with the works of Franz Kafka.

Never have I seen a case of genuine guilt or regret after abortion. I have seen great relief. I have seen women take desperate suicidal chances to obtain abortion, and I have seen genuine suicide attempts. Where abortion could not be obtained I have seen marital relations worsen and the mothering care to other children in the family deteriorate. A few women have expressed *a priori* feelings of guilt over a planned abortion, but I believe their statements are fearful distortions of more complex dynamics. Issues in such a case are frequently confused, and it is impossible for even the most astute psychiatrist to make rapid psychiatric judgments about their validity.

One patient who was referred to me for psychiatric evaluation was four months pregnant. She had made numerous unsuccessful efforts, first to obtain a legal abortion then an illegal one. When I discovered that she had refused a $600 abortion because her boyfriend would not pay for one costing $1,000, I asked her how she could have rejected what she had sought so desperately.

"I guess I don't really want an abortion," she said. "After all, I'd feel guilty. It's a child, after all, it's killing a child."

When she noted my incredulous reaction, her anger flared. "That's right," she said. "That bastard wouldn't marry me, so I got pregnant to *make* him. He insisted that I get an abortion and I'm going to make him pay. He's paid plenty already. And I'm going to give birth to that child, and I'll haul him into court and get blood tests to establish the paternity, and he's going to pay, one way or another. And when I'm done with the kid, I'll give it up for adoption. There are plenty of people who want kids. When I don't want it, let them take over."

This woman had been hospitalized briefly in mental institutions, and her raging, vindictive behavior was probably a paranoid schizophrenic reaction. Examination of her statements shows that her "feeling guilty" is a clever, linguistic mask, the use of society's attitudes to disguise her goals and to bolster her position. If this woman carries out her threatened intentions her self-esteem will be further damaged and she will ultimately become more seriously disturbed. It would have been fortunate for society if she had received an abortion at her first request, when her reluctance to be pregnant was paramount and her rage and vindictiveness were latent. Her case points up a more urgent issue: should a disturbed and vindictive woman be allowed to conceive a child only as a weapon against a man?

Torn

Alfred Kinsey once observed that biases tend to elicit irrational thinking. He was taken aback by the ease with which events that follow each other are assigned a causal relationship. The psychiatrist recognizes this kind of thought as primitive, infantile or paleologic. Unfortunately we all have islands of irrationality. Professional status renders no one immune, and some statements that have been made about damage to a woman's mental health are categorized by this same kind of primitive thought. Some professionals seem torn by conflicting attitudes. It is hard to understand the position of Dr. André Hellegers of Georgetown University who, on the one hand, espouses the World Health Organization's criteria of health as reflecting the physical, mental and social health of the individual, and on the other hand opposes abortion for any reason other than to save the mother's life.

Perhaps an unvoiced aspect of the problem is our concern over changing and disintegrating sex mores. Instead of meeting the problem with education we refuse to liberalize or repeal abortion laws. In this way we punish the offending woman. We would be better advised to direct our attention to the exploitation of sex by big business, to the sex in the sales pitch that sells everything from cars to shaving cream to "The Sexier Chutney."

British psychiatrist J. G. Howells, one of the first to emphasize the woman's needs in abortion, has called attention to the inconsistency of our attitudes. We stress family planning but when contraception fails, we refuse to back it up with abortion. Psychiatrist Robert White has gone a step further. He believes that some male attitudes may reflect psychosexual problems.

Psychoanalyst Kate Van Leeuwen has observed that deep repression and reaction formation have interfered with an objective appraisal of man's envy of woman. Society's attitude toward abortion infects even the women whose profession is to alleviate suffering. Abraham Heller, a Denver psychiatrist who has conducted research on the consequence of therapeutic abortion, was struck by the unkindness of nurses to women hospitalized for therapeutic abortion.

Fantasy

Frequently a pregnant girl will say that she does not want an abortion. This is understandable when we realize that pregnancy in unmarried girls is often a sign of emotional ill-health. Such a girl follows her bitter course because she is so emotionally damaged, so alienated that she feels she has no human tie and no prospect of one. Her only chance to belong to the world is through producing a creature of her own. Her pregnancy is the result of a parthenogenetic fantasy in which the man is of little interest except to impregnate her and so fulfill her wish. Sometimes a girl may use a pregnancy to retaliate against her parents, threatening their social position which she has come to feel, often correctly, is more important to them than she is. Certainly some out-of-wedlock pregnancies occur in girls who simply have been caught. These girls seek abortion—a healthy effort to avoid being the victim of circumstance.

Distress

Some psychiatrists believe that the desire for abortion reveals a sick person. Like Iago Galdston they postulate that the desire to propagate is a tenacious and fulfilling one, hence hostility and guilt inevitably follow upon abortion. I find it strange that this "biologic disappointment" does not give rise to concern about the unfertilized egg, or to society's concern for the biologic, sexual and social distress of the woman who has not found a mate. Perhaps lack of clarity comes from viewing the woman as though she were in a test tube or were a biological organism in the feral state, ignoring the fact that she lives in her civilized social setting.

Psychoanalyst Therese Benedek has concluded that psychic factors dominate woman's sexual impulse; we must realize that they dominate her reproductive impulse as well. Failure to recognize this suggests masculine lack of empathy, an ignorance of the degree to which pregnancy alters a woman's life and a deeper ignorance of the fact that it is the kind of alteration that determines the acceptability of the child.

Sequence

The typical unwelcome pregnancy goes through four phases:

1. The initial reaction is surprise, disbelief, anger and desperation. Threats of suicide—sometimes carried out—and depression are more prevalent than is generally supposed. I know of several instances in which, when desperate attempts to get an abortion failed, the woman attempted suicide by automobile; one woman drove her car into a rock wall. Had these women died, no one would have suspected that pregnancy had motivated their deaths.

2. Along with suicidal thoughts, depression and the gamut of psychiatric disorders in the second trimester, a major way of expressing rejection is vomiting—a symbolic effort to vomit the fetus out. The normal physiological imbalance that causes morning sickness becomes extended and elaborated and may ultimately turn into the pernicious vomiting of pregnancy. Other psychopatho-physiological responses are hypertensive; they are vascular somatic expressions of rejection. The migraine headache is an example.

3. A calmer psychological state seems to prevail in the last trimester. Aside from endocrinological changes that might account for this, the pregnancy is well established; the social group has been informed. The woman is, as the poet Rainer Maria Rilke said, "weighted down by the fruit of her body" and has little energy for protest. Most statistical surveys show fewer psychotic breakdowns at this time.

4. Shortly after delivery serious trouble may occur—a renewed rejection of the child and feelings of inadequacy as a mother. The biphasic curve of brief euphoria (partly due to relief that the delivery is over) and slump into depression (a complex physical and psychological post-creative slump), *always* present to some degree in the early postpartum period, may herald anything from mild depression to delirial excitement and schizophrenic breakdown with paranoid reactions. One patient expressed the delusion that she was paralyzed by polio—a symbolic statement of the harm done to her by the pregnancy and of her inability to care for the infant.

Hum

Three or four years ago a hum was heard across the land. It was the early mumbling of protest against suffering by a special underprivileged group—women. Perhaps they were encouraged by the stirrings in England for abortion-law reform, and together they evoked in 1967 perhaps the first serious attention to the problem: the First International Conference on Abortion, sponsored by the Joseph P. Kennedy Jr. Foundation and the Harvard Divinity School. A year later another and broader conference was held by the Association for the Study of Abortion. Here information from many sources pointed in one inevitable direction: the repeal of all abortion laws.

Since that time volumes have been published on abortion; numerous test cases have been brought to court and legal victories have been won. Among them was the famous Leon P. Belous case, in which the conviction of a Beverly Hills physician on abortion charges (in this case, referral of a woman to another physician for abortion) was reversed, and the U.S. Supreme Court refused to hear an appeal. This followed the reform of the California abortion law. Among the more recent developments is the Supreme Court decision in Washington, D.C. outlawing a 1901 Washington law and ruling that abortions by doctors are legal. On behalf of 135 women, Drs. Robert Hall, Louis M. Hellman and Alan F. Guttmacher, New York obstetrician-gynecologists, have brought a case challenging the constitutionality of New York State's abortion laws. The American Medical Women's Association has called for legalization of abortion, as have the National Association for Mental Health and the American Public Health Association. The Group for the Advancement of Psychiatry of the American Psychiatric Association has declared that a woman has as much right to decide whether or not to abort as she has to decide whether or not to marry. Hawaii recently became the first state to pass a rational abortion law: abortion is available on demand, provided the woman has been a Hawaii resident for 90 days and the surgery is performed by a licensed physician in a licensed hospital.

Not all the agitation is confined to the courts: concerned by the high cost of illegal abortion, a group of New York doctors have banded together to perform abortions "openly but illegally" for only $75.

Access

In early pregnancy the fetus is not a reality, not a child to the woman. This is the time when women should have ready access to abortion on request, as a matter between a woman and her physician. Hospitals should have separate contraceptive and abortion facilities where, should the woman feel unclear, trained social workers can discuss personal issues without bias, and where immediate action can be taken as necessary. And where, should any problems arise after the abortion, the woman can return to talk things over.

It is not enough to reform our present abortion laws. Simple reform forces the physician, on brief contact and with insufficient information, to judge the woman's ability to stand the duress of an unwelcome pregnancy. Or, if her reason for abortion is not legally admissible, he must become a criminal or an accessory if he wishes to help her. Physicians are needed to help her. Physicians are needed to help the ill, not to judge them.

Repeal of all abortion laws—which were adopted to protect women at a time when abortion meant almost certain death—is the only decent answer to the problem. If repeal creates a demand for additional health services, let us create them.

Joy

Those who continue to oppose repeal of these obsolete laws must ask themselves searching questions: How can a woman raging against pregnancy be a devoted wife and a good mother? What is the effect on a woman when the sometimes expressed pregnancy fantasy of creating a monster (a reflection of damaged self-esteem) is augmented by certainty of fetal malformation? How does the guilt caused by the secret hate of an unwanted child affect a woman? Or of abandoning her child? What is the good of compounding a sexual mistake? What is good preventive psychiatry?

Our society devotes great effort and expense to caring for and helping the physically and mentally handicapped. It is time for measures that free us to aid the healthy and encourage the gifted. Let us educate men to responsibility and women to proper use and mastery of their reproductive function. Let us espouse the philosophy of John Dewey by encouraging development instead of stultifying it with restriction and punishment. Let us believe that, free of compulsion, women will want to have children, will see motherhood as a joy.

In Rilke's words: "The beauty of a virgin, a being that has not yet achieved anything, is motherhood that begins to sense itself and to prepare, anxious and yearning. And the mother's beauty is ministering motherhood, and in the old woman there is a great remembering."

Maxine Williams

WHY WOMEN'S LIBERATION IS IMPORTANT TO BLACK WOMEN, 1970

22

*Maxine Williams is a member of the New York City Young
Socialist Alliance and Third World Women's Alliance.*

SOURCE
*Maxine Williams, "Why Women's Liberation Is Important to Black
Women,"* The Militant, *July 3, 1970, pp. 3–11.*
*Portrait: Harry Ring/*The Militant.

In the early part of the sixties, social scientists became more and more interested in the family structure of blacks. Unemployment and so-called crime among blacks was increasing, and some of these "scientists" decided that the problems of the black community were caused by the family pattern among black people.

Since blacks were deviating from the "norm"—more female heads of households, higher unemployment, more school "dropouts"—these pseudoscientists claimed that the way to solve these problems was to build up a more stable black family in accord with the American patriarchal pattern.

In 1965, the U.S. government published a booklet entitled *The Negro Family—The Case for National Action.* The author (U.S. Dept. of Labor) stated, "In essence, the Negro community has been forced into a matriarchal structure which, because it is so out of line with the rest of the American society, seriously retards the progress of the group as a whole."

According to this theory, the institution of slavery led to a breakdown in the black family and the development of a so-called matriarchy, in which the black woman was "dominant." This "matriarchal" structure was held responsible, in turn, for contributing to the "emasculation" of the black man. In other words, as these people would have it, the oppression of black people was partly caused by the chief victims of this oppression, black women!

This myth of the black matriarchy has had widespread influence and is even widely believed in the black community today. To show just how wrong this theory is, let's look at the real condition and history of the so-called dominant black woman.

Under slavery, once arriving on American soil, the African social order of black people was broken down. Tribes were separated and shipped to different plantations. Slaves underwent a process of desocialization and had to adopt a new culture and language.

Up until 1840, black men greatly outnumbered black women. Sociologist E. F. Frazier indicates, in his book *The Negro Family in the U.S.*, that this probably led to "numerous cases of sex relations between Negro slaves and indentured white women." The "marriage" rate between black men and white women became so high that interracial "marriages" were banned.

Prior to this time, black men were encouraged to "marry" white women in order to enrich the slavemaster's plantation with more human labor. The black man in some instances was able to select a mate of his choice. However, in contrast, the black woman had little choice in the selection of her mate. Living in a patriarchal society, she became a mere breeding instrument.

Just as black men were chained and branded under slavery, so were black women. Lying nude on the slave ship, some women gave birth to children in the scorching hot sun.

There were economic interests involved in the black woman having as many offspring as she could bear. After her child was born, she was allowed to nurse and fondle the infant only at the slavemaster's discretion. There are cases of black women who greatly resisted being separated from their children and having them placed on the auction block, even though they were subject to flogging. And in some cases, the black woman took the lives of her own children rather than submit them to the oppression of slavery.

There are those who say that because the black woman was in charge of caring for the slavemaster's children, she became an important figure in the household. Nothing could be further from the truth. The black woman became the most exploited "member" of the master's household. She scrubbed the floors, washed dishes, cared for the children and was often subjected to the lustful advances of Miss Ann's husband. She became an unpaid domestic. However, she worked outside as well.

Still today many black women continue to work in households as underpaid domestics. And as W. E. B. Du Bois stated in his essay *The Servant in the House*, "The personal degradation of their work is so great that any white man of decency would rather cut his daughter's throat than let her grow up to such a destiny."

In this way arose the "mammy" image of black women—an image so embedded in the system that its impact is still felt today. Until recently, the mass media has aided in reinforcing this image, portraying a black woman as weighing 200 pounds, holding a child to her breast, and/or scrubbing floors with a rag around her head. For such a one, who was constantly portrayed with her head to the floor and her behind facing the ceiling, it is ludicrous to conceive of any dominant role.

Contrary to popular opinion, all black women do not willingly submit to the sexual advances of white men. Probably every black woman has been told the old myth that the only ones who have had sexual freedom in this country are the white man and the black woman. But in many instances, even physical force has been used to compel black women to submit. Frazier gives a case in his book where a black woman who refused the sexual advances of a white man was subdued and held to the ground by black men while the "master" stood there whipping her.

In some instances, black women stood in awe of the white skin of their masters and felt that copulation with a white man would enhance their slave status. There was also the possibility that her mulatto offspring would achieve emancipation. Her admiration of white skin was not very different from the slave mentality of some blacks which caused them to identify with their masters.

In some cases, the black woman who submitted herself sexually played a vital role in saving the life of the black man. If she gave the master a "good lovin'," she could sometimes prevent her husband from being horsewhipped or punished.

The myth that is being perpetuated in the black community states that somehow the black woman has managed to escape much of the oppression of slavery and that all avenues of opportunity were opened to her. Well, this is highly interesting, since in 1870 when the Fifteenth Amendment guaranteed citizens the right to vote, this right did not apply to the black woman.

During Reconstruction those blacks who served as justices of the peace and superintendents of education, and in municipal and state governments, were men. Although the Reconstruction period was far from being an era of "black rule," it is estimated that thousands of black men used their votes to help keep the Republicans in power. The black women remained on the outside.

To be sure, the black man had a difficult time exercising his right to vote. Mobs of whites waited for him at the voting booth. Many were threatened with the loss of jobs and subjected to the terror of Klan elements. The political activity for the black man was relatively ephemeral, but while it lasted, many offices for the first time were occupied by them.

The loose ties established between black men and women during slavery were in many cases dissolved after emancipation. In order to test their freedom, some black men who remained with their wives began flogging them. Previously, this was a practice reserved only for the white master.

In the late 1860s and early 1870s, female heads of households began to crop up. Black men who held jobs as skilled craftsmen, carpenters, etc., were being driven out of these occupations. Since the Republicans no longer needed the black vote after 1876, the "welfare" of blacks was placed in southern hands. Black men found it very difficult to obtain jobs and, in some instances, found employment only as strikebreakers. Black men, who were made to feel "less of a man" in a racist oppressive system, turned toward black women and began to blame them for the position they occupied.

The black woman, in some cases left to herself with children to feed, also went looking for employment. Many went to work in the white man's kitchen. Du Bois in the same essay mentioned earlier, *The Servant in the House*, gives a vivid portrayal of the exploitation of domestic workers. He speaks of the personal degradation of their work, the fact that they are still in some instances made to enter and exit by the side door, that they are referred to by their first name, paid extremely low wages and subjected to the sexual exploitation of the "master."

All of this proves that because the black woman worked, it did not make her more "independent" than the white woman. Rather she became more subject to the brutal exploitation of capitalism—as black, as worker, as woman.

I mentioned earlier that after emancipation, black men had a difficult time obtaining employment, that after emancipation he was barred from many of the crafts he had been trained in under slavery. The labor market for black women also proved to be a disaster. Black women entered the needle trades in New York in the 1900s, as a cheap source of labor for the employers; and in Chicago in 1917, black women, who were willing to work for lower wages, were used to break a strike.

There was great distrust between black and white workers, and in some cities, white workers refused to work beside black women and walked off their jobs.

The black woman has never held high status in this society. Under slavery she was mated like cattle and used as a mere breeding instrument. Today, the majority of black women are still confined to the most menial and lowest-paid occupations— domestic and laundry workers, file clerks, counter workers and other service occupations. These jobs in most cases are not yet unionized.

Today at least 20 percent of black women are employed as private household workers, and their median income is $1,200. These women have the double exploitation of first doing drudgery in someone else's home and then having to take care of their own households as well. Some are forced to leave their own children without adequate supervision in order to earn money by taking care of someone else's children.

Sixty-one percent of black married women were in the labor force in 1966. Almost one-fourth of black families are headed by females, double the percentage for whites. Due to the shortage of black men, most black women are forced to accept a relationship on male terms. In black communities there sometimes exists a type of serial polygamy—a situation where many women share the same man, one at a time.

As if black women did not have enough to contend with— being exploited economically as a worker, being used as a source of cheap labor because she is a female and being treated even worse because she is black—she also finds herself fighting the beauty "standards" of a white Western society.

Years ago it was a common sight to see black women wearing blond wigs and rouge, the object being to get as close to the white beauty standard as one possibly could. But, in spite of the fact that bleaching creams and hair straighteners were used, the trick just didn't work. Her skin was still black instead of fair and her hair kinky instead of straight. She was constantly being compared to the white woman, and she was the antithesis of what was considered beautiful. Usually when she saw a black man with a white woman, the image she had of herself became even more painful.

But now "black is beautiful," and the black woman is playing a more prominent role in the movement. But there is a catch! She is still being told to step back and let the black man come forward and lead. It is ironic that at a time when all talents and abilities should be utilized to aid in the struggle of national liberation, Stokely Carmichael comes along and declares that the position of women in the movement should be "prone."

And some years later, Eldridge Cleaver in referring to the status of women said they had "pussy power." Since then, the Black Panther Party has somewhat altered its view, saying "women are our other half."

When writing their political statement, the Republic of New Africa stated they wanted the right of all black men to have as many wives as they can afford. This was based on their conception that this is the way things were in Africa. (In their publication, *The New Africa*, written in December 1969, one of the points in their Declaration of Independence seeks "to assure equality of rights for the sexes." Whether this means that the black woman would be allowed to have as many husbands as she can afford, I have no way of knowing.)

So today the black woman still finds herself up the creek. She feels that she must take the nod from "her man," because if she "acts up," then she just might lose him to a white woman. She must still subordinate herself, her own feelings and desires, especially when it comes to the right of having control of her own body.

When the birth-control pill first came into use, it was experimentally tested on Puerto Rican women. It is therefore not surprising that Third World people look at this example and declare that both birth control and abortion are forms of genocide—devices to elminate Third World people.

However, what is at issue is the right of women to control their own bodies. Enforced motherhood is a form of male supremacy; it is reactionary and brutal. During slavery, the plantation masters forced motherhood on black women in order to enrich their plantations with more human labor.

It is women who must decide whether they wish to have children or not. Women must have the right to control their own bodies. And this means that we must also speak out against forced sterilization and against compelling welfare mothers to accept contraceptive methods against their will.

There is now a women's liberation movement growing in the United States. By and large, black women have not played a prominent role in this movement. This is due to the fact that many black women have not yet developed a feminist consciousness. Black women see their problem mainly as one of national oppression.

The middle-class mentality of some white women in the movement has also helped to make the issue of women's liberation seem to be irrelevant to black women's needs. For instance, at the November 1969 Congress to Unite Women in New York, some of the participants did not want to take a stand against the school tracking system, that is, the system school authorities use to channel students into certain types of occupations on the basis of their so-called intelligence. These women feared that "good" students thrown in with "bad" ones would cause the "brilliant" students to leave school, thus lowering the standards. One white woman had the gall to mention to me that she felt women living in Scarsdale were more oppressed than Third World women trapped in the ghetto. There was also little attempt to deal with the problems of poor women, for example, the fact that women in Scarsdale exploit black women as domestics.

The movement must take a clearer stand against the horrendous conditions in which poor women are forced to work. Some women in the movement are in favor of eliminating the state protective laws for women, that is, the laws which regulate women's working conditions. But poor women who are forced to work in sweatshops, factories and laundries need those laws on the books. Not only must the state protective laws for women remain on the books, but we must see that they are enforced and made even stronger. I do not mean that those laws which are so "protective" that women are protected right out a job should be kept. But any laws that better the working conditions for women should be strengthened, and extended to men!

Women in the women's liberation movement assert that they are tired of being slaves to their husbands, confined to the household performing menial tasks. While the black woman can sympathize with this view, she does not feel that breaking her ass every day from nine to five is any form of liberation.

She has always had to work. Before the Emancipation Proclamation, she worked in the fields of the plantation, as Malcolm X put it, "from can't see in the morning until can't see at night."

And what is liberation under this system? Never owning what you produce, you are forced to become a mere commodity on the labor market. Workers are never secure, and their length of employment is subject to the ups and downs in the economy.

Women's liberation must relate to these problems. What is hampering it now is not the fact that it is still composed of mainly white, "middle-class" women. Rather it is the failure to engage in enough of the type of actions that would draw in and link up with the masses of women not yet in the movement, including working and Third World women. Issues such as day care, support for the striking telephone workers, support for the laws which improve working conditions for women and the campaign to free Joan Bird are steps in the right direction. (Joan Bird is one of the New York Black Panther members, who was unjustly held in jail for months awaiting trial, because of the excessively high bond demanded by the courts.)

I don't feel, however, that white women sitting around a room, browbeating one another for their "racism," saying, "I'm a racist, I'm a racist," as some women have done, is doing a damn thing for the black woman. What is needed is action.

Women's liberation must not isolate itself from the masses of women or the Third World community. At the same time, white women cannot speak for black women. Black women must speak for themselves.

The Third World Women's Alliance has been formed in New York to begin to do this. We felt there was a need for a revolutionary black women's movement to speak to the oppression of black women as blacks, as workers, as women. We are involved in reading, discussion, consciousness-raising and taking action.

We feel that black women will have a difficult time relating to the more bitter antimale sentiment in the women's liberation movement, fearing that it will be a device to keep black men and women fighting among themselves and diverting their energies from the real enemy. Many black women realize it will take both men and women to wage an effective struggle. However, this does not negate the necessity of women building our own movement, because we must build our struggle now and continue it after the revolution if we are to achieve real emancipation.

When the Third World woman begins to recognize the depth of her oppression, she will move to form alliances with all revolutionary forces available and settle for nothing less than complete destruction of this racist, capitalist, male-dominated system.

Pamela Newman

TAKE A GOOD LOOK AT OUR PROBLEMS, 1970

*A recent graduate of Overbrook High School in Philadelphia
where she was a member of the Black Socialist Alliance, Pamela
Newman, now a member of the Young Socialist Alliance, is
particularly concerned with the relationship between Women's
Liberation and Third World women.*

SOURCE
Pamela Newman, *"Take a Good Look at Our Problems,"* The Militant,
October 30, 1970, pp. 12–15.
Portrait: The Militant.

When women's liberation is mentioned, there are often two reactions. One is that this is just a bunch of frustrated women who are going to separate themselves from men. The other is that this is something that is a white thing, which doesn't concern black women.

The truth is that the exploitation of black women goes deeper than that of white women. Unity of all black women is needed to push for such demands as self-determination, equal pay, free abortion and child-care centers. We should realize the need for the women of the black nation to have a liberation movement of women as part of our movement for total liberation of our people.

The black man has been led to believe that office and skilled jobs are given to the black woman by the white capitalists to make the black man feel inferior. In reality, there aren't enough jobs for everyone, and the black woman suffers the most from law pay and unemployment.

When our men get jobs where they make enough to keep a family, they often insist that the woman's place is in the home with the children. But raising children can be done just as well by the man as the woman. Because a woman is able to have babies doesn't mean she knows more about caring for them and raising them.

The very idea that women are here on earth just for having children isn't true either. We have minds and have the right to determine what we do and say. Child rearing should be a profession, not an automatic duty.

Usually black children are taken care of by older women who can't find work. As a result, the children are separated from other children because these women aren't able to take care of more than one or two children. The mother often has to run home from work to take the child off the older woman's hands. There are no facilities for child care in the black community and few qualified people to take care of teaching the children in a progressive manner.

Ask yourself, have you ever been told, this is a man's conversation, so be quiet or keep out because woman's work is only dishwashing, sewing or laundry. This, my sisters, is male chauvinism, not by the system but by the brothers because of the illusions that capitalism has produced.

How many of you sisters come home from work and have to cook dinner and clean the house, and if the brother comes in before you finish, he immediately gets angry because you are not in the best mood. Somehow we must make him understand that we are human as much as he is. We aren't tools of pleasure to be called to his side and put down if we dare not come.

Just look at the newspaper ads, how they use sex to sell products, and also use race. Before the rise of black power, you never saw a product for black people. But they did have lighteners and brighteners on the market to make women "look beautiful." Not until it was profitable could you buy a bush comb, bush wig or Afro-Sheen. Most of these black products are for women because of their general lack of a strong sense of worth and dignity, which makes women more exploitable than men and better consumers.

And don't you think it is wrong that women who can't afford to keep their children have no say in where their child is sent? Isn't it wrong that after a certain number of "illegal" children, you are sterilized without your permission? Don't you think that we should have community control of abortion hospitals in our communities?

No doubt you or almost anyone can somehow get an abortion, but it is either expensive or risky. It would be nice to see the day when we have free abortion by recognized doctors in the community. But with hospital costs what they are now, and with most of us making only about $75 a week, we can't afford this.

Why not lower the cost of medical care or make it free? Reason: the system of medical care would cut from the profits of all the companies, including the drug companies. The system wouldn't want Bayer Aspirin or Excedrin or any other company that makes drugs and sells them at ridiculously high rates to be unhappy. But still people are dying in the black community without the care they desperately need, and children are being brought up in conditions that some rats would turn down.

It is time that we started struggles against every aspect of our oppression.

Take a look at our problems: medical care, housing, jobs, police repression, child care, abortion . . . To solve these problems we need to gain control of our communities. We have to stop letting our communities be controlled by white, rich politicians and capitalists. We can't go on voting for the two parties controlled by these dictators. Both parties protect not the interest of the people but the white ruling class which controls the economic system. For the total liberation of our people, we need an independent black political party which we can control.

With the demand for self-determination, we are demanding total control of everything that affects our lives. Is it wrong to ask for the right to make the decisions affecting the lives of your children and yourself? If you think so, then you are against women's liberation, black liberation and democracy.

It is very important that black women's groups be formed now, because the capitalists are not going to give money out of their pockets to finance twenty-four-hour child-care centers and meet our other needs. A black women's liberation group would also bring out other demands directly related to women, such as welfare. They could fight for new clothes and for free food which is not surplus but fresh meat and other products which are good for the body.

This money-greedy ruling class can't and won't give us free medical care and other necessities. The only way to get these things is to fight for them. In the process of this fight, many women will begin to realize that our struggle is against capitalism and imperialism. We should be dedicated to building a socialist society inside the United States where profits would be outlawed and the total means of production and distribution placed in the hands of the working class. That struggle must be led by black people, who are concerned about the humanity of this world.

The revolutionary vanguard of America will be the black nation. The total working class must be liberated, including the women, and of course the black woman shall have to be liberated *first* because of the multi-oppression which she suffers.

All over the world, black and Third World people have stopped turning their cheeks. We need to organize to struggle against every aspect of our oppression. Black women's liberation could not and will not be a diversion from the liberation of our people. The organization of black women to fight for our needs as well as the needs of all black people will help intensify the struggle.

Gloria Steinem

WHAT IT WOULD BE LIKE IF WOMEN WIN, 1970

24

Seldom do utopias pass from dream to reality, but it is often an illuminating exercise to predict what could happen if they did. The following very personal and partisan speculations on how the world might be different if Women's Lib had its way were written for Time *by Gloria Steinem, a contributing editor of* New York *magazine, whose journalistic curiosity ranges from show business to Democratic politics. Miss Steinem admits to being not only a critical observer but also a concerned advocate of the feminist revolt.*

SOURCE
Gloria Steinem, "What It Would Be Like If Women Win," Time,
August 31, 1970, pp. 22–23.

Any change is fearful, especially one affecting both politics and sex roles, so let me begin these utopian speculations with a fact. To break the ice.

Women don't want to exchange places with men. Male chauvinists, science-fiction writers and comedians may favor that idea for its shock value, but psychologists say it is a fantasy based on the ruling-class ego and guilt. Men assume that women want to imitate them, which is just what white people assumed about blacks. An assumption so strong that it may convince the second-class group of the need to imitate, but for both women and blacks that stage has passed. Guilt produces the question. What if they could treat us as we have treated them?

That is not our goal. But we do want to change the economic system to one more based on merit. In Women's Lib Utopia, there will be free access to good jobs—and decent pay for the bad ones women have been performing all along, including housework. Increased skilled labor might lead to a four-hour workday, and higher wages would encourage further mechanization of repetitive jobs now kept alive by cheap labor.

With women as half the country's elected representatives, and a woman President once in a while, the country's *machismo* problems would be greatly reduced. The old-fashioned idea that manhood depends on violence and victory is, after all, an important part of our troubles in the streets, and in Viet Nam. I'm not saying that women leaders would eliminate violence. We are not more moral than men; we are only uncorrupted by power so far. When we do acquire power, we might turn out to have an equal impulse toward aggression. Even now, Margaret Mead believes that women fight less often but more fiercely than men, because women are not taught the rules of the war game and fight only when cornered. But for the next 50 years or so, women in politics will be very valuable by tempering the idea of manhood into something less aggressive and better suited to this crowded, post-atomic planet. Consumer protection and children's rights, for instance, might get more legislative attention.

Men will have to give up ruling-class privileges, but in return they will no longer be the only ones to support the family, get drafted, bear the strain of power and responsibility. Freud to the contrary, anatomy is not destiny, at least not for more than nine months at a time. In Israel, women are drafted, and some have gone to war. In England, more men type and run switchboards. In India and Israel, a woman rules. In Sweden, both parents take care of the children. In this country, come Utopia, men and women won't reverse roles; they will be free to choose according to individual talents and preferences.

If role reform sounds sexually unsettling, think how it will change the sexual hypocrisy we have now. No more sex arranged on the barter system, with women pretending interest, and men never sure whether they are loved for themselves or for the security few women can get any other way. (Married or not, for sexual reasons or social ones, most women still find it second nature to Uncle-Tom.) No more men who are encouraged to spend a lifetime living with inferiors; with housekeepers, or dependent creatures who are still children. No more domineering wives, emasculating women, and "Jewish mothers," all of whom are simply human beings with all their normal ambition and drive confined to the home. No more unequal partnerships that eventually doom love and sex.

In order to produce that kind of confidence and individuality, child rearing will train according to talent. Little girls will no longer be surrounded by air-tight, self-fulfilling prophecies of natural passivity, lack of ambition and objectivity, inability to exercise power, and dexterity (so long as special aptitude for jobs requiring patience and dexterity is confined to poorly paid jobs; brain surgery is for males).

Schools and universities will help to break down traditional sex roles, even when parents will not. Half the teachers will be men, a rarity now at preschool and elementary levels; girls will not necessarily serve cookies or boys hoist up the flag. Athletic teams will be picked only by strength and skill. Sexually segregated courses like auto mechanics and home economics will be taken by boys and girls together. New courses in sexual politics will explore female subjugation as the model for political oppression, and women's history will be an academic staple, along with black history, at least until the white-male-oriented textbooks are integrated and rewritten.

As for the American child's classic problem—too much mother, too little father—that would be cured by an equalization of parental responsibility. Free nurseries, school lunches, family cafeterias built into every housing complex, service companies that will do household cleaning chores in a regular, businesslike way, and more responsibility by the entire community for the children: all these will make it possible for both mother and father to work, and to have equal leisure time with the children at home. For parents of very young children, however, a special job category, created by Government and unions, would allow such parents a shorter work day.

The revolution would not take away the option of being a housewife. A woman who prefers to be her husband's housekeeper and/or hostess would receive a percentage of his pay determined by the domestic relations courts. If divorced, she might be eligible for a pension fund, and for a job-training allowance. Or a divorce could be treated the same way that the dissolution of a business partnership is now.

If these proposals seem farfetched, consider Sweden, where most of them are already in effect. Sweden is not yet a working Women's Lib model; most of the role-reform programs began less than a decade ago, and are just beginning to take hold. But that country is so far ahead of us in recognizing the problem that Swedish statements on sex and equality sound like bulletins from the moon.

Our marriage laws, for instance, are so reactionary that Women's Lib groups want couples to take a compulsory written exam on the law, as for a driver's license, before going through with the wedding. A man has alimony and wifely debts to worry about, but a woman may lose so many of her civil rights that in the U.S. now, in important legal ways, she becomes a child again. In some states, she cannot sign credit agreements, use her maiden name, incorporate a business, or establish a legal residence of her own. Being a wife, according to most social and legal definitions, is still a 19th century thing.

Assuming, however, that these blatantly sexist laws are abolished or reformed, that job discrimination is forbidden, that parents share financial responsibility for each other and the children, and that sexual relationships become partnerships of equal adults (some pretty big assumptions), then marriage will probably go right on. Men and women are, after all, physically complementary. When society stops encouraging men to be exploiters and women to be parasites, they may turn out to be more complementary in emotion as well. Women's Lib is not trying to destroy the American family. A look at the statistics on divorce—plus the way in which old people are farmed out with strangers and young people flee the home—shows the destruction that has already been done. Liberated women are just trying to point out the disaster, and build compassionate and practical alternatives from the ruins.

What will exist is a variety of alternative life-styles. Since the population explosion dictates that childbearing be kept to a minimum, parents-and-children will be only one of many "families": couples, age groups, working groups, mixed communes, blood-related clans, class groups, creative groups. Single women will have the right to stay single without ridicule, without the attitudes now betrayed by "spinster" and "bachelor." Lesbians or homosexuals will no longer be denied legally binding marriages, complete with mutual-support agreements and inheritance rights. Paradoxically, the number of homosexuals may get smaller. With fewer overpossessive mothers and fewer fathers who hold up an impossibly cruel or perfectionist idea of manhood, boys will be less likely to be denied or reject their identity as males.

Changes that now seem small may get bigger:

Men's Lib

Men now suffer from more diseases due to stress, heart attacks, ulcers, a higher suicide rate, greater difficulty living alone, less adaptability to change and, in general, a shorter life span than women. There is some scientific evidence that what produces physical problems is not work itself, but the inability to choose which work, and how much. With women bearing half the financial responsibility, and with the idea of "masculine" jobs gone, men might well feel freer and live longer.

Religion

Protestant women are already becoming ordained ministers; radical nuns are carrying out liturgical functions that were once the exclusive property of priests; Jewish women are rewriting prayers—particularly those that Orthodox Jews recite every morning thanking God they are not female. In the future, the church will become an area of equal participation by women. This means, of course, that organized religion will have to give up one of its great historical weapons: sexual repression. In most structured faiths, from Hinduism through Roman Catholicism, the status of women went down as the position of priests ascended. Male clergy implied, if they did not teach, that women were unclean, unworthy and sources of ungodly temptation, in order to remove them as rivals for the emotional forces of men. Full participation of women in ecclesiastical life might involve certain changes in theology, such as, for instance, a radical redefinition of sin.

Literary Problems

Revised sex roles will outdate more children's books than civil rights ever did. Only a few children had the problem of a *Little Black Sambo*, but most have the male-female stereotypes of "Dick and Jane." A boomlet of children's books about mothers who work has already begun, and liberated parents and editors are beginning to pressure for change in the textbook industry. Fiction writing will change more gradually, but romantic novels with wilting heroines and swashbuckling heroes will be reduced to historical value. Or perhaps to the sado-masochist trade. (*Marjorie Morningstar,* a romantic novel that took the '50s by storm, has already begun to seem as unreal as its '20s predecessor, *The Sheik.*) As for the literary plots that turn on forced marriages or horrific abortions, they will seem as dated as Prohibition stories. Free legal abortions and free birth control will force writers to give up pregnancy as the *deus ex machina.*

Manners and Fashion

Dress will be more androgynous, with class symbols becoming more important than sexual ones. Pro- or anti-Establishment styles may already be more vital than who is wearing them. Hardhats are just as likely to rough up antiwar girls as antiwar men in the street, and police understand that women are just as likely to be pushers or bombers. Dances haven't required that one partner lead the other for years, anyway. Chivalry will transfer itself to those who need it, or deserve respect: old people, admired people, anyone with an armload of packages. Women with normal work identities will be less likely to attach their whole sense of self to youth and appearance; thus there will be fewer nervous breakdowns when the first wrinkles appear. Lighting cigarettes and other treasured niceties will become gestures of mutual affection. "I like to be helped on with my coat," says one Women's Lib worker, "but not if it costs me $2,000 a year in salary."

For those with nostalgia for a simpler past, here is a word of comfort. Anthropologist Geoffrey Gorer studied the few peaceful human tribes and discovered one common characteristic: sex roles were not polarized. Differences of dress and occupation were at a minimum. Society, in other words, was not using sexual blackmail as a way of getting women to do cheap labor, or men to be aggressive.

Thus Women's Lib may achieve a more peaceful society on the way toward its other goals. That is why the Swedish government considers reform to bring about greater equality in the sex roles one of its most important concerns. As Prime Minister Olof Palme explained in a widely ignored speech delivered in Washington this spring: "It is *human beings* we shall emancipate. In Sweden today, if a politician should declare that the woman ought to have a different role from man's, he would be regarded as something from the Stone Age." In other words, the most radical goal of the movement is egalitarianism.

If Women's Lib wins, perhaps we all do.

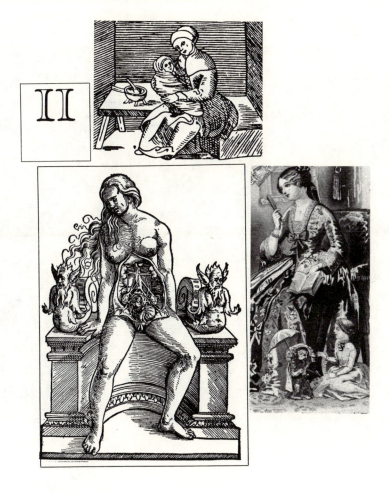

Family life and relationships between men and women are undergoing profound changes in the second half of the twentieth century. The extended family has disappeared as a basic social unit and there is considerable dissatisfaction with the nuclear family that has replaced it. The traditional definitions of woman as "homemaker" and man as "breadwinner" are being challenged: women are demanding a place in the world outside the home, and men are beginning to take a more active responsibility for childcare and housework. These changing patterns of responsibility provide an opportunity for more "authentic" relationships—relationships with emotional integrity rather than alliances based on rigid role definitions.

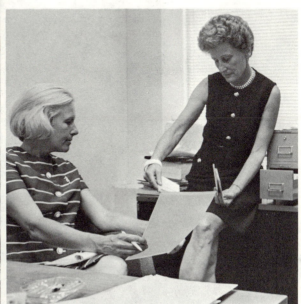

Progress toward social equality is slow, and women protest that they are still domestic servants. Even communes, which purport to be experimental, are often very retrogressive for women. However, women are striving to share their lives with men on a more equal basis and are even entering men's recreational clubs such as McSorley's Old Ale House, which was forced by New York City law to admit women.

Although the issues have shifted from suffrage to equal employment opportunities and practices abortion, and day-care centers, the tactics remain the same. Women are still employing civil disobedience and picketing in protest of the abridgments of their rights.

Frances Wright

FREE ENQUIRY, 1829

Frances Wright was born in Dundee, Scotland, September 6, 1795. Her questioning mind rejected her early religious upbringing and turned to the philosophy of Epicurus; this new influence led to a life's devotion to the rational progress of humankind. A turning point in her life came when she and her sister Camilla sailed to the United States.

Frances began her career in America as a dramatist; shortly after the production of her play Altorf, *she began a tour of the northern and eastern states, followed by the publication of a collection of letters entitled* Views of Society and Manners in America. *In this work she attacked both slavery and the enslavement of women. She writes, "Hitherto the education of women has been slightly attended to. Married without knowing anything of life . . . then quickly immersed in household affairs and the rearing of children, they command but few of the opportunities by which their husbands are daily improving . . . The wonderful advance which this nation has made . . . may yet be doubly accelerated when the education of the women shall be equally a national concern with that of the other sex."*

SOURCE
Frances Wright, "Free Enquiry," Course of Popular Lectures, *Lecture II, New York, 1829, pp. 52–57.*

197

Troubled by her first encounter with slavery while visiting the homes of ex-Presidents Madison and Jefferson, Frances Wright began to formulate a plan for its eradication. After investigating several cooperative communities, she established Nashoba, where slaves could work for their freedom and at the same time repay the southern planters for their loss.

Leaving Nashoba in 1828, Frances then joined Robert Dale Owen in publishing and editing the New Harmony Gazette, *and in 1829, she began her own newspaper,* The Free Enquirer. *Both papers were dedicated to examining the social, political, and religious issues of the time; in addition, they advocated, among other things, abolition of capital punishment and imprisonment for debt and supported social, pecuniary, and political equality for women—in short, equal civil rights for all human beings.*

Frances began, also in 1829, a lecture tour concentrating on contemporary social issues. About feminism, one of the outstanding issues, she said, "Until women assume the place in society which good sense and good feeling alike assign to them, human improvement must advance but feebly."

Frances Wright became closely associated with the working class movement in New York and the promotion of a "system of equal universal republican education." This led to the organization in New York City of the Association for the Protection of Industry and for the Promotion of National Education; these, and similar societies, became known as "Fanny Wright Societies."

In 1831, Frances Wright married William Phiquepal D'Arusmont in France and retired from public life for several years. On her return to the United States in 1835 she renewed her activism. She died on December 13, 1853, in Cincinnati, where she had spent the last few years of her life.

Who, then, shall say, enquiry is good for him and not good for his children? Who shall cast error from himself, and allow it to be grafted on the minds he has called into being? Who shall break the chains of his own ignorance, and fix them, through his descendants, on his race? But, there are some who, as parents, make one step in duty, and halt at the second. We see men who will aid the instruction of their sons, and condemn only their daughters to ignorance. "Our sons," they say, "will have to exercise political rights, may aspire to public offices, may fill some learned profession, may struggle for wealth and acquire it. It is well that we give them a helping hand; that we assist them to such knowledge as is going, and make them as sharp witted as their neighbors. But for our daughters," they say—if indeed respecting them they say any thing—"for our daughters, little trouble or expense is necessary. They can never *be any thing;* in fact, *they are nothing.* We had best give them up to their mothers, who may take them to Sunday's preaching; and, with the aid of a little music, a little dancing, and a few fine gowns, fit them out for the market of marriage."

Am I severe? It is not my intention. I know that I am honest, and I fear that I am correct. Should I offend, however I may regret, I shall not repent it; satisfied to incur displeasure, so that I render service.

But to such parents I would observe, that with regard to their sons, as to their daughters, they are about equally mistaken. If it be their duty, as we have seen, to respect in their children the same natural liberties which they cherish for themselves—if it be their duty to aid as guides, not to dictate as teachers—to lend assistance to the reason, not to command its prostration,—then have they nothing to do with the blanks or the prizes in store for them, in the wheel of worldly fortune. Let possibilities be what they may in favor of their sons, they have no calculations to make on them. It is not for them to ordain their sons magistrates nor statesmen; nor yet even lawyers, physicians, or merchants. They have only to improve the one character which they receive at the birth. They have only to consider them as *human beings,* and to ensure them the fair and thorough development of all the faculties, physical, mental, and moral, which distinguish their nature. In like manner, as respects their daughters, they have nothing to do with the injustice of laws, nor the absurdities of society. Their duty is plain, evident, decided. In a daughter they have in charge a human being; in a son, the same. Let them train up these *human*

199

beings, under the expanded wings of liberty. Let them seek *for* them and *with* them just knowledge; encouraging, from the cradle upwards, that useful curiosity will lead them unbidden in the paths of free enquiry; and place them, safe and superior to the storms of life, in the security of well regulated, self-possessed minds, well grounded, well reasoned, conscientious opinions, and self-approved, consistent practice.

I have as yet, in this important matter, addressed myself only to the reason and moral feelings of my audience; I could speak also to their interests. Easy were it to show, that in proportion as your children are enlightened, will they prove blessings to society and ornaments to their race. But if this be true of all, it is more especially true of the now more neglected half of the species. Were it only in our power to enlighten part of the rising generation, and should the interests of the whole decide our choice of the portion, it were the females, and not the males, we should select.

When, now a twelvemonth since, the friends of liberty and science pointed out to me, in London, the walls of their rising university, I observed, with a smile, that they were beginning at the wrong end: "Raise such an edifice for your young women, and ye have enlightened the nation." It has already been observed, that women, wherever placed, however high or low in the scale of cultivation, hold the destinies of humankind. Men will ever rise or fall to the level of the other sex; and from some causes in their conformation, we find them, however armed with power or enlightened with knowledge, still held in leading strings even by the least cultivated female. Surely, then, if they knew their interests, they would desire the improvement of those who, if they do not advantage, will injure them; who, if they elevate not their minds and meliorate not their hearts, will debase the one and harden the other; and who, if they endear not existence, most assuredly will dash it with poison. How many, how omnipotent are the interests which engage men to break the mental chains of women! How many, how dear are the interests which engage them to exalt rather than lower their condition, to multiply their solid acquirements, to respect their liberties, to make them their equals, to wish them even their superiors! Let them enquire into these things. Let them examine the relation in which the two sexes stand, and ever must stand, to each other. Let them perceive, that, mutually dependent, they must ever be giving and receiving, or they must be losing;—receiving or losing in knowledge, in virtue, in enjoyment. Let them perceive how immense the loss, or how immense the gain. Let them not imagine that they know aught of the delights which intercourse with the other sex can give, until they have felt the sympathy of mind with mind, and heart with heart; until they bring into that intercourse every affection, every talent, every confidence, every refinement, every respect. Until power is annihilated on one side, fear and obedience on the other, and both restored to their birthright—equality. Let none think that affection can reign without it; or friendship, or esteem. Jealousies, envyings, suspicions, reserves, deceptions—these are the fruits of inequality. Go, then! and remove the evil first from the minds of women, then from their condition, and then from your laws. Think it no longer indifferent whether the mothers of the rising generation are wise or foolish. Think it not indifferent whether your own companions are ignorant or enlightened. Think it not indifferent whether those who are to form the opinions, sway the habits, decide the destinies, of the species—and that not through their children only, but through their lovers and husbands—are enlightened friends or capricious mistresses, efficient coadjutors or careless servants, reasoning beings or blind followers of superstition.

There is a vulgar persuasion, that the ignorance of women, by favoring their subordination, ensures their utility. 'Tis the same argument employed by the ruling few against the subject many in aristocracies; by the rich against the poor in democracies; by the learned professions against the people in all countries. And let us observe, that if good in one case, it should be good in all; and that, unless you are prepared to admit that you are yourselves less industrious in proportion to your intelligence, you must abandon the position with respect to others. But, in fact, who is it among men that best struggle with difficulties? —the strong minded or the weak? Who meet with serenity adverse fortune?—the wise or the foolish? Who accommodate themselves to irremediable circumstances? or, when remediable, who control and mould them at will?—the intelligent or the ignorant? Let your answer in your own case, be your answer in that of women.

If the important enquiry which engaged our attention last evening was satisfactorily answered, is there one who can doubt the beneficial effects of knowledge upon every mind, upon every heart? Surely it must have been a misconception of the nature of knowledge which could alone bring it into suspicion. What is the danger of truth? Where is the danger of fact? Error and ignorance, indeed, are full of danger. They fill our imagination with terrors. They place us at the mercy of every external circumstance. They incapacitate us for our duties as members of the human family, for happiness as sentient beings, for improvement as reasoning beings. Let us awake from this illusion. Let us understand what knowledge is. Let us clearly perceive that accurate knowledge regards all equally; that truth, or fact, is the same thing for all human-kind; that there are not truths for the rich and truths for the poor, truths for men and truths for women; there are simply *truths*, that is, *facts*, which all who open their eyes and their ears and their understandings can perceive. There is no mystery in these facts. There is no witchcraft in knowledge. Science is not a trick; not a puzzle. The philosopher is not a conjuror. The observer of nature who envelops his discoveries in mystery, either knows less than he pretends, or feels interested in *withholding* his knowledge. The teacher whose lessons are difficult of comprehension, is either clumsy or he is dishonest.

Books by Frances Wright (D' Arusmont)

Altorf, a tragedy. Philadelphia: 1819.

Views of Society and Manners in America. London: 1821.

A Few Days in Athens. London: 1822.

Course of Popular Lectures. New York: 1829.

Course of Popular Lectures. Vol. 2. Philadelphia: 1838.

Fables. New York: 1830.

What Is the Matter? New York: 1838.

Tracts on Republican Government and National Education Addressed to the Inhabitants of the United States of America. London: 1840.

Biography, Notes, and Political Letters of Frances Wright D'Arusmont. New York: 1844.

England the Civilizer: Her History Developed in Its Principles. London: 1848.

Newspapers with which Miss Wright was associated

New Harmony Gazette, New Harmony, Indiana.

New Harmony and Nashoba Gazette or Free Enquirer. New Harmony, Indiana.

Free Enquirer. New York.

Margaret Fuller

WOMAN IN THE NINETEENTH CENTURY AND KINDRED PAPERS, 1855

Sarah Margaret Fuller was born May 23, 1810, in Cambridge, Massachusetts. Her early childhood was spent in educational pursuits that were extraordinary for her age: Her father, Timothy Fuller, a prominent lawyer and Harvard graduate, tutored her in English literature and in eight languages, including Latin and Greek, which she could read before she was in her teens.

After leaving school, Margaret taught at Bronson Alcott's progressive school for several years and became acquainted, through Alcott, with the New England Transcendentalists. She was accepted as an equal into the literary circle of Alcott, Emerson, Hawthorne, William Henry Channing, George Ripley, and others; she became an integral part of their philosophical trend and was active in their affairs.

Margaret supported herself from 1839 to 1844 as a conductress of an extremely popular women's discussion series that dealt with social and literary topics. Her Woman in the Nineteenth Century *(1845), an outgrowth of the discussions, presented an impassioned but clearheaded argument for woman's development as an individual and also exhorted the woman suffrage movement. Earlier, from 1840 to 1842, at the request of her Transcendentalist friends, Margaret coedited the Transcendentalist magazine* The Dial *with Emerson and Ripley. She was also interested in the founding of Brook Farm, and*

SOURCE
Margaret Fuller, Woman in the Nineteenth Century and Kindred Papers. *Cleveland, John Jewett, 1855.*

although she disagreed with certain aspects of its conception, she enrolled one of her younger brothers there. In 1844 Margaret went to New York to live with the Horace Greeleys, and, writing literary criticism for the Tribune, *she established a fine reputation. Her investigation of prisons and asylums supplied the newspaper with many articles.*

Margaret broadened her literary acquaintances through a trip to Europe in 1846, visiting Thomas Carlyle, William Wordsworth, and George Sand. Settling in Rome in 1847, she involved herself in Giuseppe Mazzini's fold, and soon married one of Mazzini's followers, the Marquis Giovanni Angelo Ossoli, bearing a son in 1848. The final two years of her life were tumultuous: the seige by the French on Rome and Ossoli's activity in the Italian liberation movement caused Margaret and her family to move to Florence, where Margaret wrote a history of the Roman revolution. A further move to New York was begun on May 17, 1850, but the family was shipwrecked off Fire Island, and Margaret, Ossoli, and their son were drowned in July 1850. Margaret's Florence manuscript was lost with them.

Margaret Fuller believed that, because men controlled society, they were therefore responsible for the world's ills, such as war and injustice; women, if they were to share equally in the management of world affairs, would greatly improve conditions. Margaret's idea of an ideal marriage included respect for one's partner as well as intellectual and spiritual communion; she resented the woman's "belonging" to the man, because it created a malignant relationship. Margaret held the progressive view that the dualities designated as masculine or feminine were not confined to men and women, respectively, but that these characteristics were present in both men and women; however, her idea of homosexuality centered on spiritual love, rather than sensual, which she viewed as the domain of heterosexuality.

Her works include a translation of Johann Peter Eckermann's Conversations with Goethe *(1839),* Summer on the Lakes *(1844), in which she optimistically viewed the expansion of the American West, and* Papers on Literature and Art *(1846);* At Home and Abroad *(1856) and* Life Without and Life Within *(1859), which was edited by Margaret's brother Arthur, were published posthumously. Mason Wade edited a one-volume selection of Margaret Fuller's writings, published in New York in 1940.*

Male and Female represent the two sides of the great radical dualism. But, in fact, they are perpetually passing into one another. Fluid hardens to solid, solid rushes to fluid. There is no wholly masculine man, no purely feminine woman.

History jeers at the attempts of physiologists to bind great original laws by the forms which flow from them. They make a rule; they say from observation what can and cannot be. In vain! Nature provides exceptions to every rule. She sends a woman to battle, and sets Hercules spinning; she enables woman to bear immense burdens, cold and frost; she enables the man, who feels maternal love, to nourish his infant like a mother. Of late she plays still gayer pranks. Not only she deprives organizations, but organs, of a necessary end. She enables people to read with the top of the head, and see with the pit of the stomach. Presently she will make a female Newton, and a male Syren. . . .

Women I hold to be especially capable. Even without equal freedom with the other sex, they have already shown themselves so, and should these faculties have free play, I believe they will open new, deeper and purer sources of joyous inspiration than have as yet refreshed the earth.

Let us be wise, and not impede the soul. Let her work as she will. Let us have one creative energy, one incessant revelation. Let it take what form it will, and let us not bind it by the past to man or woman, black or white. Jove sprang from Rhea, Pallas from Jove. So let it be.

Every relation, every gradation of nature is incalculably precious, but only to the soul which is poised upon itself, and to whom no loss, no change can bring dull discord, for it is in harmony with the central soul.

If any individual live too much in relations, so that he becomes a stranger to the resources of his own nature, he falls, after a while, into a distraction, or imbecility, from which he can only be cured by a time of isolation, which gives the renovating fountains time to rise up. With a society it is the same. Many minds, deprived of the traditionary or instinctive means of passing a cheerful existence, must find help in self impulse, or perish. It is therefore that, while any elevation in the view of union, is to be hailed with joy, we shall not decline celibacy as the great fact of the time. It is one form which no vow, no arrangement, can at present save a thinking mind. For now the rowers are passing on their oars. They wait a change before they can pull together. All tend to illustrate the thought of a wise contemporary. Union is only possible to those who are units. To be fit for relations in time, souls, whether of Man or Woman, must be able to do without them in spirit.

It is therefore that I would have Woman lay aside all thought such as she habitually cherishes, of being taught and led by men. I would have her, like the Indian girl, dedicate herself to the Sun, the Sun of Truth, and go nowhere if his beams did not make clear the path. I would have her free from compromise, from complaisance, from helplessness, because I would have her good enough and strong enough to love one and all beings, from the fullness, not the poverty of being.

Men, as at present instructed, will not help this work, because they also are under the slavery of habit. I have seen with delight their poetic impulses. A sister is the fairest ideal, and how nobly Wordsworth, and even Byron have written of a sister!

There is no sweeter sight than to see a father with his little daughter. Very vulgar men become refined to the eyes when leading a little girl by the hand. At that moment, the right relation between sexes seems established, and you feel as if the man would aid the noblest purpose, if you ask him in behalf of his little daughter. Once, two fine figures stood before me, thus. The father of very intellectual aspect, his falcon eye softened by affection as he looked down on his fair child; she the image of himself, only more graceful and brilliant in expression. I was reminded of Southey's Kehama; when, lo, the dream was rudely broken! They were talking of education, and he said.

"I shall not have Maria brought too forward. If she knows too much, she will never find a husband; superior women hardly ever can."

"Surely," said his wife, with a blush, "you wish Maria to be as wise and as good as she can, whether it will help her to marriage or not."

"No," he persisted, "I want her to have a sphere and a home, and someone to protect her when I am gone."

It was a trifling incident, but made a deep impression. I felt the holiest relations fail to instruct the unprepared and perverted mind. If this man, indeed, could have looked at it on the other side, he was the last that would have been willing to have been taken himself for the home and protection he could give, but would have been much more likely to repeat the tale of Alcibiades with his phials.

But men do not look at both sides, and women must leave off asking them and being influenced by them, but retire within themselves, and explore the ground-work of life till they find their peculiar secret. Then, when they come forth again, renovated and baptized, they will know how to turn all dross to gold, and will be rich and free though they live in a hut, tranquil in a crowd. Then their sweet singing shall not be from passionate impulse, but the lyrical overflow of a divine rapture and a new music shall be evolved from the many-chorded wild.

Grant her, then, for a while the armor and the javelin. Let her put from her the press of other minds, and meditate in virgin loneliness. The same idea shall reappear in due time as Muse or Ceres, the all kindly patient Earth Spirit.

Books by Margaret Fuller

At Home and Abroad. Arthur B. Fuller, ed. Boston: Crosby, Nicholas & Co., 1856.

The Dial: a Magazine for Literature, Philosophy and Religion, S. M. Ossoli, ed. 4 vols. New York: Russell & Russell, 1961.

Memoirs of Margaret Fuller Ossoli. Boston: Phillips, Sampson & Co., 1852.

Woman in the Nineteenth Century. Boston: J. J. Jewett & Co., New York: Sheldon, Lampart & Co., 1855.

Books about Margaret Fuller

ANTHONY, KATHARINE SUSAN. *Margaret Fuller, A Psychological Biography.* New York: Harcourt Brace Jovanovich, 1920.

BEACH, SETH CURTIS. *Daughters of the Puritans; a group of brief biographies.* Freeport, N.Y.: Books for Libraries Press, 1967.

BELL, MARGARET. *Margaret Fuller, a Biography.* New York: C. Boni, 1930.

BROWN, ARTHUR W. *Margaret Fuller.* New York: Twayne, 1964.

HIGGINSON, THOMAS WENTWORTH. *Margaret Fuller Ossoli.* Boston and New York: Houghton Mifflin, 1884.

STERN, MADELEINE BETTINE. *The Life of Margaret Fuller.* New York: Dutton, 1942.

WADE, MASON. *The Writings of Margaret Fuller.* New York: Viking, 1941.

Elizabeth Blackwell

LETTER, 1881

*The first woman to break the monopoly of men in the practice
of medicine was Elizabeth Blackwell. Born near Bristol,
England, she emigrated to New York City with her parents
when she was ten. She taught school in Cincinnati between
1842 and 1847. When she decided to enter medical school she
endured eight rejections before she was accepted at Geneva
Medical College (now a part of Syracuse University) in 1847. After
graduation, she went to Paris, where she was permitted to
practice only as a student-midwife. The famous La Maternité
Hospital refused to honor her physician's diploma.*

*She contracted ophthalmia and lost the sight of one eye. Her
hopes of becoming a surgeon were diminished; yet she went on to
London for further study. There her friendship with Florence
Nightingale began. After returning to New York, she was
ostracized by the medical profession and abused in anonymous
letters. In 1853 she opened a small dispensary in the slums where
contact with living conditions of the poor refired her zeal for
sanitary reform.*

*Her sister Emily and a third woman, Marie Zakrzewska,
joined her in opening the New York Infirmary for Indigent
Women and Children. In 1868 they opened the Women's Medical
College of New York Infirmary, the first of its kind in America.
The infirmary even today is staffed entirely with women doctors.*

*Dr. Blackwell returned to London in 1869, where she taught
at the London School of Medicine for Women. She was the first
woman to be entered in the British Medical Registry and fought
for medical recognition of women doctors in England, as well
as for hygiene and social reform. She died in Sussex, England,
on May 31, 1910.*

SOURCE
Elizabeth Blackwell, "Letter," History of Woman Suffrage, I, *1881, p. 90.*

Philadelphia, August 12, 1848

Dear Madam:

Your letter, I can assure you, met with a hearty welcome from me. And I can not refrain from writing to you a warm acknowledgment of your cordial sympathy, and expressing the pleasure with which I have read your brave words. It is true, I look neither for praise nor blame in pursuing the path which I have chosen. With firm religious enthusiasm, no opinion of the world will move me, but when I receive from a woman an approval so true-hearted and glowing, a recognition so clear of the motives which urge me on, then my very soul bounds at the thrilling words, and I go on with renewed energy, with hope, and holy joy in my inmost being.

My whole life is devoted unreservedly to the service of my sex. The study and practice of medicine is in my thought but one means to a great end, for which my very soul yearns with intensest passionate emotion, of which I have dreamed day and night, from my earliest childhood, for which I would offer up my life with triumphant thanksgiving, if martyrdom could secure that glorious end:—the true ennoblement of woman, the full harmonious development of her unknown nature, and the consequent redemption of the whole human race. "Earth waits for her queen." Every noble movement of the age, every prophecy of future glory, every throb of that great heart which is laboring throughout Christendom, call on woman with a voice of thunder, with the authority of a God, to listen to the mighty summons to awake from her guilty sleep, and rouse to glorious action to play her part in the great drama of the ages, and finish the work that man has begun.

Most fully do I respond to all the noble aspirations that fill your letter. Women are feeble, narrow, frivolous at present: ignorant of their own capacities, and undeveloped in thought and feeling; and while they remain so, the great work of human regeneration must remain incomplete; humanity will continue to suffer, and cry in vain for deliverance, for woman has her work to do, and no one can accomplish it for her. She is bound to rise, to try her strength, to break her bonds;—not with noisy outcry, not with fighting or complaint; but with quiet strength, with gentle dignity, firmly, irresistibly, with a cool determination that never wavers, with a clear insight into her own capacities, let her do her duty, pursue her highest conviction of right, and firmly grasp whatever she is able to carry.

Much is said of the oppression woman suffers; man is

209

reproached with being unjust, tyrannical, jealous. I do not so read human life. The exclusion and constraint woman suffers, is not the result of purposed injury or premeditated insult. It has arisen naturally, without violence, simply because woman has desired nothing more, has not felt the soul too large for the body. But when woman, with matured strength, with steady purpose, presents her lofty claim, all barriers will give way, and man will welcome, with a thrill of joy, the new birth of his sister spirit, the advent of his partner, his co-worker, in the great universe of being.

If the present arrangements of society will not admit of woman's free development, then society must be remodeled, and adapted to the great wants of all humanity. Our race is one, the interests of all are inseparably united, and harmonic freedom for the perfect growth of every human soul is the great want of our time. It has given me heartfelt satisfaction, dear madam, that you sympathize in my effort to advance the great interests of humanity. I feel the responsibility of my position, and I shall endeavor, by wisdom of action, purity of motive, and unwavering steadiness of purpose, to justify the noble hope I have excited. To me the future is full of glorious promise, humanity is arousing to accomplish its grand destiny, and in the fellowship of this great hope, I would greet you, and recognize in your noble spirit a fellow-laborer for the true and the good.

Elizabeth Blackwell

Books by Elizabeth Blackwell

Pioneer Work in Opening the Medical Profession to Women. London: Longmans, 1895.

The Laws of Life—In Reference to the Physical Education of Girls. New York: Putnam, 1852.

Books about Elizabeth Blackwell

BAKER, RACHEL. *The First Woman Doctor—The Story of Elizabeth Blackwell, M.D.* New York: Messner, 1944.

ROSS, ISHBEL. *Child of Destiny—The Life Story of the First Woman Doctor.* New York: Harper & Row, 1949.

WILSON, DOROTHY CLARKE. *Lone Woman.* Boston: Little, Brown, 1970.

Jane Addams

FILIAL RELATIONS, 1902

Born in September 1860 of well-to-do Quaker parents in
Cedarville, Illinois, young Jane Addams witnessed the great
debates of the times in which her father's friend Abraham
Lincoln was a key figure.

Her mother's death when she was two left her father in
total charge of her development. At an age when young girls
were expected to prepare themselves for their future roles as
housewives and mothers, Jane Addams emulated her father
in her desire for public life, yet was horrified by the poverty of
the workers who labored in her father's mills.

Her desire to attend the recently opened Smith College for
Women was frustrated by her father, who decided to send her
to the local Rockford (Illinois) Seminary. After graduation in
1881 she traveled in Europe, avoiding the historic sites and
cathedrals, which were considered the post-graduate courses for
young scholars of the wealthy classes. Instead she visited the
centers of poverty and the headquarters of the social reform
movement in Great Britain, Toynbee Hall, the first university
settlement.

After several years she returned to the United States and
enrolled at the Woman's Medical College in Philadelphia, later
leaving because of ill health.

In 1889 Jane Addams and her friend Ellen Gates Starr went
to Chicago and bought a large red-brick mansion, once the home

SOURCE
"Filial Relations," Democracy and Social Ethics, 1902, pp. 82–90.

of Charles J. Hull, in the heart of Chicago's West Side immigrant neighborhoods. Hull House grew rapidly and became the most famous neighborhood settlement house in America, initiating many social services for the sick and indigent, victims of widespread deprivation.

Her experience with the problems of the poor and the ethnically diverse groups who came to Hull House gave her the reputation of an authority on many social matters. She wrote and lectured on child labor, public health, woman suffrage, unemployment, and old-age insurance. She was a city inspector of streets and alleys for three years. In 1909 she became president of the National Conference of Charities and Correction, now known as the National Conference of Social Welfare.

In her 75 years she dedicated herself to many interests. She worked for world peace and helped to found the Women's International Peace Congress, of which she was president from 1915 to 1929. Thereafter she was made honorary international president. Her concern with the role of women and their exploitation in the labor market forced her to speak out frequently.

At times her efforts were directed toward securing the rights of women to stay home and care for their children, which working women were forced to sacrifice under the economic imperative of dire poverty. The playgrounds of Hull House cared for many children left to the streets and alleys while their parents worked in the mills and processing plants of Chicago. Among the reforms with which she was closely associated was the first eight-hour law for working women.

Jane Addams thought a great deal about the role of women. From her early days at Rockford Seminary, she aimed at independence for herself and a new perspective in the relationship between the sexes. She wanted to preserve what she believed was still good in the traditional roles and at the same time help to formulate a new view that would accept a wider range of possible life styles for women. Her own life was an example, and Hull House offered great encouragement and help in socializing women's roles and organizing women to view their problems in a social rather than an individual way.

In 1931 she shared the Nobel Peace Prize with Nicholas Murray Butler. She continued to be in the vanguard of social reform movements until her death.

It is always difficult for the family to regard the daughter otherwise than as a family possession. From her babyhood she has been the charm and grace of the household, and it is hard to think of her as an integral part of the social order, hard to believe that she has duties outside of the family, to the state and to society in the larger sense. This assumption that the daughter is solely an inspiration and refinement to the family itself and its own immediate circle, that her delicacy and polish are but outward symbols of her father's protection and prosperity, worked very smoothly for the most part so long as her education was in line with it. When there was absolutely no recognition of the entity of woman's life beyond the family, when the outside claims upon her were still wholly unrecognized, the situation was simple, and the finishing school harmoniously and elegantly answered all requirements. She was fitted to grace the fireside and to add lustre to that social circle which her parents selected for her. But this family assumption has been notably broken into, and educational ideas no longer fit it. Modern education recognizes woman quite apart from family or society claims, and gives her the training which for many years has been deemed successful for highly developing a man's individuality and freeing his powers for independent action. Perplexities often occur when the daughter returns from college and finds that this recognition has been but partially accomplished. When she attempts to act upon the assumption of its accomplishment, she finds herself jarring upon ideals which are so entwined with filial piety, so rooted in the tenderest affections of which the human heart is capable, that both daughter and parents are shocked and startled when they discover what is happening, and they scarcely venture to analyze the situation. The ideal for the education of woman has changed under the pressure of a new claim. The family has responded to the extent of granting the education, but they are jealous of the new claim and assert the family claim as over against it.

The modern woman finds herself educated to recognize a stress of social obligation which her family did not in the least anticipate when they sent her to college. She finds herself, in addition, under an impulse to act her part as a citizen of the world. She accepts her family inheritance with loyalty and affection, but she has entered into a wider inheritance as well, which, for lack of a better phrase, we call the social claim. This claim has been recognized for four years in her training, but after her return from college the family claim is again exclusively and strenuously asserted. The situation has all the discomfort of transition and compromise. The daughter finds a constant and totally unnecessary conflict between the social and the family claims. In most cases the former is repressed and gives way to the family claim, because the latter is concrete and definitely asserted, while the social demand is vague and unformulated. In such instances the girl quietly submits, but she feels wronged whenever she allows her mind to dwell upon the situation. She either hides her hurt, and splendid reserves of enthusiasm and capacity go to waste, or her zeal and emotions are turned inward, and the result is an unhappy woman, whose heart is consumed by vain regrets and desires.

If the college woman is not thus quietly reabsorbed, she is even reproached for her discontent. She is told to be devoted to her family, inspiring and responsive to her social circle, and to give the rest of her time to further self-improvement and enjoyment. She expects to do this, and responds to these claims to the best of her ability, even heroically sometimes. But where is the larger life of which she has dreamed so long? That life which surrounds and completes the individual and family life? She has been taught that it is her duty to share this life, and her highest privilege to extend it. This divergence between her self-centered existence and her best convictions becomes constantly more apparent. But the situation is not even so simple as a conflict between her affections and her intellectual convictions, although even that is tumultuous enough, also the emotional nature is divided against itself. The social claim is a demand upon the emotions as well as upon the intellect, and in ignoring it she represses not only her convictions but lowers her springs of vitality. Her life is full of contradictions. She looks out into the world, longing that some demand be made upon her powers, for they are too untrained to furnish an initiative. When her health gives way under this strain, as it often does, her physician invariably advises a rest. But to be put to bed and fed on milk is not what she requires. What she needs is simple, health-giving activity, which, involving the use of all her faculties, shall be a response to all the claims which she so keenly feels.

It is quite true that the family often resents her first attempts to be part of a life quite outside their own, because the college woman frequently makes these first attempts most awkwardly; her faculties have not been trained in the line of action. She lacks the ability to apply her knowledge and theories to life itself and to its complicated situations. This is largely the fault of her training and of the one-sidedness of educational methods. The colleges have long been full of the best ethical teaching, insisting that the good of the whole must ultimately be the measure of effort, and that the individual can only secure his own rights as he labors to secure those of others. But while the teaching has included an ever-broadening range of obligation and has insisted upon the recognition of the claims of human brotherhood, the training has been singularly individualistic; it has fostered ambitions for personal distinction, and has trained the faculties almost exclusively in the direction of intellectual accumulation. Doubtless, woman's education is at fault, in that it has failed to recognize certain needs, and has failed to cultivate and guide the larger desires of which all generous young hearts are full.

During the most formative years of life, it gives the young girl no contact with the feebleness of childhood, the pathos of suffering, or the needs of old age. It gathers together crude youth in contact only with each other and with mature men and women who are there for the purpose of their mental direction. The tenderest promptings are bidden to bide their time. This could only be justifiable if a definite outlet were provided when they leave college. Doubtless the need does not differ widely in men and women, but women not absorbed in professional or business life, in the years immediately following college, are baldly brought face to face with the deficiencies of their training. Apparently every obstacle is removed, and the college woman is at last free to begin the active life, for which, during so many years, she has been preparing. But during this so-called preparation, her faculties have been trained solely for accumulation, and she has learned to utterly distrust the finer impulses of her nature, which would naturally have connected her with human interests outside of her family and her own immediate social circle. All through school and college the young soul dreamed of self-sacrifice, of succor to the helpless and of tenderness to the unfortunate. We persistently distrust these desires, and, unless they follow well-defined lines, we repress them with every device of convention and caution.

Books by Jane Addams

Democracy and Social Ethics. 1902.

The Spirit of Youth and The City Streets. 1909.

A New Conscience and an Ancient Evil. 1911.

Women at The Hague. 1915.

Newer Ideals of Peace. 1915.

Peace and Bread in Time of War. 1922.

Charlotte Perkins Gilman

AS TO HUMANNESS, 1904

*One of the first feminists to speak out from the public platform
on the need to change women's role from a domestic to a
social and economic one, was Charlotte Perkins Gilman. Born
in July 1860 in Hartford, Connecticut, she began her public life
in 1890 after her first marriage ended in divorce.*

*Her lectures covered a wide range of topics; ethics,
economics, sociology, labor problems, and the liberation of
women from domestic slavery were her themes. She was invited
to lecture in Europe at least five times between 1896 and 1913.*

When Charlotte Gilman became the sole editor of The
Forerunner Magazine *(1909–1916), she had already published
some of her revolutionary ideas in her book* Woman and
Economics *(1899). The ideas she develops are so radical that
there are still only a few women today prepared to argue their
validity. She says:*

SOURCE
Charlotte Perkins Gilman, "As to Humanness," The Man-Made World,
1904, pp. 16–27.
Portrait: Brown Brothers.

The home would cease to be to us a workshop or a museum, and would become far more the personal expression of its occupants. The place of peace and rest, of love and privacy that it can be in its present condition of *arrested industrial development* [editor's emphasis]. And woman will fill her place in those industries with far better results than are now provided by her ceaseless struggles, her conscientious devotion, her pathetic ignorance and efficiency.

Her other books are equally provocative and brilliantly argued: The Man-Made World: Androcentric Culture *(1911)*, His Religion and Hers *(1923)*, In This Our World *(verse), and* Problems of Civilization *(co-authored, 1929). In the latter book, Charlotte Gilman views the gains of women as an historical challenge to traditionally accepted values. She recognized in 1929 that modern society overemphasizes the importance of sex-conditioned characteristics (the too-feminine woman, the too-masculine man) to the detriment of both. She believed the feminist movement would raise the social awareness of men and women to match the inevitable changes brought about by technology. She saw women wage-earners becoming economically self-sufficient in 1929. As their self-images underwent tremendous changes, she predicted that their statuses and work-roles in the family would be greatly affected.*

On other important issues, such as the problem of uncontrolled fertility, she projected the need for quality rather than quantity in reproduction of the human species in the "new" role of motherhood. She challenged the validity of monogamy, maintaining that it can only continue to exist in a male-dominated society where it is of advantage to males. She supported the ideal male-female relationship that would emerge because of "mutual attractions, based on legitimate distinctions, with no additional advantage to be gained."

Her death in 1935 did not receive the public attention it deserved. Society lost a uniquely original thinker, one whose contributions will only be appreciated in the next few years.

Partridge-cock, farmyard-cock, peacock, from sparrow to ostrich, observe his mien! To strut and languish; to exhibit every beauteous lure; to sacrifice ease, comfort, speed, everything, to beauty—for her sake—this is the nature of the he-bird of any species; the characteristic, not of the turkey, but of the cock! With drumming of loud wings, with crow and quack and bursts of glorious song, he woos his mate; displays his splendours before her; fights fiercely with his rivals. To butt—to strut—to make a noise—all for love's sake; these acts are common to the male.

We may now generalise and clearly state: That is masculine which belongs to the male—to any or all males, irrespective of species. That is feminine which belongs to the female, to any or all females, irrespective of species. That is ovine, bovine, feline, canine, equine, or asinine which belongs to that species, irrespective of sex.

In our own species all this is changed. We have been so taken up with the phenomena of masculinity and femininity, that our common humanity has largely escaped notice. We know we are human, naturally, and are very proud of it; but we do not consider in what our humanness consists, nor how men and women may fall short of it, or overstep its bounds, in continual insistence upon their special differences. It is "manly" to do this; it is "womanly" to do that; but what a human being should do under the circumstances is not thought of.

The only time when we do recognize what we call "common humanity" is in extreme cases, matters of life and death; when both men and women are expected to behave as if they were also human creatures. Since the range of feeling and action proper to humanity, as such, is far wider than that proper to either sex, it seems at first somewhat remarkable that we have given it so little recognition.

A little classification will help us here. We have certain qualities in common with inanimate matter, such as weight, opacity, resilience. It is clear that these are not human. We have other qualities in common with all forms of life,—cellular construction, for instance, the reproduction of cells, and the need of nutrition. These again are not human. We have others, many others, common to the higher mammals, which are not exclusively ours—are not distinctively human. What then are true human characteristics? In what way is the human species distinguished from all other species?

Our humanness is seen most clearly in three main lines: it is mechanical, physical, and social. Our power to make and use things is essentially human; we alone have extra-physical tools. We have added to our teeth the knife, sword, scissors, mowing machine; to our claws the spade, harrow, plough, drill, dredge. We are a protean creature, using the larger brain power through a wide variety of changing weapons. This is one of our main and vital distinctions. Ancient animal races are traced and known by mere bones and shells, ancient human races by their buildings, tools, and utensils.

That degree of brain development which gives us the human mind is a clear distinction of race. The savage who can count a hundred is more human than the savage who can count ten.

More prominent than either of these is the social nature of humanity. We are by no means the only group-animal; that ancient type of industry, the ant, and even the well-worn bee, are social creatures. But insects of their kind are found living alone, human beings never. Our humanness begins with some low form of social relation and increases as that relation develops.

Human life of any sort is dependent upon what Kropotkin calls "mutual aid," and human progress keeps step absolutely with that interchange of specialised services which makes society organic. The nomad, living on cattle as ants live on theirs, is less human than the farmer, raising food by intelligently applied labour; and the extension of trade and commerce, from mere village market-places to the world-exchanges of to-day, is extension of humanness as well.

Humanity, thus considered, is not a thing made at once and unchangeable, but a stage of development; and is still, as Wells describes it, "in the making." Our humanness is seen to lie not so much in what we are individually, as in our relations to one another; and even our individuality is but the result of our relations to one another. It lies in what we do and how we do it, rather than in what we are. Some, philosophically inclined, exalt "being" over "doing." To them this question may be put: "Can you mention any form of life that merely *is*, without *doing* anything?"

Taken separately and physically, we are animals, *genus homo;* taken socially and physically, we are, in varying degree, human; and our real history lies in the development of this humanness.

Our historic period is not very long. Real written history only goes back a few thousand years, beginning with the stone records of ancient Egypt. During this period we have had almost universally what is here called an Androcentric Culture. The history, such as it was, was made and written by men.

The mental, the mechanical, the social development, was almost wholly theirs. We have, so far, lived and suffered and died in a man-made world. So general, so unbroken, has been this condition, that to mention it arouses no more remark than the statement of a natural law. We have taken it for granted, since the dawn of civilisation, that "man-kind" meant men-kind, and that the world was theirs.

Women we have sharply delimited. Women were a sex; "the sex," according to chivalrous toasts; they were set apart for special services peculiar to femininity. As one English scientist put it, in 1888, "Women are not only not the race—they are not even half the race, but a sub-species told off for reproduction only."

This mental attitude toward women is even more clearly expressed by Mr. H. B. Marriott-Watson in his article on "The American Woman" in the *Nineteenth Century* for June, 1904, where he says: "Her constitutional restlessness has caused her to abdicate those functions which alone excuse or explain her existence." This is a peculiarly unhappy and condensed expression of the relative position of women during our androcentric culture. The man was accepted as the race type without one dissentient voice; and the woman—a strange, diverse creature, quite disharmonious in the accepted scheme of things—was excused and explained only as a female.

She has needed volumes of such excuse and explanation; also, apparently, volumes of abuse and condemnation. In any library catalogue we may find books upon books about women: physiological, sentimental, didactic, religious—all manner of books about women, as such. Even to-day in the works of Marholm, poor young Weininger, Mœbius, and others, we find the same perpetual discussion of women—as such.

This is a book about men—as such. It differentiates between the human nature and the sex nature. It will not go so far as to allege man's masculine traits to be all that excuse or explain his existence; but it will point out what are masculine traits as distinct from human ones, and what has been the effect on our human life of the unbridled dominance of one sex.

We can see at once, glaringly, what would have been the result of giving all human affairs into female hands. Such an extraordinary and deplorable situation would have "feminised" the world. We should have all become "effeminate."

See how in our use of language the case is clearly shown. The adjectives and derivatives based on woman's distinctions are alien and derogatory when applied to human affairs; "effeminate" —too female, connotes contempt, but has no masculine analogue; whereas "emasculate"—not enough male, is a term of reproach, and has no feminine analogue. "Virile"—manly, we oppose to "puerile"—childish, and the very word "virtue" is derived from "vir"—a man.

Even in the naming of other animals we have taken the male as the race type, and put on a special termination to indicate "his female," as in lion, lioness; leopard, leopardess; while all our human scheme of things rests on the same tacit assumption;

man being held the human type, woman a sort of accompaniment and subordinate assistant, merely essential to the making of people.

She has held always the place of a preposition in relation to man. She has been considered above him or below him, before him, behind him, beside him, a wholly relative existence—"Sydney's sister," "Pembroke's mother"—but never by any chance Sydney or Pembroke herself.

Acting on this assumption, all human standards have been based on male characteristics, and when we wish to praise the work of a woman, we say she has "a masculine mind."

It is no easy matter to deny or reverse a universal assumption. The human mind has had a good many jolts since it began to think, but after each upheaval it settles down as peacefully as the vine-growers on Vesuvius, accepting the last lava crust as permanent ground.

What we see immediately around us, what we are born into and grow up with, be it mental furniture or physical, we assume to be the order of nature.

If a given idea has been held in the human mind for many generations, as almost all our common ideas have, it takes sincere and continued effort to remove it; and if it is one of the oldest we have in stock, one of the big, common, unquestioned world ideas, vast is the labour of those that seek to change it.

Nevertheless, if the matter is one of importance, if the previous idea was a palpable error, of large and evil effect, and if the new one is true and widely important, the effort is worth making.

The task here undertaken is of this sort. It seeks to show that what we have all this time called "human nature" and deprecated, was in great part only male nature, and good enough in its place: that what we have called "masculine" and admired as such, was in large part human, and should be applied to both sexes; that what we have called "feminine" and condemned, was also largely human and applicable to both. Our androcentric culture is so shown to have been, and still to be, a masculine culture in excess, and therefore undesirable.

In the preliminary work of approaching these facts it will be well to explain how it can be that so wide and serious an error should have been made by practically all men. The reason is simply that they were men. They were males, and saw women as females—and not otherwise.

So absolute is this conviction that the man who reads will say, "Of course! How else are we to look at women except as females? They are females, aren't they?" Yes, they are, as men are males unquestionably; but there is possible the frame of mind of the old marquise who was asked by an English friend how she could bear to have the footman serve her breakfast in bed—to have a man in her bed-chamber—and replied sincerely, "Call you that thing there a man?"

The world is full of men, but their principal occupation is human work of some sort; and women see in them the human distinction preponderantly. Occasionally some unhappy lady marries her coachman—long contemplation of broad shoulders having an effect, apparently; but in general women see the human creature most, the male creature only when they love.

To the man, the whole world was his world, his because he was male; and the whole world of woman was the home, because she was female. She had her prescribed sphere, strictly limited to her feminine occupations and interests; he had all the rest of life, and not only so, but, having it, insisted on calling it male.

This accounts for the general attitude of men toward the now rapid humanisation of women. From her first faint struggles towards freedom and justice, to her present valiant efforts towards full economic and political equality, each step has been termed "unfeminine," and resented as an intrusion upon man's place and power. Here shows the need of our new classification, of the three distinct fields of life—masculine, feminine, and human.

As a matter of fact, there is a "woman's sphere," sharply defined and quite different from his; there is also a "man's sphere," as sharply defined and even more limited; but there remains a common sphere—that of humanity which belongs to both alike.

In the early part of what is known as "the woman's movement," it was sharply opposed on the ground that women would become "unsexed." Let us note in passing that they have become unsexed in one particular, most glaringly so, and no one has noticed or objected to it.

As part of our androcentric culture, we may point to the peculiar reversal of sex characteristics which makes the human female carry the burden of ornament. She alone, of all female creatures, has adopted the essentially masculine attribute of special sex-decoration; she does not fight for her mate, as yet, but she blooms forth as do the peacock and the bird of paradise, in poignant reversal of nature's laws, even wearing masculine feathers to further her feminine ends.

Woman's natural work as a female is that of the mother; man's natural work as a male is that of the father; their mutual relation to this end being a source of joy and well-being when rightly held: but human work covers all our life outside of these specialties. Every handicraft, every profession, every science, every art, all normal amusements and recreations, all government, education, religion, the whole living world of human achievement—all this is human.

That one sex should have monopolised all human activities, called them "man's work," and managed them as such, is what is meant by the phrase "Androcentric Culture."

Books by Charlotte Perkins Gilman

"Feminism and Social Progress." *Problems of Civilization.* Baker Boswell, ed. New York: Van Nostrand Reinhold, 1929.

Women and Economics. Carl Degler, ed. New York: Harper & Row, 1966.

Books about Charlotte Perkins Gilman

GRAVES, ERNEST. *The American Woman.* New York: Greenberg, 1937.

Emma Goldman

MARRIAGE AND LOVE, 1917

The New York Times *bade good riddance to a "pernicious anarchist" when, in 1919, Emma Goldman was deported from the United States to her homeland, Russia. It is likely that the* Times *spoke for most Americans, who viewed Emma Goldman as a rather plump, dowdy, middle-aged fanatic who railed against capitalism, the State, and organized religion, and at the same time espoused her own brand of radical feminism.*

Born in Lithuania on June 27, 1869, Emma Goldman emigrated to the United States in 1886, after a youthful repugnance for regimentation. Finding employment in a clothing factory in Rochester, New York, she also found loneliness. She soon married, but early disillusionment led to a separation.

Her conversion to radicalism was influenced primarily by the "judicial murder" of the Haymarket anarchists in Chicago in 1887 and also by the ideas of Johann Most, a labor agitator whom she personally befriended. Emma's political activism resulted in a one-year jail sentence, in 1893 on Blackwells Island

SOURCE
Emma Goldman, "Marriage and Love," Anarchism and Other Essays, *Mother Earth Publishing Association, 1917. Reprinted by Dover Publications, 1969.*
Portrait: Brown Brothers.

in New York City, for her speeches and action inciting workers to riot. After her release, she went to Vienna to train as a nurse and midwife, all the while developing her anarchistic philosophy and theories. Her friendship with Alexander Berkman, among others, and her political activities and lectures resulted in her implication, in 1901, in the McKinley assassination.

With Berkman, Emma published the anarchist journal Mother Earth *from 1906 to 1917; she and Berkman were arrested in 1917 for opposing the draft and served two years in prison. They were both deported to Russia in the "Red Scare" of 1919.*

Disillusioned with the Bolsheviks, they left in 1921; Emma, living in both England and Canada, continued to write and lecture on such topics as birth control, women's rights, and libertarianism. She published her autobiography, Living My Life, *in 1931 and in 1934 was allowed to reenter the United States on a lecture tour that, despite enthusiasm, proved a financial failure. A trip to Spain in 1936 to aid Spanish anarchists in the civil war, was followed by a move to Toronto, where, still working for her causes, she died on May 14, 1940.*

Emma Goldman's feminism can be best understood in the context of her anarchism: as an anarchist, she worked passionately to "free man from the phantoms that hold him captive"; as a feminist, therefore, she faced the additional labor of freeing women from those "phantoms" that were the singular plagues of women. The institution of marriage offended Emma, who saw it as an economic and sexual prison, for which the woman pays with "her name, her property, her self respect, her very life." She scornfully rejected puritanical chastity as an "artificial imposition upon nature," which, because of the double standard, harmed women much more than it did men. She was one of the earliest champions of contraception, which she felt made possible "fewer and better children, begotten and reared in love and free choice." Unlike most feminists of her day, Emma Goldman opposed universal suffrage, because it perpetuated the State, an establishment already responsible for untold crimes against humanity.

The popular notion about marriage and love is that they are synonymous, that they spring from the same motives, and cover the same human needs. Like most popular notions this also rests not on actual facts, but on superstition.

Marriage and love have nothing in common; they are as far apart as the poles; are, in fact, antagonistic to each other. No doubt some marriages have been the result of love. Not, however, because love could assert itself only in marriage; much rather is it because few people can completely outgrow a convention. There are to-day large numbers of men and women to whom marriage is naught but a farce, but who submit to it for the sake of public opinion. At any rate, while it is true that some marriages are based on love, and while it is equally true that in some cases love continues in married life, I maintain that it does so regardless of marriage, and not because of it.

On the other hand, it is utterly false that love results from marriage. On rare occasions one does hear of a miraculous case of a married couple falling in love after marriage, but on close examination it will be found that it is a mere adjustment to the inevitable. Certainly the growing-used to each other is far away from the spontaneity, the intensity, and beauty of love, without which the intimacy of marriage must prove degrading to both the woman and the man.

Marriage is primarily an economic arrangement, an insurance pact. It differs from the ordinary life insurance agreement only in that it is more binding, more exacting. Its returns are insignificantly small compared with the investments. In taking out an insurance policy one pays for it in dollars and cents, always at liberty to discontinue payments. If, however, woman's premium is a husband, she pays for it with her name, her privacy, her self-respect, her very life "until death doth part." Moreover, the marriage insurance condemns her to life-long dependency, to parasitism, to complete uselessness, individual as well as social. Man, too, pays his toll, but as his sphere is wider, marriage does not limit him as much as woman. He feels his chains more in an economic sense.

Thus Dante's motto over Inferno applies with equal force to marriage: "Ye who enter here leave all hope behind."

That marriage is a failure none but the very stupid will deny. One has but to glance over the statistics of divorce to realize how bitter a failure marriage really is. Nor will the stereotyped Philistine argument that the laxity of divorce laws and the growing looseness of woman account for the fact that: first, every twelfth marriage ends in divorce; second, that since 1870 divorces have increased from 28 to 73 for every hundred thousand population; third, that adultery, since 1867, as ground for divorce, has increased 270.8 per cent.; fourth, that desertion increased 369.8 per cent.

Added to these startling figures is a vast amount of material, dramatic and literary, further elucidating this subject. Robert Herrick, in *Together;* Pinero, in *Mid-Channel;* Eugene Walker, in *Paid in Full*, and scores of other writers are discussing the barrenness, the monotony, the sordidness, the inadequacy of marriage as a factor for harmony and understanding.

The thoughtful social student will not content himself with the popular superficial excuse for this phenomenon. He will have to dig down deeper into the very life of the sexes to know why marriage proves so disastrous.

Edward Carpenter says that behind every marriage stands the life-long environment of the two sexes; an environment so different from each other that man and woman must remain strangers. Separated by an insurmountable wall of superstition, custom, and habit, marriage has not the potentiality of developing knowledge of, and respect for, each other, without which every union is doomed to failure.

Henrik Ibsen, the hater of all social shams, was probably the first to realize this great truth. Nora leaves her husband, not—as the stupid critic would have it—because she is tired of her responsibilities or feels the need of woman's rights, but because she has come to know that for eight years she had lived with a stranger and borne him children. Can there be anything more humiliating, more degrading than a life-long proximity between two strangers? No need for the woman to know anything of the man, save his income. As to the knowledge of the woman—what is there to know except that she has a pleasing appearance? We have not yet outgrown the theologic myth that woman has no soul, that she is a mere appendix to man, made out of his rib just for the convenience of the gentleman who was so strong that he was afraid of his own shadow.

Perchance the poor quality of the material whence woman comes is responsible for her inferiority. At any rate, woman has no soul—what is there to know about her? Besides, the less soul a woman has the greater her asset as a wife, the more readily will she absorb herself in her husband. It is this slavish acquiescence to man's superiority that has kept the marriage institution seemingly intact for so long a period. Now that woman is coming into her own, now that she is actually growing aware of herself as a being outside of the master's grace, the sacred institution of marriage is gradually being undermined, and no amount of sentimental lamentation can stay it.

From infancy, almost, the average girl is told that marriage is her ultimate goal; therefore her training and education must be directed toward that end. Like the mute beast fattened for slaughter, she is prepared for that. Yet, strange to say, she is allowed to know much less about her function as wife and mother than the ordinary artisan of his trade. It is indecent and filthy for a respectable girl to know anything of the marital relation. Oh, for the inconsistency of respectability, that needs the marriage vow to turn something which is filthy into the purest and most sacred arrangement that none dare question or criticize. Yet that is exactly the attitude of the average upholder of marriage. The prospective wife and mother is kept in complete ignorance of her only asset in the competitive field—sex. Thus she enters into life-long relations with a man only to find herself shocked, repelled, outraged beyond measure by the most natural and healthy instinct, sex. It is safe to say that a large percentage of the unhappiness, misery, distress, and physical suffering of matrimony is due to the criminal ignorance in sex matters that is being extolled as a great virtue. Nor is it at all an exaggeration when I say that more than one home has been broken up because of this deplorable fact.

If, however, woman is free and big enough to learn the mystery of sex without the sanction of State or Church, she will stand condemned as utterly unfit to become the wife of a "good" man, his goodness consisting of an empty head and plenty of money. Can there be anything more outrageous than the idea that a healthy, grown woman, full of life and passion, must deny nature's demand, must subdue her most intense craving, undermine her health and break her spirit, must stunt her vision, abstain from the depth and glory of sex experience until a "good" man comes along to take her unto himself as a wife? That is precisely what marriage means. How can such an arrangement end except in failure? This is one, though not the least important, factor of marriage, which differentiates it from love.

Ours is a practical age. The time when Romeo and Juliet risked the wrath of their fathers for love, when Gretchen exposed herself to the gossip of her neighbors for love, is no more. If, on rare occasions, young people allow themselves the luxury of romance, they are taken in care by the elders, drilled and pounded until they become "sensible."

The moral lesson instilled in the girl is not whether the man has aroused her love, but rather is it, "How much?" The important and only God of practical American life: Can the man make a living? Can he support a wife? That is the only thing that justifies marriage. Gradually this saturates every thought of the girl; her dreams are not of moonlight and kisses, of laughter and tears; she dreams of shopping tours and bargain counters. This soul-poverty and sordidness are the elements inherent in the marriage institution. The State and the Church approve of no other ideal, simply because it is the one that necessitates the State and Church control of men and women.

Doubtless there are people who continue to consider love above dollars and cents. Particularly is this true of that class whom economic necessity has forced to become self-supporting. The tremendous change in woman's position, wrought by that mighty factor, is indeed phenomenal when we reflect that it is but a short time since she has entered the industrial arena. Six million women wage-earners; six-million women, who have the equal right with men to be exploited, to be robbed, to go on strike; aye, to starve even. Anything more, my lord? Yes, six million wage-workers in every walk of life, from the highest brain work to the most difficult menial labor in the mines and on the railroad tracks; yes, even detectives and policemen. Surely the emancipation is complete.

Yet with all that, but a very small number of the vast army of women wage-workers look upon work as a permanent issue, in the same light as does man. No matter how decrepit the latter, he has been taught to be independent, self-supporting. Oh, I know that no one is really independent in our economic treadmill; still, the poorest specimen of a man hates to be a parasite; to be known as such, at any rate.

The woman considers her position as worker transitory, to be thrown aside for the first bidder. That is why it is infinitely harder to organize women than men. "Why should I join a union? I am going to get married, to have a home." Has she not been taught from infancy to look upon that as her ultimate calling? She learns soon enough that the home, though not so large a prison as the factory, has more solid doors and bars. It has a keeper so faithful that naught can escape him. The most tragic part, however, is that the home no longer frees her from wage-slavery; it only increases her task.

According to the latest statistics submitted before a Committee "on labor and wages, and congestion of population," ten per cent of the wage workers in New York City alone are married, yet they must continue to work at the most poorly paid labor in the world. Add to this horrible aspect the drudgery of housework, and what remains of the protection and glory of the home? As a matter of fact, even the middle-class girl in marriage can not speak of her home, since it is the man who creates her sphere. It is not important whether the husband is a brute or a darling. What I wish to prove is that marriage guarantees woman a home only by the grace of her husband. There she moves about in *his* home, year after year, until her aspect of life and human affairs becomes as flat, narrow, and drab as her surroundings. Small wonder if she becomes a nag, petty, quarrelsome, gossipy, unbearable, thus driving the man from the house. She could not go, if she wanted to; there is no place to go. Besides, a short period of married life, of complete surrender of all faculties, absolutely incapacitates the average woman for the outside world. She becomes reckless in appearance, clumsy in her movements, dependent in her decisions, cowardly in her judgment, a weight and a bore, which most men grow to hate and despise. Wonderfully inspiring atmosphere for the bearing of life, is it not?

But the child, how is it to be protected, if not for marriage? After all, is not that the most important consideration? The sham, the hypocrisy of it! Marriage protecting the child, yet thousands of children destitute and homeless. Marriage protecting the child, yet orphan asylums and reformatories overcrowded, the Society for the Prevention of Cruelty to Children keeping busy in rescuing the little victims from "loving" parents, to place them under more loving care, the Gerry Society. Oh, the mockery of it!

Marriage may have the power to "bring the horse to water," but has it ever made him drink? The law will place the father under arrest, and put him in convict's clothes; but has that ever stilled the hunger of the child? If the parent has no work, or if he hides his identity, what does marriage do then? It invokes the law to bring the man to "justice," to put him safely behind closed doors; his labor, however, goes not to the child, but to the State. The child receives but a blighted memory of its father's stripes.

As to the protection of the woman,—therein lies the curse of marriage. Not that it really protects her, but the very idea is so revolting, such an outrage and insult on life, so degrading to human dignity, as to forever condemn this parasitic institution.

It is like that other parental arrangement—capitalism. It robs man of his birthright, stunts his growth, poisons his body, keeps him in ignorance, in poverty and dependence, and then institutes charities that thrive on the last vestige of man's self-respect.

The institution of marriage makes a parasite of woman, an absolute dependent. It incapacitates her for life's struggle, annihilates her social consciousness, paralyzes her imagination, and then imposes its gracious protection, which is in reality a snare, a travesty on human character.

If motherhood is the highest fulfillment of woman's nature, what other protection does it need save love and freedom? Marriage but defiles, outrages, and corrupts her fulfillment. Does it not say to woman, Only when you follow me shall you bring forth life? Does it not condemn her to the block, does it not degrade and shame her if she refuses to buy her right to motherhood by selling herself? Does not marriage only sanction motherhood, even though conceived in hatred, in compulsion? Yet, if motherhood be of free choice, of love, of ecstasy, of defiant passion, does it not place a crown of thorns upon an innocent head and carve in letters of blood the hideous epithet, Bastard? Were marriage to contain all the virutes claimed for it, its crimes against motherhood would exclude it forever from the realm of love.

Love, the strongest and deepest element in all life, the harbinger of hope, of joy, of ectasy; love, the defier of all laws, of all conventions; love, the freest, the most powerful moulder of human destiny; how can such an all-compelling force be synonymous with that poor little State and Church-begotten weed, marriage?

Free love? As if love is anything but free! Man has bought brains, but all the millions in the world have failed to buy love. Man has subdued bodies, but all the power on earth has been unable to subdue love. Man has conquered whole nations, but all his armies could not conquer love. Man has chained and fettered the spirit, but he has been utterly helpless before love. High on a throne, with all the splendor and pomp his gold can command, man is yet poor and desolate, if love passes him by. And if it stays, the poorest hovel is radiant with warmth, with life and color. Thus love has the magic power to make of a beggar a king. Yes, love is free; it can dwell in no other atmosphere. In freedom it gives itself unreservedly, abundantly, completely. All the laws on the statutes, all the courts in the universe, cannot tear it from the soil, once love has taken root. If, however, the soil is sterile, how can marriage make it bear fruit? It is like the last desperate struggle of fleeting life against death.

Love needs no protection; it is its own protection. So long as love begets life no child is deserted, or hungry, or famished for the want of affection. I know this to be true. I know women who became mothers in freedom by the men they loved. Few children in wedlock enjoy the care, the protection, the devotion free motherhood is capable of bestowing.

The defenders of authority dread the advent of a free motherhood, lest it will rob them of their prey. Who would fight wars? Who would create wealth? Who would make the policeman, the jailer, if woman were to refuse the indiscriminate breeding of children? The race, the race! shouts the king, the president, the capitalist, the priest. The race must be preserved, though woman be degraded to a mere machine,—and the marriage institution is our only safety valve against the pernicious sex-awakening of woman. But in vain these frantic efforts to maintain a state of bondage. In vain, too, the edicts of the Church, the mad attacks of rulers, in vain even the arm of the law. Woman no longer wants to be a party to the production of a race of sickly, feeble, decrepit, wretched human beings, who have neither the strength nor moral courage to throw off the yoke of poverty and slavery. Instead she desires fewer and better children, begotten and reared in love and through free choice; not by compulsion, as marriage imposes. Our pseudo-moralists have yet to learn the deep sense of responsibility toward the child, that love in freedom has awakened in the breast of woman. Rather would she forego forever the glory of motherhood than bring forth life in an atmosphere that breathes only destruction and death. And if she does become a mother, it is to give to the child the deepest and best her being can yield. To grow with the child is her motto; she knows that in that manner alone can she help build true manhood and womanhood.

Ibsen must have had a vision of a free mother, when, with a master stroke, he portrayed Mrs. Alving. She was the ideal mother because she had outgrown marriage and all its horrors, because she had broken her chains, and set her spirit free to soar until it returned a personality, regenerated and strong. Alas, it was too late to rescue her life's joy, her Oswald; but not too late to realize that love in freedom is the only condition of a beautiful life. Those who, like Mrs. Alving, have paid with blood and tears for their spiritual awakening, repudiate marriage as an imposition, a shallow, empty mockery. They know, whether love last but one brief span of time or for eternity, it is the only creative, inspiring, elevating basis for a new race, a new world.

In our present pygmy state love is indeed a stranger to most people. Misunderstood and shunned, it rarely takes root; or if it does, it soon withers and dies. Its delicate fiber can not endure the stress and strain of the daily grind. Its soul is too complex to adjust itself to the slimy woof of our social fabric. It weeps and moans and suffers with those who have need of it, yet lack the capacity to rise to love's summit.

Some day, some day men and women will rise, they will reach the mountain peak, they will meet big and strong and free, ready to receive, to partake, and to bask in the golden rays of love. What fancy, what imagination, what poetic genius can foresee even approximately the potentialities of such a force in the life of men and women. If the world is ever to give birth to true companionship and oneness, not marriage, but love will be the parent.

Books by Emma Goldman

A Beautiful Ideal. Chicago: J. C. Hart, 1908.

Anarchism and Other Essays. New York: Mother Earth Publishing Association, 1910. Reprinted by Dover.

The Social Significance of Modern Drama. Boston: R. G. Badger, 1914.

The Crushing of the Russian Revolution. London: Freedom Press, 1922.

My Disillusionment in Russia. Garden City, N.Y.: Doubleday, 1923.

My Further Disillusionment in Russia. Garden City, N.Y.: Doubleday, 1924.

Living My Life. New York: Knopf, 1931.

Voltairine de Cleyre. Berkeley Heights, N.J.: Oriole Press, 1932.

Trotsky Protests Too Much. Glasgow: Anarchist Communist Federation, 1938.

Books about Emma Goldman

DRINNON, RICHARD. *Rebel in Paradise.* Chicago: The University of Chicago Press, 1961.

ISHILL, JOSEPH. *Emma Goldman, a Challenging Rebel.* Berkeley Heights, N.J.: Oriole Press, 1957.

WEINBERGER, HARRY. *Emma Goldman.* Berkeley Heights, N. J.: Oriole Press, 1940.

Margaret Sanger

BIRTH CONTROL—A PARENTS' PROBLEM OR A WOMAN'S? 1920

31

Margaret Higgins Sanger was born in Corning, New York,
in September 1883, the sixth of eleven children. Her mother's
death at 48, brought on by endless labor and extreme fatigue,
greatly influenced Margaret's future life's work.

Financially unable to realize her dream to become a
physician, Margaret Higgins entered the nursing school at White
Plains Hospital, New York, in 1899. While a student, she met a
young architect, William Sanger. They married in 1902.

As a nurse on New York's Lower East Side, Margaret
became sharply aware of the daily inhumanity perpetrated on
thousands of poverty-stricken women, slowly dying of diseases
aggravated by multiple unwanted pregnancies. Witnessing the
self-inflicted torment of mothers, she said, "It is apparent that
nothing short of contraceptives can put an end to the horrors
of abortion and infanticide." At considerable risk to her reputation and career, she began to distribute illegal birth control
information to these hopeless women. The infamous Comstock
Law of 1873 prohibited the dispensation of contraceptive information, let alone devices, even by a physician. Not until 1936 was
this repressive law legally challenged, and then it was merely
revised.

SOURCE
Margaret Sanger, "Birth Control—A Parents' Problem or A Woman's?"
Woman and the New Race, New York: Truth Press, 1920, pp. 93–99.
Portrait: Brown Brothers.

In 1912 her first two articles were published in a woman's magazine, The Call: *"What Every Girl Should Know" and "What Every Mother Should Know." She established the National Birth Control League in 1914, dedicated to the widest dissemination of contraceptive information. She also founded a magazine,* The Woman Rebel, *in which she urged women "to look the whole world in the face with a go-to-hell look in the eyes; to have an ideal; to speak and act in defiance of convention."*

Her first brush with the law came in 1915 when her pamphlet Family Limitation *was circulated. The indictment was dropped, but the following year the police closed down the first American birth control clinic in Brooklyn and she was jailed for 30 days. Hardly "rehabilitated," she founded* The Birth Control Review *that same year; the magazine continued until 1928.*

Margaret Sanger's work did not interfere with her motherhood (she had three children), nor did her divorce in 1921 and remarriage to J. N. Slee the following year prevent her from expanding her life's work. In 1927 she organized the World Population Conference in Geneva, which led to the formation of the International Union for Scientific Investigation of Population Problems. The book she coedited with Dr. Hannah M. Stone, The Practice of Contraception, *recorded the results of an international conference in 1930 initiated by her to discuss this vital problem for the first time.*

Her organization of a National Committee for Federal Legislation of Birth Control in 1932 provided the necessary impetus to challenge the Comstock Law for the first time in 1936. It won the right of physicians to dispense birth control information and devices. Finally, in 1937, the American Medical Association courageously endorsed birth control. In 1942 Margaret Sanger organized the National Birth Control League with its neighborhood clinics, later known as Planned Parenthood Association and finally International Planned Parenthood Federation.

In her total involvement with freeing women from reproductive slavery, Margaret Sanger recognized that freedom and equality depended on such knowledge. Ignorance combined with victorian attitudes toward sex "exploited and enslaved women, and killed their opportunity for self-expression."

Her vision went beyond the legalistic oppression of women; her battle was not against acceptance of the biblical imperative, "Be fruitful and multiply"; she aimed her weaponry at those who wished to keep woman "barefoot and pregnant."

235

The problem of birth control has arisen directly from the effort of the feminine spirit to free itself from bondage. Woman herself has wrought that bondage through her reproductive powers and while enslaving herself has enslaved the world. The physical suffering to be relieved is chiefly woman's. Hers, too, is the love life that dies first under the blight of too prolific breeding. Within her is wrapped up the future of the race—it is hers to make or mar. All of these considerations point unmistakably to one fact—it is woman's duty as well as her privilege to lay hold of the means of freedom. Whatever men may do, she cannot escape the responsibility. For ages she has been deprived of the opportunity to meet this obligation. She is now emerging from her helplessness. Even as no one can share the suffering of the overburdened mother, so no one can do this work for her. Others may help, but she and she alone can free herself.

The basic freedom of the world is woman's freedom. A free race cannot be born of slave mothers. A woman enchained cannot choose but give a measure of that bondage to her sons and daughters. No woman can call herself free who does not own and control her body. No woman can call herself free until she can choose consciously whether she will or will not be a mother.

It does not greatly alter the case that some women call themselves free because they earn their own livings, while others profess freedom because they defy the conventions of sex relationship. She who earns her own living gains a sort of freedom that is not to be undervalued, but in quality and in quantity it is of little account beside the untrammeled choice of mating or not mating, of being a mother or not being a mother. She gains food and clothing and shelter, at least, without submitting to the charity of her companion, but the earning of her own living does not give her the development of her inner sex urge, far deeper and more powerful in its outworkings than any of these externals. In order to have that development, she must still meet and solve the problem of motherhood.

With the so-called "free" woman, who chooses a mate in defiance of convention, freedom is largely a question of character and audacity. If she does attain to an unrestricted choice of a mate, she is still in a position to be enslaved through her reproductive powers. Indeed, the pressure of law and custom upon the woman not legally married is likely to make her more of a slave than the woman fortunate enough to marry the man of her choice.

Look at it from any standpoint you will, suggest any solution you will, conventional or unconventional, sanctioned by law or in defiance of law, woman is in the same position, fundamentally, until she is able to determine for herself whether she will be a mother and to fix the number of her offspring. This unavoidable situation is alone enough to make birth control, first of all, a woman's problem. On the very face of the matter, voluntary motherhood is chiefly the concern of the woman.

It is persistently urged, however, that since sex expression is the act of two, the responsibility of controlling the results should not be placed upon woman alone. Is it fair, it is asked, to give her, instead of the man, the task of protecting herself when she is, perhaps, less rugged in physique than her mate, and has, at all events, the normal, periodic inconveniences of her sex?

We must examine this phase of her problem in two lights—that of the ideal, and of the conditions working toward the ideal. In an ideal society, no doubt, birth control would become the concern of the man as well as the woman. The hard, inescapable fact which we encounter to-day is that man has not only refused any such responsibility, but has individually and collectively sought to prevent woman from obtaining knowledge by which she could assume this responsibility for herself. She is still in the position of a dependent to-day because her mate has refused to consider her as an individual apart from his needs. She is still bound because she has in the past left the solution of the problem to him. Having left it to him, she finds that instead of rights, she has only such privileges as she has gained by petitioning, coaxing and cozening. Having left it to him, she is exploited, driven and enslaved to his desires.

While it is true that he suffers many evils as the consequence of this situation, she suffers vastly more. While it is true that he should be awakened to the cause of these evils, we know that they come home to her with crushing force every day. It is she who has the long burden of carrying, bearing and rearing the unwanted children. It is she who must watch beside the beds of pain where lie the babies who suffer because they have come into overcrowded homes. It is her heart that the sight of the deformed, the subnormal, the undernourished, the overworked child smites first and oftenest and hardest. It is *her* love life that dies in the fear of undesired pregnancy. It is her opportunity for self expression that perishes first and most hopelessly because of it.

Conditions, rather than theories, facts, rather than dreams, govern the problem. They place it squarely upon the shoulders of woman. She has learned that whatever the moral responsibility of the man in this direction may be, he does not discharge it. She has learned that, lovable and considerate as the individual husband may be, she has nothing to expect from men in the mass, when they make laws and decree customs. She knows that regardless of what ought to be, the brutal, unavoidable fact is that she will never receive her freedom until she takes it for herself.

Having learned this much, she has yet something more to learn. Women are too much inclined to follow in the footsteps of men, to try to think as men think, to try to solve the general problems of life as men solve them. If after attaining their freedom, women accept conditions in the spheres of government, industry, art, morals and religion as they find them, they will be but taking a leaf out of man's book. The woman is not needed to do man's work. She is not needed to think man's thoughts. She need not fear that the masculine mind, almost universally dominant, will fail to take care of its own. Her mission is not to enhance the masculine spirit, but to express the feminine; hers is not to preserve a man-made world, but to create a human world by the infusion of the feminine element into all of its activities.

Woman must not accept; she must challenge. She must not be awed by that which has been built up around her; she must reverence that within her which struggles for expression. Her eyes must be less upon what is and more clearly upon what should be. She must listen only with a frankly questioning attitude to the dogmatized opinions of man-made society. When she chooses her new, free course of action, it must be in the light of her own opinion—of her own intuition. Only so can she give play to the feminine spirit. Only thus can she free her mate from the bondage which he wrought for himself when he wrought hers. Only thus can she restore to him that of which he robbed himself in restricting her. Only thus can she remake the world.

Books about Margaret Sanger

KENNEDY, DAVID M. *Birth Control in America: The Career of Margaret Sanger*. New Haven, Conn.: Yale University Press, 1970.

ROVINSKY, J. J., STONE, ABRAHAM, AND HIMES, NORMAN E. *Planned Parenthood—A Practical Guide to Birth Control Methods*. New York: Macmillan, 1965.

Isadora Duncan

EXCERPT FROM MY LIFE, *1927*

Isadora Duncan was born in San Francisco on May 27, 1878.
Her innovations in the art of the dance were foreshadowed
when, because of her family's fall into deep poverty, she began
a dancing school in which she taught six-year-old neighborhood
children. In her "new system," improvisations arose from the
interpretation of poetry, music, and the rhythms of nature.
Her move to Chicago at seventeen afforded scant success;
disillusioned by a further attempt in New York City, where she
performed in Augustin Daly's Company, she went with her
family to London. There they spent much time studying Greek
art, which later profoundly influenced Isadora's dancing.

In London, a chance meeting with Mrs. Patrick Campbell,
an earlier acquaintance, led to Isadora's introduction to an
appreciative intellectual circle. After successful performances
in London, she went to Paris and then travelled throughout
Europe, trying many times to establish a dancing school.
Finally, she seized an opportunity, and became the instructress
of forty children on the outskirts of Berlin.

SOURCE
Isadora Duncan, My Life, *New York, Liveright Publishing Company,*
1955, pp. 17–19.

Although her daughter Diedre was born in 1905, Isadora adhered to her childhood pledge to avoid marriage, influenced by her own parents' separation and her father's waywardness; therefore, her lover, Edward Gordon Craig, an English stage designer, actor, and producer, did not become her husband. A son, Patrick, was born, in 1908, out of an alliance with an art-loving friend, whom Isadora called "Lohengrin." Both Patrick and Diedre were drowned in 1913, when their automobile went over a Seine bridge in Paris and they and their nurse were unable to escape. The disaster came as a great shock to Isadora, who was at the peak of her career.

After unsuccessful attempts to establish schools throughout Europe, South America, and the United States, Isadora received an invitation from the Soviet government to form a school in Moscow. There she married a partially mad Russian poet, Sergei Yessenin, in 1922: It appeared that the Russian marriage laws were liberal enough to persuade her to break her oath. The marriage was doomed, however, by Yessenin's often violent, uncontrollable attacks; he committed suicide in 1925, when Isadora's dancing abilities had declined. She began a new artistic undertaking, the authorship of her autobiography, My Life (1926–1927). On September 14, 1927, after several years of financial and personal upset, Isadora was instantly strangled when her long scarf caught in the wheel of her companion's racing car.

Arnold Genthe described Isadora Duncan as "poised, in terrible impatience, arms tensely extended, a militant and a mighty woman, the symbol and the veritable leader of those who put on their courage like armour and fought for affirmation of life in America." Isadora introduced new possibilities to the dance: She interpreted the "Marseillaise," Marche slave, and Marche funebre in her own adventurous style; she replaced the traditional tights and ballet slippers with flowing Grecian draperies and the bare feet, which at first shocked audiences.

Although chiefly exemplified by her intensive dedication to the dance, in itself her reason for living, Isadora Duncan contributed to feminism through her avant garde life style, her reevaluation of the marital institution, and her remarkable aggressiveness to pursue her interests, whether they be dancing, teaching, or living according to her own personal ethics.

I am relating something of the history of my father because these early impressions had a tremendous effect on my after life. On one hand I was feeding my mind with sentimental novels, while on the other I had a very practical example of marriage before my eyes. All my childhood seemed to be under the black shadow of this mysterious father of whom no one would speak, and the terrible word divorce was imprinted upon the sensitive plate of my mind. As I could not ask any one for the explanation of these things I tried to reason them out for myself. Most of the novels I read ended in marriage and a blissfully happy state of which there was no more reason to write. But in some of these books, notably George Eliot's "Adam Bede," there is a girl who does not marry, a child that comes unwanted, and the terrible disgrace which falls upon the poor mother. I was deeply impressed by the injustice of this state of things for women, and putting it together with the story of my father and mother, I decided, then and there, that I would live to fight against marriage and for the emancipation of women and for the right for every woman to have a child or children as it pleased her, and to uphold her right and her virtue. These may seem strange ideas for a little girl of twelve years old to reason out, but the circumstances of my life had made me very precocious. I enquired into the marriage laws and was indignant to learn of the slavish condition of women. I began to look enquiringly at the faces of the married women friends of my mother, and I felt that on each was the mark of the green-eyed monster and the stigmata of the slave. I made a vow then and there that I would never lower myself to this degrading state. This vow I always kept, even when it cost me the estrangement of my mother and the miscomprehension of the world. One of the fine things the Soviet Government has done is the abolishment of marriage. With them two people sign their names in a book and under the signature is printed: "This signature involves no responsibility whatever on the part of either party, and can be annulled at the pleasure of either party." Such a marriage is the only convention to which any free-minded woman could consent, and is the only form of marriage to which I have ever subscribed.

At the present time I believe my ideas are more or less those of every free-spirited woman, but twenty years ago my refusal to marry and my example in my own person of the right of the woman to bear children without marriage, created a considerable misunderstanding. Things have changed and there has been so great a revolution in our ideas that I think to-day every intelligent woman will agree with me that the ethics of the marriage code are an impossible proposition for a free-spirited woman to accede to. If in spite of this, intelligent women continue to marry, it is simply because they have not the courage to stand up for their convictions, and if you will read through a list of the divorces of the last ten years you will realize that what I say is true. Many women to whom I have preached the doctrine of freedom have weakly replied, "But who is to support the children?" It seems to me that if the marriage ceremony is needed as a protection to insure the enforced support of children, then you are marrying a man who, you suspect, would under certain conditions, refuse to support his children, and it is a pretty low-down proposition. For you are marrying a man whom you already suspect of being a villain. But I have not so poor an opinion of men that I believe the greater percentage of them to be such low specimens of humanity.

Books by Isadora Duncan

The Art of the Dance. New York: Theatre Arts, Inc., 1928.
My Life. New York: Boni and Liveright, 1927, 1942.

Books about Isadora Duncan

DESTI, MARY. *The Untold Story: The Life of Isadora Duncan, 1921–1927.* New York: Liveright, 1929.

GENTHE, ARNOLD. *Isadora Duncan: Twenty-Four Studies.* New York and London: M. Kennerley, 1929.

MACDOUGALL, ALLAN ROSE. *Isadora: A Revolutionary in Art and Love.* New York: T. Nelson, 1960.

MAGRIEL, PAUL DAVID, ed. *Isadora Duncan.* New York: Holt, Rinehart and Winston, 1947.

Barbara Welter

THE CULT OF TRUE WOMANHOOD, 1966

*Barbara Welter is a professor of history at Hunter College in
New York City.*

SOURCE
Barbara Welter, *"The Cult of True Womanhood: 1820–1860,"* American
Quarterly, *Vol. XVIII, Summer 1966, pp. 151–162, 173–174.*

The nineteenth-century American man was a busy builder of bridges and railroads, at work long hours in a materialistic society. The religious values of his forebears were neglected in practice if not in intent, and he occasionally felt some guilt that he had turned this new land, this temple of the chosen people, into one vast countinghouse. But he could salve his conscience by reflecting that he had left behind a hostage, not only to fortune, but to all the values which he held so dear and treated so lightly. Woman, in the cult of True Womanhood[1] presented by the women's magazines, gift annuals and religious literature of the nineteenth century, was the hostage in the home.[2] In a society where values changed frequently, where fortunes rose and fell with frightening rapidity, where social and economic mobility provided instability as well as hope, one thing at least remained the same—a true woman was a true woman, wherever she was found. If anyone, male or female, dared to tamper with the complex of virtues which made up True Womanhood, he was

[1] Authors who addressed themselves to the subject of women in the mid-nineteenth century used this phrase as frequently as writers on religion mentioned God. Neither group felt it necessary to define their favorite terms; they simply assumed—with some justification—that readers would intuitively understand exactly what they meant. Frequently what people of one era take for granted is most striking and revealing to the student from another. In a sense this analysis of the ideal woman of the mid-nineteenth century is an examination of what writers of that period actually meant when they used so confidently the vague phrase True Womanhood.

[2] The conclusions reached in this article are based on a survey of almost all of the women's magazines published for more than three years during the period 1820–1860 and a sampling of those published for less than three years; all the gift books cited in Ralph Thompson, *American Literary Annuals and Gift Books, 1825–1865* (New York, 1936) deposited in the Library of Congress, the New York Public Library, the New-York Historical Society, Columbia University Special Collections, Library of the City College of the University of New York, Pennsylvania Historical Society, Massachusetts Historical Society, Boston Public Library, Fruitlands Museum Library, the Smithsonian Institution and the Wisconsin Historical Society; hundreds of religious tracts and sermons in the American Unitarian Society and the Galatea Collection of the Boston Public Library; and the large collection of nineteenth-century cookbooks in the New York Public Library and the Academy of Medicine of New York. Corroborative evidence not cited in this article was found in women's diaries, memoirs, autobiographies and personal papers, as well as in all the novels by women which sold over 75,000 copies during this period, as cited in Frank Luther Mott, *Golden Multitudes: The Story of Best Sellers in the United States* (New York, 1947) and H. R. Brown, *The Sentimental Novel in America, 1789–1860* (Durham, N.C., 1940). This latter information also indicated the effect of the cult of True Womanhood on those most directly concerned.

damned immediately as an enemy of God, of civilization and of the Republic. It was a fearful obligation, a solemn responsibility, which the nineteenth-century American woman had—to uphold the pillars of the temple with her frail white hand.

The attributes of True Womanhood, by which a woman judged herself and was judged by her husband, her neighbors and society could be divided into four cardinal virtues—piety, purity, submissiveness and domesticity. Put them all together and they spelled mother, daughter, sister, wife—woman. Without them, no matter whether there was fame, achievement or wealth, all was ashes. With them she was promised happiness and power.

Religion or piety was the core of woman's virtue, the source of her strength. Young men looking for a mate were cautioned to search first for piety, for if that were there, all else would follow.[3] Religion belonged to woman by divine right, a gift of God and nature. This "peculiar susceptibility" to religion was given her for a reason: "the vestal flame of piety, lighted up by Heaven in the breast of woman" would throw its beams into the naughty world of men.[4] So far would its candle power reach that the "Universe might be enlightened, Improved, and Harmonized by WOMAN!!"[5] She would be another, better Eve, working in cooperation with the Redeemer, bringing the world back "from its revolt and sin."[6] The world would be reclaimed for God through her suffering, for "God increased the cares and sorrows of woman, that she might be sooner constrained to accept the terms of salvation."[7] A popular poem by Mrs. Frances Osgood, "The Triumph of the Spiritual Over the Sensual" expressed just this sentiment, woman's purifying passionless love bringing an erring man back to Christ.[8]

Dr. Charles Meigs, explaining to a graduating class of medical students why women were naturally religious, said that "hers is a pious mind. Her confiding nature leads her more readily than

[3] As in "The Bachelor's Dream," in *The Lady's Gift: Souvenir for All Seasons* (Nashua, N.H., 1849), p. 37.

[4] *The Young Ladies' Class Book: A Selection of Lessons for Reading in Prose and Verse*, ed. Ebenezer Bailey, Principal of Young Ladies' High School, Boston (Boston, 1831), p. 168.

[5] A Lady of Philadelphia, *The World Enlightened, Improved, and Harmonized by WOMAN! ! !* A lecture, delivered in the City of New York, before the Young Ladies' Society for Mutual Improvement, on the following question, proposed by the society, with the offer of $100 for the best lecture that should be read before them on the subject proposed; —What is the power and influence of woman in moulding the manners, morals and habits of civil society? (Philadelphia, 1840), p. 1.

[6] *The Young Lady's Book: A Manual of Elegant Recreations, Exercises, and Pursuits* (Boston, 1830), p. 29.

[7] *Woman As She Was, Is, and Should Be* (New York, 1849), p. 206.

[8] "The Triumph of the Spiritual Over the Sensual: An Allegory," in *Ladies' Companion: A Monthly Magazine Embracing Every Department of Literature, Embellished with Original Engravings and Music*, XVII (New York, 1842), 67.

men to accept the proffered grace of the Gospel."[9] Caleb Atwater, Esq., writing in *The Ladies' Repository*, saw the hand of the Lord in female piety: "Religion is exactly what a woman needs, for it gives her that dignity that best suits her dependence."[10] And Mrs. John Sandford, who had no very high opinion of her sex, agreed thoroughly:" Religion is just what woman needs. Without it she is ever restless or unhappy. . . ."[11] Mrs. Sandford and the others did not speak only of that restlessness of the human heart, which St. Augustine notes, that can only find its peace in God. They spoke rather of religion as a kind of tranquilizer for the many undefined longings which swept even the most pious young girl, and about which it was better to pray than to think.

One reason religion was valued was that it did not take a woman away from her "proper sphere," her home. Unlike participation in other societies or movements, church work would not make her less domestic or submissive, less a True Woman. In religious vineyards, said the *Young Ladies' Literary and Missionary Report*, "you may labor without the apprehension of detracting from the charms of feminine delicacy." Mrs. S. L. Dagg, writing from her chapter of the Society in Tuscaloosa, Alabama, was equally reassuring: "As no sensible woman will suffer her intellectual pursuits to clash with her domestic duties" she should concentrate on religious work "which promotes these very duties."[12]

The women's seminaries aimed at aiding women to be religious, as well as accomplished. Mt. Holyoke's catalogue promised to make female education "a handmaid to the Gospel and an efficient auxiliary in the great task of renovating the world."[13] The Young Ladies' Seminary at Bordentown, New Jersey, declared its most important function to be "the forming of a sound and virtuous character."[14] In Keene, New Hampshire, the Seminary tried to instill a "consistent and useful character" in its students, to enable them in this life to be "a good friend, wife and mother" but more important, to qualify them for "the enjoyment of Celestial Happiness in the life to come."[15] And Joseph M' D. Matthews, Principal of Oakland Female Seminary in Hills-

[9] *Lecture on Some of the Distinctive Characteristics of the Female*, delivered before the class of the Jefferson Medical College, January 1847 (Philadelphia, 1847), p. 13.
[10] "Female Education," *Ladies' Repository and Gatherings of the West: A Monthly Periodical Devoted to Literature and Religion*, I (Cincinnati), 12.
[11] *Woman, in Her Social annd Domestic Character* (Boston, 1842), pp. 41–42.
[12] *Second Annual Report of the Young Ladies' Literary and Missionary Association of the Philadelphia Collegiate Institution* (Philadelphia, 1840), pp. 20, 26.
[13] *Mt. Holyoke Female Seminary: Female Education. Tendencies of the Principles Embraced, and the System Adopted in the Mt. Holyoke Female Seminary* (Boston, 1839), p. 3.
[14] *Prospectus of the Young Ladies' Seminary at Bordentown, New Jersey* (Bordentown, 1836), p. 7.
[15] *Catalogue of the Young Ladies' Seminary in Keene, New Hampshire* (n.p., 1832), p. 20.

borough, Ohio, believed that "female education should be pre-eminently religious."[16]

If religion was so vital to a woman, irreligion was almost too awful to contemplate. Women were warned not to let their literary or intellectual pursuits take them away from God. Sarah Josepha Hale spoke darkly of those who, like Margaret Fuller, threw away the "One True Book" for others, open to error. Mrs. Hale used the unfortunate Miss Fuller as fateful proof that "the greater the intellectual force, the greater and more fatal the errors into which women fall who wander from the Rock of Salvation, Christ the Saviour. . . ."[17]

One gentleman, writing on "Female Irreligion" reminded his readers that "Man may make himself a brute, and does so very often, but can woman brutify herself to his level—the lowest level of human nature—without exerting special wonder?" Fanny Wright, because she was godless, "was no woman, mother though she be." A few years ago, he recalls, such women would have been whipped. In any case, "woman never looks lovelier than in her reverence for religion" and, conversely, "female irreligion is the most revolting feature in human character."[18]

Purity was as essential as piety to a young woman, its absence as unnatural and unfeminine. Without it she was, in fact, no woman at all, but a member of some lower order. A "fallen woman" was a "fallen angel," unworthy of the celestial company of her sex. To contemplate the loss of purity brought tears; to be guilty of such a crime, in the women's magazines at least, brought madness or death. Even the language of the flowers had bitter words for it: a dried white rose symbolized "Death Preferable to Loss of Innocence."[19] The marriage night was the single great event of a woman's life, when she bestowed her greatest treasure upon her husband, and from that time on was completely dependent upon him, an empty vessel,[20] without legal or emotional existence of her own.[21]

[16] "Report to the College of Teachers, Cincinnati, October, 1840" in *Ladies' Repository*, I (1841), 50.
[17] *Woman's Record: or Sketches of All Distinguished Women from 'The Beginning' Till A. D. 1850* (New York, 1853), pp. 665, 669.
[18] "Female Irreligion," *Ladies' Companion*, XIII (May-October 1840), 111.
[19] *The Lady's Book of Flowers and Poetry*, ed. Lucy Hooper (New York, 1842), has a "Floral Dictionary" giving the symbolic meaning of floral tributes.
[20] See, for example, Nathaniel Hawthorne, *The Blithedale Romance* (Boston, 1852), p. 71, in which Zenobia says: "How can she be happy, after discovering that fate has assigned her but one single event, which she must contrive to make the substance of her whole life? A man has his choice of innumerable events."
[21] Mary R. Beard, *Woman As Force in History* (New York, 1946) makes this point at some length. According to common law, a woman had no legal existence once she was married and therefore could not manage property, sue in court, etc. In the 1840s and 1850s laws were passed in several states to remedy this condition.

Therefore all True Women were urged, in the strongest possible terms, to maintain their virtue, although men, being by nature more sensual than they, would try to assault it. Thomas Branagan admitted in *The Excellency of the Female Character Vindicated* that his sex would sin and sin again, they could not help it, but woman, stronger and purer, must not give in and let man "take liberties incompatible with her delicacy." "If you do," Branagan addressed his gentle reader, "You will be left in silent sadness to bewail your credulity, imbecility, duplicity, and premature prostitution."[22]

Mrs. Eliza Farrar, in *The Young Lady's Friend*, gave practical logistics to avoid trouble: "Sit not with another in a place that is too narrow; read not out of the same book; let not your eagerness to see anything induce you to place your head close to another person's."[23]

If such good advice was ignored the consequences were terrible and inexorable. In *Girlhood and Womanhood: or Sketches of My Schoolmates*, by Mrs. A. J. Graves (a kind of mid-nineteenth-century *The Group*), the bad ends of a boarding school class of girls are scrupulously recorded. The worst end of all is reserved for "Amelia Dorrington: The Lost One." Amelia died in the almshouse "the wretched victim of depravity and intemperance" and all because her mother had let her be "high-spirited not prudent." These girlish high spirits had been misinterpreted by a young man, with disastrous results. Amelia's "thoughtless levity" was "followed by a total loss of virtuous principle" and Mrs. Graves editorializes that "the coldest reserve is more admirable in a woman a man wishes to make his wife, than the least approach to undue familiarity."[24]

A popular and often-reprinted story by Fanny Forester told the sad tale of "Lucy Dutton." Lucy "with the seal of innocence upon her heart, and a rose-leaf on her cheek" came out of her vine-covered cottage and ran into a city slicker. "And Lucy was beautiful and trusting, and thoughtless: and he was gay, selfish and profligate. Needs the story to be told? . . . Nay, censor, Lucy was a child—consider how young, how very untaught—oh! her innocence was no match for the sophistry of a gay, city youth! Spring came and shame was stamped upon the cottage at the foot of the hill." The baby died: Lucy went mad at the funeral and finally died herself. "Poor, poor Lucy Dutton! The grave is a blessed couch and pillow to the wretched. Rest thee there, poor Lucy!"[25] The frequency with which derangement follows loss of

[22] *Excellency of the Female Character Vindicated: Being an Investigation Relative to the Cause and Effects on the Encroachments of Men Upon the Rights of Women, and the Too Frequent Degradation and Consequent Misfortunes of The Fair Sex* (New York, 1807), pp. 277, 278.
[23] By a Lady (Eliza Ware Rotch Farrar), *The Young Lady's Friend* (Boston, 1837), p. 293.
[24] *Girlhood and Womanhood: or, Sketches of My Schoolmates* (Boston, 1844), p. 140.
[25] Emily Chubbuck, *Alderbrook* (2nd. ed., Boston, 1847) II, 121, 127.

virtue suggests the exquisite sensibility of woman, and the possibility that, in the women's magazines at least, her intellect was geared to her hymen, not her brain.

If, however, a woman managed to withstand man's assaults on her virtue, she demonstrated her superiority and her power over him. Eliza Farnham, trying to prove this female superiority, concluded smugly that "the purity of women is the everlasting barrier against which the tides of man's sensual nature surge."[26]

A story in *The Lady's Amaranth* illustrates this dominance. It is set, improbably, in Sicily, where two lovers, Bianca and Tebaldo, have been separated because her family insisted she marry a rich old man. By some strange circumstance the two are in a shipwreck and cast on a desert island, the only survivors. Even here, however, the rigid standards of True Womanhood prevail. Tebaldo unfortunately forgets himself slightly, so that Bianca must warn him: "We may not indeed gratify our fondness by caresses, but it is still something to bestow our kindest language, and looks and prayers, and all lawful and honest attentions on each other." Something, perhaps, but not enough, and Bianca must further remonstrate: "It is true that another man is my husband, but you are my guardian angel." When even that does not work she says in a voice of sweet reason, passive and proper to the end, that she wishes he wouldn't but "still, if you insist, I will become what you wish; but I beseech you to consider, ere that decision, that debasement which I must suffer in your esteem." This appeal to his own double standards holds the beast in him at bay. They are rescued, discover that the old husband is dead, and after "mourning a decent season" Bianca finally gives in, legally.[27]

Men could be counted on to be grateful when women thus saved them from themselves. William Alcott, guiding young men in their relations with the opposite sex, told them that "Nothing is better calculated to preserve a young man from contamination of low pleasures and pursuits than frequent intercourse with the more refined and virtuous of the other sex." And he added, one assumes in equal innocence, that youth should "observe and learn to admire, that purity and ignorance of evil which is the characteristic of well-educated young ladies, and which, when we are near them, raises us above those sordid and sensual considerations which hold such sway over men in their intercourse with each other."[28]

The Rev. Jonathan F. Stearns was also impressed by female chastity in the face of male passion, and warned woman never

---

[26] *Woman and Her Era* (New York, 1864), p. 95.
[27] "The Two Lovers of Sicily," *The Lady's Amaranth: A Journal of Tales, Essays, Excerpts—Historical and Biographical Sketches, Poetry and Literature in General* (Philadelphia), II (Jan. 1839), 17.
[28] *The Young Man's Guide* (Boston, 1833), pp. 229, 231.

to compromise the source of her power: "Let her lay aside delicacy, and her influence over our sex is gone."[29]

Women themselves accepted, with pride but suitable modesty, this priceless virtue. *The Ladies' Wreath*, in "Woman the Creature of God and the Manufacturer of Society" saw purity as her greatest gift and chief means of discharging her duty to save the world: "Purity is the highest beauty—the true pole-star which is to guide humanity aright in its long, varied, and perilous voyage."[30]

Sometimes, however, a woman did not see the dangers to her treasure. In that case, they must be pointed out to her, usually by a male. In the nineteenth century any form of social change was tantamount to an attack on woman's virtue, if only it was correctly understood. For example, dress reform seemed innocuous enough and the bloomers worn by the lady of that name and her followers were certainly modest attire. Such was the reasoning only of the ignorant. In another issue of *The Ladies' Wreath* a young lady is represented in dialogue with her "Professor." The girl expresses admiration for the bloomer costume—it gives freedom of motion, is healthful and attractive. The "Professor" sets her straight. Trousers, he explains, are "only one of the many manifestations of that wild spirit of socialism and agrarian radicalism which is at present so rife in our land." The young lady recants immediately: "If this dress has any connexion with Fourierism or Socialism, or fanaticism in any shape whatever, I have no disposition to wear it at all . . . no true woman would so far compromise her delicacy as to espouse, however unwittingly, such a cause."[31]

America could boast that her daughters were particularly innocent. In a poem on "The American Girl" the author wrote proudly:

Her eye of light is the diamond bright,
Her innocence the pearl,
And these are ever the bridal gems
That are worn by the American girl.[32]

Lydia Maria Child, giving advice to mothers, aimed at preserving that spirit of innocence. She regretted that "want of confidence between mothers and daughters on delicate subjects" and suggested a woman tell her daughter a few facts when she reached the age of twelve to "set her mind at rest." Then Mrs.

[29] *Female Influence: and the True Christian Mode of Its Exercise; a Discourse Delivered in the First Presbyterian Church in Newburyport, July 30, 1837* (Newburyport, 1837), p. 18.
[30] W. Tolles, "Woman The Creature of God and the Manufacturer of Society," *Ladies' Wreath* (New York), III (1852), 205.
[31] Prof. William M. Heim, "The Bloomer Dress," *Ladies' Wreath*, III (1852), 247.
[32] *The Young Lady's Offering: or Gems of Prose and Poetry* (Boston, 1853), p. 283. The American girl, whose innocence was often connected with ignorance, was the spiritual ancestress of the Henry James heroine. Daisy Miller, like Lucy Dutton, saw innocence lead to tragedy.

Child confidently hoped that a young lady's "instinctive modesty" would "prevent her from dwelling on the information until she was called upon to use it."[33] In the same vein, a book of advice to the newly-married was titled *Whisper to a Bride*.[34] As far as intimate information was concerned, there was no need to whisper, since the book contained none at all.

A masculine summary of this virtue was expressed in a poem "Female Charms":

> I would have her as pure as the snow on the mount—
>   As true as the smile that to infamy's given—
> As pure as the wave of the crystalline fount,
>   Yet as warm in the heart as the sunlight of heaven.
> With a mind cultivated, not boastingly wise,
>   I could gaze on such beauty, with exquisite bliss;
> With her heart on her lips and her soul in her eyes—
>   What more could I wish in dear woman than this.[35]

Man might, in fact, ask no more than this in woman, but she was beginning to ask more of herself, and in the asking was threatening the third powerful and necessary virtue, submission. Purity, considered as a moral imperative, set up a dilemma which was hard to resolve. Woman must preserve her virtue until marriage and marriage was necessary for her happiness. Yet marriage was, literally, an end to innocence. She was told not to question this dilemma, but simply to accept it.

Submission was perhaps the most feminine virtue expected of women. Men were supposed to be religious, although they rarely had time for it, and supposed to be pure, although it came awfully hard to them, but men were the movers, the doers, the actors. Women were the passive, submissive responders. The order of dialogue was, of course, fixed in Heaven. Man was "woman's superior by God's appointment, if not in intellectual dowry, at least by official decree." Therefore, as Charles Elliott argued in *The Ladies' Repository*, she should submit to him "for the sake of good order at least."[36] In *The Ladies' Companion* a young wife was quoted approvingly as saying that she did not think woman should "feel and act for herself" because "When, next to God, her husband is not the tribunal to which her heart and intellect appeals—the golden bowl of affection is broken."[37]

---

[33] *The Mother's Book* (Boston, 1831), pp. 151, 152.
[34] Mrs. L. H. Sigourney, *Whisper to a Bride* (Hartford, 1851), in which Mrs. Sigourney's approach is summed up in this quotation: "Home! Blessed bride, thou art about to enter this sanctuary, and to become a priestess at its altar!," p. 44.
[35] S. R. R., "Female Charms," *Godey's Magazine and Lady's Book* (Philadelphia), XXXIII (1846), 52.
[36] Charles Elliott, "Arguing With Females," *Ladies' Repository*, I (1841), 25.
[37] *The Ladies' Companion*, VIII (Jan. 1838), 147.

Women were warned that if they tampered with this quality they tampered with the order of the Universe.

The Young Lady's Book summarized the necessity of the passive virtues in its readers' lives: "It is, however, certain, that in whatever situation of life a woman is placed from her cradle to her grave, a spirit of obedience and submission, pliability of temper, and humility of mind, are required from her."[38]

Woman understood her position if she was the right kind of woman, a true woman. "She feels herself weak and timid. She needs a protector," declared George Burnap, in his lectures on *The Sphere and Duties of Woman.* "She is in a measure dependent. She asks for wisdom, constancy, firmness, perseverance, and she is willing to repay it all by the surrender of the full treasure of her affections. Woman despises in man every thing like herself except a tender heart. It is enough that she is effeminate and weak; she does not want another like herself."[39] Or put even more strongly by Mrs. Sandford: "A really sensible woman feels her dependence. She does what she can, but she is conscious of inferiority, and therefore grateful for support."[40]

Mrs. Sigourney, however, assured young ladies that although they were separate, they were equal. This difference of the sexes did not imply inferiority, for it was part of the same order of Nature established by Him "who bids the oak brave the fury of the tempest, and the alpine flower lean its cheek on the bosom of eternal snows."[41] Dr. Meigs had a different analogy to make the same point, contrasting the anatomy of the Apollo of the Belvedere (illustrating the male principle) with the Venus de Medici (illustrating the female principle). "Woman," said the physician, with a kind of clinical gallantry, "has a head almost too small for intellect but just big enough for love."[42]

This love itself was to be passive and responsive. "Love, in the heart of a woman," wrote Mrs. Farrar, "should partake largely of the nature of gratitude. She should love, because she is already loved by one deserving her regard."[43]

Woman was to work in silence, unseen, like Wordsworth's Lucy. Yet "working like nature, in secret" her love goes forth to the world "to regulate its pulsation, and send forth from its heart, in pure and temperate flow, the life-giving current."[44] She was to work only for pure affection, without thought of money or ambition. A poem, "Woman and Fame," by Felicia Hermans, widely quoted in many of the gift books, concludes with a spirited renunciation of the gift of fame:

[38] *The Young Lady's Book* (New York, 1830), American edition, p. 28. (This is a different book than the one of the same title and date of publication cited in note 6.)
[39] *Sphere and Duties of Woman* (5th ed., Baltimore, 1854), p. 47.
[40] *Woman,* p. 15.
[41] *Letters to Young Ladies* (Hartford, 1835), p. 179.
[42] *Lecture,* p. 17.
[43] *The Young Lady's Friend,* p. 313.
[44] Maria J. McIntosh, *Woman in America: Her Work and Her Reward* (New York, 1850), p. 25.

Away! to me, a woman, bring
Sweet flowers from affection's spring.[45]

"True feminine genius," said Grace Greenwood (Sara Jane Clarke) "is ever timid, doubtful, and clingingly dependent: a perpetual childhood." And she advised literary ladies in an essay on "The Intellectual Woman"—"Don't trample on the flowers while longing for the stars."[46] A wife who submerged her own talents to work for her husband was extolled as an example of a true woman. In *Women of Worth: A Book for Girls*, Mrs. Ann Flaxman, an artist of promise herself, was praised because she "devoted herself to sustain her husband's genius and aid him in his arduous career."[47]

Caroline Gilman's advice to the bride aimed at establishing this proper order from the beginning of a marriage: "Oh, young and lovely bride, watch well the first moments when your will conflicts with his to whom God and society have given the control. Reverence his *wishes* even when you do not his *opinions*."[48]

Mrs. Gilman's perfect wife in *Recollections of a Southern Matron* realizes that "the three golden threads with which domestic happiness is woven" are "to repress a harsh answer, to confess a fault, and to stop (right or wrong) in the midst of self-defense, in gentle submission." Woman could do this, hard though it was, because in her heart she knew she was right and so could afford to be forgiving, even a trifle condescending. "Men are not unreasonable," averred Mrs. Gilman. "Their difficulties lie in not understanding the moral and physical nature of our sex. They often wound through ignorance, and are surprised at having offended." Wives were advised to do their best to reform men, but if they couldn't, to give up gracefully. "If any habit of his annoyed me, I spoke of it once or twice, calmly, then bore it quietly."[49]

A wife should occupy herself "only with domestic affairs—wait till your husband confides to you those of a high importance—and do not give your advice until he asks for it," advised the *Lady's Token*. At all times she should behave in a manner becoming a woman, who had "no arms other than gentleness." Thus "if he is abusive, never retort."[50] *A Young Lady's Guide to the Harmonious Development of a Christian Character* suggested

---

[45] *Poems and a Memoir of the Life of Mrs. Felicia Hemans* (London, 1860), p. 16.

[46] Letter "To an Unrecognized Poetess, June, 1846" (Sara Jane Clarke), *Greenwood Leaves* (2nd ed., Boston, 1850), p. 311.

[47] "The Sculptor's Assistant: Ann Flaxman," in *Women of Worth: A Book for Girls* (New York, 1860), p. 263.

[48] Mrs. Clarissa Packard (Mrs. Caroline Howard Gilman), *Recollections of a Housekeeper* (New York, 1834), p. 122.

[49] *Recollections of a Southern Matron* (New York, 1838), pp. 256, 257.

[50] *The Lady's Token: or Gift of Friendship*, ed. Colesworth Pinckney (Nashua, N.H., 1848), p. 119.

that females should "become as little children" and "avoid a controversial spirit."[51] *The Mother's Assistant and Young Lady's Friend* listed "Always Conciliate" as its first commandment in "Rules for Conjugal and Domestic Happiness." Small wonder that these same rules ended with the succinct maxim: "Do not expect too much."[52]

As mother, as well as wife, woman was required to submit to fortune. In *Letters to Mothers* Mrs. Sigourney sighed: "To bear the evils and sorrows which may be appointed us, with a patient mind, should be the continual effort of our sex.... It seems, indeed, to be expected of us; since the passive and enduring virtues are more immediately within our province." Of these trials "the hardest was to bear the loss of children with submission" but the indomitable Mrs. Sigourney found strength to murmur to the bereaved mother: "The Lord loveth a cheerful giver."[53] *The Ladies' Parlor Companion* agreed thoroughly in "A Submissive Mother," in which a mother who had already buried two children and was nursing a dying baby saw her sole remaining child "probably scalded to death. Handing over the infant to die in the arms of a friend, she bowed in sweet submission to the double stroke." But the child "through the goodness of God survived, and the mother learned to say 'Thy will be done.' "[54]

Woman then, in all her roles, accepted submission as her lot. It was a lot she had not chosen or deserved. As *Godey's* said, "the lesson of submission is forced upon woman." Without comment or criticism the writer affirms that "To suffer and to be silent under suffering seems the great command she has to obey."[55] George Burnap referred to a woman's life as "a series of suppressed emotions."[56] She was, as Emerson said, "more vulnerable, more infirm, more mortal than man."[57] The death of a beautiful woman, cherished in fiction, represented woman as the innocent victim, suffering without sin, too pure and good for this world but too weak and passive to resist its evil forces.[58] The best

[51] Harvey Newcomb, *Young Lady's Guide to the Harmonious Development of Christian Character* (Boston, 1846), p. 10.
[52] "Rules for Conjugal and Domestic Happiness," *Mother's Assistant and Young Lady's Friend*, III (Boston), (April 1843), 115.
[53] *Letters to Mothers* (Hartford, 1838), p. 199. In the diaries and letters of women who lived during this period the death of a child seemed consistently to be the hardest thing for them to bear and to occasion more anguish and rebellion, as well as eventual submission, than any other event in their lives.
[54] "A Submissive Mother," *The Ladies' Parlor Companion: A Collection of Scattered Fragments and Literary Gems* (New York, 1852), p. 358.
[55] "Woman," *Godey's Lady's Book*, II (August 1831), 110.
[56] *Sphere and Duties of Woman*, p. 172.
[57] Ralph Waldo Emerson, "Woman," *Complete Writings of Ralph Waldo Emerson* (New York, 1875), p. 1180.
[58] As in Donald Fraser, *The Mental Flower Garden* (New York, 1857). Perhaps the most famous exponent of this theory is Edgar Allan Poe who affirms in "The Philosophy of Composition" that "the death of a beautiful woman is unquestionably the most poetical topic in the world. . . ."

refuge for such a delicate creature was the warmth and safety of her home. . . .

"Women's Rights" meant one thing to reformers, but quite another to the True Woman. She knew her rights,

The right to love whom others scorn,
The right to comfort and to mourn,
The right to shed new joy on earth,
The right to feel the soul's high worth . . .
Such women's rights, and God will bless
And crown their champions with success.[59]

The American woman had her choice—she could define her rights in the way of the women's magazines and insure them by the practice of the requisite virtues, or she could go outside the home, seeking other rewards than love. It was a decision on which, she was told, everything in her world depended. "Yours it is to determine," the Rev. Mr. Stearns solemnly warned from the pulpit, "whether the beautiful order of society . . . shall continue as it has been" or whether "society shall break up and become a chaos of disjointed and unsightly elements."[60] If she chose to listen to other voices than those of her proper mentors, sought other rooms than those of her home, she lost both her happiness and her power—"that almost magic power, which, in her proper sphere, she now wields over the destinies of the world."[61]

But even while the women's magazines and related literature encouraged this ideal of the perfect woman, forces were at work in the nineteenth century which impelled woman herself to change, to play a more creative role in society. The movements for social reform, westward migration, missionary activity, utopian communities, industrialism, the Civil War—all called forth responses from woman which differed from those she was trained to believe were hers by nature and divine decree. The very perfection of True Womanhood, moreover, carried within itself the seeds of its own destruction. For if woman was so very little less than the angels, she should surely take a more active part in running the world, especially since men were making such a hash of things.

Real women often felt they did not live up to the ideal of True Womanhood: some of them blamed themselves, some challenged the standard, some tried to keep the virtues and enlarge the scope of womanhood.[62] Somehow through this mixture of

[59] Mrs. E. Little, "What Are the Rights of Women?," *Ladies' Wreath*, II (1848–1849), 133.
[60] *Female Influence*, p. 18.
[61] Ibid., p. 23.
[62] Even the women reformers were prone to use domestic images, i.e., "sweep Uncle Sam's kitchen clean," and "tidy up our country's house."

challenge and acceptance, of change and continuity, the True Woman evolved into the New Woman—a transformation as startling in its way as the abolition of slavery or the coming of the machine age. And yet the stereotype, the "mystique" if you will, of what woman was and ought to be persisted, bringing guilt and confusion in the midst of opportunity.[63]

The women's magazines and related literature had feared this very dislocation of values and blurring of roles. By careful manipulation and interpretation they sought to convince woman that she had the best of both worlds—power and virtue—and that a stable order of society depended upon her maintaining her traditional place in it. To that end she was identified with everything that was beautiful and holy.

"Who Can Find a Valiant Woman?" was asked frequently from the pulpit and the editorial pages. There was only one place to look for her—at home. Clearly and confidently these authorities proclaimed the True Woman of the nineteenth century to be the Valiant Woman of the Bible, in whom the heart of her husband rejoiced and whose price was above rubies.

[63] The "Animus and Anima" of Jung amounts almost to a catalogue of the nineteenth-century masculine and female traits, and the female hysterics whom Freud saw had much of the same training as the nineteenth-century American woman. Betty Friedan, *The Feminine Mystique* (New York, 1963), challenges the whole concept of True Womanhood as it hampers the "fulfillment" of the twentieth-century woman.

Wendy Martin

SEDUCED AND ABANDONED IN THE NEW WORLD, 1970

The Fallen Woman in American Fiction

Wendy Martin received her Ph.D. in American literature from the University of California in 1968 and teaches at Queens College of the City University of New York. She has written several articles on the early American novel and women in American fiction.

SOURCE
Wendy Martin, "Seduced and Abandoned in the New World: The Fallen Woman in American Fiction," Woman in Sexist Society, *New York, Basic Books, 1971.*

And the Lord God said unto the woman,
What is this that thou has done? And
the woman said, the serpent beguiled me,
and I did eat (Genesis 3:13).

Unto the woman he said, I will greatly multiply
thy sorrow and thy conception; in sorrow thou
shalt bring forth children; and thy desire shall
be to thy husband, and he shall rule over thee
(Genesis 3:16).

Ever since Susanna Rowson wrote *Charlotte Temple*—the first American best-seller—in 1794, heroines of American fiction have reenacted Eve's fall from grace and thereby inherited the legacy of Eden. As daughters of Eve, American heroines are destined to lives of dependency and servitude as well as to painful and sorrowful childbirth because, like their predecessor, they have dared to disregard authority or tradition in the search for wisdom or happiness; like Eve, heroines of American fiction are fallen women, eternally cursed for eating the apple of experience. *Charlotte Temple*, a Richardsonian tale of passion and its penalties, narrates the story of a naive young woman whose lover, Montraville, persuades her to accompany him on a military mission to the United States. Shortly after arriving in New York, he abandons her for a wealthy socialite, whereupon grief-stricken, guilt-ridden Charlotte dies after giving birth to an illegitimate daughter. The American novel has never outgrown the sentimental and sensational plot of its first best-seller, and heroines from Hester Prynne to Catherine Barkley have been condemned to variations of Charlotte's fate.

Because the concept of the fallen woman is central to Christianity, it is not surprising that the fiction of a nation founded by Puritans, who were obsessed with salvation and the scriptures, should reflect this bias. The American novel has inherited the Puritan conviction that life is a continual moral struggle and that man, and especially woman, is a frail creature. Like the Puritan sermon, the eighteenth-century novel attempted to instruct by example, exhorting readers to lead virtuous lives: sermons relied on homily and plain style to bring the message home; the sentimental novel used example and emotion to achieve the same result—the guilt and anguish that Charlotte experiences as a result of her transgressions are the same emotions evoked by Jonathan Edwards' sermon, "Sinners in the

Hands of an Angry God." Thus, the Puritan heritage of the spirit warring with the flesh is evident in American fiction; and, like the sermon, the novel attempts to instruct the audience in the ways of virtue and to illustrate the wages of sin. The archetype of the fallen woman, which is central to Christian, Puritan mythology, is perpetuated in American fiction where women are perceived as morally inferior creatures who, beguiled by their own passions, are destined to tragic lives if they deviate from the laws of God and man.

In addition to reinforcing Puritan morality, American fiction conditions its readers to accept bourgeois economic values which are an outgrowth of Puritan morality as Tawney and Weber demonstrate, by encouraging women to be virtuous so that they can make a good marriage—that is, a financially respectable match. As Ian Watt argues in *The Rise of the Novel*,[1] the moral values of the novel reinforce bourgeois economic reality in which women are totally dependent on marriage for economic survival (the wage for women in the late eighteenth-century was approximately a quarter of a man's wage, and a woman's property automatically became her husband's upon marriage). In this economic system, virtue is a commodity to be sold to the highest bidder, and virginity relinquished before marriage inevitably means that a woman is less marketable and is therefore less likely to survive economically. The virtuous Pamela was rewarded with financial security in marriage; Charlotte Temple would have died of starvation had she not first died in childbirth.

This polarization of economic roles that occurred on a widespread scale in the eighteenth century was accompanied by a polarization of psychological roles that required that women be emotionally passive and weak as well as economically dependent. (The principle that man is the breadwinner and woman the helpmate and homemaker as we have seen, has biblical antecedents.) This myth provides a basis for the economic and social system of industrial society, which requires that men be strong in order to face the harsh world of the competitive marketplace, to be captains of industry, to steer the ship of state, and that women, the weaker sex, withdraw from the rough world for which they are not suited, in order to nurture children and preserve culture within the home. The novel reflects this social definition of woman as a private creature, reinforcing purity, piety, and submissiveness as the proper feminine virtues and punishing those women who fail to comply with a behavior code that is economically viable in addition to being Christian.

Because many of the most important American novels from *Charlotte Temple* to *A Farewell to Arms* define women as essentially passive, dependent creatures who are doomed to tragic

[1] Ian Watt, *The Rise of the Novel; Studies in De Foe, Richardson, and Fielding*, Berkeley, University of California Press, 1959.

lives if they deviate from convention, an analysis of the numerous ways in which some of these novels perpetuate the archetype of the fallen woman, thereby conditioning women to accept their inferior status, reveals the extent to which a myth can influence behavior long after widespread belief in the formal religious or economic mythology that gave rise to it has ceased to exist. In addition, such an analysis reveals the ways in which fiction not only reflects and expresses social values but transmits them to future generations. A thorough understanding of this conditioning process as it occurs in the American novel—a conditioning process that in turn represents an aspect of larger cultural conditioning—is necessary in order to sensitize readers to the often subtle but pervasive negative influence of destructive archetypes.

Hester Prynne in Nathaniel Hawthorne's *The Scarlet Letter* (1850)[2] is one of the better known heiresses of Eve's legacy.

Doomed to wear the scarlet A—the sign of adultery—Hester's fall from grace is underscored by her loss of beauty: "All the light and graceful foliage of her character had been withered up by this red hot brand, and had long ago fallen away, leaving a bare and harsh outline which might have been repulsive, had she possessed friends or companions to be repelled by it." Her diminished beauty is a source of yet greater pain when it is finally revealed as existing, stifled beneath the burden of her cruel public punishment. Flinging away the scarlet letter, she is suddenly free and her luxurious beauty and vitality are again revealed.

The stigma gone, Hester heaved a long, deep sigh, in which the burden of shame and anguish departed from her spirit. O exquisite relief! She had not known the weight until she felt the freedom! By another impulse, she took off the formal cap that confined her hair; and down it fell upon her shoulders, dark and rich, with at once a shadow and a light in its abundance, and imparting the charm of softness to her features. There played around her mouth and beamed out of her eyes a radiant and tender smile, that seemed gushing from the very heart of womanhood. A crimson flush was glowing on her cheek, that had been long so pale. Her sex, her youth, and the whole richness of her beauty, came back from what men call the irrevocable past, and clustered themselves, with her maiden hope and a happiness before unknown, within the magic circle of this hour.

However, her efforts to free herself are useless and she must forfeit her sexuality; she must gather up "the heavy tresses of her hair, confined them beneath her cap . . . her beauty, the warmth and richness of her womanhood departed."

Hawthorne reminds his readers that independent thought and emotion, that is, self-reliance, can be dangerous for women: he

[2] Nathaniel Hawthorne, *The Scarlet Letter*, New York, New American Library, 1959.

tells us that the scarlet letter had been "her passport into regions where other women dared not tread. Shame, Despair, Solitude! These had been her teachers—stern and wild ones—and they had made her strong, but taught her much amiss." This is an ironic observation in view of the fact that self-reliance is an American virtue, and male protagonists in American fiction are praised for their courage in breaking out of the confines of traditional society. Hester, however, does harsh penance for her moment of passion and demonstrates her piety by spending the rest of her days comforting and counselling women "in the continuing trials of wounded, wronged, misplaced or erring and sinful passion." Hawthorne further undermines Hester's position by concluding that "no mission of divine and mysterious truth should be confided to a woman stained with sin, bowed down with shame, or even burdened with lifelong sorrow. The angel and apostle of the coming revelation must be a woman, indeed, but lofty, pure, and beautiful; and wise, moreover, not through dusky grief, but the ethereal medium of joy." Yet, the questioning reader remembers the dramatic scene in the woods in which Hester flings the scarlet letter away and lets down her hair; he cannot help wondering what authorial perversity prevents Hester from being the prophetess of "a whole relation between man and woman on a surer ground of mutual happiness." Why must she bear the burden of such a complicated set of spiritual values that she is ultimately denied her human portion of understanding and generosity?

The Blithedale Romance[3] is Hawthorne's secular version of The Scarlet Letter. A study of the activities of a commune similar to Brook Farm, the novel portrays two women, Zenobia and Priscilla, who represent passion and piety, respectively: Zenobia, named after a queen who ruled Palmyra between 267 and 273 A.D., is stately and commanding; Priscilla, passive and pristine as her name suggests, is a "delicate instrument" with nerves like "fragile harp strings." Many critics think Zenobia is based on Margaret Fuller, who was associated with Brook Farm and who knew Hawthorne; like Margaret Fuller, Zenobia is a champion of women's rights, and she asks the narrator, Coverdale:

Did you ever see a happy woman in your life? Of course, I do not mean a girl, like Priscilla, and a thousand others,—for they are all alike, while on the sunny side of experience,—but a grown woman. How can she be happy, after discovering that fate has assigned her but one single event, which she must contrive to make the substance of her whole life? A man has his choice of innumerable events.

Hawthorne's descriptions of Zenobia's opulent beauty resemble his description of Hester in the woods—like Hester,

[3] Nathaniel Hawthorne, The Blithedale Romance, New York, Norton, 1958.

Zenobia is depicted as being warm, generous, and, above all, passionate:

Zenobia has a rich, though varying color. It was, most of the while, a flame, and anon a sudden paleness. Her eyes glowed, so that their light sometimes flashed upward to me, as when the sun throws a dazzle from some bright object on the ground. Her gestures were free and strikingly impressive. The whole woman was alive with a passionate intensity, which I now perceived to be the phase in which her beauty culminated. Any passion would have become her well; and passionate love, perhaps, the best of all.

... her beauty was set off by all that dress and ornament could do for it. And they did much. Not, indeed, that they created or added anything to what Nature had lavishly done for Zenobia. But, those costly robes which she had on, those flaming jewels around her neck, served as lamps to display the personal advantages which required nothing less than such an illumination to be fully seen.

Ironically, instead of recognizing her own strength and beauty, Zenobia submits to Hollingsworth's egotism and capitulates to his very traditional definition of woman as man's subordinate:

She is the most admirable handiwork of God, in her true place and character. Her place is at man's side. Her office, that of sympathizer, the unreserved, unquestioning believer; the recognition, withheld in every other manner, but given, in pity, through woman's heart, lest man should utterly lose faith in himself. . . . All the separate action of woman is, and ever has been, and always shall be, false, foolish, vain, destructive of her own best and holiest qualities, void of every good effect, and productive of intolerable mischiefs! Man is a wretch without woman; but woman is a monster— thank Heaven, an almost impossible and hitherto imaginary monster—without man as her acknowledged principal! . . . if there was a chance of their attaining the end which these petticoated monstrosities have in view, I would call upon my own sex to use its physical force, the unmistakable evidence of sovereignty, to scourge them back within their proper bounds! But it will not be needful. The heart of true womanhood knows where its own sphere is, and never seeks to stray beyond it.

Coverdale observes that women always acquiesce to man's definition of them and wonders, somewhat patronizingly, if women are innately frail: "Women almost invariably behave thus ... what does the fact mean? Is it their nature? Or is it, at last, the result of ages of compelled degradation? And, in either case, will it be possible to redeem them?" Although Zenobia struggles against Hollingsworth's edict of women's dependency denouncing his egotism, "It's all self! Nothing else; nothing but self, self, self"; she confides her despair and defeat to Coverdale: "In the battlefield of life, the downright stroke, that would only fall on a man's steel head-piece, is sure to light on a woman's heart, over which she wears no breastplate, and whose wisdom it is, therefore, to keep out of the conflict ... the woman who swerves one hair's breadth, . . . that, with that one hair's breadth, she goes all astray, and never sees the world in its true aspect afterwards."

In a moment of self-abasement, Zenobia drowns herself, and Coverdale mourns, "It was a woeful thought, that a woman of Zenobia's diversified capacity should have fancied herself irretrievably defeated on the broad battle-field of life, and with no refuge, save to fall on her own sword, merely because Love had gone against her." Yet, in spite of his railing against the male egotism that confines women to the sphere of emotions defining them as failures if they are not loved, Coverdale reveals his own chauvinism in the concluding sentence of the novel: "I—I myself —was in love—with *Priscilla*"—Priscilla, whom he had described earlier as a "gentle parasite, the soft reflection of a more powerful existence" who sat at Hollingsworth's feet in mute adoration while Zenobia struggled against him for her womanhood and recognition as a human being. In revealing his own preference for the "gentle parasite" Priscilla, Coverdale was perhaps echoing Hawthorne himself, who had strong antifeminist predilections as revealed by his statement in 1855 that "America is now wholly given over to a damn mob of scribbling women, and I should have no chance of success while the public taste is occupied with their trash."

Perhaps the "scribbling women" Hawthorne was referring to were women like Verena Tarrant and Olive Chancellor, the feminist heroines of Henry James's *The Bostonians*,[4] which was published in 1881. Verena, an articulate and passionate public speaker for the cause of women's rights, and Olive, a theoretician of the movement; both vow "to become great not to be obscure, and powerful, in order not to be useless." Convinced that "it is women in the end who had paid for everything," Olive, who is politically more sophisticated than Verena, rejects men as a class; but Verena takes a vow of celibacy, simply to please Olive. It is suggested that Olive has a sexual interest in Verena, but Verena is sexually attracted to Basil Ransom, who insists that "the use of a truly amiable woman is to make some honest man happy"; he despises feminists and paternalistically asserts that they are ineffectual in public life. His statements to Verena reveal his immense hostility to her values:

The whole generation is womanized; the masculine tone is passing out of the world; it's a feminine, a nervous, hysterical, chattering, canting age, an age of hollow phrases and false delicacy and exaggerated solicitudes and coddled sensibilities, which, if we don't look out, will usher in a reign of mediocrity, of the feeblest, flattest and most pretentious that has ever

[4] Henry James, *The Bostonians*, New York, Modern Library, 1956.

been. The masculine character, the ability to dare and endure, to know and yet not fear reality, to look the world in the face and take it for what it is—a very queer and partly very base mixture—that is what I want to preserve, or rather, as I may say, to recover; and I must tell you that I don't in the least care what becomes of you ladies while I make the attempt.

The crisis in the novel occurs when Ransom attempts to convince Verena to give herself to a man rather than a movement, assuring her that "the dining-table itself shall be our platform." Olive entreats Verena to live her own life, devoting herself to the cause of women's rights rather than sitting at the feet of Ransom thereby providing their adversaries "with consummate proof of the fickleness, the futility, the predestined servility of women." Verena despises Ransom's philosophy but confesses with anguish to Olive that she is irresistibly drawn to him; "I like him—I can't help it—I do like him. I don't want to marry him, I don't want to embrace his ideas, which are unspeakably false and horrible; but I like him better than any gentleman I have seen."

In the tug of war between Olive Chancellor and Basil Ransom for Verena's allegiance, Ransom gets the upper hand, forcing the issue minutes before Verena is scheduled to speak on women's rights to a huge Boston audience. Paralyzed and unable to bring herself to address the crowd without Ransom's permission, Verena allows herself to be "wrenched away" by "muscular force" in a scene very much like the one in which Montraville abducts Charlotte Temple. (It is interesting to note the frequent occurrence in fiction of woman who faint at the crucial moment, thereby relinquishing conscious choice or, if they fail to cooperate by swooning, of how often men assert their physical strength over them.) James reveals his own misgivings about Verena's fate by confiding that Ransom cannot fulfill his namesake and redeem Verena: "He presently discovered that with the union, so far from brilliant, into which she was about to enter, those were not the last [tears] she was destined to shed." The conclusion of the novel reveals James' essential sympathy for Verena; yet he places her in a double bind, an either/or situation. Because she has to make a choice between a husband and her ideals, Verena is damned if she does and damned if she doesn't, and in order to cut the Gordian knot, she must sacrifice an important part of herself, giving up her ability to function effectively in the world in order to play a supporting role in Ransom's domestic drama.

Isabel Archer in Henry James's *The Portrait of a Lady* (1881)[5] is a much stronger person than Verena and one of the most interesting and engaging American heroines: Attractive, articulate, and intelligent Isabel reveals her capacity for existential consciousness in her wish to actively shape her life:

[5] Henry James, *The Portrait of a Lady*, New York, New American Library, 1963.

She was intelligent and generous; it was a fine free nature;
but what was she going to do with herself? This question was
irregular, for with most women one had no occasion to ask it.
Most women did with themselves nothing at all; they waited
in attitudes more or less gracefully passive, for a man to
come their way and furnish them with a destiny. Isabel's
originality was that she gave one an impression of having
intentions of her own.

Because she wants to see life for herself, she declines to marry
her two most ardent suitors—Lord Warburton, a kind and gentle
British aristocrat, and Casper Goodwood, a sturdy American
industrialist. Although Isabel insists that she "doesn't want to
begin life by marrying," she admits to herself that she liked
Warburton "too much to marry him, that was the point, something told her that she should not be satisfied, and to inflict
upon a man who offered so much, a tendency to criticize would
be a particularly discreditable act." The reader is told that
Isabel is really "frightened of herself"; yet it is difficult to
imagine the cause of this fear unless she has internalized the
conventional definition of wife and worries that her ego is too
assertive to permit her to be pious, passive, and supportive. On
the one hand, Isabel wishes to choose her fate, to know "something of human affairs beyond what other people think it compatible with propriety to tell me" but, on the other hand, she is
afraid of not being able to meet social expectations, and her
newly inherited fortune simply compounds her fear and guilt:
"I try to care more about the world than about myself—but I
always come back to myself. It is because I am afraid. . . . A large
fortune means freedom, and I am afraid of that. It's such a fine
thing, and one should make such good use of it. If one shouldn't,
one would be ashamed."

Encouraged and manipulated by Madam Merle, Isabel
ignores the advice of her cousin Ralph and marries Gilbert
Osmond, a sterile dilettante whom Isabel mistakes for a man
of sensitivity. Isabel had hoped that her fortune could expand
Osmond's life, but a year after her marriage, she admits to herself that "she had not read him right." Although her life as
Mrs. Osmond is one in which "suffering is an active condition,"
she remains committed to her marriage vow and remains with
her husband in order to care for his daughter Pansy whom she
genuinely loves. Isabel is unwilling or afraid to act for her own
happiness and becomes a martyr in marriage. Ironically, she is
imprisoned by her own sense of duty and no longer dares to live
her own life.

A decade later, Edna Pontellier in Kate Chopin's *The
Awakening*,[6] unlike Isabel, worries less about social convention

[6] Kate Chopin, *The Awakening and Other Stories*, New York, Holt, Rinehart and Winston, 1970.

and more about her own fulfillment. *The Awakening* is the first American novel to focus on the perceptions and experience of a woman who finds that her marriage damages her sense of self —Edna Pontellier's story begins where Isabel's left off. At twenty-eight she has been married for six years to a New Orleans financier and is the mother of two children; in the course of the novel, she is gradually awakened to her "position in the universe as a human being, and to recognize her relations as an individual to the world within her and without her." From her youth, Edna has understood "the dual life—that outward existence which conforms, the inward life which questions"; although she loves her husband and children, she experiences "indescribable oppression, which seemed to generate in some unfamiliar part of her consciousness, filled her being with anguish." The novel captures the flux of Edna's moods as she moves from a stereotyped perception of herself as wife and mother to that of self-aware person. As she becomes less and less repressed, her will asserts itself more strongly; her first act of freedom is minor—she defiantly refuses to comply with her husband's request to come indoors at bedtime; then she fails to meet her social obligations to the wives of her husband's business associates. Later, she begins to keep her own hours, and, finally, she moves into a small house of her own.

Edna's yearning for independence confuses and frightens her at first, but as the novel progresses, she becomes more and more sure of her need for solitude which is reflected by the increasingly frequent appearance of bird and sea imagery, and her stature heightens. Like Zenobia, Edna is characterized by her queenlike magnificence:

The golden shimmer of Edna's satin gown spread in rich folds on either side of her. There was a soft fall of lace encircling her shoulders. It was the color of her skin, without the glow, the myriad living tints that one may sometimes discover in vibrant flesh. There was something in her attitude, in her whole appearance when she leaned her head against the highbacked chair and spread her arms, which suggested the regal woman, the one who rules, who looks on, who stands alone.

Edna's appearance is in direct contrast to the madonnalike Madame Ratingnole with her hair like "spun gold" and eyes "like nothing but sapphires; two lips that pouted, that were so red that one could only think of cherries or some other delicious fruit in looking at them.... Never were hands more exquisite than hers, and it was a joy to look at them when she threaded her needle or sewed away on little night drawers or fashioned a bodice or a bib."

Although Edna feels affection for her children, she asserts, "I would give my life for my children, but I wouldn't give myself." She resents being a victim of nature's "torture" and feels dread while witnessing Madame Ratingnole's labor pains. In spite of Edna's efforts to divest herself of the illusions that nature provides in order to "secure mothers for the race," she feels immeshed by social pressures to meet her obligations as wife and mother. Madame Reiz had told her that "the bird that would soar above the level plain of tradition must have strong wings. It is a sad spectacle to see the weaklings, bruised, exhausted, fluttering back to earth." However, in spite of Edna's yearning for the unconventional life, her wings are really not strong enough for the flight.

Like so many heroines in American fiction, she is not able to bear the rejection of the man she loves: "Dependency had come upon her there in the wakeful night, and had never lifted. There was no one thing in the world that she desired. There was no human being whom she wanted near her except Robert; and she even realized that the day would come when he, too, and the thought of him would melt out of her existence, leaving her alone. The children appeared before her like antagonists who had overcome her, who had overpowered and sought to drag her into the soul's slavery for the rest of her days." Just before Edna drowns herself, she sees a bird with a "broken wing beating the air above, reeling, fluttering, circling disabled down, down to the water." Perhaps Edna is foolish to look for freedom in solitude, but, after all, solitude is the essential basis for the profound American belief in self-reliance. In any case, the significance of the novel lies in its depiction of Edna's desire to free herself from biological determinants—a necessary prerequisite to becoming a whole person rather than an extension of nature.

Edith Wharton's *The Age of Innocence* (1920)[7] has both a dark and a fair heroine but this time the protagonist, Newland Archer, prefers the exotic Ellen Olenska to his compliant, fair wife May. May is described as having the "vacant serenity of a young marble athlete," while Ellen looks very much like Zenobia or Edna Pontellier: "[she] sat half-reclined, her head propped on a hand and her wide sleeve leaving the arm bare to the elbow . . . heedless of tradition, [she] was attired in a long robe of red velvet bordered about the chin and down the front with glossy black fur."

Although his marriage to May is proclaimed "the most brilliant of the year," Archer feels himself sinking into a black abyss; he feels claustrophobic, "as though he were being buried alive by the future." Because he knows that May will never surprise him "by an unexpected mood, by a weakness, a cruelty, or an emotion," he cannot avoid feeling that he has missed "the flower of life." However, like Isabel Archer, he resigns himself to honoring his marriage commitment: "It did not matter so much if marriage was a dull duty: lapsing from that, it became a

[7] Edith Wharton, *The Age of Innocence*, New York, New American Library, 1962.

battle of ugly appetites." Interestingly, Newland Archer, one of the few male protagonists in American fiction who appreciates women who are people rather than extensions of his ego, is a creation of a woman novelist; although Archer is a somewhat atypical protagonist, his appreciation and concern for Ellen Olenska reveal the other possible dimensions in human relationships than those designated by breadwinner, homemaker recipe.

Although it is obvious that human relationships are complex, and Edith Wharton's novel reveals that men as well as women suffer from thwarted love, the happiness of American heroines is sacrificed more readily than that of their male counterparts. In order to meet the demands of a conventional marriage, most women must submerge their individual identities; Newland Archer may feel that he has "missed the flower of life," but he has not lost his sense of self—his ego survives and his place in society is not questioned. Ellen Olenska, however, has a very uncertain future; she depends on family and friends for support, and it is clear that she will never have the financial, social, or professional freedom that Newland Archer has.

In Willa Cather's *My Mortal Enemy*,[8] Myra Henshawe gives up an inheritance in order to marry for love. Myra is as dramatically beautiful as the women who precede her in the gallery of dark American heroines:

Her deep-set, flashing grey eyes seemed to be taking me in altogether—estimating me. For all that, she was no taller than I, I felt quite overpowered by her—and stupid; hopelessly clumsy and stupid. Her black hair was done high on her head, a la Pompadour, and there were curious zigzag, curly streaks of glistening white in it, which made it look like the fleece of a Persian goat or some animal that bore silky fur. I could not meet the playful curiosity of her eyes at all, so I fastened my gaze upon a necklace of carved amethysts she wore inside the square-cut neck of her dress.

In spite of her romantic disposition, Myra confides to the narrator, Nellie, that her marriage has not really been satisfying, that she has had to relinquish so many of her own needs—a sacrifice she regretted bitterly:

People can be lovers and enemies at the same time, you know. We were . . . A man and a woman draw apart from that long embrace, and see what they have done to each other. Perhaps I can't forgive him for the harm I did him. Perhaps that's it. When there are children, that feeling goes through natural changes. But when it remains so personal . . . something gives way in one. In age we lose everything, even the power to love.

Convinced that she has permitted her romantic illusions to rob her of self-hood, Myra cries, "Why must I die like this, alone with my mortal enemy?" Her cry is sufficiently ambiguous so that the reader does not know if she considers her mortal enemy

8 Willa Cather, *My Mortal Enemy*, New York, Random House, 1956.

to be her husband or herself. The ambiguity is interesting, because she made the decision to marry and is therefore responsible for the erosion of self she has experienced in marriage. Myra Henshawe is very much like Edna Pontellier—dissatisfied with the limitations of her married life but without sufficient conviction and strength to create an alternative life for herself.

In *Love and Death in the American Novel*,[9] Leslie Fiedler observes that the American heroine is bifurcated into the "Fair Virgin and Dark Lady," that is, into the good blonde girl and the evil dark woman. According to Fiedler, the male protagonist in American fiction is essentially antisexual; the dark heroines in American fiction represent authorial masturbatory fantasies and must be destroyed because they are too threatening. The Priscilla–Zenobia, Olive–Verena, Edna Pontellier–Madame Ratingnole, and Ellen Olenska–May Welland rivalries corroborate Fiedler's perception of the schizophrenic split between good and evil or passion and frigidity in American literature. This duality also reveals the Puritan bias in our literature characterized by the need to *punish* women for original sin as well as the imperative to reward those women who are content to be subservient to men's needs. This need indicates that the dual image of goddess and temptress manifests man's terrible fear of his own sexuality—in the shadow of this image most women have lived out their lives.

Some of the most widely read novels of the twentieth century, such as *A Farewell to Arms* and *An American Dream*, reveal that the stigma of original sin still taints American heroines. *A Farewell to Arms* (1929)[10] is a contemporary reenactment of Eden. Catherine Barkley is the subservient, compliant companion par excellence. As nurse-mistress to Frederic Henry, she is passive femininity incarnate; when they make love, she obsessively asks, "I'm good, aren't I good . . . I do what you want." Henry feels that the relationship is blissful, and it should be for him because there is only one ego—his. "Oh, darling, I want you so much I want to be you too," Catherine says. "You are," Henry responds, "we're the same one." Although Catherine cleaves to Frederic, ironically she still cannot escape pain and destruction: She experiences intense agony in labor and, like Charlotte Temple, dies in childbirth. The labor room scene, depicting the consequences of God's wrath on adulteresses, could be right out of a Puritan sermon. Catherine's pain is horrifying, and the pitiful moralizing of Frederic Henry does not diminish its terror: "Poor, poor dear Cat. And this was the price you paid for sleeping together." While Henry mouths platitudes, Catherine

---

[9] Leslie A. Fiedler, *Love and Death in the American Novel*, New York, Dell, 1966.
[10] Ernest Hemingway, *A Farewell to Arms*, New York, Scribner, 1957.

screams in agony because the gas is no longer sufficient to subdue the pain:

"I'm just a fool, darling," Catherine said. "But it [the gas] doesn't work anymore." She began to cry. "Oh, I wanted so much to have this baby and not make trouble, and now I'm all done and gone to pieces and it doesn't work. Oh, darling, it doesn't work at all. I don't care if only it will stop. There it comes. Oh Oh Oh!" She breathed sobbingly into the mask. "It doesn't work. It doesn't work. It doesn't work. Don't mind me, darling."

Catherine dies, thereby expiating their sin, and Henry, with a stiff upper lip, leaves the hospital and walks back to the hotel in the rain.

In Norman Mailer's *An American Dream* (1965)[11] Stephen Richards Rojack echos Frederic Henry's manly fortitude when he says, "If one wished to be a lover, one could not find one's sanity in another, that was the iron law of romance: one took the vow to be brave." Obviously, this is one lesson American heroines have never learned. However, it appears that Rojack has not really learned it either; he makes such statements as, "Women must murder us unless we possess them altogether," and then proceeds to murder his wife because he feels possessed by her. Sex is a battle for Rojack in which wills meet "locked in an exchange of stares which goes on and on." Rojack decides he loves the nightclub singer Cherry and prays for a romantic idyll much like that of Catherine and Frederic: "Let me love that girl, and become a father and try to be a good man," but because his courage fails him, she is killed as retribution for his cowardice and egotism. Again, the grief-stricken hero leaves, but this time he valiantly heads for Yucatán instead of resolutely returning to the hotel as Frederic Henry does.

Perhaps the woman who comes closest to taking Rojack's vow of courage is the narrator of Mary McCarthy's *The Company She Keeps* (1942)[12]—a brilliant novel that has received little critical attention to date. This novel chronicles a twentieth-century woman's attempts to resist biblical strictures and to attain self-hood on her own terms. It begins with her divorce, which she regards ironically and self-deprecatingly; nevertheless, it permits her to begin to take responsibility for her own life. To prove her social emancipation, she becomes sexually aggressive but nevertheless worries about becoming a spinster; she experiences a strange combination of timidity and defiance and is alternately predatory and victimized. Her favorite quotation is from Chaucer's *Criseyde*: "I am my owene woman, wel at ese." Although she is sexually liberated, she continues to be psychologically enslaved because she persists in looking for her identity in a man. She remarries, this time to a successful architect, but

[11] Norman Mailer, *An American Dream*, New York, Dell, 1965.
[12] Mary McCarthy, *The Company She Keeps*, New York, Harcourt Brace Jovanovich, 1942.

the marriage does not create self-hood. Finally, with an analyst's help, she begins to make the transition from dependency to self-hood, realizing that *she* is her greatest enemy and that her failures are because of insufficient self-love to which both her childhood and cultural conditioning contribute:

Now for the first time she saw her own extremity, saw that it
was some failure in self-love that obliged her to snatch blindly
at love of others, hoping to love herself through them,
borrowing their feelings, as the moon borrowed light. She
herself was a dead planet.

Yet this new knowledge frightens her (her fear is not surprising—this is the first perception of its kind to be made by a woman in American fiction); she wonders and perhaps even hopes that it is a therapeutic lie: "There was no use talking. *She knew*. Only a man . . . she was under a terrible enchantment, like the beleagured princesses in the fairy tales." In spite of the emotional red herring with which she tries to distract herself, she realizes that no man can ever create self-love; she must do that for herself. The novel concludes somewhat ironically because her prayer for continued insight, "O di reddite me hoc pro pietate mea," is belied by the fact that she does not believe in God. The novel reveals our culture's dire need for a new mythology for women, and although, as Freud has demonstrated, psychoanalysis is often as confining as Christianity, it has at least made us aware of the extent of psychic damage resulting from a failure of self-love. It is important, however, to realize that insufficient self-love continues to be the norm by which our culture measures adjustment for women, and self-abnegation is considered to be a form of feminine maturity.

The problem of self-doubt still plagues the American heroine; unfortunately, not much progress has been made since *The Company She Keeps*. As has been pointed out, major social and economic changes will have to take place before improvements in the female psyche can occur. But fiction can contribute to changing female consciousness and men's concept of women by providing a vision of a new Eve, of a woman who is self-actualizing, strong, risk-taking, and independent but also capable of loving and being loved. Women like this have existed in real life—consider Anne Bradstreet, Elizabeth Cady Stanton, Margaret Fuller, Frances Wright, Amelia Bloomer, Amelia Earhart. Why have our novelists persisted in ignoring these examples of strong women, reinforcing instead the image of women as forlorn, helpless creatures, who are certain to be destroyed or hopelessly embittered unless they devote themselves exclusively to their domestic lives and duties as wives and mothers? Why have novelists persisted (consciously or unconsciously) in perpetuating the tradition of the fallen woman, consistently punishing her for her frailty? Why have novelists insisted that heroines can redeem themselves only if they forgo sexuality? Furthermore, why have women internalized cultural concepts of themselves, defining them as inferior or potentially evil creatures when their own experience often tells them otherwise? These questions are not easy to answer, but it is time to attempt to reverse the effects of the centuries of conditioning that have reinforced the biblical perception of women as fallen creatures who must do penance for original sin. Unfortunately, most women as well as most men, unquestionably accept this myth that renders one-half of the race less than human. Sacrificing the humanity of slightly more than fifty percent of the species is a pretty high price to pay for eating an apple—and it was probably a rotten apple at that.

Florence Howe

THE EDUCATION OF WOMEN, 1970

*Florence Howe has taught at Goucher for several years and is
presently teaching at the State University of New York at Old
Westbury. In addition to writing many articles on the education
of women, she has taught in the Freedom Schools in Mississippi
and in the Upward Bound Program. She has been active in
Resist and the New University Conference and has coauthored*
The Conspiracy of the Young *with her husband, Paul Lauter.
In 1970, Florence was elected vice president of the Modern
Language Association—the professional association of college
and university language and literature teachers, and she also
serves that association as chairwoman of the Commission of
the Place of Women in the Profession.*

SOURCE
Florence Howe, "The Education of Women," Liberation, *August–
September 1969, pp. 49–55.
Portrait: United Press International.*

Recently, on a train, a Goucher College student met the editor of a relatively new magazine. "Why don't we get your magazine?" she queried.

"Isn't Goucher a girls' school?"

"Sure, but what's that got to do with it?"

"Well, we didn't think you'd be interested—it's about careers."

This is a perfectly commonplace attitude. Even in 1969, it is assumed that women who go to college are generally sitting out four years of their lives before becoming wives and mothers. During my nine years at Goucher, I have found little encouragement for any other view. Unfortunately, statistics bear me out only too well. Though more women than ever before go to college, and even receive degrees, fewer proportionately go on to graduate school. The faculties of colleges and universities naturally reflect this condition: there are fewer women on the faculties of women's colleges than there were in the 30's; the percentage of women on the faculty of the University of Chicago has dropped from 8 per cent at the end of the nineteenth century to a recent low of 2 per cent; and a number of university departments are searching currently for their token female. And as studies continue to show, when men and women of comparable education and experience are employed, women's salaries and rates of promotion are significantly inferior to men's. In spite of a century of sporadic hue and cry about women's rights, and in spite of our rhetoric about the equality of women, even in spite of the pill and the recent outburst of women's liberation groups, women remain a passive majority of second class citizens.

Our education is chiefly to blame, but of course after one has said that, one must add at once that education reflects the values of our society and is to a major extent controlled by those values. That is to say that we do not think of our girl students as we do our boys—and this is true from the beginning of their school years as well as on to graduate school where women are openly discriminated against for reasons which I do not here need to list. What would happen to men if women were, indeed, allowed to compete in a system equally open to them? This is, of course, a rhetorical question, since it is not likely to happen. We do know that white men, in our culture, are by and large loath to compete with black men, and our friends tell us that women will have to wait until those male racial and economic problems are solved.

Economic and political problems cannot, obviously, be solved by educational institutions. But colleges can educate their students quite deliberately to those problems, and even, if they will, to work towards their solution. Generally speaking, the purpose of those responsible for the education of women has been to perpetuate their subordinate status. There is a hoary story still being told about the difference between educating men and women. It goes like this: "When you educate a man, you educate an individual, but when you educate a woman, you educate a family." Obviously, the story is meant to compliment women as traditional carriers of culture. But more to the point is the role that woman is channelled into by her culture. The question of purpose in education is dependent upon a prior notion of hierarchy. Put another way, education is prophecy fulfilled: imagine women educated for a push-button household and a consumer's life and you create institutions to effect that. To illustrate, I want to look at the views of five men—I choose men because for the most part they have been responsible for our history and our education.

First, Plato and Aristotle, who illustrate two poles: the revolutionary believer in equality between the sexes and the conservative believer in the inferiority of women. Plato, as revolutionary, writes in the *Republic* that, "There is no occupation concerned with the management of social affairs which belongs either to woman or to man, as such. Natural gifts are to be found here and there in both creatures alike; and every occupation is open to both, so far as their natures are concerned." He concludes, therefore, that "we shall not have one education for men and another for women, precisely because the nature to be taken in hand is the same." When he describes roles for women, he allows them "their full share with men" in all areas of life, "whether they stay at home or go out to war." He continues, "Such conduct will not be unwomanly, but all for the best and in accordance with the natural partnership of the sexes." Obviously, Plato's notions have not only not prevailed; they are hardly known today.

To read Aristotle on the same subject is to learn how little a student may learn from a teacher. For to the question "why educate women?" Aristotle would have answered, "Certainly not." This is his key statement, from the *Politics*: "We may thus conclude that it is a general law that there should be naturally ruling elements and elements naturally ruled. . . . The rule of the freeman over the slave is one kind of rule; that of the male over the female another. . . . The slave is entirely without the faculty of deliberation; the female indeed possesses it, but in a form which remains inconclusive. . . . It is thus clear that while moral goodness is a quality of all the persons mentioned, the fact still remains that temperance—and similarly fortitude and justice— are not, as Socrates held, the same in a woman as they are in a man." Aristotle thus offers no education to women. Or if we think of her in a category close to the slave's, only such education as will make her more useful to man, her master. The defining of capability—or "role definition"—controls education. And Aristotle's voice has prevailed. He and the early Church fathers settled the non-education of women for nearly two thousand years.

Milton's is a useful voice to illustrate the perpetuation of woman's subordinate status in a form somewhat more subtle than Aristotle's. In fact, Milton is my favorite example of such a view, one that I find still dominant today. To Goucher students, I usually say, study him closely: he is the enemy. You must understand your enemy if you are to defeat him. Women are teachable, Milton says, though just barely and only under careful conditions. Certainly, they need to be observed and looked after constantly or trouble may follow, as it did for Eve in the garden. But the order is plain enough: God teaches man and man teaches woman, just a bit of this or that, enough to keep her in her place. Milton's main idea is hierarchy: woman is subordinate in status, inferior in intellect, and even less reliable than man in matters of the heart.

In matters of the heart, Jonathan Swift has argued, either sex might claim distinction—for foolishness and corruption. "I am ignorant of any one quality," he writes in "A Letter to a Young Lady on her Marriage," "that is amiable in a Man, which is not equally so in a Woman; I do not except Modesty and Gentleness of Nature. Nor do I know one Vice or Folly which is not equally detestable in both." If women are more full of "nonsense and frippery" than men, their parents are to blame for failing "to cultivate" their minds. "It is a little hard," Swift continues, "that one Gentleman's daughter in a thousand should be brought to read or understand her own natural Tongue, or be judge of the easiest Books that are written in it. . . ." Swift's remedy is to offer himself as tutor for the young lady in question; in *Gulliver's Travels*, he recommends education for both sexes.

When I asked my students what they thought of Swift— expecting at least some delight or surprise at his modernity—one sophomore said, "Why, he's insulting. I didn't like him at all." She added that his attitude was patronizing and demeaning: "He doesn't care anything about the girl. All he cares about is that she please her husband. That's why he wants her to be able to read. So that she can carry on a conversation with him."

Marianne's sharp disgust surprised me and some of the other students present, one of whom commented gently and slightly in wonderment: "But that's just why I'm going to college and taking English courses. My boy friend is at college and I think that I should be able to keep up to his interests and his friends. You know, I want to know what he's talking and thinking about."

Both students had in mind a passage in which Swift offers his young lady a rationale for the education of her intellect: "to acquire or preserve the Friendship and Esteem of a Wise Man, who soon grows weary of acting the Lover and treating his Wife like a Mistress, but wants a reasonable Companion, and a true Friend through every Stage of his Life. It must be therefore your Business to qualify yourself for those Offices." That is, to function interestingly for one's husband—or children. The question of self or vocation is entirely absent, as it is from the concerns of the majority of women in college today.

About a hundred years after Swift wrote his essay, Harriet Taylor and John Stuart Mill began a long and complex intellectual relationship, one of the results of which was a book that Mill published in 1869 called *The Subjection of Women*. Like Swift, Mill believed that sexual differences do not entirely, if at all, control the intellect. Women are not a separate and lesser species but, as Mill put it, they are a separate class or caste, created and controlled by men through a process of socialization that includes depriving women of education.

I want to quote from Mill's book at some length because I think it is still the best single piece of analysis and because it is his only significant work not available in paperback. First, his argument about the alleged inferiority of woman's "nature": "Standing on the ground of common sense, and the constitution of the human mind, I deny that anyone knows, or can know, the nature of the two sexes, as long as they have only been seen in their present relation to one another. If man had ever been found in society without women, or women without men, or if there had been a society of men and women in which the women were not under the control of the men, something might have been positively known about the mental and moral differences which may be inherent in the nature of each. What is now called the nature of women is an eminently artificial thing—the result of forced repression in some directions, unnatural stimulation in others. It may be asserted without scruple, that no other class of dependents have had their character so entirely distorted from its natural proportions by their relation with their masters. . . ."

Women's relations with their "masters," according to Mill, are unique for an "enslaved class," for two reasons: their universality in time and space, their perpetuation seemingly without "force." "The subjection of women to men being a universal custom," Mill begins urbanely, "any departure from it quite naturally appears unnatural." On the other hand, most women accept their state. In fact, "All causes, social and natural, combine to make it unlikely that women should be collectively rebellious to the power of men." Thence follows an analysis by a "master" of the master's point of view: "Women," Mill begins,

are so far in a position different from all other subject classes, that their masters require something more from them than actual service. Men do not want solely the obedience of women, they want their sentiments. All men, except the most brutish, desire to have, in the women most nearly connected with them, not a forced slave but a willing one, not a slave merely, but a favorite. They have therefore put everything in practice to enslave their minds. The masters of all other slaves rely, for maintaining obedience, on fear—either fear of themselves, or religious fears. The masters of women wanted more than simple obedience, and they turned the whole force of education to effect their purpose. All women are brought up from the very earliest years in the belief that their ideal of character is the very opposite to that of men; not self-will and government by self-control, but submission and yielding to the control of others. All the moralities tell them that it is the duty of women, and all the current sentimentalities that it is their nature, to live for others, to make complete abnegation of themselves, and to have no life but in their affections. And by their affections are meant the only ones that they are allowed to have—those to the men with whom they are connected, or to the children who constitute an additional and indefeasible tie between them and a man. When we put together three things—first, the natural attraction between opposite sexes; secondly, the wife's entire dependence on the husband, every privilege or pleasure she has being either his gift, or depending entirely on his will; and lastly, that the principal object of human pursuit, consideration, and all objects of social ambition, can in general be sought or obtained by her only through him, it would be a miracle if the object of being attractive to men had not become the polar star of feminine education and formation of character. And this great means of influence over the minds of women having been acquired, an instinct of selfishness made men avail themselves of it to the utmost as a means of holding women in subjection, by representing to them meekness, submissiveness, and resignation of all individual will into the hands of a man, as an essential part of sexual attractiveness.

Mill concludes this section of his book by summarizing: "In no instance except this, which comprehends half the human race, are the higher social functions closed against anyone by a fatality of birth which no exertions, and no change of circumstances can overcome; for even religious disabilities . . . do not close any career to the disqualified person in case of conversion." The remedies Mill proposes are changes in law and the opening of educational and vocational opportunities to women. His ideal is "freedom of individual choice" regardless of sex: "If the principle is true, we ought to act as if we believed it, and not to ordain that to be born a girl instead of a boy, any more than to be born black instead of white, or a commoner instead of a nobleman, shall decide the person's position through all life—shall interdict people from all the more elevated social positions, and from all, except a few, respectable occupations."

It is a pity to spoil Mill's peroration with a sour note, but he makes, in the end, a nineteenth-century distinction between married and unmarried women. Whatever her talents and inclinations, the married woman ought to stay at home—for practical reasons at least. No housekeeper can replace her with economy and efficiency both. When he pleads for woman's presence in the university and at the bar, Mill is pleading for the unmarried woman alone.

Obviously, in 1969 we do not officially hold to Mill's distinction between married and unmarried women. And yet our suburban style of life institutionalizes Mill's notion of economy: by the time a woman pays for a baby-sitter and a commuter's ticket, she might just as well stay at home. In fact, though our forms may look different, essentials have not been altered for the majority of women since Mill's day. And some beliefs about us harken back to Aristotle and Milton, though now they are part of the unconscious of college-educated females. For example, the basic assumption about women's biological inferiority, dealt what one might have expected to be a death-blow in the 1940's by Simone de Beauvoir, comes to college annually in the heads and hearts of freshmen women.

Four years ago, I began to use as a theme in a freshman writing course "the identity of woman." Some of the corollary reading assigned has included D. H. Lawrence's *Sons and Lovers*, Elizabeth Bowen's *The Death of the Heart*, Doris Lessing's *The Golden Notebook*, Mary McCarthy's *The Group*, Kate Chopin's *The Awakening*, Simone de Beauvoir's *The Second Sex*, a collection of essays entitled *Women in America*, and Ralph Ellison's *Invisible Man*. In every class I have taught, someone has asked, "Why are our books only by women?" or "Why do we have to read mostly women writers—they're always inferior to men." Even in something as simple as athletics, girls have been eager to point out that female swimmers are inevitably inferior to male swimmers. Only once in all the classes I have taught did a student point out that males of some cultures, say Vietnam, may be physically "weaker" than females of another culture, say the Soviet Union or the U.S. And I have typically received lengthy essays "proving" that women must be inferior since in the whole length of recorded history so few have been truly great. At the same time, I should point out that a questionnaire I used did not verify the impression I gained from class discussion and student themes. It was as though the students answered the questionnaire in terms of what was "supposed to be."

The same split occurred with regard to the question of women's social equality. On paper, the students indicated a belief in its existence. In class and on themes, they gave evidence that they lived their lives in the chains Mill described and analyzed. Their dependence on male approval came out particularly in discussions of coeducation, though with varying degrees of openness and consciousness. Close to the surface and freely aired was the question of dressing for boys. It was a relief, students said, to be able to live whole days at Goucher in jeans and no make-up. And they joked about looking very different—sometimes unrecognizably so—when they left the campus for a date or a weekend. Very few students said that they dressed in a particular way to please themselves. Much more difficult to get at was the deeper question of sexual role in the classroom's intellectual life. I have had only a few students able to say, as one did this year, at the beginning of an essay, "Men distract me." In fact, that was why she had come to Goucher. In high school classes, Virginia became aware of her unwillingness to be herself: either she was silly or silent. Here at Goucher, she said, she was able to say what she thought without worry about what boys would think of her. Moreover, she was going to be a lawyer because that was the most "male" occupation she could think of. She wanted to show that she could do what any man could. If she could manage that, then she could be "independent," and that, she said, was a meaningful goal.

Virginia is an exception. Obviously women go to college today in numbers that would boggle Mill's brain. But most come without genuine purpose, or, when they discover purpose, it is in Mill's or Swift's terms. About halfway through one term, my freshmen were talking about the motivation of a character in a story by Doris Lessing. Joan tried to make a point about the complexities of motivation by saying that she had come to Goucher only because her parents had wanted her to go to college and this was as good a place as any and that for nearly a whole term she had been wondering what she was doing here, but now she understood what her purpose might be, not only here but for the rest of her life. The class hung on her words, but she grew suddenly shy of naming her discovery. Finally she said, "Enjoyment. I think that I am here to enjoy not myself but life—and also later on, after I get out of college." Joan was immediately chastized for "selfishness": "The purpose of life," another student said, "is to help other people." Most of the twenty students sitting in the circle proceeded to take sides; a few tried to reconcile the two positions: "helping other people might itself be enjoyable." "If you enjoyed tutoring in Baltimore slums," one girl retorted, "then you weren't doing your job properly." The discussion raged as few classroom discussions do. I said nothing, except at the end when we had to stop for supper. Then I commented that no one had mentioned, in more than an hour, earning money or having an ambition or vocation; no one had talked about the fulfillment of her identity in terms of satisfying and useful work. The girls were not particularly astonished; my terms meant very little to them, at least at that time. The girls who were most numerous and most vocal were those who thought that "service" or "helping people" should be performed for its own sake, because that was morally right, not as an enjoyable act for the individual to perform or for any other reason. This is the woman-slave mentality that Mill was describing a hundred years ago.

It is clear that a social order sends girls to college who are generally unconscious of their position in that society. And on the whole, colleges do very little to sort out the conflicts girls feel. How can they please themselves and please their (future) husbands and/or satisfy the demands of class and society? Their conflicts have grown sharper, more fierce and destructive, since Mill's day. For women a hundred years ago, the problem was to fight for the right to an education or to be allowed to vote. Women have these rights. But in fact a woman is—unless she closes her eyes completely—pulled terrifically in two opposing directions. They are not parallel lines: marriage and career.

On the one hand, she is still playing with dolls, dressing to suit boys, and pretending to be dumb in a co-ed high school class. She is still a continual disappointment to her mama if she returns from college each term without an engagement ring. She wants—and naturally so—to get married and have children. To assume that a career would not conflict with marriage and child-rearing, at least as our present society is arranged, is an error.

On the other hand, her college education assumes that even if she is not going on to a career or graduate school, she should specialize for two years in some particular area of knowledge. The curriculum, moreover, doesn't help her to work out the dual roles she may have to assume, that is, if she is not simply a housewife. It assumes, largely, that the problem doesn't exist. The curriculum is geared to vocation, however narrowly conceived. An English major will send you to graduate schools, for example. But nothing I can think of at Goucher prepared women for marriage or motherhood.

Why do we educate women? Cynically, I might answer, to keep them off the streets. Certainly, we are not thinking of them even as we do think of men—as the future engineers and administrators of a complex bureaucracy. Then why design curricula for women that are remarkably similar to those for men? Why, especially when they and their teachers assume a lesser degree of serious intellectual commitment from female than from male students, even from those avoiding the draft? I have heard a few male professors at women's colleges candidly admit either the "ease" with which it is possible to teach women or the "bore" it is. And women like me fret about the "passivity" of our students. But mostly we do little to promote a reawakening or an altering of students' or faculty's consciousness. "There, there," one professor was overheard saying to a weeping freshman, "don't cry about that paper. In a few years, you'll be washing dishes and you won't even remember this course."

I have spent a lot of time on the purpose of education because I think that we must be conscious of our motives. Are we, as one student put it recently, educating girls to become "critical housewives"? I for one am not, not at least any more than Hopkins' professors are educating "critical husbands." We can do better than that for our students and I think we should.

Women and men both need work lives and private relationships. Women need to be educated for consciousness about themselves as members of a society they can learn to change. Even if women are to spend some years of their lives at home with small children part or all of the day, these are few years when compared to a lifetime. Without what I call a "work-identity," moreover, women, their families, and society generally lose a great deal.

But now I want to turn to the means: what can colleges do for the education of women? I am not speaking simply of women's colleges, for even if we were to inaugurate instant co-education, the problems would remain the same. If we consider the candor with which some administrators of hitherto male colleges have discussed the function of incoming female students, in fact, the problems may multiply. As one dean put it to me, "The girls will keep our men on campus weekends." The three programmatic suggestions that follow are aimed at coeducational institutions as well as women's colleges. The first two are curricular in nature.

1. The most traditional approach is to recruit women to programs hitherto open chiefly to men (e.g., architecture, engineering, international relations) or to create new institutions to train women professionally in those careers. For example, a woman's college might add to its campus a school of architecture that gives graduate degrees. By and large, this is the way that the education of women has proceeded in the past, though women have been channeled into nursing, teaching, social work, rather than allegedly "male" careers. I do not wish to disparage this procedure—obviously it is useful that it continue—but by itself it can do little more than to open doors for handfuls of individual women, leaving the bulk of their sisters behind. Philosophically, moreover, it does nothing more than to say, see, women can be architects, if you, the male world, will allow them to be. We know that already.

2. The second approach is one that has come historically out of the civil rights movement, and recently out of an analogy to black and third world studies programs: the development of *consciousness* about the psychology and sociology of sexual differentiation in western and other societies. A freshman study program that combines literature, sociology, psychology, and history, would usefully introduce the subject to students; interdepartmental women's studies programs may be devised or particular courses (e.g. in the history or sociology of women) be added to existing departmental offerings. I value this curricular direction because it calls not for competition with men but for the growth of understanding by both men and women about how society is arranged. Such understanding is essential to intelligent action for social change as opposed to individual advancement.

3. The third suggestion would commit the institution to educate the rest of its members. That is, the administration of a

college, the procedures and literature of its admissions or vocational placement offices, for example, ought to reflect a conscious militancy about the education of women. The education of faculty members and administrators, male and female together, would support and promote the curricular program suggested for students. Such a program would not be easy to arrange. It is difficult, in reality, for men to see women as their replacements. And women who have come up through the usual channels of individual competition with men may not readily understand the need to reexamine their perceptions about sexual differentiation.

Needless to say, instituting a series of programs at one or even several colleges can hardly correct a condition that is fundamental to our society. But colleges can raise consciousness and offer students some tools with which to solve problems as well as the optimism necessary for any political solution.

Matina Horner

A BRIGHT WOMAN IS CAUGHT IN A DOUBLE BIND, 1969

Matina Horner teaches psychology at Harvard University. She is married to a physicist and has three children.

SOURCE
Matina Horner, "A Bright Woman Is Caught in a Double Bind,"
Psychology Today, *November 1969, pp. 36, 38, 69.*

Consider Phil, a bright young college sophomore. He has
always done well in school, he is in the honors program, he
has wanted to be a doctor as long as he can remember. We ask
him to tell us a story based on one clue: *"After first-term finals,
John finds himself at the top of his medical-school class."* Phil
writes:

John is a conscientious young man who worked hard. He is
pleased with himself. John has always wanted to go into
medicine and is very dedicated . . . John continues working
hard and eventually graduates at the top of his class.

Now consider Monica, another honors student. She too has
always done well and she too has visions of a flourishing career.
We give her the same clue, but with "Anne" as the successful
student—*after first-time finals, Anne finds herself at the top of
her medical-school class.* Instead of identifying with Anne's
triumph, Monica tells a bizarre tale:

Anne starts proclaiming her surprise and joy. Her fellow
classmates are so disgusted with her behavior that they jump
on her in a body and beat her. She is maimed for life.

Next we ask Monica and Phil to work on a series of achievement tests by themselves. Monica scores higher than Phil.
Finally we get them together, competing against each other on
the same kind of tests. Phil performs magnificently, but Monica
dissolves into a bundle of nerves.

The glaring contrast between the two stories and the dramatic changes in performance in competitive situations illustrate
important differences between men and women in reacting to
achievement.

In 1953, David McClelland, John Atkinson and colleagues
published the first major work on the "achievement motive."
Through the use of the Thematic Apperception Test (TAT), they
were able to isolate the psychological characteristic of a *need
to achieve.* This seemed to be an internalized standard of excellence, motivating the individual to do well in any achievement-
oriented situation involving intelligence and leadership ability.

Subsequent investigators studied innumerable facets of achievement motivation: how it is instilled in children, how it is expressed, how it relates to social class, even how it is connected to the rise and fall of civilizations. The result of all this research is an impressive and a theoretically consistent body of data about the achievement motive—in men.

Women, however, are conspicuously absent from almost all of the studies. In the few cases where the ladies were included, the results were contradictory or confusing. So women were eventually left out altogether. The predominantly male researchers apparently decided, as Freud had before them, that the only way to understand woman was to turn to the poets. Atkinson's 1958 book, *Motives in Fantasy, Action and Society*, is an 800-page compilation of all of the theories and facts on achievement motivation in men. Women got a footnote, reflecting the state of the science.

To help remedy this lopsided state of affairs, I undertook to explore the basis for sex differences in achievement motivation. But where to begin?

My first clue came from the one consistent finding on the women: they get higher test-anxiety scores than do the men. Eleanor Maccoby has suggested that the girl who is motivated to achieve is defying conventions of what girls "should" do. As a result, the intellectual woman pays a price in anxiety. Margaret Mead concurs, noting that intense intellectual striving can be viewed as "competitively aggressive behavior." And of course Freud thought that the whole essence of femininity lay in repressing aggressiveness (and hence intellectuality).

Thus consciously or unconsciously the girl equates intellectual achievement with loss of femininity. A bright woman is caught in a double bind. In testing and other achievement-oriented situations she worries not only about failure, but also about success. If she fails, she is not living up to her own standards of performance; if she succeeds she is not living up to societal expectations about the female role. Men in our society do not experience this kind of ambivalence, because they are not only permitted but actively encouraged to do well.

For women, then, the desire to achieve is often contaminated by what I call the *motive to avoid success*. I define it as the fear that success in competitive achievement situations will lead to negative consequences, such as unpopularity and loss of femininity. This motive, like the achievement motive itself, is a stable disposition within the person, acquired early in life along with other sex-role standards. When fear of success conflicts with a desire to be successful, the result is an inhibition of achievement motivation.

I began my study with several hypotheses about the motive to avoid success:

1. Of course, it would be far more characteristic of women than of men.

2. It would be more characteristic of women who are capable of success and who are career-oriented than of women not so motivated. Women who are not seeking success should not, after all, be threatened by it.

3. I anticipated that the anxiety over success would be greater in competitive situations (when one's intellectual performance is evaluated against someone else's) than in noncompetitive ones (when one works alone). The aggressive, masculine aspects of achievement are certainly more pronounced in competitive settings, particularly when the opponent is male. Women's anxiety should therefore be greatest when they compete with men.

I administered the standard TAT achievement motivation measures to a sample of 90 girls and 88 boys, all undergraduates at the University of Michigan. In addition, I asked each to tell a story based on the clue described before: *After first-term finals, John (Anne) finds himself (herself) at the top of his (her) medical-school class.* The girls wrote about Anne, the boys about John.

Their stories were scored for "motive to avoid success" if they expressed any negative imagery that reflected concern about doing well. Generally, such imagery fell into three categories:

1. The most frequent Anne story reflected strong fears of social rejection as a result of success. The girls in this group showed anxiety about becoming unpopular, unmarriageable and lonely.

Anne is an acne-faced bookworm. She runs to the bulletin board and finds she's at the top. As usual she smarts off. A chorus of groans is the rest of the class's reply. . . . She studies 12 hours a day, and lives at home to save money. "Well it certainly paid off. All the Friday and Saturday nights without dates, fun—I'll be the best woman doctor alive." And yet a twinge of sadness comes thru—she wonders what she really has. . . .

Although Anne is happy with her success she fears what will happen to her social life. The male med. students don't seem to think very highly of a female who has beaten them in their field . . . She will be a proud and successful but alas a very *lonely* doctor.

Anne doesn't want to be number one in her class . . . she feels she shouldn't rank so high because of social reasons. She drops down to ninth in the class and then marries the boy who graduates number one.

Anne is pretty darn proud of herself, but everyone hates and envies her.

2. Girls in the second category were less concerned with issues of social approval or disapproval; they were more worried about definitions of womanhood. Their stories expressed guilt and despair over success, and doubts about their femininity or normality.

Unfortunately Anne no longer feels so certain that she really
wants to be a doctor. She is worried about herself and
wonders if perhaps she isn't normal . . . Anne decides not to
continue with her medical work but to take courses that have
a deeper personal meaning for her.

Anne feels guilty . . . She will finally have a nervous
breakdown and quit medical school and marry a successful
young doctor.

Anne is pleased. She had worked extraordinarily hard and
her grades showed it. "It is not enough," Anne thinks. "I am
not happy." She didn't even want to be a doctor. She is not
sure what she wants. Anne says to hell with the whole
business and goes into social work—not hardly as glamorous,
prestigious or lucrative; but she is happy.

3. The third group of stories did not even try to confront the
ambivalence about doing well. Girls in this category simply
denied the possibility that any mere woman could be so successful. Some of them completely changed the content of the
clue, or distorted it, or refused to believe it, or absolved Anne
of responsibility for her success. These stories were remarkable
for their psychological ingenuity:

Anne is a *code name* for a nonexistent person created by a
group of med. students. They take turns writing exams for
Anne . . .

Anne is really happy she's on top, though *Tom is higher
than she*—though that's as it should be . . . Anne doesn't mind
Tom winning.

Anne is talking to her counselor. Counselor says she will
make a fine *nurse*.

It was *luck* that Anne came out on top because she didn't
want to go to medical school anyway.

Fifty-nine girls—over 65 per cent—told stories that fell into
one or another of the above categories. But only eight boys,
fewer than 10 per cent, showed evidence of the motive to avoid
success. (These differences are significant at better than the
.0005 level.) In fact, sometimes I think that most of the young
men in the sample were incipient Horatio Algers. They expressed
unequivocal delight at John's success (clearly John had worked
hard for it), and projected a grand and glorious future for him.
There was none of the hostility, bitterness and ambivalence that
the girls felt for Anne. In short, the differences between male
and female stories based on essentially the same clue were
enormous.

Two of the stories are particularly revealing examples of
this male-female contrast. The girls insisted that Anne give up
her career for marriage:

Anne has a boyfriend, Carl, in the same class and they are
quite serious . . . She wants him to be scholastically higher
than she is. Anne will deliberately lower her academic
standing the next term, while she does all she subtly can to
help Carl. His grades come up and Anne soon drops out of
medical school. They marry and he goes on in school while
she raises their family.

But of course the boys would ask John to do no such thing:

John has worked very hard and his long hours of study have
paid off . . . He is thinking about his girl, Cheri, whom he
will marry at the end of med. school. He realizes he can give
her all the things she desires after he becomes established.
He will go on in med. school and be successful in the long run.

Success inhibits social life for the girls; it enhances social life
for the boys.

Earlier I suggested that the motive to avoid success is especially aroused in competitive situations. In the second part of
this study I wanted to see whether the aggressive overtones of
competition against men scared the girls away. Would competition raise their anxiety about success and thus lower their
performance?

First I put all of the students together in a large competitive
group, and gave them a series of achievement tests (verbal and
arithmetic). I then assigned them randomly to one of three other
experimental conditions. One-third worked on a similar set of
tests, each in competition with a member of the same sex. One-
third competed against a member of the opposite sex. The last
third worked by themselves, a non-competitive condition.

Ability is an important factor in achievement motivation
research. If you want to compare two persons on the strength
of their *motivation* to succeed, how do you know that any differences in performance are not due to initial differences in
ability to succeed? One way of avoiding this problem is to use
each subject as his own control; that is, the performance of an
individual working alone can be compared with his score in
competition. Ability thus remains constant; any change in score
must be due to motivational factors. This control over ability
was, of course, possible only for the last third of my subjects:
the 30 girls and 30 boys who had worked alone *and* in the large
group competition. I decided to look at their scores first.

Performance changed dramatically over the two situations.
A large number of the men did far better when they were in
competition than when they worked alone. For the women the
reverse was true. Fewer than one-third of the women, but more
than two-thirds of the men, got significantly higher scores in
competition.

When we looked at just the girls in terms of the motive to
avoid success, the comparisons were even more striking. As
predicted, the students who felt ambivalent or anxious about
doing well turned in their best scores when they worked by
themselves. Seventy-seven per cent of the girls who feared success did better alone than in competition. Women who were low
on the motive, however, behaved more like the men: 93 per
cent of them got higher scores in competition. (Results significant at the .005 level.)

As a final test of motivational differences, I asked the students to indicate on a scale from 1 to 100 "How important was it for you to do well in this situation?" The high-fear-of-success girls said that it was much more important for them to do well when they worked alone than when they worked in either kind of competition. For the low-fear girls, such differences were not statistically significant. Their test scores were higher in competition, as we saw, and they thought that it was important to succeed no matter what the setting. And in all experimental conditions—working alone, or in competition against males or females—high-fear women consistently lagged behind their fearless comrades on the importance of doing well.

These findings suggest that most women will fully explore their intellectual potential only when they do not need to compete—and least of all when they are competing with men. This was most true of women with a strong anxiety about success. Unfortunately, these are often the same women who could be very successful if they were free from that anxiety. The girls in my sample who feared success also tended to have high intellectual ability and histories of academic success. (It is interesting to note that all but two of these girls were majoring in the humanities and in spite of very high grade points aspired to traditional female careers: housewife, mother, nurse, schoolteacher. Girls who did not fear success, however, were aspiring to graduate degrees and careers in such scientific areas as math, physics and chemistry.)

We can see from this small study that achievement motivation in women is much more complex than the same drive in men. Most men do not find many inhibiting forces in their path if they are able and motivated to succeed. As a result, they are not threatened by competition; in fact, surpassing an opponent is a source of pride and enhanced masculinity.

If a women sets out to do well, however, she bumps into a number of obstacles. She learns that it really isn't ladylike to be too intellectual. She is warned that men will treat her with distrustful tolerance at best, and outright prejudice at worst, if she pursues a career. She learns the truth of Samuel Johnson's comment, "A man is in general better pleased when he has a good dinner upon his table, than when his wife talks Greek." So she doesn't learn Greek, and the motive to avoid success is born.

In recent years many legal and educational barriers to female achievement have been removed; but it is clear that a psychological barrier remains. The motive to avoid success has

---

Female Fear of Success and Performance

	Perform better working alone	Perform better in competition
High fear of success	13	4
Low fear of success	1	12

an all-too-important influence on the intellectual and professional lives of women in our society. But perhaps there is cause for optimism. Monica may have seen Anne maimed for life, but a few of the girls forecast a happier future for our medical student. Said one:

Anne is quite a lady—not only is she tops academically, but she is liked and admired by her fellow students—quite a trick in a man-dominated field. She is brilliant—but she is also a woman. She will continue to be at or near the top. And . . . always a lady.

Naomi Weisstein

WOMAN AS NIGGER, 1969

*Naomi Weisstein is assistant professor of psychology at Loyola
University (Chicago) where she is conducting research on visual
perception. With a B.A. from Wellesley College, she began her
graduate training in the clinical personality program but
switched to perceptual and cognitive psychology for her Ph.D.
from Harvard. She completed a year of postdoctoral research
on the Committee on Mathematical Biology at the University
of Chicago.*

SOURCE
Naomi Weisstein, "Woman as Nigger," Psychology Today, *October 1969,
pp. 21–22, 58.*

Psychology has nothing to say about what women are really like, what they need and what they want, for the simple reason that psychology does not know. Yet psychologists will hold forth endlessly on the true nature of woman, with dismaying enthusiasm and disquieting certitude.

Bruno Bettelheim, of the University of Chicago, tells us:

> We must start with the realization that, as much as women want to be good scientists or engineers, they want first and foremost to be womanly companions of men and to be mothers.

Erik Erikson, of Harvard University, explains:

> Much of a young woman's identity is already defined in her kind of attractiveness and in the selectivity of her search for the man (or men) by whom she wishes to be sought.

Some psychiatrists even see in women's acceptance of woman's role the solution to problems that rend our society. Joseph Rheingold, a psychiatrist at Harvard Medical School, writes:

> ... when women grow up with dread of their biological functions and without subversion by feminist doctrine and ... enter upon motherhood with a sense of fulfillment and altruistic sentiment, we shall attain the goal of a good life and a secure world in which to live.

These views reflect a fairly general consensus among psychologists, and the psychologists' idea of woman's nature fits the common prejudice. But it is wrong. There isn't the tiniest shred of evidence that these fantasies of childish dependence and servitude have anything to do with woman's true nature, or her true potential. Our present psychology is less than worthless in contributing to a vision that could truly liberate women.

And this failure is not limited to women. The kind of psychology that is concerned with how people act and who they are has failed in general to understand why people act the way they do and what might make them act differently. This kind of psychology divides into two professional areas: academic personality research, and clinical psychology and psychiatry. The basic reason for the failure is the same in both these areas: the central assumption for most psychologists of human personality has been that human behavior rests primarily on an individual and inner dynamic. This assumption is rapidly losing ground, however, as personality psychologists fail again and again to get consistency in the assumed personalities of their subjects, and as the evidence collects that what a person does and who he believes himself to be will be a function of what people around him expect him to be, and what the overall situation in which he is acting implies that he is.

Academic personality psychologists are looking, at least, at the counter evidence and changing their theories; no such corrective is occurring in clinical psychology and psychiatry. Freudians and neo-Freudians, Adlerians and neo-Adlerians, classicists and swingers, clinicians and psychiatrists, simply refuse to look at the evidence against their theory and practice. And they support their theory and their practice with stuff so transparently biased as to have absolutely no standing as empirical evidence.

If we inspect the literature of personality theory that has been written by clinicians and psychiatrists, it is immediately obvious that the major support for theory is "years of intensive clinical experience." Now a person is free to make up theories with any inspiration that works: divine revelation, intensive clinical practice, a random numbers table. He is not free to claim any validity for this theory until it has been tested. But in ordinary clinical practice, theories are treated in no such tentative way.

Consider Freud. What he accepted as evidence violated the most minimal conditions of scientific rigor. In *The Sexual Enlightenment of Children*, the classic document that is supposed to demonstrate the existence of a castration complex and its connection to a phobia, Freud based his analysis on reports from the little boy's father, himself in therapy and a devotee of Freud. Comment on contamination in this kind of evidence is unnecessary.

It is remarkable that only recently has Freud's classic theory on female sexuality—the notion of the double orgasm—been tested physiologically and found just plain wrong. Now those who claim that 50 years of psychoanalytic experience constitute evidence of the essential truth of Freud's theory should ponder the robust health of the double orgasm. Before Masters and Johnson did women believe they were having two different kinds of orgasm? Did their psychiatrists coax them into reporting something that was not true? If so, were other things they reported also not true? Did psychiatrists ever learn anything that conflicted with their theories? If clinical experience means anything, surely we should have been done with the double-orgasm myth long before Masters and Johnson.

But, you may object, intensive clinical experience is the only reliable measure in a discipline that rests its findings on insight, sensitivity and intuition. The problem with insight, sensitivity and intuition is that they tend to confirm our biases. At one time people were convinced of their ability to identify witches. All it required was sensitivity to the workings of the devil.

Clinical experience is not the same thing as empirical evidence. The first thing an experimenter learns is the concept of the double blind. The term comes from medical experiments, in which one group takes a drug that is supposed to change behavior in a certain way, and a control group takes a placebo. If the observers or subjects know which group took which drug, the result invariably confirms the new drug's effectiveness. Only when no one knows which subject took which pill is validity approximated.

When we are judging human behavior, we must test the reliability of our judgments again and again. Will judges, in a blind experiment, agree in their observations? Can they repeat their judgments later? In practice, we find that judges cannot judge reliably or consistently.

Evelyn Hooker of U.C.L.A. presented to a group of judges, chosen for their clinical expertise, the results of three widely used clinical projective tests—the Rorschach, the Thematic Apperception Test (TAT) and the Make-A-Picture Story Test (MAPS)—that had been given to homosexuals and a control group of heterosexuals. The ability of these judges to distinguish male heterosexuals from male homosexuals was no better than chance. Any remotely Freudian-like theory assumes that sexuality is of fundamental importance in the deep dynamic of personality. If gross sexual deviance cannot be detected, then what do psychologists mean when they claim that "latent homosexual panic" is at the basis of paranoid psychosis? They can't identify homosexual *anything*, let alone "latent homosexual panic."

More astonishing, the diagnoses of expert clinicians are not consistent. In the Kenneth Little and Edwin S. Shneidman study, on the basis of both tests and interviews, judges described a number of normals as psychotic, assigning them to such categories as "schizophrenic with homosexual tendencies," or "schizoid character with depressive trends." When the same judges were asked to rejudge the same test results several weeks later, their diagnoses of the same subjects differed markedly from their initial judgments. It is obvious that even simple descriptive conventions in clinical psychology cannot be applied consistently. These descriptive conventions, therefore, have no explanatory significance.

I was a member of a Harvard graduate seminar to which two piles of TAT tests were presented. We were asked to identify which pile had been written by males and which pile by females. Although the class had spent one and a half months intensively studying the psychological literature on the differences between the sexes, only four students out of 20 identified the piles correctly. Since this result is far below chance, we may conclude that there is a consistency here. Within the context of psychological teaching, the students judged knowledgeably; the teachings themselves are erroneous.

Some might argue that while clinical theory may be scientifically unsound, it at least cures people. There is no evidence that it does. In 1952, Hans Eysenck of the University of London reported the results of an "outcome-of-therapy" study of neurotics that showed that 44 per cent of the patients who received psychoanalysis improved; 64 per cent of the patients who received psychotherapy improved; and 72 per cent of the patients who received no treatment at all improved. These findings have never been refuted, and later studies have confirmed their negative results, no matter what type of therapy was used. In Arnold Goldstein and Sanford Dean's recent book, *The Investigation of Psychotherapy*, five different outcome-of-therapy studies with negative results are reported.

How, in all good conscience, can clinicians and psychiatrists continue to practice? Largely by ignoring these results and taking care not to do outcome-of-therapy studies.

Since clinical experience and tools are shown to be worse than useless when they are tested for consistency, efficacy and reliability, we can safely conclude that clinical theories about women are also worse than useless.

But even academic personality research that conforms to a rigorous methodology has only limited usefulness. As stated above, most psychologists of human personality have assumed that human behavior rests on an individual and inner dynamic, perhaps fixed in infancy, perhaps fixed by genitalia, perhaps simply arranged in a rigid cognitive network. But they have failed repeatedly to find consistency in the assumed personalities of their subjects. A rigid authoritarian on one test will be unauthoritarian on another. The reason for this inconsistency seems to depend more on the social situation in which a person finds himself than on the person himself.

In a series of experiments, Robert Rosenthal and his co-workers at Harvard showed that if experimenters have one hypothesis about what they expect to find and another group of experimenters has the opposite hypothesis, each group will obtain results that are in accord with its hypothesis. Experimenters who were told that their rats had been bred for brightness found that their rats learned to run mazes better than did the rats of experimenters who believed their animals had been bred for dullness. These results would have happened by chance one out of 100 times.

In a recent study, Robert Rosenthal and Lenore Jacobson extended their analysis to the classroom. They found that when teachers expected randomly selected students to "show great promise," the I.Q.s of these students increased significantly.

Thus, even in carefully controlled experiments, our hypotheses will influence the behavior of both animals and people. These studies are extremely important when we assess psychological studies of women. Since it is fairly safe to say that most of us start with hypotheses as to the nature of men and women, the validity of a number of observations on sex differences is questionable, even when these observations have been made under carefully controlled situations. In important ways, people are what you expect them to be, or at least they behave as you expect them to behave. If, as Bruno Bettelheim has it, women want first and foremost to be good wives and mothers, it is likely that this is what Bettelheim wants them to be.

The obedience experiments of Stanley Milgram point to the inescapable effect of social context. A subject is told that he is administering a learning experiment, and that he is to deal out shocks each time the other "subject" (a confederate of the experimenter) answers incorrectly. The equipment appears to provide graduated shocks ranging from 15 to 450 volts; for each four consecutive voltages there are verbal descriptions such as "mild shock," "danger," "severe shock," and finally, for the 435- and 450-volt switches, simply a red XXX marked over the switches. Each time the stooge answers incorrectly, the subject is supposed to increase the voltage. As the voltage increases, the stooge cries in pain; he demands that the experiment stop; finally, he refuses to answer at all. When he stops responding, the experimenter instructs the subject to continue increasing the voltage; for each shock administered, the stooge shrieks in agony. Under these conditions, about 62.5 per cent of the subjects administered shocks that they believed to be lethal.

No tested individual differences predicted which subjects would continue to obey and which would break off the experiment. When 40 psychiatrists predicted how many of a group of 100 subjects would go on to give the lethal shock, their predictions were far below the actual percentage; most expected only one tenth of one per cent of the subjects to obey to the end.

Even though psychiatrists have no idea how people will behave in this situation, and even though individual differences do not predict which subjects will obey and which will not, it is easy to predict when subjects will be obedient and when they will be defiant. All the experimenter has to do is change the social situation. In a variant of Milgram's experiment, two stooges were present in addition to the "victim"; these worked with the subject in administering electric shocks. When the stooges refused to go on with the experiment, only 10 per cent of the subjects continued to the maximum voltage. This is critical for personality theory. It says that the lawful behavior is the behavior that can be predicted from the social situation, not from the individual history.

Finally, Stanley Schachter and J. E. Singer gave a group injections of adrenalin, which produces a state of physiological arousal almost identical to a state of extreme fear. When they were in a room with a stooge who acted euphoric, they became euphoric; when they were placed in a room with a stooge who acted angry, they became extremely angry.

It is obvious that a study of human behavior requires a

study of the social contexts in which people move, the expectations as to how they will behave, and the authority that tells them who they are and what they are supposed to do.

We can now dispose of two biological theories of the nature of women. The first theory argues that females in primate groups are submissive. and passive. Until we change the social organization of these groups and watch their subsequent behavior, we must conclude that—since primates are at present too stupid to change their own social conditions—the innateness and fixedness of these sexual differences in behavior are simply not known. Applied to humans, the primate argument becomes patently irrelevant, for the salient feature of human social organization is its variety, and there are a number of cultures in which there is at least a rough equality between men and women.

The second theory argues that since females and males differ in their sex hormones, and since sex hormones enter the brain, there must be innate differences in *psychological nature*. But this argument tells us only that there are differences in *physiological state*. From the adrenalin experiment we know that a particular physiological state can lead to varied emotional states and outward behavior, depending on the social situation.

Our culture and our psychology characterize women as inconsistent, emotionally unstable, lacking in a strong superego, weaker, nurturant rather than productive, intuitive rather than intelligent, and—if they are at all normal—suited to the home and family. In short, the list adds up to a typical minority-group stereotype—woman as nigger—if she knows her place (the home), she is really a quite lovable, loving creature, happy and childlike. In a review of the intellectual differences between little boys and little girls, Eleanor Maccoby has shown that no difference exists until high school, or, if there is a difference, girls are slightly ahead of boys. In high school, girls begin to do worse on a few intellectual tasks, and beyond high school the productivity and accomplishment of women drops off even more rapidly.

In light of the social expectations about women, it is not surprising that women end up where society expects them to; the surprise is that little girls don't get the message that they are supposed to be stupid until they get into high school. It is no use to talk about women being different-but-equal; all the sex-difference tests I can think of have a "good" outcome and a "bad" outcome. Women usually end up with the bad outcome.

Except for their genitals, I don't know what immutable differences exist between men and women. Perhaps there are some other unchangeable differences; probably there are a number of irrelevant differences. But it is clear that until social expectations for men and women are equal, until we provide equal respect for both sexes, answers to this question will simply reflect our prejudices.

Della Cyrus

WHY MOTHERS FAIL, 1947

A graduate of Tufts College, Della Cyrus has worked as a family welfare caseworker, is married to a Unitarian minister, and has two children.

SOURCE
Della Cyrus, "Why Mothers Fail," Atlantic, March 1947, pp. 57–60.

1

The significant thing about women in America is that all of them are either rebelling against or trying to fit into a social pattern for women which was originally intended as a pattern for full-time mothers—the homemaker-mother pattern. The much talked about freedom of American women is not freedom in any real sense at all. It is simply freedom for some women to break away from the homemaker pattern if they have the personal courage and energy which breaking away from an established pattern requires. *And neither the woman who conforms to the pattern nor the woman who breaks away can express her whole self as a woman and a person.*

The homemaker way of life once applied to mothers who kept on having babies for the greater part of their lives, and to a time when most of the work of the world was done within the home. In present-day urban life, with almost all of the world's work being done outside the home, our mores and our mechanics of living still compel most women to be homemakers if they want to be mothers. Women may, and significantly do, renounce motherhood and refuse to be homemakers, but in spite of our toleration and even admiration for women who "do things" in the world, we have no ideal which permits us to *expect* any achievement from women beyond the achievement of homemaking. As long as women are forced to be homemakers in order to be mothers, we are compelled to hold fast to our one inadequate ideal for women—the homemaker-mother ideal.

It is difficult to understand why the plight of mothers has so long been ignored. *Motherhood apparently is regarded as a condition so holy or so occult that it must never be subjected to rational criticism and analysis.* We have finally—under protest—allowed medical science to intrude into the sacred sphere of motherhood. We have even produced, through psychology and psychoanalysis, more books than any mother will ever read on how she can be good for her child.

But what we haven't done, and what for some reason we suppose we needn't do, *is to make our modern American institution of motherhood satisfying or even bearable to mothers themselves.* We assume that motherhood is a condition so synonymous with life itself that its problems are inexorable, so that to ask the question how to make life bearable for mothers is as vague and sophomoric as to ask the question how to make *life* bearable. *About all we can actually manage is to pay a confused and embarrassed tribute to mothers once a year.*

When we consider that the old Christian problem of over-
coming hate and fear with love, now recognized as the basic
problem in psychiatry (if not yet in international relations!),
has always been first of all a mother-child problem, the question
of a satisfactory life for mothers appears in a more urgent perspective. It is now a psychiatric truism that the first act of the
human drama of love and hate is played between the mother
and her child, and that all other acts in that drama are in a
profound sense dependent upon and conditioned by this relationship. The sweeping tribute, "The hand that rocks the cradle
is the hand that rules the world," is a shallow statement of the
truth. The mother has always had in her keeping such power
to create love and hate in her child, and therefore in the world,
that there really isn't any question to take precedence over the
question, Why do mothers fail?

That mothers are failing in ever increasing numbers is
hardly a matter of argument. Their obvious failures are recorded
every day in newspapers throughout the country in stories of
neglect, desertion, delinquency, abortion, and divorce. But these
glaring failures are merely the eruptions, the symptoms of
a way of life which is difficult for all mothers. Most mothers
don't neglect or desert their children. On the other hand, many
mothers who are scrupulously conscientious about motherhood
are failing their children in ways just as destructive though less
dramatic. The evidence of this kind of failure is not so generally
recognized, but it exists in its most obvious forms in steadily
increasing quantities, and in the offices of psychologists, psychiatrists, psychoanalysts, child guidance clinics, and social
workers.

The case records of professional people who work with
"problem" children are full of conclusive evidence that children
often lie, steal, destroy property, commit sex crimes, fail in
school and at work, or are crippled with emotional and mental
illnesses in direct response to mothers who have somehow failed
in the kind of *feeling* they bring to their children. These same
professional people are constantly thwarted in their efforts to
save promising and intelligent children because they can do
nothing at all to change the destructive, though often well-
intentioned, attitudes of mothers. One distinguished psychoanalyst has said that all American cities are desperately in need of
institutions for girls—not for girls whose mothers are neglecting
them, but for girls who will be emotionally and morally ruined
if some way cannot be found to separate them from their
mothers.

Every woman brings her own unique problems of love and
hate to her relationship to her child, and there have always been
women in all ages who, because of distortions and failures in
their own development, have been "bad" mothers. Such women

are properly the concern of psychoanalysts. But when literally thousands of mothers in our time are unsuccessful at providing for their children the kind of emotional atmosphere necessary for the average healthy growth of personality, then perhaps we must look for something other than exclusively personal failure. When so definite a trend of failure exists it is logical to suppose that destructive forces are at work on all mothers which account not only for the dramatic breakdowns printed in the newspapers and for the child clients of psychiatrists and social workers, but which account also for the dissatisfaction, frustration, and semi-failure of almost all mothers.

2

Every modern mother feels—in some degree—a conflict between the kind of life she is trained in America to want and expect, and the kind of life she must in fact lead as a mother. More than that, it is a conflict between the kind of woman she hoped to become and the kind of woman our homemaker-mother ideal usually compels her to be.

This difference between what women are educated to be and what they must in fact become can be described almost entirely in terms of their relationship to men and to the world outside the family. Up to the point of marriage most women participate fully in the work, the recreation, and the aspirations of the males of their own age. From kindergarten to graduate school they read the same books, compete in many of the same contests, talk the same talk, follow the same daily routine, eat in the same drug-stores and cafeterias, make the same plans for exploring or dazzling or remaking the world. For them there is no such thing as "woman's work" or a "man's world." There are only men and women and the world's work and the world's pleasure.

No one can estimate the shock which getting married and having a child gives to this American educated woman. From the exhilarating threshold of the world with all its problems and possibilities, from the daily companionship of men and other women, she is catapulted into a house—a house, further-more, from which she has no escape. Her husband disappears into the outside world on business of his own, while for hours and days at a time she has no companion except her child, and the hands with which she had planned to remake the world are, incredibly enough, in the laundry tubs, the dishpan, and the scrub bucket. And so her first experience of what it means to be a mother, however much she may love her baby, is an experience full to overflowing with confusion, disappointment, humiliation, and above all, loneliness.

Usually the shock of becoming a homemaker-mother is more devastating to the college-educated woman than to the woman with less education, as our birth statistics significantly indicate. But almost no woman is free from some dissatisfaction with the isolation and bondage of motherhood. As long as we educate women, even partially, to be interested in and responsible for the needs and problems of their world, and then isolate them in houses as soon as they become mothers and load them with work which they spent their youth learning to regard as menial and unintelligent, we should stop being surprised if they emerge finally with no faith in themselves and no real interest in anybody or anything but their own narrowed and distorted desires.

Women who at best are lonely and disappointed, and who are separated from their husbands in so many important ways, are almost doomed to failure as mothers. It isn't only that they see too much of their children and too little of anybody else, or even that they particularly resent doing a certain amount of sordid and trivial work. *Most of them carry, whether they know it or not, a burden of unused ability and frustrated purpose which falls resentfully on the child.* To make the day-long occupations of washing, ironing, cooking, and scrubbing an inevitable condition of motherhood is obviously as wasteful of the miracle and variety of human talent as it would be to make gardening, street cleaning, and bookkeeping a necessary condition of fatherhood. It means that all mothers who have trained themselves to be violinists, teachers, actresses, business women, or just plain citizens of their world, are struggling under permanent vocational maladjustment.

The question is often asked, *What would mothers do if freed from housework? Many women aren't capable of anything else. Wouldn't they be worse off in factories and stores? These questions condemn our whole society and all its values, or lack of them. They reflect our belief that people work only because they have to and only to earn money.* No one would think to ask what women would do if we took it for granted that the right work for a woman is as important as the right husband—if we took it for granted that women from earliest childhood were training their minds and developing their abilities, not to fill in the time until marriage and motherhood, but in order to contribute their serious share to the enrichment of all life for as long as they live.

Many mothers do adjust to modern conditions of motherhood. They may have sought in marriage an escape from parents or from the boredom of an uncongenial job. They may have hoped to find in marriage an escape from inner emptiness and lack of personal direction. Bringing to marriage a great residue of childish needs, they may sink gratefully into the protection of a comfortable home. Accepting as inevitable the separation of their husbands' interests from their own, they may resign themselves and finally adapt themselves to life in a child's world. While their children are young they give up, and then forget they ever had, a need for privacy in which to read or think. They make do with the limited and meager opportunities for adult relationships open to them and they sometimes manage, by stunting their own growth, to love their children without undue conflict or resentment.

One sometimes hears the "well-adjusted" mother express her self-abnegation in heroic terms. "After all," she says, "the children come first. They're all that really matters."

To such an attitude there is only one possible response. If the purpose of an adult human being is to rear a child or two so that those children can in turn rear children, ad infinitum, then life is unquestionably the absurd treadmill it sometimes seems and there is nothing to do but relax. How can the mother who believes she herself doesn't matter rear her children *for* anything? The only bearable theory is that we bring our children up to adulthood because we believe in adulthood—in its satisfactions and in the possibilities it offers for infinite growth and development.

The mother who adjusts to a life which forces her to be less than an adult is not only betraying herself and the purposes for which she was intended. She is not only, by example, belittling for her children the importance of full maturity. She is, worst of all, depriving them of a mother who has real wisdom about the world. And in this time, no other kind of mother will do. No other kind of mother can begin to prepare her children for the conflict of interests, the confusion of values, the groping for new forms of living, which make up the world in which those same children must some day try to be adults.

So we come to the ironic truth that the mothers who make the best adjustment to the conditions now implicit in our homemaker-mother ideal are by that very adjustment incapable of fulfilling their full obligations as mothers. In their immaturity and isolation they tend to teach their children that it is more important to keep their feet dry than it is to know and understand their world. They are the mothers one hears lamenting the basic principle of life by wishing that their little babies would not grow up. In their loneliness and lack of any real job apart from motherhood, they hover over, lean on, and dominate their children, paralyzing their wills, blocking their way to independence.

In a recent news story a psychiatrist, Edward A. Strecker, flatly states that most of the 2,400,000 psychoneurotics uncovered by the Army are the victims of clinging and domineering mothers. *Is it inevitable that the "good" mother in our society will smother her child with love, security, and peace at home, and then, painfully and belatedly, turn him out into a world which, to the complete surprise of both mother and child, commands him to kill and be killed? Surely we require more of motherhood than this.*

3

How can modern mothers serve at the same time their children, their men, themselves, and their world? Obviously only by becoming the vital and complete citizens of the world which they wanted and expected to be in the beginning. The answer is so simple that we can only conclude that some overwhelming obstacle stands in the way.

That obstacle, of course, is the homemaker-mother pattern and, more significantly, the prevailing notion, embodied in the modern distortion of that pattern, that mothers must be the constant, hour by hour, day by day, nursemaids and supervisors of their own children.

Child psychologists, who know what havoc a mother can work with her children, have been greatly responsible for perpetuating this notion. Because they see what destruction the wrong maternal feelings can bring to a child, they assume that an equal dose of the right maternal feelings will have the opposite effect. But they are as conspicuously unsuccessful as anybody else in producing the right feelings, and it is unlikely that anyone will be able to produce them by shutting mature women up with small children in crowded city houses for twenty-four hours a day, three hundred and sixty-five days a year.

The dilemma grows out of a complete confusion over the difference between quantity and quality in a mother-child relationship. So much emphasis has been placed on the emotional meanings involved in feeding a child or taking it to the toilet or introducing it to a new experience, that conscientious mothers are frequently tense and self-conscious all the time they are with their children and worried all the time their children are with someone else. Because a new sense of their importance and responsibility has been loaded onto mothers at a time when they are least able to accept the traditional pattern of motherhood, the more well-intentioned they are, the more guilty they feel over their longing to spend part of their lives somewhere else. Dissatisfaction, then, leads to guilt, and guilt to despair as they find themselves, consciously or unconsciously, incapable of giving their little children the one thing little children need most— simple, relaxed, wholehearted love.

Intelligent people in all ages have understood that educated women must do *something* besides tend the very young. Our great-grandmothers took this for granted, and from the perspective of their importantly busy lives would probably be horrified at the concentrated relationship between the modern mother and her child. Though their life was far from ideal, it might even be true that little children brought up by Negro mammies in the South, for instance, were happier, better cared for, and more sensibly loved than the average child now under its educated mother's constant supervision in a modern apartment.

The intelligent, urban-civilized woman has serious shortcomings as a mother. The more "civilized" her way of life, the more eager she is to civilize her child quickly. But this is in direct conflict with the child's own need to progress calmly at its own pace. Perhaps one of the very worst things educated mothers do to their little children is to hurry them. Not because they want to do something really important after the child has hurried, but because they *feel* they have something else important to do.

Could it be that the much maligned "dumb" nursemaid had her points after all, when she was easygoing, relaxed, unambitious, foolishly contented, and childlike with her young charges? Perhaps the superstitions and vulgarities she taught them were far less dangerous than the overanxious, impatient expectations of the intelligent and discontented mother. Not that anyone wants to turn children over to uncivilized or moronic women. But does the sharp conflict between a newborn child and society suggest that babies need totally different qualities in a mother from the qualities required by older, intellectually developing children?

Perhaps the solution to the dilemma is not the seemingly hopeless one of making a good hour after hour after hour relationship between mother and little child, but rather lies in the direction *of spreading out the mother role to include significant relationships for the child with father, friends, teachers, and other children.* This is exactly what did happen in an earlier rural society, when life was more leisurely, families were large and included many relatives, and fathers had time really to be fathers. Perhaps the very intensity of the modern continuous, exclusive relationship between mother and child is at the root of two opposite problems—the problem of why mothers neglect and desert their children, and the problem of why they ruin them with too much concentration and too many of the wrong feelings.

Surely if one woman is to be in complete charge of a child twenty-four hours a day for the first five or six years of its life, then it should be a woman who in the depths of her mind and soul honestly has nothing else to do and nowhere else to go. Either we should deprive women of all their education and civilization and send them back to some primitive state of instinctual and timeless life so that they can be happy full-time mothers of small children (a well-known and valuable fascist technique), or *we should find a satisfactory way to care for children away from their mothers part of the time so that mothers can be a fully developed, responsible part of the world their children will inherit.*

The problem is inherent in the education of women, as many people knew and feared that it would be. It is intrinsic in the fact that the urban way of life has deprived mothers of significant work, separated them from their husbands, and created a physical environment incompatible with the raising of children. It is not a problem which mothers can solve by themselves, nor can psychoanalysts or social workers solve it, though all can bring their knowledge and experience to its solution. It is a social problem which must be solved by whole communities. It means some kind of community plan for the care of homes and of children—and not for a few odd hours now and then, but for several absolutely dependable hours every day.

It is not merely a need for first-class nursery schools in every neighborhood, and community services to reduce the mechanics of homemaking far below the present minimum. *It is a need for a new philosophy and pattern of community life, not to destroy the privacy of the family, but to end the isolation of individual mothers and children.* It is a need for community plan which at the same time stimulates more significant relationships and offers more meaningful privacy than most mothers now have.

Only with practical, specific plans for making time available to mothers can we justify our claim that American women are emancipated, and create a new ideal for all women which demands the fullest use of their talent and power. When we have freed all women from the modern curse of the full-time homemaker-mother ideal, more intelligent women will have babies, more women will love and cherish the babies they have, and more women without babies will use their lives to some good end. *Without a new ideal and a new plan, women can never be really free or really mature or really appealing, or for that matter, really mothers.*

Ann Eliasberg

ARE YOU HURTING YOUR DAUGHTER WITHOUT KNOWING IT? 1971

Ann Eliasberg teaches at Queens College, is married, and has three children.

SOURCE
Ann Eliasberg, *"Are You Hurting Your Daughter Without Knowing It?,"*
Family Circle, *February 1971, pp. 38, 76–77.*
Portrait: Jay Eliasberg.

Recently, a delegation of young women—university teachers and students—presented their ideas about discrimination against females and stereotyping in the schools to an all-male group of school superintendents attending a two-week conference at Columbia University. The conference subject was early childhood education. And yet, as the women who politely crashed the conference pointed out to these men, they had not even considered a "vital aspect of the early education of all children, namely the ways in which children learn that they are male and female and what they learn about being male and female."

The young women presented a well-documented argument to support their case that in school, girls are taught to have fewer aspirations than men, because fewer opportunities lie open to them. The argument was so persuasive that one conference observer, a mother with daughters, 12 and 16, and a son of 10, was moved to conduct an informal survey of books commonly found in children's libraries or used in schools throughout the country.

"I was appalled," she reports. "I thought the suffragettes had solved the whole question of women's right and that any problems that still remained were settled in the 1920s and 1940s. But to read some of these books, you'd think that women not only haven't achieved anything in science or art or politics, but that they aren't even interested in such matters."

The same mother discovered, in books for preschool children and in the elementary-grade readers and recreational literature to be found on any school or public library shelf, how limited a role in society we mark out for women. For example, in a series of basic readers used in many private and public schools, a second-grade reader starts out with a description of how our country might look to an astronaut. The country he surveys has men taking most of the active, achieving roles, and women generally portrayed as homemakers, nurses or teachers. In a book that focuses on historical figures, youngsters learn about George Washington Carver, King Alfred, Robert Bruce, William Tell, Alexander the Great, Copernicus, Galileo, Johannes Kepler, Henry Ford and the Wright brothers. Searching for feminine greats (Queen Elizabeth, perhaps, or Joan of Arc?), a diligent reader will finally come upon two: Nurse Florence Nightingale (not pioneer doctor Elizabeth Blackwell) and the Negro educator Mary McLeod Bethune. Mrs. Bethune and Negro contralto Marian Anderson are often among the few women who appear in books about important people in American life; rather a one-token-buys-two-rides approach.

Moving down the shelf, a book that offers brief biographies of Benjamin West, Benjamin Franklin and most of the presidents of the United States, also informs its readers that William Cullen Bryant was America's first great poet. Why no mention of Emily Dickinson, whom most critics consider far greater? Or Anne Bradstreet, first poet of either sex on American shores?

Children invest a great deal of their intellects and imaginations in the world they meet in schoolbooks. What kind of women inhabit this world? Many books have invented a vapid, generalized, "typical" American woman. We meet this feminine figure in, for example, a series of children's books about a school-age boy named Peter. Peter's father, Mr. Sills, works at a proving ground for space missiles that conveniently allows Peter to be in on the excitement of rocket building, rocket testing, moon shooting and the like. Throughout the series, Peter's mother and his sister, Linda, never visit the proving ground or show any interest in space matters. At one point, Mrs. Sills invites Dr. Dan, a scientist friend of her husband, to visit the Sills' home. She adds archly, "I will even let you and John talk about space now and then." When one considers this literary characterization in light of the fact that approximately 40 million women, as compared with 36 million men, viewed our astronauts' first step on the moon in July, 1969, one wants to ask where the author of the Peter series (a woman) gets her ideas about female America.

The fact is, more children's books are about boys than about girls, and the girls and women who do appear are usually passive, undifferentiated characters. When Mark and Rich, in another children's series, visit the Mayan ruins of Mexico, their professor-guide is a man, and when they make an undersea journey, they are again part of an all-male team. A reasonably well-informed woman will feel puzzled as she browses through such juveniles. Didn't archaeologist Iris Love head a team that discovered a temple of Aphrodite in Turkey? And didn't five women aquanauts spend two weeks in an undersea laboratory habitat, studying the ecology of sea life? Or if these events are too recent, what about Marie Curie's discovery of radium or Lise Meitner's contribution to the splitting of the atom?

Of course, there are books in which girls figure as principal characters: Cherry Ames is a student nurse, Vicki Barr a flight stewardess, and Peggy Lane an aspiring actress. But these girls seem somewhat pallid beside Tom Swift, budding scientist, and Tom Corbett, space explorer. The one exception, the girl who outsells them all—more than a million copies in one year as compared with 40,000 for Cherry Ames—is Nancy Drew, who tootles about the country in her roadster, solving mysteries and living a life of freedom and adventure. Interestingly, a psychoanalyst, the late Dr. Lili Peller, discovered in a study on the reading habits of school-age boys and girls that Nancy Drew's image satisfies the young girl's daydream that "maybe I can be a boy."

Educational and vocational guidance counselors should, of course, help every student, girl and boy, to set his or her sights as high as abilities warrant. But, as specialists in this area have discovered, not all of them do. Eli Ginzberg, director of Columbia University's Conservation of Human Resources Project, points out that girls often receive inferior vocational and educational guidance. "A lot of vocational counselors have outdated ideas about men's jobs and women's jobs," he declares. Also, many parents still think in terms of career aspirations for their sons but not necessarily for their daughters.

Of course, realists will point out that men are usually the chief breadwinners. But doesn't the male-breadwinner argument conveniently ignore the fact that of the approximately 30 million women in our labor force, the majority of them work from financial necessity, many because they head their households? Denying them equal education and job opportunities merely restricts them to jobs that require low skills and pay low wages. Many girls settle for low-skill jobs in fields only vaguely related to the one they really care about, which might be law, medicine, or social work. Furthermore, most graduate schools do not encourage women who have interrupted their studies for marriage to come back on a part-time basis, although many women have successfully earned graduate degrees while running a home and rearing children.

Perhaps this is as good a time as any to rake over that old chestnut about a woman's work-life damaging her children. Research has not really shown a causal relationship between maladjustment in children and a mother's hours outside the home, but the main fallacy is the either/or that is built into the argument. "Unquestionably," says Dr. Aaron Esman, psychiatrist, "the best climate for the development of a child's sense of self and his relationships with other people is a close, loving and consistent association with his mother, or mother-person, until about his third year." But that doesn't mean that a child must be in his mother's sole care 24 hours a day. In fact, Dr. Esman sees some definite advantages in a pattern whereby both a wife and husband might share breadwinning and child-rearing responsibilities, and when the crucial early years are passed, psychiatrists agree that some pattern that involves a woman in meaningful outside work is usually better for her, her husband and her children than total concentration on the home.

Parents still tend to be fearful that girls who love sports and excel in math or science are "masculine," while boys who help with the dishes and like music and poetry are "feminine." But there is simply no valid reason for discouraging a girl's or boy's natural inclinations. If Judy likes to refinish furniture, experiment with test tubes or stargaze through a telescope, and her father or mother can enjoy these activities with her, Judy is a lucky girl. She gains a sense of acceptance by her parents that is like courage in the bank for future challenge.

How often, though, do parents unconsciously undermine the work they consciously try to do, praising a girl for her looks and her clothes and a boy for his ideas and achievements, thereby setting up a double standard that children will surely detect?

The consensus of psychological thought relates the disparities in the achievement of boys and girls to early conditioning as often as to inherent factors of superiority or inferiority.

The message is clear. Setting overly protective limits on the world a small girl can explore both physically and mentally, playing up her looks and playing down her ideas, setting standards for her that are subtly different from those set for her brother, concentrating on his educational and vocational goals to the neglect of hers—in all these ways parents, often unintentionally, restrict their daughter's total growth. As she comes to accept (or resign herself to) such restrictions, she may also come to identify herself with the passive female stereotypes she meets in books, in movies and on television. She is especially likely to accept them if we, as parents, provide no more satisfactory models. And the diminished self-image that is a natural consequence of such conditioning may be permanently fixed as she is guided toward educational goals below her capabilities. The common rationale for this all-too-common practice is: "You'll marry and have children anyway."

She probably will. So do most men. And in the course of a long life she will be called upon to play many other roles. Reared according to our current attitudes and methods, how well will she be equipped to enjoy them? Will she be a well-stacked, well-deodorized expert at keeping white clothes white, or will she be a fully functioning adult human being?

Clara Thompson

SOME EFFECTS OF THE DEROGATORY ATTITUDE TOWARD FEMALE SEXUALITY, 1950

Clara Thompson was the first executive director of the William Alanson White Institute of Psychiatry, Psychoanalysis, and Psychology, one of the most respected institutes in the United States. Her innovative research and writings in feminine psychology have contributed greatly to reversing the negative image promulgated by Freudian theory.

SOURCE
Clara Thompson, "Some Effects of the Derogatory Attitude Toward Female Sexuality," Psychiatry, Vol. XIII, 1950, 349–354.
Portrait: The William Alanson White Institute.

In an earlier paper[1] I stressed the fact that the actual envy of the penis as such is not as important in the psychology of women as their envy of the position of the male in our society. This position of privilege and alleged superiority is symbolized by the possession of a penis. The owner of this badge of power has special opportunities while those without have more limited possibilities. I questioned in that paper whether the penis in its own right as a sexual organ was necessarily an object of envy at all.

That there are innate biological differences between the sexual life of man and woman is so obvious that one must apologize for mentioning it. Yet those who stress this aspect most are too often among the first to claim knowledge of the psychic experiences and feelings of the opposite sex. Thus for many centuries male writers have been busy trying to explain the female. In recent years a few women have attempted to present the inner life of their own sex, but they themselves seem to have had difficulty in freeing their thinking from the male orientation. Psychoanalysts, female as well as male, seem for the most part still to be dominated by Freud's thinking about women.

Freud was a very perceptive thinker but he was a male, and a male quite ready to subscribe to the theory of male superiority prevalent in the culture. This must have definitely hampered his understanding of experiences in a woman's life, especially those specifically associated with her feminine role.

Of course this thinking can be carried to extreme lengths and one can say that no human being can really know what another human being actually experiences about anything. However, the presence of similar organs justifies us in thinking that we can at least approximate an understanding of another person's experiences in many cases. A headache, a cough, a pain in the heart, intestinal cramps, weeping, laughter, joy, a sense of well-being—we assume that all of these feel to other people very similar to what we ourselves experience under those titles.

In the case of sexual experiences, however, one sex has no adequate means of identifying with the experience of the other sex. A woman, for instance, cannot possibly be sure that she knows what the subjective experience of an erection and male

[1] Clara Thompson, "Penis Envy in Women," *Psychiatry* (1943) 6: 123–125.

orgasm is. Nor can a man identify with the tension and sensations of menstruation, or female genital excitation, or child birth. Since for many years most of the psychoanalysts were men this may account for the prevalence of some misconceptions about female sexuality. Horney pointed out in 1926 that Freud's theory that little girls believed they had been castrated and that they envied boys their penises is definitely a male orientation to the subject.[2] In this paper she listed several ideas which little boys have about girls' genitals. These ideas, she shows, are practically identical with the classical psychoanalytic conception of the female. The little boys' ideas are based on the assumption that girls also have penises, which results in a shock at the discovery of their absence. A boy, reasoning from his own life experience, assumes this is a mutilation, as a punishment for sexual misdemeanor. This makes more vivid to him any castration threats which have been made to him. He concludes that the girl must feel inferior and envy him because she must have come to the same conclusions about her state. In short, the little boy, incapable of imagining that one could feel complete without a penis, assumes that the little girl must feel deprived. It is doubtless true that her lack of a penis can activate any latent anxiety the boy may have about the security of his own organ, but it does not necessarily follow that the girl feels more insecure because of it.

In the "Economic Problem of Masochism"[3] Freud assumes that masochism is a part of female sexuality, but he gives as his evidence the phantasies of passive male homosexuals. What a passive male homosexual imagines about the experience of being a woman is not necessarily similar to female sexual experience. In fact, a healthy woman's sexual life is probably not remotely similar to the phantasies and longings of a highly disturbed passive male personality.

Recently I heard to my amazement that a well-known psychiatrist had told a group of students that in the female sexual life there is no orgasm. I can only explain such a statement by assuming that this man could not conceive of orgasm in the absence of ejaculation. If he had speculated that the female orgasm must be a qualitatively different experience from that of the male because of the absence of ejaculation, one could agree that this may well be the case. I think these examples suffice to show that many current ideas about female psychosexual life may be distorted by being seen through male eyes.

In "Sex and Character"[4] Fromm has pointed out that the biological differences in the sexual experience may contribute to

[2] Karen Horney, "Flight from Womanhood," *Internat. J. Psycho-Analysis* (1926) 7: 324–339.
[3] Freud, *Collected Papers* 2: 255–268; London, Hogarth Press, 1925.
[4] Erich Fromm, "Sex and Character," *Psychiatry* (1943) 6: 21–31.

greater emphasis on one or the other character trends in the two sexes. Thus he notes that for the male it is necessary to be able to perform, while no achievement is required of the female. This, he believes, can have a definite effect on the general character trends. This gives the man a greater need to demonstrate, to produce, to have power, while the woman's need is more in the direction of being accepted, being desirable. Since her satisfaction is dependent on the man's ability to produce, her fear is in being abandoned, being frustrated, while his is fear of failure. Fromm points out that the woman can make herself available at any time and give satisfaction to the man, but the man's possibility of satisfying her is not entirely within his control. He cannot always produce an erection at will.

The effect of basic sexual differences on the character structure is not pertinent to this paper. Fromm's thesis that the ability to perform is important in male sexual life, that it is especially a matter of concern to the male because it is not entirely within his control, and that the female may perform at all times if she so wishes, are points of importance in my thesis. But I should like to develop somewhat different aspects of the situation. Fromm shows that the woman can at any time satisfy the male, and he mentions the male's concern over successfully performing for the female, but he does not at any point discuss how important obtaining satisfaction for themselves is in the total reaction.

In general the male gets at least some physiological satisfaction out of his sexual performance. Some experiences are more pleasurable than others, to be sure, and there are cases of orgasm without pleasure. However, for the very reason that he cannot force himself to perform, he is less likely to find himself in the midst of a totally uncongenial situation.

The female, however, who permits herself to be used when she is not sexually interested or is at most only mildly aroused frequently finds herself in the midst of an unsatisfactory experience. At most she can have only a vicarious satisfaction in the male's pleasure. I might mention parenthetically here that some male analysts, for example Ferenczi, are inclined to think that identification with the male in his orgasm constitutes a woman's true sexual fulfillment. This I would question.

One frequently finds resentment in women who have for some reason consented to being used for the male's pleasure. This is in many cases covered by an attitude of resignation. A frequent answer from women when they are asked about marital sexual relations is: "It is all right. He doesn't bother me much." This attitude may hold even when in other respects the husband and wife like each other; that is, such an attitude may exist even when the woman has not been intimidated by threats or violence. She simply assumes that her interests are not an important consideration.

Obviously the sexual act is satisfactory to the woman only when she actively and from choice participates in her own characteristic way. If she considered herself free to choose, she would refuse the male except when she actually did desire to participate.

This being the case, it might be fruitful to examine the situations in which the woman submits with little or no interest. There are, of course, occasions when she genuinely wishes to do this for the man's sake; this does not create a problem. More frequently the cause is a feeling of insecurity in the relationship; this insecurity may arise from external factors—that is, the male concerned may insist on his satisfaction or else! The insecurity may also arise from within because of the woman's own feelings of inadequacy. These feelings may arise simply from the fact that the woman subscribes to the cultural attitude that her needs are not as insistent as the man's; but in addition she may have personal neurotic difficulties.

The question arises, How has it become socially acceptable for a man to insist on his sexual rights whenever he desires? Is this because rape is a possibility, and the woman is physically relatively defenseless? This must have had some influence in the course of society's development. However, it has often been proved that even rape is not easy without some cooperation from the woman. The neurotic condition of vaginismus illustrates that in some conditions even unconscious unwillingness on the part of the woman may effectively block male performance. So while the superior physical power of the male may be an important factor in the frequency of passive compliance, there must be other factors. These other factors are not of a biological nature, for the participation in sexual relations without accompanying excitement is most obviously possible in human females, although not definitely impossible in other animals.

One must look to cultural attitudes for the answer. There are two general concepts which are significant here, and to which both men and women subscribe in our culture. One is that the female sexual drive is not as pressing or important as the male. Therefore there is less need to be concerned in satisfying it or considering it. The other is the analytically much discussed thesis that the female sex organs are considered inferior to those of the male.

In recent years there has been a definite tendency to move away from the first idea as far as actual sexual performance is concerned. With the increasing tendency to be more open in observing facts about sex, women in many groups have become able not only to admit to themselves but also to men that their sexual needs are important. However, this is still not true of all groups. Moreover, at almost the same time another important aspect of woman's sexual life has diminished in importance; that is, the bearing of children. Woman's specific type of creativeness is no longer highly desired in many situations. This is an important subject in itself and will not be discussed here.

As we know, during the Victorian era a woman's sexual needs were supposed to be practically nonexistent. A woman was expected to be able to control her sexual desires at all times. Thus an extramarital pregnancy was allegedly entirely due to the woman's weakness or depravity. The man's participation in such an extramarital relationship was looked upon with more tolerance, and there was little or no social disgrace attached to him. The double standard of sexual morality also implied an assumption that woman's sexual drive was not as insistent as the male's.

The fact that evidence of erotic excitement could be concealed much better by a woman than by a man made the development of such thinking possible. Since she was not supposed to be erotic and since the man must have his satisfaction, a pattern was developed in which the dutiful wife offered herself to her husband without actively participating in the act herself. I am sure many women were sufficiently normal to find nonparticipation difficult, and doubtless many men did not subscribe to the feeling that they should be horrified at any evidence of passion in their wives. Nevertheless as recently as twenty years ago a woman, who consulted me about her marital difficulties, reported that her husband felt disgust, it seemed, whenever she responded sexually to him. She tried to conceal her sexual responses, including orgasm, from him, then would lie awake the rest of the night in misery and rage. Since I saw this woman only twice, I am not in a position to say how much this situation contributed to her suicide about a year later. Undoubtedly there were many other difficulties in her relation to her husband of which the sexual may have been only one expression. Certainly this extreme denial of sexual interest is seldom required of women today, but an attenuated form still remains, especially in marriage. Here it is found not only in frigid women who, realizing their inadequacy as mates, make amends as best they can by a nonparticipating offering of themselves. But one also finds the attitude even in women with adequate sexual responsiveness in many situations. They have accepted the idea that the male's needs are greater than their own and that therefore his wishes and needs are paramount.

So the feeling that woman's sexual life is not as important or insistent as the male's may produce two unfortunate situations. It may inhibit the woman's natural expressions of desire for fear of appearing unwomanly, or it may lead her to feel she must be ready to accommodate on all occasions—that is, she has no rights of her own. Both extremes mean an interference with her natural self-expression and spontaneity with resulting resentment and discontent.

Moreover, since the male has often been indoctrinated with the idea that woman's sexual life is not important, he may not exert himself much to make her interested. He fails to see the importance of the art of love.

When an important aspect of a person's life becomes under-valued, this has a negative effect on the self-esteem. What a woman actually has to offer in sexual responsiveness becomes undervalued, and this in turn affects her own evaluation of herself as a person.

The second way in which our culture has minimized woman's sexual assets is in the derogation of her genitals. This in classical terminology is connected with the idea of penis envy. I wish to approach the problem differently. As I said earlier, the idea of penis envy is a male concept. It is the male who experiences the penis as a valuable organ and he assumes that women also must feel that way about it. But a woman cannot really imagine the sexual pleasure of the penis—she can only appreciate the social advantages its possessor has.[5] What a woman needs rather is a feeling of the importance of her own organs. I believe that much more important than penis envy in the psychology of woman is her reaction to the undervaluation of her own organs. I think we can concede that the acceptance of one's body and all its functions is a basic need in the establishment of self-respect and self-esteem.

The short plump brunette girl may feel that she would be more acceptable if she were a tall thin blonde—in other words, if she were somebody else. The solution of her problem lies not in becoming a blonde but in finding out why she is not accepting of what she is. The history will show either that some significant person in her early life preferred a tall blonde or that being a brunette has become associated with other unacceptable characteristics. Thus in one case in which this envy of the blond type was present, being brunette meant being sexy, and being sexy was frowned upon.

Sex in general has come under the disapproval of two kinds of thinking in our culture. The puritan ideal is denial of body pleasure, and this makes sexual needs something of which to be ashamed. Traces of this attitude still remain today in the feelings of both sexes.

We also have another attitude which derogates sexuality, especially female sexuality. We are people with great emphasis on cleanliness. In many people's minds the genital organs are classed with the organs of excretion and thus become associated with the idea of being unclean. With the male some of the curse is removed because he gets rid of the objectionable product. The female, however, receives it, and when her attitude is strongly influenced by the dirty excretion concept, this indicates her feeling of unacceptability. Moreover, the men who feel the sexual product is unclean reinforce the woman's feeling that her genitals are unclean.

[5] I do not wish to leave the impression that there is never a woman who thinks she desires to possess the male genital as such, but I believe such women are found relatively rarely.

The child's unrestrained pleasure in his body and its products begins to be curbed at an early age. This is such a fundamental part of our basic training that most of us would have difficulty imagining the effect on our psychic and emotional life of a more permissive attitude. What has happened is that this training has created a kind of moral attitude towards our body products. Sphincter morality, as Ferenczi has called it, extends to more than the control of urine and feces. To some extent genital products come also under the idea of sphincter morality. Obviously this especially has an influence on attitudes towards the female genitals where no sphincter control is possible. My attention was first called to this by a paper written in German by Bertram Lewin twenty years ago.[6] In this paper he presented, among other things, clinical data in which the menses were compared to an unwanted loss of feces and urine due to lack of sphincter control. In one case which he reported the woman had become very proficient at contracting the vaginal muscles so that she attained some semblance of control of the quantity of menstrual flow. Although in my own practice I have never encountered a patient who actually tried to produce a sphincter, I have frequent evidence that the inability not only to control menstruation but all secretions of the female genitals has contributed to a feeling of unacceptability and dirtiness. One patient on being presented by her mother with a perineal napkin on the occasion of her first menses refused to use it. To her it meant a baby's diaper, and she felt completely humiliated. Obviously she presently felt even more humiliated because of the inevitable consequences of her refusal.

Also because of the culture's overevaluation of cleanliness another attribute of the female genital can be a source of distress, that is, the fact that it has an odor. Thus one of the chief means by which the female attracts the male among animals has been labelled unpleasant, to many even disgusting. For example, a female patient whose profession requires her appearing before audiences has been greatly handicapped for many years by a feeling of being "stinking" which is greatly augmented whenever she is in a position to have her body observed. Thus she can talk over the radio but not before an audience. Another patient felt for years that she could never marry because she would not be able to keep her body clean at every moment in the presence of her husband. Whenever she had a date with a man she prepared for it by a very vigorous cleansing of the genitals especially trying to make them dry. When she finally had sexual relations she was surprised and greatly helped in her estimation of her body by discovering that this highly prized dryness was just the opposite of what was pleasing to the man.

In two cases the feeling of genital unacceptability had been a factor in promiscuity. In each case an experience with a man

[6] B. Lewin, "Kotschmieren, Menses und weibliches über-Ich," *Internat. Zschr. Psychoanal.* (1930) 16: 43–56.

who kissed her genitals in an obviously accepting way was the final step in bringing about a complete transformation of feeling. In both cases all need to be promiscuous disappeared, and each of the women felt loved for the first time.

I am obviously oversimplifying these cases in order to make my point clear. I do not wish to leave the impression that the feeling of dirtiness connected with the genitals was the sole cause of a feeling of unacceptability in these patients. There was in each case a feeling from early childhood of not being acceptable, produced by specific attitudes in the parents. The feeling of unacceptability became focused on the genitals eventually for different reasons in each case. For example, in three cases the woman had risen above the lowly social position of her parents and with each of these three women the feeling of having dirty genitals became symbolic of her lowly origin of which she was ashamed. The parents had not placed such an emphasis on baths as they found to be the case in the new social milieu. Therefore any evidence of body secretion or odor betrayed them, and this made sex itself evidence of lower-class origin. On the other hand, two other patients suffered from their own mothers' over-emphasis on body cleanliness. In each of these two cases the mother was cold and puritanical as well as overclean, and the patient felt humiliated because she had a more healthy sexual drive which she felt was proclaimed to the world by her body's odors and secretions.

From these observations I hope I have emphasized the fact that the problem of a woman's sexual life is not in becoming reconciled to having no penis but in accepting her own sexuality in its own right. In this she is hampered by certain attitudes in the culture such as that her sexual drive is not important and her genitals are not clean. With these two deprecatory cultural attitudes in the background of women's lives it is to be expected that both are important points at which difficulties in inter-personal relations may be expressed.

Susan Lydon

UNDERSTANDING ORGASM, 1968

*Susan Lydon, active in the Women's Liberation Movement in
Berkeley, California is a free-lance writer whose articles have
appeared in* Ramparts, *the* New York Times *magazine, and in*
Rolling Stone.

SOURCE
Susan Lydon, "Understanding Orgasm," Ramparts, *December 1968, pp.
59–63.*
Portrait: Craig Pyes.

[Aristotle is said to have concluded—on the basis of pure theory—that women have fewer teeth than men. Apparently he never checked to see. In this essay, Susan Lydon shows that Freud's pontifical speculations regarding female sexuality were scarcely sounder than Aristotle's about female denture—but they have been far more fateful. They have, in fact, been among the cruelest and most effective means of obfuscating women's efforts to break free of their man-made identity. Along with Ann Koedt's pamphlet, "The Myth of the Vaginal Orgasm," Lydon's essay has been one of the most influential writings on the sexual aspect of women's liberation.]

Tiresias, who had been both man and woman, was asked, as Ovid's legend goes, to mediate in a dispute between Jove and Juno as to which sex got more pleasure from lovemaking. Tiresias unhesitatingly answered that women did. Yet in the intervening 2000 years between Ovid's time and our own, a mythology has been built up which not only holds the opposite to be true, but has made this belief an unswerving ideology dictating the quality of relations between the sexes. Women's sexuality, defined by men to benefit men, has been downgraded and perverted, repressed and channeled, denied and abused until women themselves, thoroughly convinced of their sexual inferiority to men, would probably be dumbfounded to learn that there is scientific proof that Tiresias was indeed right.

The myth was codified by Freud as much as anyone else. In *Three Essays on the Theory of Sexuality,* Freud formulated his basic ideas concerning feminine sexuality: for little girls, the leading erogenous zone in their bodies is the clitoris; in order for the transition to womanhood to be successful, the clitoris must abandon its sexual primacy to the vagina; women in whom this transition has not been complete remain clitorally oriented, or "sexually anaesthetic," and "psychosexually immature." In the context of Freud's total psychoanalytic view of women—that they are not whole human beings but mutilated males who long all their lives for a penis and must struggle to reconcile themselves to its lack—the requirement of a transfer of erotic sensation from clitoris to vagina became a *prima facie* case for their inevitable sexual inferiority. In Freud's logic, those who struggle to become what they are not must be inferior to that to which they aspire.

Freud himself admitted near the end of his life that his knowledge of women was inadequate. "If you want to know more about femininity, you must interrogate your own experience, or turn to the poets, or wait until science can give you more profound and more coherent information," he said; he also hoped the female psychoanalysts who followed him would be able to find out more. But the post-Freudians adhered rigidly to the doctrine of the master, and, as with most of his work, what Freud hoped would be taken as a thesis for future study became instead a kind of canon law.

While the neo-Freudians haggled over the correct reading of the Freudian bible, watered-down Freudianism was wending its way into the cultural mythology via Broadway plays, novels, popular magazines, social scientists, marriage counselors and experts of various kinds who found it useful in projecting desired images of woman. The superiority of the vaginal over the clitoral orgasm was particularly useful as a theory since it provided a convenient basis for categorization: clitoral women were deemed immature, neurotic, bitchy and masculine; women who had vaginal orgasms were maternal, feminine, mature, and normal. Though frigidity should technically be defined as total inability to achieve orgasm, the orthodox Freudians (and pseudo-Freudians) preferred to define it as inability to achieve vaginal orgasm, by which definition, in 1944, Edmond Bergler adjudged between 70 and 80 per cent of all women frigid. The clitoral versus vaginal debate raged hot and heavy among the sexologists—Kinsey's writings stressed the importance of the clitoris to female orgasm and contradicted Bergler's statistics —but it became clear that there was something indispensable to society in the Freudian view which allowed it to remain unchallenged in the public consciousness.

In 1966, Dr. William H. Masters and Mrs. Virginia E. Johnson published *Human Sexual Response*, a massive clinical study of the physiology of sex. Briefly and simply, the Masters and Johnson conclusions about the female orgasm, based on observation of and interviews with 487 women, were these:

1. That the dichotomy of vaginal and clitoral orgasms is entirely false. Anatomically, all orgasms are centered in the clitoris, whether they result from direct manual pressure applied to the clitoris, indirect pressure resulting from the thrusting of penis during intercourse, or generalized sexual stimulation of other erogenous zones like the breast.

2. That women are naturally multiorgasmic; that is, if a woman is immediately stimulated following orgasm, she is likely to experience several orgasms in rapid succession. This is not an exceptional occurrence, but one of which most women are capable.

3. That while women's orgasms do not vary in kind, they vary in intensity. The most intense orgasms experienced by the research subjects were by masturbatory manual stimulation, followed in intensity by manual stimulation by the partner; the least intense orgasms were experienced during intercourse.

4. That there is an "infinite variety in female sexual response" as regards intensity and duration of orgasms.

To anyone acquainted with the body of existing knowledge of feminine sexuality, the Masters and Johnson findings were truly revolutionary and liberating in the extent to which they demolished the established myths. Yet two years after the study was published, it seems hardly to have made any impact at all. Certainly it is not for lack of information that the myths persist; *Human Sexual Response,* despite its weighty scientific language, was an immediate best seller, and popular paperbacks explicated it to millions of people in simpler language and at a cheaper price. The myths remain because a male-dominated American culture has a vested interest in their continuance.

Before Masters and Johnson, men defined feminine sexuality in a way as favorable to themselves as possible. If woman's pleasure was obtained through the vagina, then she was totally dependent on the man's erect penis to achieve orgasm; she would receive her satisfaction only as a concomitant of man's seeking his. With the clitoral orgasm, woman's sexual pleasure was independent of the male's, and she could seek her satisfaction as aggressively as the man sought his, a prospect which didn't appeal to too many men. The definition of feminine sexuality as normally vaginal, in other words, was a part of keeping women down, of making them sexually as well as economically, socially and politically subservient.

In retrospect, particularly with the additional perspective of our own times, Freud's theory of feminine sexuality appears an historical rationalization for the realities of Victorian society. A prisoner of the Victorian ethos, Freud had to play the paterfamilias. Freud's analysis implied that woman's low status had not been conferred upon her by men, but by God, who created her without a penis.

The superiority of the vaginal orgasm seems almost a demoniac determination on Freud's part to complete the Victorians' repression of feminine eroticism, to stigmatize the remaining vestiges of pleasure felt by women and thus make them unacceptable to the women themselves. For there were still women whose sexuality hadn't been completely destroyed, as evidenced by one Dr. Issac Brown Baker, a surgeon who performed numerous clitoridectomies on women to prevent the sexual excitement which, he was convinced, caused "insanities," "catalepsy," "hysteria," "epilepsy" and other diseases. The Victorians needed to repress sexuality for the success of Western industrialized society; in particular, the total repression of woman's sexuality was crucial to ensure her subjugation. So the Victorians honored only that aspect of sexuality which was necessary to the survival of the species—the male ejaculation; made women submissive to sex by creating a mystique of the sanctity of motherhood; and, supported by Freud, passed on to us the heritage of the double standard.

When Kinsey laid to rest the part of the double standard that maintained women got no pleasure at all from sex, everyone cried out that there was a sexual revolution afoot. But such talk, as usual, was deceptive. Morality, outside the marriage bed, remained the same, and children were socialized as though Kinsey had never described what they would be like when they grew up. Boys were taught that they should get their sex where they could find it, "go as far" as they could. On the old assumption that women were asexual creatures, girls were taught that since they needed sex less than boys did, it was up to them to impose sexual restraints. In whatever sex education adolescents did manage to receive, they were told that men had penises and women vaginas; the existence of the clitoris was not mentioned, and *pleasure* in sex was never discussed at all.

Adolescent boys growing up begging for sexual crumbs from girls frightened for their "reputations"—a situation that remains unchanged to this day—hardly constitutes the vanguard of a sexual revolution. However, the marriage manual craze that followed Kinsey assumed that a lifetime of psychological destruction could, with the aid of a little booklet, be abandoned after marriage, and that husband and wife should be able to make sure that the wife was not robbed of her sexual birthright to orgasm, just so long as it was *vaginal* (though the marriage manuals did rather reluctantly admit that since the clitoris was the most sexually sensitive organ in the female body, a little clitoral stimulation was in order), and so long as their orgasms were *simultaneous*.

The effect of the marriage manuals of course ran counter to their ostensible purpose. Under the guise of frankness and sexual liberation, they dictated prudery and restraint. Sex was made so mechanized, detached and intellectual that it was robbed of its sensuality. Man became a spectator of his own sexual experience. And the marriage manuals put new pressure on women. The swing was from repression to preoccupation with the orgasm. Men took the marriage manuals to mean that their sexuality would be enhanced by bringing women to orgasm and, again coopting feminine sexuality for their own ends, they put pressure on women to perform. The marriage manuals' endorsement of the desirability of vaginal orgasm insured that women would be asked not only, "Did you come?" but also, "Did you conform to Freud's conception of a psychosexually mature woman, and thereby validate my masculinity?"

Appearances notwithstanding, the age-old taboos against conversation about personal sexual experience haven't yet been broken down. This reticence has allowed the mind-manipulators of the media to create myths of sexual supermen and superwomen. So the bed becomes a competitive arena, where men and women measure themselves against these mythical rivals, while simultaneously trying to live up to the ecstasies promised them by the marriage manuals and the fantasies of the media ("If the earth doesn't move for me, I must be missing something"). Our society has made sex a sport, with its record-breakers, its judges, its rules and its spectators.

As anthropologists have shown, woman's sexual response is culturally conditioned; historically, women defer to whatever model of their sexuality is offered them by men. So the sad thing for women is that they have participated in the destruction of their own eroticism. Women have helped make the vaginal orgasm into a status symbol in a male-dictated system of values. A woman would now perceive her preference for clitoral orgasm as a "secret shame," ignominious in the eyes of other women as well as those of men. This internalization can be seen in literature: Mary McCarthy and Doris Lessing's writings on orgasm do not differ substantially from Ernest Hemingway's, and Simone de Beauvoir, in *The Second Sex*, refers to vaginal orgasm as the only "normal satisfaction."

One factor that has made this possible is that female sexuality is subtle and delicate, conditioned as much by the emotions as by physiology and sociology. Masters and Johnson proved that the orgasm experienced during intercourse, the misnamed vaginal orgasm, did not differ *anatomically* from the clitoral orgasm. But this should not be seen as their most significant contribution to the sexual emancipation of women. A difference remains in the *subjective* experience of orgasm during intercourse and orgasm apart from intercourse. In the complex of emotional factors affecting feminine sexuality, there is a whole panoply of pleasures: the pleasure of being penetrated and filled by a man, the pleasure of sexual communication, the pleasure of affording a man his orgasm, the erotic pleasure that exists even when sex is not terminated by orgasmic release. Masters and Johnson's real contribution was to show this "infinite variety in female sexual response"; that one experience is not better than another, but merely different.

There is no doubt that Masters and Johnson were fully aware of the implications of their study to the sexual liberation of women. As they wrote, "With orgasmic physiology established, the human female now has an undeniable opportunity to develop realistically her own sexual response levels." Two years later this statement seems naïve and entirely too optimistic. Certainly the sexual problems of our society will never be solved until there is real and unfeigned equality between men and women. This idea is usually misconstrued: sexual liberation for women is wrongly understood to mean that women will adopt all the forms of masculine sexuality. As in the whole issue of women's liberation, that's really not the point. Women don't aspire to imitate the mistakes of men in sexual matters, to view sexual experiences as conquest and ego-enhancement, to use other people to serve their own ends. But if the Masters and Johnson material is allowed to filter into the public consciousness, hopefully to replace the enshrined Freudian myths, then woman at long last will be allowed to take the first step toward her emancipation: to define and enjoy the forms of her own sexuality.

Dana Densmore

SEX ROLES AND FEMALE OPPRESSION, 1970

Dana Densmore has been active in Women's Liberation in the Boston area.

SOURCE
Dana Densmore, Sex Roles and Female Oppression, *Boston, New England Free Press, 1970.*

And what of the throat-catching excitement of new romance? The pregnant frightened seriousness of its first encounters and the joys of sexual conquest, the cliff-hanging excruciating suspense, the intense role-playing for tangible immediate stakes?

The ideal woman is created out of the frail mortal that was you. She is witty, shy, laughing, a little bold, downcast eyes smoldering. Everything is done with just the right touch, just the right timing....

One could not help but take pride in a job so well done: fine acting and consummate artistry, the creation of a Desirable Woman out of a simple female body transformed by your imagination.

You are not passive, although that must be the chief impression conveyed to the man so that he will think the conquest entirely his.

You do not sit by and through just BEING lure him into your net, no, being a woman is an active thing, you MAKE yourself a woman, you create the role and play it.

To be a woman you must please and attract the man, and to do that a thousand little postures and tricks are required, all tailored to the demands of the moment.

False, all false, admitted. But, you may argue, since that is your definition, why then you truly ARE this bundle of falsehoods. And, false or not, the game is rewarding.

There are the rewards of self-satisfaction reaped by any actress who plays her role superbly, heightened here by the fact that success brings not mere applause from an audience but the conquest and enchantment of an exciting man who adores the "woman" you have created and moreover believes absolutely that this incredible creature is you. Which means, for practical purposes, that he adores you—and you did EARN it, didn't you?

But no, it's not the same. In fact, it's not the same at all. It's deception and unreal and the conquest it engineers is the ignoble manipulation of another human being, however he begs for it, however much he himself contributes to his own deception by demanding the false qualities and blinding himself to others that are yours most rightfully.

No, no, no more conquests. You work for your conquest, but you are begging this man to master you, not meeting him honorably halfway. Your success, your conquest, is only in being conquered.

You tempt him, entice him, titillate him, until he can't resist any longer and he takes you. Then you are possessed. You.

He thinks it's that little doll you showed him who was begging for a master and will treat you accordingly. If the little doll was more docile and more subservient than you, watch out.

He thinks he knows how you want to be treated and adds the weight of this datum to his opinion on how ALL women want to be treated.

Maybe for you the conquest has been made, the suspense is over, and it's time to get back on a more realistic basis.

But it's too late. He adores that role-playing little doll and he's not about to give it up.

So you did wrong. Never mind that your plain unvarnished self never would have landed him at all. When women stoop to conquer they relinquish all rights to respect later and set the stage for the whole act by declaring themselves traditional role-playing women who delight in their own degradation.

And while we're at it, maybe you should ask yourself how much you've internalized all this role-playing.

To what extent do you believe you ARE this bundle of falsehoods? To what extent has it seeped into your consciousness, penetrated below what you intellectually recognize about yourself to condition everything and cause you to fall into role-playing instinctively without a deliberate conscious decision?

It is almost inevitable that some of the mass of propaganda about our sexual identity that constantly bombards us should condition our own self-image.

We can't always be on guard against definition from without, and in fact most of it occurred before it was us that they were defining, when it was "woman," a mysterious or strange and distasteful other we only later realized we would grow into one day.

By the time we could measure the reality of ourselves against the myth, it was too late for us to make a totally objective judgement about what we were.

But look particularly hard at the sexual myths you have internalized.

Psychologists (male) have defined you as a creature whose ego development demands a delicate balance of narcissism and masochism.

This is the "scientific" view of woman, as opposed to the purely mythic and male-wish-fulfillment identities.

What is your own sexual self-image? How much narcissism and masochism are in it? And how much does your sexual self-image condition your whole self-image?

In the heady joy of the sexual encounter are you reveling in masochism euphemistically calling your surrender "womanly"?

Why should you like being dominated by a man? What is there to recommend a man who makes decisions without consulting you, who expects you to conform to his ideas about how women should act?

He isn't being virile and manly, he's showing disrespect for you and disregard for your wishes and needs; he is demanding that you yield up your liberty, your mind and will; he is crushing your ego.

Virility is the euphemism. The real word is sadism.

Radical Lesbians

THE WOMAN-IDENTIFIED WOMAN, 1970

*Radical Lesbians is one of the first groups to explore the political
implications of what is usually referred to as deviant sexuality.
In addition to the fact that they are women who have chosen to
love other women, radical lesbians analyze the socialization of
women which results in the "male identified" female—that is,
the woman who has internalized values which may not actually
reflect her own convictions or experience.*

SOURCE
*Ellen Bedoz, Rita Mae Brown, Barbara XX, Lois Hart, Cynthia Funk,
March Hoffman, "The Woman-Identified Woman," copyright © 1970 by
the Radical Lesbians. All rights reserved.*
Photo: United Press International.

What is a lesbian? A lesbian is the rage of all women condensed to the point of explosion. She is the woman who, often beginning at an extremely early age, acts in accordance with her inner compulsion to be a more complete and freer human being than her society—perhaps then, but certainly later—cares to allow her. These needs and actions, over a period of years, bring her into painful conflict with people, situations, the accepted ways of thinking, feeling and behaving, until she is in a state of continual war with everything around her, and usually with her self. She may not be fully conscious of the political implications of what for her began as personal necessity, but on some level she has not been able to accept the limitations and oppression laid on her by the most basic role of her society—the female role. The turmoil she experiences tends to induce guilt proportional to the degree to which she feels she is not meeting social expectations, and/or eventually drives her to question and analyze what the rest of her society more or less accepts. She is forced to evolve her own life pattern, often living much of her life alone, learning usually much earlier than her "straight" (heterosexual) sisters about the essential aloneness of life (which the myth of marriage obscures) and about the reality of illusions. To the extent that she cannot expel the heavy socialization that goes with being female, she can never truly find peace with herself. For she is caught somewhere between accepting society's view of her—in which case she cannot accept herself—and coming to understand what this sexist society has done to her and why it is functional and necessary for it to do so. Those of us who work that through find ourselves on the other side of a tortuous journey through a night that may have been decades long. The perspective gained from that journey, the liberation of self, the inner peace, the real love of self and of all women, is something to be shared with all women—because we are all women.

It should first be understood that lesbianism, like male homosexuality, is a category of behaviour possible only in a sexist society characterized by rigid sex roles and dominated by male supremacy. Those sex roles dehumanize women by defining us as a supportive/serving caste *in relation to* the master caste of men, and emotionally cripple men by demanding that they be alienated from their own bodies and emotions in order to perform their economic/political/military functions effectively. Homosexuality is a by-product of a particular way of setting up roles (or approved patterns of behaviour) on the basis of sex; as such it is an inauthentic (not consonant with "reality") category. In a society in which men do not oppress women, and

sexual expression is allowed to follow feelings, the categories
of homosexuality and heterosexuality would disappear.

But lesbianism is also different from male homosexuality,
and serves a different function in the society. "Dyke" is a different kind of put-down from "faggot," although both imply you are
not playing your socially assigned sex role . . . are not therefore
a "real woman" or a "real man." The grudging admiration felt
for the tomboy, and the queasiness felt around a sissy boy point
to the same thing: the contempt in which women—or those who
play a female role—are held. And the investment in keeping
women in that contemptuous role is very great. Lesbian is the
word, the label, the condition that holds women in line. When a
woman hears this word tossed her way, she knows she is stepping out of line. She knows that she has crossed the terrible
boundary of her sex role. She recoils, she protests, she reshapes
her actions to gain approval. Lesbian is a label invented by the
man to throw at any woman who dares to be his equal, who
dares to challenge his prerogatives (including that of all women
as part of the exchange medium among men), who dares to
assert the primacy of her own needs. To have the label applied
to people active in women's liberation is just the most recent
instance of a long history; older women will recall that not so
long ago, any woman who was successful, independent, not ori-
enting her whole life about a man, would hear this word. For in
this sexist society, for a woman to be independent means she
can't be a woman—she must be a dyke. That in itself should tell
us where women are at. It says as clearly as can be said: women
and person are contradictory terms. For a lesbian is not considered a "real woman." And yet, in popular thinking, there is
really only one essential difference between a lesbian and other
women: that of sexual orientation—which is to say, when you
strip off all the packaging, you must finally realize that the
essence of being a "woman" is to get fucked by men.

"Lesbian" is one of the sexual categories by which men
have divided up humanity. While all women are dehumanized as
sex objects, as the objects of men they are given certain compensations: identification with his power, his ego, his status, his
protection (from other males), feeling like a "real woman," finding social acceptance by adhering to her role, etc. Should a
woman confront herself by confronting another woman, there
are fewer rationalizations, fewer buffers by which to avoid the
stark horror of her dehumanized condition. Herein we find the
overriding fear of many women towards being used as a sexual
object by a woman, which not only will bring her no male-
connected compensations, but also will reveal the void which is
woman's real situation. This dehumanization is expressed when a
straight woman learns that a sister is a lesbian; she begins to
relate to her lesbian sister as her potential sex object, laying a

surrogate male role on the lesbian. This reveals her heterosexual conditioning to make herself into an object when sex is potentially involved in a relationship, and it denies the lesbian her full humanity. For women, especially those in the movement, to perceive their lesbian sisters through this male grid of role deformities is to accept his male cultural conditioning and to oppress their sisters much as they themselves have been oppressed by men. Are we going to continue the male classification system of defining all females in sexual relation to some other category of people? Affixing the label lesbian not only to a woman who aspires to be a person, but also to any situation of real love, real solidarity, real primacy among women is a primary form of divisiveness among women: it is the condition which keeps women within the confines of the feminine role, and it is the debunking/scare term that keeps women from forming any primary attachments, groups, or associations among ourselves.

Women in the movement have in most cases gone to great lengths to avoid discussion and confrontation with the issue of lesbianism. It puts people up-tight. They are hostile, evasive, or try to incorporate it into some "broader issue." They would rather not talk about it. If they have to, they try to dismiss it as a "lavender herring." But it is no side issue. It is absolutely essential to the success and fulfillment of the women's liberation movement that this issue be dealt with. As long as the label "dyke" can be used to frighten women into a less militant stand, keep her separate from her sisters, keep her from giving primacy to anything other than men and family—then to that extent she is controlled by the male culture. Until women see in each other the possibility of a primal commitment which includes sexual love, they will be denying themselves the love and value they readily accord to men, thus affirming their second-class status. As long as male acceptability is primary—both to individual women and to the movement as a whole—the term lesbian will be used effectively against women. Insofar as women want only more privileges within the system, they do not want to antagonize male power. They instead seek acceptability for women's liberation, and the most crucial aspect of the acceptability is to deny lesbianism—i.e., deny any fundamental challenge to the basis of the female. It should also be said that some younger, more radical women have honestly begun to discuss lesbianism, but so far it has been primarily as a sexual "alternative" to men. This, however, is still giving primacy to men, both because the idea of relating more completely to women occurs as a negative reaction to men, and because the lesbian relationship is being characterized simply by sex, which is divisive and sexist. On one level, which is both personal and political, women may withdraw emotional and sexual energies from men, and work out various alternatives for those energies in their own lives. On a different political/psychological level, it must be understood that what is crucial is that women begin disengaging from male-defined response patterns. In the privacy of our own psyches, we must cut those cords to the core. For irrespective of where our love and sexual energies flow, if we are male-identified in our heads we cannot realize our autonomy as human beings.

But why is it that women have related to and through men? By virtue of having been brought up in a male society, we have internalized the male culture's definition of ourselves. That definition consigns us to sexual and family functions, and excludes us from defining and shaping the terms of our lives. In exchange for our psychic servicing and for performing society's non-profit-making functions, the man confers on us just one thing: the slave status which makes us legitimate in the eyes of the society in which we live. This is called "femininity" or "being a real woman" in our cultural lingo. We are authentic, legitimate, real to the extent that we are the property of some man whose name we bear. To be a woman who belongs to no man is to be invisible, pathetic, inauthentic, unreal. He confirms his image of us—of what we have to be in order to be acceptable by him— but not our real selves; he confirms our womanhood—as he defines it, in relation to him—but cannot confirm our person-hood, our own selves as absolutes. As long as we are dependent on the male culture for this definition, for this approval, we cannot be free.

The consequence of internalizing this role is an enormous reservoir of self-hate. This is not to say the self-hate is recognized or accepted as such; indeed most women would deny it. It may be experienced as discomfort with her role, as feeling empty, as numbness, as restlessness, a paralyzing anxiety at the center. Alternatively, it may be expressed in shrill defensiveness of the glory and destiny of her role. But it does exist, often beneath the edge of her consciousness, poisoning her existence, keeping her alienated from herself, her own needs, and render-ing her a stranger to other women. They try to escape by identi-fying with the oppressor, living through him, gaining status and identity from his ego, his power, his accomplishments. And by not identifying with other "empty vessels" like themselves. Women resist relating on all levels to other women who will reflect their own oppression, their own secondary status, their own self-hate. For to confront another woman is finally to con-front one's self—the self we have gone to such lengths to avoid. And in that mirror we know we cannot really respect and love that which we have been made to be.

As the source of self-hate and the lack of real self are rooted in our male-given identity, we must create a new sense of self. As long as we cling to the idea of "being a woman," we will sense some conflict with that incipient self, that sense of I, that sense of a whole person. It is very difficult to realize and accept that being "feminine" and being a whole person are irrecon-cilable. Only women can give to each other a new sense of self.

That identity we have to develop with reference to ourselves, and not in relation to men. This consciousness is the revolutionary force from which all else will follow, for ours is an organic revolution. For this we must be available and supportive to one another, give our commitment and our love, give the emotional support necessary to sustain this movement. Our energies must flow toward our sisters, not backwards toward our oppressors. As long as woman's liberation tries to free women without facing the basic heterosexual structure that binds us in one-to-one relationship with our oppressors, tremendous energies will continue to flow into trying to straighten up each particular relationship with a man, how to get better sex, how to turn his head around—into trying to make the "new man" out of him, in the delusion that this will allow us to be the "new woman." This obviously splits our energies and commitments, leaving us unable to be committed to the construction of the new patterns which will liberate us.

It is the primacy of women relating to women, of women creating a new consciousness of and with each other which is at the heart of women's liberation, and the basis for the cultural revolution. Together we must find, reinforce and validate our authentic selves. As we do this, we confirm in each other that struggling incipient sense of pride and strength, the divisive barriers begin to melt, we feel this governing solidarity with our sisters. We see ourselves as prime, find our centers inside of ourselves. We find receding the sense of alienation, of being cut off, of being behind a locked window, of being unable to get out what we know is inside. We feel a real-ness, feel at last we are coinciding with ourselves. With that real self, with that consciousness, we begin a revolution to end the imposition of all coercive identifications, and to achieve maximum autonomy in human expression.

Sally Kempton

CUTTING LOOSE, 1970

A Private View of the Women's Uprising

Sally Kempton is a free-lance writer and has written extensively for The Village Voice, *New York's popular, hip-oriented, weekly newspaper.*

SOURCE
Sally Kempton, "Cutting Loose: A Private View of the Women's Uprising," Esquire, *July 1970.*
Portrait: Fred W. McDarrah.

Once another woman and I were talking about male resistance to Woman's Liberation, and she said that she didn't understand why men never worry about women taking their jobs away
but worry only about the possibility that women may stop making love to them and bearing their children. And once I was
arguing with a man I know about Woman's Liberation, and he
said he wished he had a motorcycle gang with which to invade
a Woman's Liberation meeting and rape everybody in it. There
are times when I understand the reason for men's feelings. I
have noticed that beyond the feminists' talk about the myth of
the vaginal orgasm lies a radical resentment of their position
in the sexual act. And I have noticed that when I feel most
militantly feminist I am hardly at all interested in sex.

Almost one could generalize from that: the feminist impulse
is anti-sexual. The very notion of women gathering in groups is
somehow anti-sexual, anti-male, just as the purposely all-male
group is anti-female. There is often a sense of genuine cultural
rebellion in the atmosphere of a Woman's Liberation meeting.
Women sit with their legs apart, carelessly dressed, barely
made-up, exhibiting their feelings or the holes at the knees of
their jeans with an unprovocative candor which is hardly seen
at all in the outside world. Of course, they are demonstrating
by their postures that they are in effect off duty, absolved from
the compulsion to make themselves attractive, and yet, as the
world measures these things, such demonstrations could in
themselves be seen as evidence of neurosis: we have all been
brought up to believe that a woman who was "whole" would
appear feminine even on the barricades.

The fact is that one cannot talk in feminist terms without
revealing feelings which have traditionally been regarded as
neurotic. One becomes concerned about women's rights, as
Simone de Beauvoir noted, only when one perceives that there
are few personal advantages to be gained from accepting the
traditional women's roles. A woman who is satisfied with her
life is not likely to be drawn into the Woman's Liberation movement: there must be advantages for her as a woman in a man's
world. To be a feminist one must be to some degree maladjusted
to that world, one must be, if you will, neurotic. And sometimes
one must be anti-sexual, if only in reaction to masculine expectations. Men do not worry about women taking their jobs
because they do not think that women could do their jobs; most

men can only be threatened by a woman in bed. A woman who
denies her sexuality, if only for an evening, denies her status as
an object of male attention, as a supplicant, successful or not,
for male favor. For a woman to deny her sexuality is to attack
the enemy in his most valuable stronghold, which is her own
need for him.

I became a feminist as an alternative to becoming a
masochist. Actually, I always was a masochist; I became a feminist because to be a masochist is intolerable. As I get older I
recognize more and more that the psychoanalytical idea that
women are natural masochists is at least metaphorically correct:
my own masochism derived from an almost worshipful respect
for masculine power. In my adolescence I screwed a lot of
guys I didn't much like, and always felt abused by them, but
I never felt free to refuse sex until after the initial encounter.
My tactic, if you can call it a tactic, was to Do It once and then
to refuse to see the boy again, and I think I succeeded, with my
demonstrations of postcoital detachment, in making several of
them feel as rejected by my lovemaking as I had felt by their
desire to make love to me without love. Yet I found in those
years that I had irretrievably marked myself a sexual rebel and
I was given to making melodramatic statements like "I'm not
the kind of girl men marry." Years later I realized that I
had been playing a kind of game, the same game boys play at
the age of sexual experimentation, except that, unlike a boy, I
could not allow myself to choose my partners and admit that
I had done so. In fact, I was never comfortable with a lover
unless he had, so to speak, wronged me. Once during my senior
year in high school I let a boy rape me (that is not, whatever
you may think, a contradiction of terms) in the bedroom of his
college suite while a party was going on next door; afterward
I ran away down the stairs while he followed shouting apologies
which became more and more abject as he realized that my
revulsion was genuine, and I felt an exhilaration which I clearly
recognized as triumph. By letting him abuse me I had won the
right to tell him I hated him; I had won the right to hurt him.

I think most American adolescents hate and fear the opposite sex: in adolescence it seems that only one's lovers can hurt
one, and I think that even young people who are entirely secure
in other relations recognize and would, if they could, disarm the
power the other sex has for them. But for adolescent boys,
sexual success is not the sole measure of worth. It is assumed
that they will grow up and work, that their most important tests
will come in areas whose criteria are extra-sexual. They can fail
with girls without failing entirely, for there remains to them the
public life, the male life.

But girls have no such comfort. Sex occupies even the
economic center of our lives; it is, we have been brought up to

feel, our live's work. Whatever else she may do, a woman is a failure if she fails to please men. The adolescent girl's situation is by definition dependent: she *must* attract, and therefore, however she may disguise it, she must compromise the sticky edges of her personality, she must arrange herself to conform with other people's ideas of what is valuable in a woman.

I was early trained to that position, trained, in the traditional manner, by my father. Like many men who are uncomfortable with adult women, my father saw his daughter as a potential antidote to his disappointment in her sex. I was someone who could be molded into a woman compatible with his needs, and also, unlike my mother, I was too impressionable to talk back. So I became the vessel into which he fed his opinions about novels and politics and sex; he fed me also his most hopeful self-image. It reached a point where I later suspected him of nourishing a sort of eighteenth-century fantasy about our relationship, the one in which the count teaches his daughter to read Virgil and ride like a man, and she grows up to be the perfect feminine companion, parroting him with such subtlety that it is impossible to tell that her thoughts and feelings, so perfectly coincident with his, are not original. I had three brothers, as it happened, and another sort of man might have chosen one of them to mold. But my father had himself a vast respect for masculine power. Boys grow up and have to kill their fathers, girls can be made to understand their place.

My father in his thirties was an attractive man, he was witty by adult standards and of course doubly so by mine, and he had a verbal facility with which he invariably demolished my mother in arguments. Masculine power in the intellectual classes is exercised verbally: it is the effort of the male supremacist intellectual to make his woman look clumsy and illogical beside him, to render her, as it were, dumb. His tactic is to goad the woman to attack him and then, resorting to rationality, to withdraw himself from the battle. In my childhood experience, subtlety appeared exclusively a masculine weapon. I never saw a woman argue except straightforwardly, and I never saw a woman best a man in a quarrel. My mother tried, but always with the conviction of ultimate failure. She attacked with pinpricks to begin with; in the end, maddened invariably by my father's ostentatious mental absence, she yelled. He was assisted in these struggles by his natural passivity. Withdrawal came easily to him; he hated, as he told us over and over again, scenes. My mother, it seemed to me, was violent, my father cool. And since it also seemed to me that he preferred me, his daughter who never disagreed with him, to his wife who did (that was a fantasy, of course, but one to which my father devoted some effort toward keeping alive), I came to feel that male power, because uncoercible, could only be handled by seduction, and that the most comfortable relation between men and women was the relation between pupil and teacher, between parent and child.

My father taught me some tricks. From him I learned that it is pleasant and useful to get information from men, pleasant because it is easier than getting it for yourself, and useful because it is seductive: men like to give information, and sometimes love the inquirer, if she is pretty and asks intelligently. From him I also learned that women are by definition incapable of serious thought. This was a comforting lesson, although it made me feel obscurely doomed, for if I was to be automatically barred from participation in the life of high intellect, there was no reason why I should work to achieve it, and thinking, after all, is difficult work. When I was fifteen my father told me that I would never be a writer because I wasn't hungry enough, by which I think he meant that there would always be some man to feed me. I accepted his pronouncement as I accepted, at that age, all pronouncements which had an air of finality, and began making other career plans.

My task, it seemed to me, was to find a man in whom there resided enough power to justify my acting the child, that is, to justify my acceptance of my own femininity. For I regarded myself as feminine only in my childlike aspect; when I presented myself as a thinking person I felt entirely sexless. The boys in my class regarded me as an intellectual and showed an almost unanimous disinterest in my company. When I was in the eighth grade I lived in trepidation lest I be cited as class bookworm, and defended myself against that threat by going steady with what surely must have been the dumbest boy in our set. He was no fonder of me than I was of him; we needed each other because you had to be part of a couple in order to get invited to parties.

I did not get the opportunity to demonstrate my skill as a child-woman until I became old enough to go out with college boys. My training had equipped me only to attract intelligent men, and a boy who was no brighter than I held no power for me. But for a man who could act as my teacher I could be submissive and seductive—I *felt* submissive and seductive; my awe of the male mind translated easily into an awe of the male person.

I was, I realize now, in tune with the demands of my time. This was in the late Fifties, Marilyn Monroe was the feminine archetype of the period, and Marilyn Monroe was sexy because of her childishness. It is not much of a step from seeing oneself as a child in relation to men to seeing oneself as their victim; obviously a child does not control its environment, obviously a child is powerless before adults. All children are potential victims, dependent upon the world's good-will. My sense of powerlessness, of feminine powerlessness, was so great that for years I trusted no man who had not indicated toward me a special favor, who had not fallen in love with me. And even toward those who had, I acted the victim, preferring to believe myself the one who loved most, for how could a man retain his power in loving me unless I gave it back to him through my submission? Years later I heard a story about how Bob Dylan so tormented a groupy that she jumped out a window while ten people looked on, and recognized the spirit of my adolescence. I never got myself into a situation even comparably extreme, my fundamental self-protectiveness having permitted me to allow only minor humiliations, but the will was there.

Masochism as clinically defined is more or less exclusively a sexual disorder: masochists are people who derive sexual pleasure from pain. Freudian psychiatrists claim that all women are to one degree or another masochistic in the sexual sense (the male penetrates the female, presumably he hurts her, and presumably she enjoys the pain as part of the pleasure), and many Freudian thinkers extend the use of the term out of the area of sex into the social area and argue that the womanly woman is correctly masochistic, must be masochistic in order to accept the male domination which is necessarily a part even of her extra-sexual life. It seems to me more useful to define masochism, insofar as the word is to be used to describe a non-clinical emotional condition, as the doing of something which one does not enjoy because someone else demands it or even because one's conscience demands it. In this sense clinical masochism can be said to be non-masochistic: if one enjoys being whipped, one is acting directly upon one's own needs, whereas if one allows oneself to be whipped for someone else's pleasure without deriving any pleasure from the act, one is behaving masochistically. A person who acts upon someone else's will, or in accordance with someone else's image of her, or who judges herself by someone else's standards, has allowed herself to be made into an object. A masochist, as I define the term, is a person who consents to be made an object. It is in that sense that I think most women are, or have been at some time in their lives, masochists. For insofar as a woman lives by the standards of the world, she lives according to the standards set by men. Men have laid down the rules and definitions by which the world is run, and one of the objects of their definitions is woman. Men define intelligence, men define usefulness, men tell us what is beautiful, men even tell us what is womanly. Constance Chatterley was a male invention; Lawrence invented her, I used to think, specifically to make me feel guilty because I didn't have the right kind of orgasms.

Lionel Trilling wrote in an essay on Jane Austen that it is the presumption of our society that women's moral life is not as men's, and that therefore we do not expect from women, in fact do not condone in them, the same degree of self-love which we expect and encourage in men. What he meant, I think, was that since women are in a sense given their lives, since women customarily choose a life-style by choosing a man rather than a path, they do not need the self-love which is necessary to carry a man to the places he has to go. Self-love is indeed a handicap to a being whose primary function is supportive, for how is a woman adequately to support another ego when her self-love demands the primacy of her own? Women learn in many ways to suppress their selfishness, and by doing so they suppress also their self-esteem. If most men hold women in contempt it is no greater than the contempt in which women hold themselves. Self-love depressed becomes self-loathing. Men are brought up to command, women to seduce: to admit the necessity of seduction is to admit that one has not the strength to command. It is in fact to accept one's own objecthood, to internalize one's oppression.

Still, I picked up some interesting lore from men, while I was studying to please them. I learned about Eliot from one boy, and about Donne from another, and about Coltrane from a third. A lover turned me on to drugs and also showed me how you were supposed to act when you were high—that is, as if you were not high. I was not surprised that he was better at this than me, cool was beginning to seem more and more a masculine talent, and I had even taken to physical retaliation in arguments, having given up the idea that I would ever win anything by verbal means. I went to Sarah Lawrence instead of Barnard because my boyfriend thought that Sarah Lawrence was a more "feminine" school. My parents got divorced and I sided with my father, at least at first, because his appeared to me to be the winning side. Men, I believed, were automatically on the winning side, which was why my oldest brother could afford to withdraw in moral outrage from my father's advances; there was for *him* no danger of branding himself a loser by consorting with my mother. Yet I envied him his integrity. How could I maintain integrity when I was willing to sell out any principle for the sake of masculine attention?

I went to Sarah Lawrence and got to love it without ever taking it very seriously, which I also supposed was the way the boys I loved in those days felt about me. In fact, Sarah Lawrence appeared to me and to most of my friends there as a sort of symbol of ourselves: like the college, we were pretty and slightly prestigious and terribly self-serious in private, but just as we laughed at the school and felt embarrassed to be identified with it publicly (I always felt that if I had been a real student I would have gone to Barnard), so we laughed publicly at our own aspirations. "I like Nancy," a Princeton boy said to me, "except she always starts talking about Kafka promptly at midnight." And I laughed, god how I laughed, at Nancy—how *Sarah Lawrence* to carry on about Kafka—and, by implication, at myself. For I too expressed my intellectualism in effusions. Men expected the effusions, even found them charming, while treating them with friendly contempt. It was important to be charming. A passion for Marxism, stumblingly expressed, an interpretation of *Moby Dick*, these tokens we offered our lovers to prove we were not simply women, but people. Yet though we displayed strong feelings about art and politics, we behaved as if we had not really done the reading. To argue a point logically was to reveal yourself as unfeminine: a man might respect your mind, but he would not love you. Wit, we believed, is frightening in a woman.

In my senior year I met a girl who knew the editor of *The Village Voice*, and after graduation she got me a job there. I went to work as a reporter without having the slightest notion of how to conduct an interview and so, to cover myself, I made up a couple of pieces out of whole cloth. They were about drugs and hippies and homosexuals, the sort of scene pieces *The Voice* later specialized in, but nobody much was writing about that stuff in 1964, and I got several book offers and invitations to cocktail parties, and my father's friends started writing me letters full of sports analogies, saying it was time I entered a main event. In fact, I felt terribly guilty about writing those pieces because they seemed frivolous and sensationalistic, the sort of thing empty-headed girl reporters did when they were too dumb to write about politics, but on the other hand they got me attention, which writing about politics would never have done. I agonized all summer, publicly and privately, over this dilemma, often spending hours telling big strong male reporters how unworthy I felt. They seemed to like it.

I had never thought of myself as ambitious; actually, I think I was too convinced of my basic incompetence to be constructively ambitious, but I quickly saw that a lady journalist has advantages denied to men. For one thing, she never has to pick up a check. For another thing, if she is even remotely serious, people praise her work much more than they would praise the work of a comparably talented man; they are amazed that a woman can write coherently on any subject not confined in interest to the readers of a woman's magazine. And finally, people tell her things they would not tell a man. Many men think the secrets they tell a woman are automatically off the record. They forget that the young woman hanging on their every word is taking it all down—often they confuse her attention with sexual interest. (That is not such an advantage. Some men, rock stars for instance, simply assumed that sex was what I had come for. They would expend a little flattery to assure me that they regarded me as a cut above other groupies, and then they would suggest that we get down to balling. They were often nasty when I refused.)

At any rate, the work was nice, and it gave me a higher status as a sexual object than I had ever had before. But it was also scary. If I was to do well at it I had to take it seriously, and the strongest belief I had retained from my childhood was my idea that nothing I could achieve was worth taking seriously. In the Autumn of 1964 I fell in love with a boy who was not sure he was in love with me, and by the time he decided he was I had quit my job and moved with him to Boston. He styled himself a revolutionary and thought the content of my work hardly worth the effort it took to produce it; I accepted his opinion with relief, telling myself that in any case I had not the emotional energy to handle both a lover and a job. My feeling for him evaporated fairly soon after I discovered that it was reciprocated, though I lived with him for several months after that, partly out of guilt and partly because living with a man made me feel grown-up in a way holding a job never could have done. But finally I left him and took a job as a staff writer on a national magazine, a classy job but underpaid. Instead of complaining about the salary, I took to not showing up for work, justifying my laziness by telling myself that I was selling out anyway by taking an uptown job and that the sooner I rid myself of it, the sooner I would regain my integrity.

In the meantime I had met a grown-up man who was powerful and smart and knocked out by my child act. We spent a few months seducing each other—"You're too young for me," he would say, and I would climb upon his lap, figuratively speaking, and protest that I was not. It was no more disgusting than most courtships. In the end we got married.

Of course, I had to marry a grown-up, a father figure if you will, and my husband, as it turned out, had to marry a child. That is, he had to have an intelligent woman, but one whose intelligence had been, as it were, castrated by some outside circumstances. My youth served that purpose; my other handicaps had not as yet emerged.

Anyway, our romantic personae lasted about a year. For a year he was kind to me and listened to my problems and put up with the psychosomatic diseases which marriage had induced in me, and for a year I brought joy and spontaneity into his drab grown-up existence. Then he began to get tired of being a father and I to resent being a child, and we began to act out what I think is a classic example of contemporary marriage.

It had turned out, I realized with horror, that I had done exactly what middle-class girls are supposed to do. I had worked for a year in the communications industry, and my glamorous job had enabled me to meet a respectable, hardworking man who made a lot of money at *his* glamorous job, and I had settled down (stopped screwing around) and straightened myself out (went into analysis), and all that was missing was babies. I defended myself by assuming that we would be divorced in a year, and sneered a lot at Design Research furniture and the other symbols of middle-class marriage, but still I could not escape the feeling that I had fallen not just into a trap but into a cliché. On the other hand, I loved my husband, and I was still a writer, that is to say, a privileged woman with a life of her own. I could afford, as I began to at that time, to read feminist literature without really applying it to my own situation.

My husband, although he is nice to women, is a male supremacist, very much in the style of Norman Mailer. That is, he invests women with more or less mystical powers of control over the inner workings of the world, but thinks that feminine power is strongest when exercised in child rearing and regards contraception as unnatural. When I had my first stirrings of feminist grievance, he pronounced the subject a bore; I used to follow him from room to room, torturing him with my recitals of the sexist atrocities I was beginning to find in my favorite novels, and when I complained that magazines were paying me less than they paid men, he accused me of trying to blame the world for my own crazy passivity. But we were engaged at that time in the usual internal power struggle, and my feminism seemed to both of us more an intellectual exercise than a genuine commitment. It was not until many months later that he began to accuse me of hating men.

We already knew that he hated women, even that he had good reasons for hating women, but I had up to that time put on such a good display of being cuddly, provocative, sexually uninhibited and altogether unlike those other women that the subject of my true feelings about men had never come up. He knew that I had a compulsion to seduce men, which argues a certain distrust of them, but as the seductions, since our marriage, were always intellectual rather than sexual, they could, if you didn't want to consider their implications, be put down simply to insecurity. I don't think even I realized how I felt. Once I told my husband about a rigmarole a friend and I had made up to dismiss men we didn't like—we would go through lists of names, pointing our fingers and saying, "Zap, you're sterile," and then collapse into giggles; my husband, who has a psychoanalytical turn of mind, thought that was Terribly Revealing and I agreed that it was, but so what? And also, I agreed that it was Terribly Revealing that I liked to pinch and bite him, that I made small hostile jokes and took an almost malicious pleasure in becoming too involved in work to pay attention to him (but only briefly; I never for very long attempted to work when he had other plans), that I would go into week-long depressions during which the bed never got made nor the dishes washed. But the degree of my hostility didn't reveal itself to me until a pattern began to emerge around our quarrels.

We had, since early in the marriage, periodically engaged in bitter fights. Because my husband was the stronger, and because he tends to be judgmental, they usually started when he attempted to punish me (by withdrawing, of course) for some offense. I would dispute the validity of his complaint, and the quarrel would escalate into shouts and blows and then into decisions to terminate the marriage. In the first year my husband always beat me hollow in those battles. I used to dissolve into tears and beg his forgiveness after twenty minutes; I could not bear his rejection and I had no talent at all for conducting a quarrel. I won only when I succeeded in making him feel guilty; if he behaved badly enough I automatically achieved the moral upper hand for at least a week following the quarrel. But after a while, the honeymoon being over, he began to refuse to feel guilty and I began to resent his superior force. Things rested there until, in the third year of our marriage, we went to live in Los Angeles because of my husband's work. During the year we spent away from home I found that I could not work, and that he was always working, and we suddenly found ourselves frozen into the textbook attitudes of male-female opposition. We fought continually, and always about the same things. He accused me of making it impossible for him to work, I accused him of keeping me dangling, dependent upon him for all emotional sustenance, he accused me of spending too much money and of keeping the house badly, I accused him of expecting me continually to subordinate my needs to his. The difficulty, I realized over and over again without being able to do much about it, was that I had gotten myself into the classic housewife's position: I was living in a place I didn't want to be, and seeing people I didn't like because that was where my man was, I was living my husband's life and I hated him for it. And the reason this was so was that I was economically dependent upon him; having ceased to earn my living I could no longer claim the breadwinner's right to attention for my special needs.

My husband told me that I was grown-up now, twenty-six years old, there were certain realities which I had to face. He was the head of the household: I had never questioned that. He had to fulfill himself: I had never questioned that. He housed and fed me and paid for my clothes, he respected my opinions and refused all his opportunities to make love to other women, and my part of the bargain should have become clear to me by now. In exchange for those things, I was supposed to keep his house and save his money and understand that if he worked sixteen hours a day for a year it was no more than necessary for his self-fulfillment. Which was all quite true. Except that it was also necessary for his fulfillment that I should be there for those few hours when he had time for me, and not complain about the hours when he did not, and that I should adapt myself to his situation or else end the marriage. It never occurred to him to consider adapting himself to mine, and it never occurred to me. I only knew that his situation was bad for me, was alien, was in fact totally paralyzing, that it kept me from working, that it made me more unhappy than I had been in my life.

I knew that I was being selfish. But he was being selfish also, the only difference being that his selfishness was somehow all right, while mine was inexcusable. Selfishness was a privilege I had earned for a while by being a writer, that is, a person who had by male standards a worthwhile place to spend her time. As soon as I stopped functioning as a writer I became to my husband and to everyone else a mere woman, somebody whose time was valueless, somebody who had no excuse for a selfish preoccupation with her own wants.

I used to lie in bed beside my husband after those fights and wish I had the courage to bash in his head with a frying pan. I would do it while he slept, since awake he would overpower me, disarm me. If only I dared, I would mutter to myself through clenched teeth, pushing back the realization that I didn't dare not because I was afraid of seriously hurting him— I would have loved to do that—but because even in the extremity of my anger I was afraid that if I cracked his head with a frying pan he would leave me. God, how absurd it was (god, how funny, I would mutter to myself, how amusing, oh wow, what a joke) that my whole life's effort had been directed toward keeping men from leaving me, toward placating them, submitting to them, demanding love from them in return for living in their style, and it all ended with me lying awake in the dark hating my husband, hating my father, hating all the men I had ever known. Probably I had always hated them. What I couldn't figure out was whether I hated them because I was afraid they would leave me or whether I was afraid they would leave me because I hated them.

Because one cannot for very long support such a rage without beginning to go crazy, I tried to think of the problem in political terms. It seemed to me too easy to say that my hatred for men was a true class hatred, that women hate men because women are an oppressed class hungering for freedom. And yet wherever there exists the display of power there is politics, and in women's relations with men there is a continual transfer of power, there is continually, politics. There are political analogies even to our deepest, our most banal fantasies. Freud maintains that the female terror of the penis is a primary fear, and that the male fear of castration by the vagina is merely a retaliatory fantasy, a guilty fear of punishment. The serf fears the overlord's knout, the overlord, guilty, fears the serf's revenge. Women are natural guerrillas. Scheming, we nestle into the enemy's bed, avoiding open warfare, watching the options, playing the odds. High, and made paranoiac by his observance of my rage, my husband has the fantasy of woman with a knife. He sees her in sexual ectasy with her eyes open to observe the ecstasy of her partner, with her consciousness awake, her consciousness the knife. It had often been my private boast that even in moments of greatest abandon, I always kept some part of my mind awake: I always searched for clues. Is he mine now, this monster? Have I disarmed him, and for how long? Men are beasts, we say, joking, parodying the Victorian rag, and then realize to our surprise that we believe it. The male has force almost beyond our overpowering, the force of laws, of science, of literature, the force of mathematics and skyscrapers and the Queensboro Bridge; the penis is only its symbol. We cannot share men's pride in the world they have mastered. If you follow that symbolism to its conclusion, we are ourselves that conquered world.

It is because they know that this is true, know it in their bones if not in their heads, that men fear the hatred of women. For women are the true maintenance class. Society is built upon their acquiescence, and upon their small and necessary labors. Restricted to the supportive role, conditioned to excel only at love, women hold for men the key to social order. It is a Marxist truism that the original exploitation, the enslavement which set the pattern for everything which came later, was the enslavement of women by men. Even the lowest worker rests upon the labor of his wife. Where no other claim to distinction exists, a man defines himself by his difference from the supportive sex: he may be a less than admirable man, but at least he is a man, at least he is not a woman.

And if women have fought, they have fought as guerrillas, in small hand-to-hand skirmishes, in pillow wars upon the marriage bed. When they attack frontally, when they come together in groups to protest their oppression, they raise psychic questions so profound as to be almost inadmissable. In E. E. Cummings' play *Him*, there is a scene in which two women sit in a Paris café and order men served up to them like plats du jour; it is an inexpressibly sinister sequence, and it has its counterparts elsewhere in the avant-garde literature of the Twenties. I do not imagine that Cummings approved of men using women like meat, but I am quite sure that he could not have treated the situation with such horror had the sexual roles been reversed. Cummings, like Leonid Andreyev and the other modernists who dealt in surreal images of female dominance, was writing during the early period of feminist protest, and I think they were expressing a fear basic to every man confronted with the idea of women's liberation. When men imagine a female uprising they imagine a world in which women rule men as men have ruled women: their guilt, which is the guilt of every ruling class, will allow them to see no middle ground. And it is a measure of the unconscious strength of our belief in natural male dominance that all of us, men and women, revolt from the image of woman with a whip, that the female sadist is one of our most deep-rooted images of perversion.

And although I believe this male fantasy of feminine equality as a euphemism for feminine dominance to be evidence of the oppressors' neurosis rather than of any supporting fact, it was part of the character of my resentment that I once fancied wresting power from men as though nothing less than total annihilation would satisfy my rage. The true dramatic conclusion of this narrative should be the dissolution of my marriage; there is a part of me which believes that you cannot fight a sexist system while acknowledging your need for the love of a man, and perhaps if I had had the courage finally to tear apart my life I could write you about my hard-working independence, about my solitary self-respect, about the new society I hope to build. But in the end my husband and I did not divorce, although it seemed at one time as if we would. Instead I raged against him for many months and joined the Woman's Liberation Movement, and thought a great deal about myself, and about whether my problems were truly all women's problems, and decided that some of them were and that some of them were not. My sexual rage was the most powerful single emotion of my life, and the feminist analysis has become for me, as I think it will for most women of my generation, as significant an intellectual tool as Marxism was for generations of radicals. But it does not answer every question. To discover that something has been wrong is not necessarily to make it right: I would be lying if I said that my anger had taught me how to live. But my life has changed because of it. I think I am becoming in many small ways a woman who takes no shit. I am no longer submissive, no longer seductive; perhaps it is for that reason that my husband tells me sometimes that I have become hard, and that my hardness is unattractive. I would like it to be otherwise. I think that will take a long time.

My husband and I have to some degree worked out our differences; we are trying to be together as equals, to separate our human needs from the needs imposed upon us by our sex roles. But my hatred lies within me and between us, not wholly a personal hatred, but not entirely political either. And I wonder always whether it is possible to define myself as a feminist revolutionary and still remain in any sense a wife. There are moments when I still worry that he will leave me, that he will come to need a woman less preoccupied with her own rights, and when I worry about that I also fear that no man will ever love me again, that no man could ever love a woman who is angry. And that fear is a great source of trouble to me, for it means that in certain fundamental ways I have not changed at all.

I would like to be cold and clear and selfish, to demand satisfaction for my needs, to compel respect rather than affection. And yet there are moments, and perhaps there always will be, when I fall back upon the old cop-outs. Why should I trouble to win a chess game or a political argument when it is so much easier to lose charmingly? Why should I work when my husband can support me, why should I be a human being when I can get away with being a child?

Woman's Liberation is finally only personal. It is hard to fight an enemy who has outposts in your head.

The Lower East Side Women's
Liberation Collective

LOVE IS JUST A FOUR-LETTER WORD, 1971

*The Lower East Side Women's Liberation Collective consists
of thirteen women in their early twenties who lived in New
York City's East Village and were part of the youth culture there.
After discovering that the East Village was not a citadel of
freedom and that being a hippie chick was far from being a
liberated woman, they joined W.I.T.C.H.—Women's International
Conspiracy from Hell—in order to protest the chauvinism of
counter-culture men and to dramatise through the guerrilla theatre
activities their belief that youth culture diverts energy from
political protest and social reform. Convinced that there must
be major economic changes in the United States before women
and other minority groups such as blacks and youth can be
truly liberated, the members of this collective are committed
to full-time radical political activity and are presently working
on such projects as organizing unions, the People's Peace
Treaty, and the Woman's Bail Fund.*

SOURCE
Hip Culture, Six Essays on Its Revolutionary Potential, *Times Change
Press, 1970, pp. 32–39.*

Hip culture: be natural, be free, do your own thing, get rid of your middle class hang-ups, turn on, drop out. Groovy? But for who? Middle class white men can sometimes find individual solutions, but oppressed people can't. Women can't find individual solutions.

In the context of this society, escape is an illusion for both sexes. Dropping out is a game open only to middle class men— they can play at an alternative while still maintaining their class privilege in a class society. Oppressed people don't have the chips required to play and the deck is clearly stacked against women. In a society such as ours, run by a wealthy few, and based on the control, division and systematic oppression of all other people, doing your *own* thing changes nothing and in fact supports that society by default. Hippy culture is not revolutionary even though that is the packaging it's sold in.

Hippies flaunt the superiority of their life style. They can choose to live in slums, but have contempt for the people who have to live there. New York hippies have even organized tours of Queens to laugh at the straights. By these attitudes hippie women are separated from their working class sisters and straight middle class sisters who are trapped *by* a straight system and don't have the option to drop out.

Straight society—the Amerikan Death Trap—is a drag. Middle class values, morals and attitudes are repressive. Women as well as men do try to drop out, but for us it's different. We gain superficial freedoms—we can go without make-up or bras, we can smoke dope and act "unladylike." But our real situation is basically unchanged and in some cases worsened. In a society based on male domination the balance of power does not change just because the style of dress does. Basic male-female role definitions remain the same.

A woman's relationship to society is that of producer of children, nurturer, stabilizer. She is responsible for the basic necessities and comforts of life, i.e., preparing food, creating a habitable environment and in general meeting the physical and emotional needs of men and children. Women who "drop out" are no exception. Of course human and social needs must be met—but by men and women!

There is a whole superstructure that applies to women, a superstructure of role definitions, of morality, of limited functions and ways to relate to the outside world. This serves to keep woman in her place regardless of what her life-style is.

Take "doing your own thing." It's very easy for men—it's the way they were raised. Men can choose their own responsibilities. Little kids are taught that men are people and women are mommys. Most men emerge from this socialization process with fairly strong egos. How many hip men do we meet who define themselves as artists, poets, political philosophers, musicians, messiahs. It even doesn't matter if they can really do these things or not. They can pretend to do them and society accepts male pretensions—especially hip society.

Woman, however, is taught from birth that her main function is to relate to society through men. To serve and to decorate. Since she is defined by her sex, she usually derives her self-image by the way in which she is responded to by men and by what type men respond to her. The woman who has developed independent talents often has to either subordinate her creativity to men or face incredible odds in male dominated fields. In the struggle to assert herself she becomes separated from other women, by feeling that she is somehow better than they are; but she is still subordinate to men in her field, resented by men, or if she has been successful in a very feminine, very groovy way —she is used as an object—a sex symbol. It's still nicer to be told you're a beautiful woman instead of that's a beautiful poem.

Most women are not allowed to be creative, except in terms of traditional female roles to bake bread, to decorate our bodies and to make love well. Hip women are allowed limited outlets for their creativity: non-threatening things like a theatrical life-style or home industry crafts like making pots, stringing beads, weaving, crocheting. To take any of these things really seriously or try to make some kind of living off them, is to threaten men. Our status depends on who we relate to, on his style, not our own.

A sister reading Jerry Rubin's *Do-It* thought—disregarding the way he talks about women—that it would be really groovy to do that stuff; but, of course, it's Jerry and Abbie doing it—it's an exclusively male style. Women can play only a supportive role to men who are running around and yipping in, talking back to everyone and saying all those groovy funny little things. A woman who did that would be considered obnoxious and would have to bear the brunt of male hatred.

Of course there's dope. "It can unleash your creative potential and free you from your hang-ups." "It's your head that's fucking you up, not your reality," he says. But women don't have hang-ups, they have political problems, and dope can't change that reality.

Some women take dope to enjoy sex more. Some women to enjoy sex. The structure is that it's not groovy to refuse a joint when it's handed to you and when you're high all the time every-thing appears beautiful—even though in reality things are often a real mess.

Walk down St. Marks Place, in New York City, especially around 5:30 when groovy, funky dressed men walk with their arms around their women, who, coming home from their jobs as receptionists, clerical workers, or maybe teachers are straightly dressed in oppressive stockings, high heels and restrictive underwear. These groovy, creative men can afford to write or paint, or be creatively blocked, or hang around and discuss philosophy, or do their "important" political work while their "old ladies" support them.

There are some women who have been able to escape the world of straight jobs, to panhandle instead maybe. But there are the problems of paying the rent, where the next meal is coming from and who's going to cook it, plus the problems of birth control, or taking care of the kids. Try dropping out of that. Men can; they do it all the time. But these things are necessary to maintain life. They've always been the responsibility of women and hip culture offers no relief.

The hippy woman cooks, washes, cleans house, and she does it without all the modern conveniences capitalist society has produced to "lighten woman's load." Preparing and cleaning up from macrobiotic meals is not much different from any other full course meal, except that it is a lot harder to fix than prepared food—like an hour and half longer. Part of the love ethic is "everybody's always welcome," which leaves women cooking (and buying food) for large unknown quantities of people, usually men, who, because they have no responsibilities, have more freedom to bum around. And if there isn't enough to go around, guess who "suddenly loses her appetite" or has to run out to the health food store. Women who have moved out to country communes to be with nature and reflect on life find that almost their entire day is spent doing household chores—no hot running water makes doing dishes alone a two-hour job. Men go out to "hunt" and "chop wood"—women keep the home fires burning—literally. Women rise at 5 to start the fire and give their men a hearty breakfast just as women in the suburbs do for their executive husbands who have to make the 7:45. A hippy woman who asks for electricity, running water, a washing machine or a vacuum cleaner is considered hopelessly bourgeois and would be put down by all the men. The point is women still serve while men do the groovy work that everyone thinks of when they talk about moving to the country.

Then there's love and sex—again be natural, be free, get rid of your hang-ups. Theoretically this is healthy and beautiful, but in a society such as ours sexual freedom and equality for women are a myth perpetuated by men. How many times has a man said, "that was beautiful," or "the best time yet," either being so absorbed in his own pleasure that he didn't realize he was the only one to come—or not caring. The role of women in hip culture is to be all loving—and more to the point—loving of all. The right to be possessive, jealous or hurt is given up with lipstick. Nobody wants to mess with a woman who might get "hung-up." That's not cool. Making demands or being emotionally vulnerable is put down as being either bourgeois or sick. This type of non-monogamy puts social pressure on women to sleep with more than one man—*very* few men feel responsibility to a woman who is not his possession. The "free" woman is great until she gets pregnant or needs a little emotional or financial support—suddenly she finds that she is not free in the way she thought she was. Not philosophically free, but free like "free beer on St. Patrick's day." As John Sinclair, self-styled hippy revolutionary, said in describing the society of the future we're all supposedly working for—"There will be free dope, free food, free clothes, and free women." "Freedom" is a male assigned role meaning one thing to women and something entirely differ-ent to men—a mean little play on words to keep us available and in our places. Real freedom implies mutual responsibility. We woman are free to give—free to meet men's needs—but not free to ask that our needs be met. Free love means that men can get it whenever they want and women have to give on demand.

For some of us non-possession means we live with a sexually free man but are his exclusive property. We never ask where he's going or when he's coming back. We are still giving on demand—knowing that there are other women in his life who are also capable of giving makes us feel very insecure—we feel we have to give more, give better so we won't lose him. The result is a society of women all trying to out-do each other in meeting men's needs—while the men sit back and manipulate what for them is a very groovy situation.

One of the basic goals mouthed by the hippy movement is the development of a human society as opposed to a technical or bureaucratic society. Yet when it comes to what we have been told is the most human of human relationships—sex—hippies have made no progress at all—even anti-progress. Hippy culture super-exploits women as sex objects. Fuck is a hate word. Paul Krassner said, "The system has to be fucked good—like a woman." Draw your own conclusions. Or take "balling"—it's obvious where that's at. By the word itself, it's clear who's the active one—the doer—and who's the receptacle. Balling doesn't even connote two people—there's the baller, he's cool, and the ballee—the one who gets it. Women become objects that men masturbate into. Love or communication becomes totally irrele-vant, and women who need and ask for love or communication are accused of being bourgeois.

Sex for its own sake is particularly oppressive—the one night stand leaves you with nothing but fantasies and the clap. Glory of sex for its own sake has also led to the proliferation of porn magazines—*Screw, EVO, Kiss, Crum* comics—whose message is "all women look the same upside down."

The concept of being natural is also often used against women. You wouldn't think of asking him to wear a condom because it would interfere with his pleasure, so it's up to the woman to risk the uncertain side-effects of the pill or the IUD or the less than sure protection of foam or a diaphragm. That is unless he is so concerned about being natural that he won't allow any birth control at all. It's not the man's responsibility if the woman gets pregnant, needs an abortion, or must bear and raise a child.

The concept of living in as natural a way of life as possible often means hip culture opposes technology and materialism. However, if we control technology it can help us survive. And, certain material things are necessary for survival, including aesthetic survival.

So what does a hippy woman drop out of? Even though she doesn't have to wear all those straight clothes she still has an image to maintain. There may be a wider range of what's groovy, but it has to be freaky, way out or cool looking—women are always looking for a way to be unique. Women who drop out of straight society must be prepared to buy a new wardrobe or they will not be accepted in hip society. At one point perhaps the idea was that you don't have to waste lots of bread buying fancy clothes, but "in" clothes—bells, leathers, suedes, antique velvets and hand fashioned sandals don't come any cheaper than straight clothes. And if you wear anything over a size nine forget it! Unless of course you go Mother Earth—and that's a whole trip in itself. There's Mama Cass, and Mama Koit, a west coast disc jockey—big mama's—warm, comforting, but who comforts them? At one point even Cass, rich, famous and creative almost killed herself by dieting—she literally had to be carried off the stage at a concert. She resented being a phenomenon rather than a person. It's so important for women to be "beautiful" that we sometimes even sacrifice our health. The benefits of not wearing a bra are overshadowed by the hassles of sexist men. "Hey baby, you look fine," he smirks, staring at your chest. Or "that's a nice pair of tits, Mama." And in a rapist society we get more than hassles—we get attacked. Men rationalize this, saying we tantalize them. After all, they say, hippie women are supposed to believe in free love and have intense, lusty orgasms. That is just a new style of the old excuse which puts the blame on us—that "women who are attacked ask for it."

Hatred of women is a visible element in hip culture. You're either "Under My Thumb" (Stones), or "You've Got to Change Your Evil Ways" (Santana)—meaning you're asserting yourself too much. Or a number one song "American Woman" (Guess Who)—"I've got better things to do than spend my time growing old with you." Rock music is made by men for men. Women who relate to musicians are always extraneous. Groupies are prostitutes paid only by their "status." Music by women, about women usually speaks of the pain of being a woman. Have you ever seen men digging on Janis Joplin? The concept of women in pain is sexually exciting to them. Our pain is considered a beautiful art form. "Woman is a loser." Women who have come to know sex and love as pain are moved by Janis, but in a different way.

We're reliving those feelings. It's not beautiful. It's horrible. It's our lives. And when rock music isn't talking about pain, it's talking about women as though we were objects to be experienced— wise in the ways of the world, a wisdom gained through having endured suffering.

Spokesmen of the hip culture claim to be struggling in solidarity with oppressed people. There's Abbie Hoffman (Right on?) who says, "The only alliance I'll make with women's liberation is in bed." (Right out!) Loving, openness, and being natural are beautiful things, but in a society based on doublethink, beautiful and liberating concepts are used to oppress us. Just as capitalism expands the war in the name of peace, Hip Culture imprisons women in the name of freedom and exploits women in the name of love.

Robin Morgan

GOODBYE TO ALL THAT, 1970

Robin Morgan is a founding member of W.I.T.C.H. and editor of Sisterhood Is Powerful *(Vintage, 1970). This essay was written to commemorate the women's take-over of* RAT.

SOURCE
Robin Morgan, "Goodbye to All That," RAT: Subterranean News, *2, 27, February 6, 1970, pp. 1–6.*
Portrait: Wide World.

So. *Rat* has been liberated, for this week, at least. Next week? If the men return to reinstate the porny photos, the sexist comic strips, the "nude-chickie" covers (along with their patronizing rhetoric about being in favor of Women's Liberation)—if this happens, our alternatives are clear. *Rat* must be taken over permanently by women—or *Rat* must be destroyed.

Why *Rat?* Why not EVO or even the obvious new pornzines (Mafia-distributed alongside the human pornography of prostitution)? First, they'll get theirs—but it won't be a takeover, which is reserved for something at least *worth* taking over. Nor should they be censored. They should just be helped not to exist—by any means necessary. But *Rat,* which has always tried to be a really radical *cum* life-style paper—that's another matter. It's the liberal co-optative masks on the face of sexist hate and fear, worn by real nice guys we all know and like, right? We have met the enemy and he's our friend. And dangerous. "What the hell, let the chicks do an issue; maybe it'll satisfy 'em for a while, it's a good controversy, and it'll maybe sell papers"—runs an unheard conversation that I'm sure took place at some point last week.

And that's what I wanted to write about—the friends, brothers, lovers in the counterfeit male-dominated Left. The good guys who think they know what "Women's Lib," as they so chummily call it, is all about—and who then proceed to degrade and destroy women by almost everything they say and do: The cover on the last issue of *Rat* (front *and* back). The token "pussy power" or "clit militancy" articles. The snide descriptions of women staffers on the masthead. The little jokes, the personal ads, the smile, the snarl. No more, brothers. No more well-meaning ignorance, no more co-optation, no more assuming that this thing we're all fighting for is the same: one revolution under *man,* with liberty and justice for all. No more.

Let's run it on down. White males are most responsible for the destruction of human life and environment on the planet today. Yet who is controlling the supposed revolution to change all that? White males (yes, yes, even with their pasty fingers back in black and brown pies again). It just could make one a bit uneasy. It seems obvious that a legitimate revolution must be led by, *made* by those who have been most oppressed: black, brown, and white *women*—with men relating to that the best they can. A genuine Left doesn't consider anyone's suffering irrelevant or titillating; nor does it function as a microcosm of capitalist economy, with men competing for power and status at the top, and women doing all the work at the bottom (and functioning as objectified prizes or "coin" as well). Goodbye to all that.

Run it all the way down.

Goodbye to the male-dominated peace movement, where sweet old Uncle Dave can say with impunity to a woman on the staff of *Liberation*, "The trouble with you is you're an aggressive woman."

Goodbye to the "straight" male-dominated Left: to PL who will allow that some workers are women, but won't see all women (say, housewives) as workers (just like the System itself); to all the old Leftover parties who offer their "Women's Liberation caucuses" to us as if that were not a contradiction in terms; to the individual anti-leadership leaders who hand-pick certain women to be leaders and then relate only to them, either in the male Left or in Women's Liberation—bringing their hang-ups about power-dominance and manipulation to everything they touch.

Goodbye to the WeatherVain, the Stanley Kowalski image and theory of free sexuality but practice of sex on demand for males. "Left Out!"—not Right On—to the Weather Sisters who, and they know better—they know, reject their own radical feminism for that last desperate grab at male approval that we all know so well, for claiming that the *machismo* style and the gratuitous violence is their own style by "free choice" and for believing that this is the way for a woman to make her revolution . . . all the while, oh my sister, not meeting my eyes because WeatherMen chose Manson as their—and your—Hero. (Honest, at least . . . since Manson is only the logical extreme of the normal American male's fantasy (whether he is Dick Nixon or Mark Rudd): master of a harem, women to do all the shitwork, from raising babies and cooking and hustling to killing people on order.) Goodbye to all that shit that sets women apart from women; shit that covers the face of any Weatherwoman which is the face of any Manson Slave which is the face of Sharon Tate which is the face of Mary Jo Kopechne which is the face of Beulah Saunders which is the face of me which is the face of Pat Nixon which is the face of Pat Swinton. *In the dark we are all the same*—and you better believe it: we're in the dark, baby. (Remember the old joke: Know what they call a black man with a Ph.D.? A nigger. Variation: Know what they call a Weatherwoman? A heavy cunt. Know what they call a Hip Revolutionary Woman? A groovy cunt. Know what they call a radical militant feminist? A crazy cunt. Amerika is a land of free choice—take your pick of titles. Left out, my Sister—don't you see? Goodbye to the illusion of strength when you run hand in hand with your oppressors; goodbye to the dream that being in the leadership collective will get you anything but gonorrhea.

Goodbye to RYM II, as well, and all the other RYMs—not that the Sisters there didn't pull a cool number by seizing control, but because they let the men back in after only *a day or so*

of self-criticism on male chauvinism. (And goodbye to the inac-
curate blanket use of that phrase, for that matter: male chauvinism is an *attitude*—male supremacy is the *objective reality,
the fact.*) Goodbye to the Conspiracy who, when lunching with
fellow sexist bastards Norman Mailer and Terry Southern in a
bunny-type club in Chicago, found Judge Hoffman at the neigh-
boring table—no surprise: *in the light they are all the same.*

Goodbye to Hip Culture and the so-called Sexual Revolution,
which has functioned toward women's freedom as did the Reconstruction toward former slaves—reinstituted oppression by another name. Goodbye to the assumption that Hugh Romney is
safe in his "cultural revolution," safe enough to refer to "our
women, who make all our clothes" without somebody not forgiving that. Goodbye to the arrogance of power indeed that lets
Czar Stan Freeman of the Electric Circus sleep without fear at
night, or permits Tomi Ungerer to walk unafraid in the street
after executing the drawings for the Circus advertising campaign
against women. Goodbye to the idea that Hugh Hefner is groovy
'cause he lets Conspirators come to parties at the Mansion—
goodbye to Hefner's dream of a ripe old age. Goodbye to Tuli
and the Fugs and all the boys in the front room—who always
knew they hated the women they loved. Goodbye to the notion
that good ol' Abbie is any different from any other up and
coming movie star (like, say Cliff Robertson) who ditches the
first wife and kids, good enough for the old days but awkward
once you're Making It. Goodbye to his hyprocritical double
standard that reeks through all the tattered charm. Goodbye to
lovely pro-Women's-Liberation Krassner, with all his astonished
anger that women have lost their sense of humor "on this issue"
and don't laugh anymore at little funnies that degrade and hurt
them; farewell to the memory of his "Instant Pussy" aerosol-can
poster, to his column for *Cavalier*, to his dream of a Rape-In
against legislators' wives, to his Scapegoats and Realist Nuns and
cute anecdotes about the little daughter he sees as often as any
proper divorced Scarsdale middle-aged (38) father; goodbye forever to the notion that he is my brother who, like Paul, buys a
prostitute for the night as a birthday gift for a male friend, or
who, like Paul, reels off the names in alphabetical order of
people in the Women's Movement he has fucked, reels off names
in the best lockerroom tradition—as proof that *he's* no sexist
oppressor.

Let it all hang out. Let it seem bitchy, catty, dykey, frustrated, crazy, Solanisesque, nutty, frigid, ridiculous, bitter, em-
barrassing, man-hating, libelous, pure, unfair, envious, intuitive,
lowdown, stupid, petty, liberating. *We are the women that men
have warned us about.*

And let's put one lie to rest for all time: the lie that men are
oppressed, too, by sexism—the lie that there can be such a thing

as "men's liberation groups." Oppression is something that one group of people commits against another group specifically because of a "threatening" characteristic shared by the latter group—skin color or sex or age, etc. The oppressors are indeed *fucked up* by being masters (racism hurts whites, sexual stereotypes are harmful to men) but those masters are not *oppressed*. Any master has the alternative of divesting himself of sexism or racism—the oppressed have no alternative—for they have no power—but to fight. In the long run, Women's Liberation will of course free men—but in the short run it's going to *cost* men a lot of privilege, which no one gives up willingly or easily. Sexism is *not* the fault of women—kill your fathers, not your mothers.

Run it on down. Goodbye to a beautiful new ecology movement that could fight to save us all if it would stop tripping off women as earth-mother types or frontier chicks, if it would *right now* cede leadership to those who have *not* polluted the planet because that action implies power and women haven't had any power in about 5,000 years, cede leadership to those whose brains are as tough and clear as any man's but whose bodies are also unavoidably aware of the locked-in relationship between humans and their biosphere—the earth, the tides, the atmosphere, the moon—. Ecology is no big shtick if you are a woman—it's always been there.

Goodbye to the complicity inherent in the Berkeley Tribesmen being part publishers of Trashman Comics; goodbye, for that matter, to the reasoning that finds whoremaster Trashman a fitting model, however comic-strip far out, for a revolutionary man—somehow related to the same Supermale reasoning that permits the first statement on Women's Liberation and male chauvinism that came out of the Black Panther Party to be made *by a man*, talkin' a whole lot 'bout how the Sisters should speak up for themselves. Such ignorance and arrogance ill befits a revolutionary.

We know how racism is worked deep into the unconscious by our System—the same way sexism is, as it appears in the very name of The Young Lords. What are you if you're a "macho woman"—a female Lord? Or, god forbid, a Young Lady? Change it, change it to The Young Gentry if you must, or never assume that the name itself is innocent of pain, of oppression.

Theory and practice—and the lightyears between them. "Do it!" says Jerry Rubin in *Rat's* last issue—but he doesn't, or every *Rat* reader would have known the pictured face next to his article as well as they know his own much-photographed face: it was Nancy Kurshan, the power behind the clown.

Goodbye to the New Nation and Earth People's Park, for that matter, conceived by men, announced by men, led by men—doomed before its birth by the rotting seeds of male supremacy which are to be transplanted in fresh soil. Was it my brother who listed human beings among the *objects* which would be easily available after the Revolution: "Free grass, free food, free women, free acid, free clothes, etc."? Was it my brother who wrote "Fuck your women till they can't stand up" and said that groupies were liberated chicks 'cause they dug a tit-shake instead of a handshake? The epitome of female exclusionism—"men will make the Revolution—and their chicks." Not my brother, no. Not my revolution. Not one breath of my support for the new counterleft Christ—John Sinclair. Just one less to worry about for ten years. I do not choose my enemy for my brother.

Goodbye, goodbye. The hell with the simplistic notion that automatic freedom for women—or non-white peoples—will come about ZAP! with the advent of a socialist revolution. Bullshit. Two evils pre-date capitalism and have been clearly able to survive and post-date socialism: sexism and racism. Women were the first property when the Primary Contradiction occurred: when one half of the human species decided to subjugate the other half, because it was "different," alien, the Other. From there it was an easy enough step to extend the Other to someone of different skin shade, different height or weight or language— or strength to resist. Goodbye to those simple-minded optimistic dreams of socialist equality all our good socialist brothers want us to believe. How liberal a politics that is! How much further we will have to go to create those profound changes that would give birth to a genderless society. *Profound*, Sister. Beyond what is male or female. Beyond standards we all adhere to now without daring to examine them as male-created, male-dominated, male-fucked-up, and in male self-interest. *Beyond all known standards*, especially those easily articulated revolutionary ones we all rhetorically invoke. Beyond, to a species with a new name, that would not dare define itself as Man.

I once said, "I'm a revolutionary, not just a woman," and knew my own lie even as I said the words. The pity of that statement's eagerness to be acceptable to those whose revolutionary zeal no one would question, i.e., any male supremacist in the counterleft. But to become a true revolutionary one must first become one of the oppressed (not organize or educate or manipulate them, but become one of them)—or realize that you *are* one of them already. No woman wants that. Because that realization is humiliating, it hurts. It hurts to understand that at Woodstock or Altamont a woman could be declared uptight or a poor sport if she didn't want to be raped. It hurts to learn that the Sisters still in male-Left captivity are putting down the crazy feminists to make themselves look okay and unthreatening to our mutual oppressors. It hurts to be pawns in those games. It hurts to try and change *each day of your life right now*—not in talk, not "in your head," and not only conveniently "out there" in the Third World (half of which is women) or the black and brown communities (half of which are women) but in your own home, kitchen, bed. No getting away, no matter how else you are oppressed, from the primary oppression of being female in a patriarchal world. It hurts to hear that the Sisters in the Gay Liberation Front, too, have to struggle continually against the male chauvinism of their gay brothers. It hurts that Jane Alpert was cheered when rapping about imperialism, racism, the Third World, and All Those Safe Topics but hissed and booed by a Movement crowd of men who wanted none of it when she began to talk about Women's Liberation. The backlash is upon us.

They tell us the alternative is to hang in there and "struggle," to confront male domination in the counterleft, to fight beside or behind or beneath our brothers—to show 'em we're just as tough, just as revolushunerry, just as whatever-image-they-now-want-of-us-as-once-they-wanted-us-to-be-feminine-and-keep-the-home-fire-burning. They will bestow titular leadership on our grateful shoulders, whether it's being a token woman on the Movement Speakers Bureau Advisory Board, or being a Conspiracy groupie or one of the "respectable" chain-swinging Motor City Nine. Sisters all, with only one real alternative: to seize our own power into our own hands, all women, separate and together, and make the Revolution the way it must be made—no priorities this time, no suffering group told to wait until after.

It is the job of revolutionary feminists to build an ever stronger independent Women's Liberation Movement, so that the Sisters in counterleft captivity will have somewhere to turn, to use their power and rage and beauty and coolness in their own behalf for once, on their own terms, on their own issues, in their own style—whatever that may be. Not for us in Women's Liberation to hassle them and confront them the way their men do, nor to blame them—or ourselves—for what any of us are: an oppressed people, but a people raising our consciousness toward something that is the other side of anger, something bright and smooth and cool, like action unlike anything yet contemplated or carried out. It is for us to survive (something the white male radical has the luxury of never really worrying about, what with all his options), to talk, to plan, to be patient, to welcome new fugitives from the counterfeit Left with no arrogance but only humility and delight, to plan, to push—to strike.

There is something every woman wears around her neck on a thin chain of fear—an amulet of madness. For each of us, there exists somewhere a moment of insult so intense that she will reach up and rip the amulet off, even if the chain tears at the flesh of her neck. And the last protection from seeing the truth will be gone. Do you think, tugging furtively every day at the chain and going nicely insane as I am, that I can be concerned with the puerile squabbles of a counterfeit Left that laughs at my pain? Do you think such a concern is noticeable when set alongside the suffering of more than half the human species for the past 5,000 years—due to a whim of the other half? No, no, no, goodbye to all that.

Women are Something Else. This time, we're going to kick out all the jams, and the boys will just have to hustle to keep up, or else drop out and openly join the power structure of which they are already the illegitimate sons. Any man who claims he is serious about wanting to divest himself of cock privileges should trip on this: all male leadership out of the Left is the only way; and it's going to happen, whether through men stepping down or through women seizing the helm. It's up to the "brothers"—after all, sexism is their concern, not ours; we're too busy getting ourselves together to have to deal with their bigotry. So they'll have to make up their own minds as to whether they will be divested of just cock privilege or—what the hell, why not say it, *say* it?—divested of cocks. How deep the fear of that loss must be, that it can be suppressed only by the building of empires and the waging of genocidal wars!

Goodbye, goodbye forever, counterfeit Left, counterleft, male-dominated cracked-glass-mirror reflection of the Amerikan Nightmare. Women are the real Left. We are rising powerful in our unclean bodies; bright glowing mad in our inferior brains; wild hair flying, wild eyes staring, wild voices keening; undaunted by blood we who hemorrhage every twenty-eight days; laughing at our own beauty we who have lost our sense of humor; mourning for all each precious one of us might have been in this one living time-place had she not been born a woman; stuffing fingers into our mouths to stop the screams of fear and hate and pity for men we have loved and love still; tears in our eyes and bitterness in our mouths for children we couldn't have, or couldn't *not* have, or didn't want, or didn't want *yet*, or wanted and had in this place and this time of horror. We are rising with a fury older and potentially greater than any force in history, and this time we will be free or no one will survive. *Power to all the people or to none.* All the way down, this time.